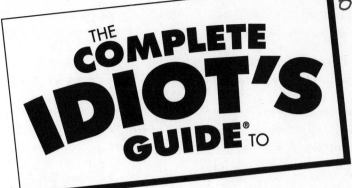

THE
COMPLETE IDIOT'S GUIDE® TO

Psychology

D1308193

Third Edition

by Joni E. Johnston, Psy.D.

ALPHA

A member of Penguin Group (USA) Inc.

ALPHA BOOKS

Published by the Penguin Group

Penguin Group (USA) Inc., 375 Hudson Street, New York, New York 10014, U.S.A.

Penguin Group (Canada), 10 Alcorn Avenue, Toronto, Ontario, Canada M4V 3B2 (a division of Pearson Penguin Canada Inc.)

Penguin Books Ltd, 80 Strand, London WC2R 0RL, England

Penguin Ireland, 25 St Stephen's Green, Dublin 2, Ireland (a division of Penguin Books Ltd)

Penguin Group (Australia), 250 Camberwell Road, Camberwell, Victoria 3124, Australia (a division of Pearson Australia Group Pty Ltd)

Penguin Books India Pvt Ltd, 11 Community Centre, Panchsheel Park, New Delhi—110 017, India

Penguin Group (NZ), cnr Airborne and Rosedale Roads, Albany, Auckland 1310, New Zealand (a division of Pearson New Zealand Ltd)

Penguin Books (South Africa) (Pty) Ltd, 24 Sturdee Avenue, Rosebank, Johannesburg 2196, South Africa

Penguin Books Ltd, Registered Offices: 80 Strand, London WC2R 0RL, England

Copyright © 2006 by Joni E. Johnston

International Standard Book Number: 1-59257-500-5
Library of Congress Catalog Card Number: 2005910784

08   07   8   7   6   5   4   3

Interpretation of the printing code: The rightmost number of the first series of numbers is the year of the book's printing; the rightmost number of the second series of numbers is the number of the book's printing. For example, a printing code of 06-1 shows that the first printing occurred in 2006.

Printed in the United States of America

Note: This publication contains the opinions and ideas of its author. It is intended to provide helpful and informative material on the subject matter covered. It is sold with the understanding that the author and publisher are not engaged in rendering professional services in the book. If the reader requires personal assistance or advice, a competent professional should be consulted.

Publisher: *Marie Butler-Knight*
Editorial Director: *Mike Sanders*
Managing Editor: *Billy Fields*
Acquisitions Editor: *Tom Stevens*
Development Editor: *Michael Thomas*
Production Editor: *Megan Douglass*
Copy Editor: *Jan Zoya*

Cartoonist: *Chris Eliopoulos*
Book Designers: *Trina Wurst/Kurt Owens*
Cover Designer: *Bill Thomas*
Indexer: *Julie Bess*
Layout: *Brian Massey*
Proofreader: *John Etchison*

Contents at a Glance

Contents

Foreword

If your mind came with an owner's manual, what would it say? *The Complete Idiot's Guide to Psychology, Third Edition*, offers you just that glimpse. Why your moods change, what motivates you and those around you, why you feel what you feel, and what turns you on and what turns you off are just a few of the questions for which you can expect to find answers.

As psychologists, we help people every day to find the solutions to some of their most haunting problems. Those answers can be complex and difficult. The beauty of *The Complete Idiot's Guide to Psychology, Third Edition*, is that it puts so many theories at your fingertips and then simplifies them in a way that helps you to apply this crucial information to your life.

The Complete Idiot's Guide to Psychology, Third Edition, is certain to give you insight into your career choices, family relationships, and love relationships. How your brain works is a fascinating adventure that has never been more understandable. To the extent that you can see how your mind and body work together to produce stress, your unique formula for bringing the stresses of everyday living under your own control will become far more understandable. Even more importantly, you will learn in simple and clear terms about the things that make you anxious, along with tips for overcoming your anxiety. If you or someone you know is depressed, it could be invaluable to gain insight into the nature of depression and how it is treated in state-of-the-art terms. Addictions, eating disorders, and sexual dysfunctions are stripped of their stigma and put into perspective.

You will understand the causes of and treatment for personality disorders as well as the more severe mental illnesses. Until now, it was extremely difficult to find so much research and bottom-line explanation for the many aspects of that vast and mysterious subject of human psychology in one place. *The Complete Idiot's Guide to Psychology, Third Edition*, gives you all the important information that you would expect to find in the finest introductory psychology textbook, without drowning you in the details or the trivia. The examples given are both user friendly and highly applicable to your life. In addition, you will learn much about the field of psychology itself: its history, the pioneers, and even some of the contemporary leaders of the field whose work continues to evolve today. This plethora of information is easy to find and fun to use.

So get ready for a wonderful adventure into who you are and how you became that way. On this incredible journey, be prepared to learn things that will help you now and in the future as well as clarify for you what may have been going on at some time in the past. You will meet many people along the way who are presented as case studies that you will highly identify with, or recognize in those people who are or have been a part of your life. Whether you are reading this book as a manual to understanding yourself, as a primer on the field, or as a study aid, enjoy your journey!

Michael S. Broder, Ph.D., and Arlene Goldman, Ph.D.
Authors of *The Secrets of Sexual Ecstasy*

Introduction

If you're into immediate gratification, then psychology is for you. What other subject can you instantly apply to every aspect of your life? And it's practical. Learn about human nature and you can't help but understand and improve your own.

The purpose of this book is to give you a quick and comprehensive overview of psychology. Although I've tried to stay off my soapbox, I'd be less than honest if I didn't tell you that my own "psychology" may at times color this book. Obviously, a book of this length can't cover everything, and you'll notice I spend more time talking about psychological disorders than psychological theory. And you'll certainly encounter my optimistic bias about human resilience (I never recovered from *The Grapes of Wrath*). However, you now hold in your hands a good place to start, a road map for your journey into the human psyche. Here's how it looks:

Part 1, "Putting It in Perspective," sets the stage for our human drama. In these chapters, we'll meet the major players in psychology and visit the various schools they started. We'll then shift to various theories of evolution—how psychology as a science evolved, how human behavior evolved, and how individual behavior evolves.

In **Part 2, "Wake Up and Smell the Coffee,"** we'll explore how we make sense of the world, starting with our ability to touch, taste, hear, see, and smell. We'll investigate how information from the world around us becomes grist for our psychic mills, and how we raise our consciousness and all the ways we alter it. We then turn to the fascinating subjects of learning and memory—how we profit from experiences and the peculiar ways we remember them, and how we organize things in our minds.

Part 3, "The Forces Are with You," unleashes the forces that drive human behavior. We'll look at motives, drives, emotions, and all the other things that rouse us to action. We'll look at our hunger and sex drives in depth, and then switch gears to examine the power of language to shape our lives. And we'll wind up with an exploration of stress—what people do when the forces in their lives get out of control.

While the first three parts look at qualities that we all share, **Part 4, "Self and Otherness,"** dares to be different. In this section, we'll cover all the characteristics that make each person unique, starting with the formation of our identity and ending with our individual brand of psychic self-defense. In between, we'll explore intelligence, personality development, and the difference between quirky personality traits and mental illness.

Part 5, "Just What Is Normal, Anyway?" serves up the meat of clinical psychology—the ability to distinguish between what's normal and what's not. The first chapter in this section takes a close look at the pros and cons of psychological diagnoses, why we have them, and who decides what they are. The next chapter looks at a relatively new branch of psychology—positive psychology—and some of the tools that can move us from surviving to thriving.

The chapters in **Part 6, "Between a Rock and a Hard Place,"** take a look at the latest weapons in the battles against mental illness, dissect the major psychological disorders, and tease out, based on scientific evidence, what psychological treatment works best for what problem.

Extras

In addition to the main narrative of *The Complete Idiot's Guide to Psychology, Third Edition*, you'll find the following other useful types of information:

Insight

Quick points or observations that shed light on a confusing topic or provide a bit of useful self-help advice.

 Brain Buster

Brief tidbits that debunk popular myths and misconceptions or warn you away from common errors or problems.

 **def•i•ni•tion**

Short summaries that define psychological terms in a fun and comprehensible way.

Psychobabble

Anecdotes or information that is too bizarre, interesting, helpful, or juicy to leave out.

Acknowledgments

Hillary Clinton once said it takes a village to raise a child. Well, it also takes a village to write a book, or, I should say, for *me* to write a book. Here's where I get to say thanks to all the people who worked in my writing "village" and raised me (sometimes, it seemed, from the dead) while I was writing this book:

- To my literary agent, Evan Fogelman (a.k.a. Hercules), who has the patience of a saint and the heart of a lion.

- To Jessica Faust, for giving me the chance to talk about psychology and then actually liking what I had to say.

◆ To the talented Nancy Gratton, Eric Heagy, and Jennifer Moore, for turning my literary lemons into lemonade.

◆ To Zach, Zane, Zhanna and Zaylin, who inspire me every day to try to master the art of motherhood (and who have motivated me to learn more than a few stress-management strategies).

◆ To my sister, Julie, a master in the psychology of sisterly love.

◆ And to my editor-in-chief, husband, and best friend—Alex Tsakiris—for everything.

Special Thanks to the Technical Reviewers

The Complete Idiot's Guide to Psychology, Third Edition, was reviewed by two experts who double-checked the accuracy of what you'll learn here, to help us ensure that this book gives you everything you need to know about psychology. Special thanks are extended to Michael S. Broder, Ph.D., and Arlene Goldman, Ph.D.

Michael S. Broder, Ph.D., and Arlene Goldman, Ph.D. are psychologists, husband and wife, and co-authors of *Secrets of Sexual Ecstasy*. Dr. Broder's other books include *The Art of Living Single, The Art of Staying Together,* and *Can Your Relationship Be Saved?* They live and practice in Philadelphia, Pennsylvania. Visit Dr. Broder at DrMichaelBroder.com.

Trademarks

Part 1

Putting It in Perspective

The study of psychology is as complex as its subject—the human psyche and human behavior. So it's no surprise that the development of the discipline took a lot of twists and turns to get to where it is today. In these first few chapters, you're going to trace the development of the various schools of psychology and the singular contributions made by their founders. From there, it's on to a discussion of how human behavior, and the behavior of individuals, has evolved.

Chapter 1

A Little Psychological Insight

In This Chapter

- Understanding psychology
- A day in the life
- Psychology's major players
- How psychologists "do" psychology
- Psychology's many points of view

Psychology has come a long way, baby, from its early years. Way back when, in the nineteenth century, much of what passed for psychological practice was based on guesswork, informed by the social prejudices of the day. It took the contributions of a great many careful researchers and deep thinkers to give birth to the modern science of psychology—and every day, new insights are achieved.

This chapter will tell you what psychology is and what it's not. You'll meet the major players in the development of the science, and you'll understand the tools psychologists use to figure people out. By the time you've finished this chapter, you'll be well on your way to thinking like a shrink!

What's Psychology?

Psychology is the science of human nature. It's all about studying the human mind and behavior so that we can figure out why people think, feel, and do what they do. How do we fall in love, communicate with each other, solve problems, and learn new things? Psychologists are constantly asking questions, developing theories, and conducting experiments so that they can better understand human nature and improve our lives. Whether they're therapists, professors, or researchers, psychologists are constantly trying to reach four goals:

◆ To describe what people do

◆ To explain why people think, feel, and act the way we do

◆ To predict what, when, and how we will do it

◆ To change the parts of human behavior that cause us pain

Let's take a look at each of these goals.

Telling It Like It Is

The first goal of psychology, describing human behavior, sounds easy: just watch what someone is doing and describe it. It's a lot tougher, though, than you might think. No matter how hard we try not to, we see each other through the filters of our prior experiences, our cultural values, and our beliefs.

For example, if you've just been dumped by the love of your life, it might be pretty hard to jump into a new relationship with complete optimism. You might try to protect yourself by watching closely for any sign of rejection. In fact, you might be so worried about getting hurt that you overlook evidence that your new love cares about you. Your mental filter has a worthy goal, to prevent more heartache, but it's still blinding you from seeing the world the way it really is.

Here's another example of how expectations and beliefs can cloud your vision: when asked to describe their newborns, parents of daughters will describe them as softer, smaller, and weaker than parents of sons, even when there is no actual difference in size, shape, or health. Even at birth, parents are "seeing" their children with eyes that reflect their expectations about gender.

Psychologists also have their share of biases, expectations, and prejudices, which, whether they're doing therapy or research, they're constantly trying to keep out of their work. That's why therapists consult with their peers: to make sure they're keeping their own "stuff" from interfering with their sessions with their patients. "Telling it like it is" is no easy task!

> **Insight**
>
> Want to start applying psychology to your life right now? Use what you learn in this book to solve just one real problem in your life—or, at least, to understand it better.

Why, Oh Why, Oh Why?

Any mystery novel buff will tell you that the motive in the whodunit is as important as who did it. Like mystery writers, psychologists often focus on the motives driving a person's behavior. They look for connections between things that happen and how people respond. Why do some—but not all—abused children become abusive adults? How does a brain tumor affect someone's personality? Does watching violent television lead to violent behavior? These are examples of the kinds of relationships psychologists try to explain.

Explanations are also useful in everyday life. People often seek therapy to make sense out of a painful situation such as a divorce or a loss. Even if we can't change what has happened to us, understanding the reason it happened gives us a sense of comfort and control, a sense that maybe we can prevent it from happening again.

What's Next?

Understanding why something happened is helpful, but being able to predict that something is going to happen gives us a lot more practical utility.

For example, here's a psychological fact of life: when it comes to human beings, the best predictor of future behavior is past behavior. How can that be useful in your day-to-day life?

Well, let's say you've been dating someone for six months and are starting to get serious. During a romantic dinner, your new love

> **Insight**
>
> Research shows that a psychologist is likely to overestimate the likelihood that prisoner Joe will become violent even after extensively interviewing and testing him. Asking a psychologist what a single person will do is like asking a physicist to predict what will happen to a particular drop of water in the ocean.

interest suddenly confesses that he's been married four times. This information might change your prediction about the odds that the two of you will turn gray together. You may be tempted to pull out your little black book of former loves and make a few calls. And you'd have good reason to do so—your dinner companion's past behavior suggests that, when it comes to long-term commitments, he's *not* a reliable candidate.

Or, at least, that's the obvious conclusion to draw. But let's look at a real-life example: well-known writer Harlan Ellison. By 1985, he had been married four times, each time for less than four years before the marriage ended in divorce. Statistically speaking, the odds of a successful fifth marriage surviving beyond his four-year-itch would seem very low. However, Ellison, apparently an eternal optimist, married again in 1986—and is still married to the same woman!

For better or worse, the best predictor of human behavior isn't always accurate. As a profession, psychology has an abominable track record for predicting what any one person will do. Real life doesn't always cooperate with what theory says should happen—especially when you're dealing with what a single individual might do in a given set of circumstances.

When it comes to predicting behavior within a group, psychology does much better. For example, what if you wanted to predict the relationship between intelligence and success? Whether a smart individual will live up to her potential will be determined by lots of variables—maybe she is lazy, has a serious medical illness, or can't get along with others. A psychologist can't easily predict that intelligence in this *particular* person will result in success in life. But psychologists *can* accurately predict that intelligent people, taken as a group, are more likely to be successful than their unintelligent counterparts.

Of course, what you're measuring is just as important as your data. Since 9/11, racial profiling—the use of demographic statistics—to justify restrictive government activity, has increased. And, historically, many African Americans have complained that they've been stopped by law enforcement for nothing more than "DWB"—driving while black.

Becoming the New, Improved Model

Human beings are always trying to improve, do better, or feel better, so it should come as no surprise that psychologists want to do more than understand human behavior. They want to shape it, mold it, and generally help people run their lives more effectively. The heart of all psychological treatment is teaching a client how to move his behavior in the desired direction—to stop drinking, to communicate more effectively, to cope with the memories of a painful childhood.

A Day in the Life of a Shrink

Take a psychologist to the movies and he or she may watch the audience instead.

Shrinks are always trying to figure out who people are and why they think, feel, and behave as they do. But there are lots of different ways they go about their work.

The Couch Trip

Most people picture a psychologist sitting behind a couch or desk and listening to people's problems all day. They visualize Robin Williams in *Good Will Hunting* or Barbra Streisand in *The Prince of Tides*. These are images of clinical psychologists, the branch of psychology that trains psychiatrists to deal with people's emotional and behavioral problems. However, although clinical psychology is the most popular area of specialization, most clinical psychologists aren't in private practice; most of them work in clinics, hospitals, or universities.

They're Everywhere, They're Everywhere!

And they do a lot more than therapy. They teach, they promote mental and physical health, they help businesses run more smoothly, and they conduct research. You can find psychiatrists in just about any place you'd find human beings—courtrooms, campuses, locker rooms, hospitals, or boardrooms.

And then there are the other branches of psychology. Not only do they study individual behavior, but they also study the relationships between individuals and anything they may do or influence. Social psychologists study how people influence one another. Environmental psychologists work with architects and city planners to improve the "relationship" between human beings and their workspaces and living quarters. Believe it or not, there's even a group, called human factors psychologists, who look at the relationships between workers and their machines!

"Doing" Psychology

There are lots of ways to study human beings. Astrologists use the moon and the stars, philosophers apply logic and reasoning, and psychics consult tea leaves and crystal balls. Psychology got *its* start when great philosophers began thinking about human nature.

How They Used to Do It

For hundreds of years, philosophers thought a lot about people, but most of them thought human nature was a spiritual matter that could not be studied scientifically. Luckily for us, in the seventeenth century, a philosopher by the name of René Descartes thought otherwise, and people slowly began changing their minds.

It wasn't until the end of the nineteenth century, though, that people went beyond just *thinking* about human nature and started *studying* it. In 1879, Wilhelm Wundt founded the first psychological laboratory at the University of Leipzig in Germany, and psychology as an academic discipline was born. This transformed psychology from philosophy to a science, and forever changed the study of human behavior.

Intuition, logic, common sense, and introspection were no longer acceptable ways to study human nature. Researchers now had to look at objective, outside evidence that either confirmed or disconfirmed their ideas about human beings. Psychologists developed a "show-me" attitude.

Psychology Today

In today's scientific climate, valid research questions about human behavior are those that are testable and replicable. They should be answerable through someone's first-hand experience, with no reliance on "experts," hearsay, or religious dogma. If I wonder whether studying before a test lowers test-taking anxiety, I'll research the question by finding students who hit the books before an exam and see whether they're less nervous than their less-studious counterparts.

Then, if you, too, are curious about the link between anxiety and studying, you can ask the same question, do the same research, and see if you get the same answer that I did. That's the *scientific method*.

Research psychologists are always checking up on each other's findings. After scientists publish results, their colleagues try to shoot holes through them, offering alternative explanations, and seeing whether they can get the same result. This asking, theorizing, predicting, testing, and retesting forms the basis of what we know about human psychology today.

But not everything can be directly observed in a laboratory or field test. Many human activities, such as reasoning, creating, or dreaming, are private; we assume they happen, but we can't see them. Psychology as a science draws its conclusions about such activities by observing what a person does, when he or she does it, and how he or she does it.

Through their careful observations of human behavior, psychologists make inferences about the mind. However, any judgments about thoughts or feelings must be checked out—after all, appearances *can* be deceiving. For example, if I greet my husband and he ignores me, I might immediately assume that he's mad at me. If I ask him about it, however, I might learn that he wasn't giving me the silent treatment on purpose. Maybe he was preoccupied with work or, more likely, is temporarily hard of hearing after watching three football games at maximum volume!

def•i•ni•tion

The **scientific method** is a way of answering questions that helps remove bias from the study. First, you form your question into a statement that can be disproved; then you test it against observable facts. Other researchers who doubt your findings can duplicate your test and see whether they get the same results.

Insight

On March 2, 2002, the state of New Mexico granted prescription privileges to clinical psychologists, making it the first state where specially trained clinical psychologists can prescribe medication for their patients. In addition to cost considerations, this groundbreaking decision was likely guided by scientific research showing that, for many mental diseases, a combination of medication and psychotherapy is most effective.

Methods to Studying Madness

Science gave psychologists some pretty clear guidelines for studying human behavior:

- Be skeptical.

- Keep your values and opinions separate from your ideas and beliefs.

- Only ask questions that you can answer yourself.

- Show other people your results.

- Make sure that other people can check your answers.

Psychology as a science dictates what kinds of questions we can ask—they must be objective and replicable. But how do we decide which questions to ask? *Theories*, my dear Watson. A theory is a set of related principles used to explain or predict something.

Because human beings are so complex, psychologists have theories for just about everything from learning to child development, from memory to mental illness. Personality theories try to explain why human beings are the way they are; development theory looks at how children become grownups. And different theoretical perspectives about what parts of human nature are important influence the questions that we can ask.

If, for instance, we theorize that mental illness is a result of painful childhood experiences, we start to wonder what particular kinds of painful childhood experiences cause the most damage. Or we may ask if the age at which the experience happens makes a difference.

def•i•ni•tion

A **theory** is a set of assumptions about a question. A **hypothesis** is an answer to the question, based on theoretical assumptions that we can test to see whether the answer can be proven wrong.

Next, we start to generate *hypotheses*, predictions about what we would expect to happen if our theory were true. If we believe that a person's childhood has a major impact on his or her adult life, for example, we might expect abused children to have some problems when they grow up. To test our hypothesis, we would conduct a study using one or more scientifically appropriate research methods, chosen to suit the kind of question we are asking. The most common research methods are *descriptive studies*, *correlation research*, and *experiments*.

Delving into the Descriptive

If the question starts with "How often," "How much," or "How many times," then a descriptive study is the way to go. In this method, the researcher describes the behavior of a person or group of people. For example, we might ask how much violence the average child sees on television. Or we might survey people to see what percentage of the population has been treated for depression. Or, if we're assessing a person's assertiveness, we might count the number of times he or she speaks up in a group.

Is There a Relationship?

Descriptive studies give us a good idea of what we're looking at, but they don't tell us what it all means. For example, discovering the level of violence a child sees on television may be interesting, but we're more concerned about discovering whether there's a relationship between watching violent television and a child's aggressive behavior. Correlational research tries to assess the relationship between two aspects of human behavior.

Researchers always have to remember a golden rule: correlation does not equal causation. *Huh?* Translated into English, that means that just because two things are related, it does not mean that one caused the other.

Let's assume we're going to do a study on TV violence and aggressive behavior in children, beginning with the theory that there is a positive relationship between watching violent television and aggressive behavior in children. Our hypothesis is that children who watch violent television are more aggressive than those who watch little or no violent television.

Brain Buster

Research is only as good as the theory behind it, and the best theories are simple, precise, and testable.

Right away, we run into problems. How are we going to measure aggression? This sounds simple but it's not. We might count the number of times a child is sent to the principal's office, but that could be misleading: some teachers run a tight ship, whereas others may be real slackers. We might rely on the number of times a sibling complains about a shoot-'em-up-show-watching child's hitting and shoving. However, depending upon tattletales introduces all kinds of problems, such as loyalty, sibling rivalry, and even the possibility of bribery! All of these extra issues can make our measurements unreliable.

One way to overcome such problems is to give the children's parents some kind of behavior-rating scale that clearly defines aggressive behavior. We'll be equally clear in defining what we want to count as exposure to violent television: do we measure the number of violent incidents in any show or just the number of violent shows? Does yelling count as violence? Do shoot-'em-up cartoons rate the same as live news coverage of terrorism?

Once we have measured both behaviors, we compare the results. If children with high violent television viewing are also rated as more aggressive than children who watch tamer fare, we have some support for our theory. If, on the other hand, children who watch violent television are less aggressive, we'd have to look for another explanation. And we'd have a new hypothesis to test: perhaps watching violent television serves as a safe outlet for children's anger and aggression and actually reduces the odds that they will act violently.

The Experimental Experience

To tease out the cause and effect between two things, the researcher changes one and sees what effect this change has on the other. The thing the experimenter changes is called the *independent* variable; the thing that is influenced by the independent variable is called the *dependent* variable.

If we want to find out whether exposure to violent television causes children to be more aggressive, we might show children violent television one hour this week, ten hours the next, and five hours the week after that. Each week, we'd see how changing the TV-watching time (the independent variable) affects aggression levels (the dependent variable).

> **Insight**
>
> In 2005, researchers announced that 20 years of the experimental method has provided a solid link between aggressive video games and short- and long-term violence in children and adolescents, especially when players see aggressive videogame characters receive no consequences for their actions.

But our experiment may still fail to give us clear-cut results. That's because of *confounding variables*—things that aren't supposed to be a part of the experiment but creep in anyway and influence the results.

In our example, parental expectations might confound the results. If parents knew the amount of violent television that their children were watching each week, they might unintentionally rate their children as being more aggressive during weeks of heavy viewing because they expected that behavior. We can try to safeguard against this by leaving the parents in the dark about the actual amount of their child's exposure to violent television during the period of our observations (but, of course, we'd get the parents' permission for this at the outset of the experiment).

Keeping Junk Science out of Your Mental Closet

"Soft drinks harmful to children." "Obesity kills 400,000 Americans each year." "Lose weight without cutting calories or exercising." Each of these 2004 news stories were based on allegedly sound scientific studies that, upon closer inspection, had more holes than Swiss cheese. Unfortunately, the weight that "science" carries in our society can make us suckers for just about any statistic we read.

"Junk science" is a term used to describe research based on faulty, insufficient, unreliable, twisted, dredged-up, or biased data. It often has a hidden agenda: the personal injury attorney trying to win money for his or her client, the scientist seeking personal fame, the corporation trying to sell its product, or the political activist seeking to support his or her political agenda. However, being able to separate the scientific wheat from the chaff is an important skill; for example, it might influence whether or not you start a certain diet, get help for a child with a learning disability, or make a life-saving phone call to your physician.

So how can you tell what's bunk from what's breakthrough? Start by asking the following questions:

◆ **Says who?** Hundreds of newspaper stories between 1993 and 2001 encouraged new parents to permanently boost their babies' I.Q. by playing Mozart music to them. However, the original study that spawned this myth (and two self-help books) was conducted with *college students* and found only a *temporary* increase in the ability to perform a specific task while listening to a Mozart sonata. A dozen subsequent studies failed to support even this. The moral of this story is to make sure you know who was involved in the study, how they were selected, who did not respond or participate, and how the study population matched—or didn't— the claims.

◆ **How did they ask "why?"** Claims based on a single or a few observations aren't "data," and statistics don't prove cause and effect. Mice aren't humans and exposure doesn't mean toxicity. Make sure you know the limits to the methods the studies used to back their claims.

◆ **What are alternative explanations?** A study claims that a new French language program is superior to its three competitors; the evidence is the superior results of a French test given to four groups, each of whom has received three months of French instruction using one of the four products. Convinced? Not yet, I hope. What do you know about the four groups? What if the new French language program was tested on Harvard seniors while the three competitors were given to college dropouts?

Multiple Perspective Disorder

If you've ever seen the movies *Sybil* or *Three Faces of Eve*, then you're aware of multiple personality disorder, a rare mental illness in which a person develops different personalities to cope with severe childhood trauma. Psychologists have their own version of this, and it has haunted the field of psychology since its early years: I call it multiple perspective disorder.

Insight

The human mind is amazingly complex. No single perspective—the biological, the behavioral, the emotional—can tell the whole story.

Imagine setting out to become the world's authority on elephants and studying only their legs. You can tell a lot about an elephant from its legs—the texture of its skin, the climate in which it lives, maybe even its travel patterns. You might even make a few guesses about its size and weight. On the other hand, you would be clueless about its mating habits, eating rituals, or defense strategies. Even if you studied for years, the best you could do is become the leading expert on elephant legs. It'd be ludicrous to claim you truly understood elephants.

Yet for years, that's exactly what some psychologists did. Some groups studied the mind, while others focused on human behavior. Some believed that childhood influences unlocked the key to our psyches and spent their time analyzing dreams and unlocking childhood memories. Others believed it was the here and now that mattered. Seven different perspectives emerged during the twentieth century, and most of them claimed to be *the* right way to study human nature. At times, battles became pretty heated over whose perspective was right.

Fortunately, psychologists today value the unique contribution of *each* psychological perspective. While some psychologists might still tell you that their beliefs about human nature fall in line with one particular perspective, in practice they are likely to apply whichever perspective best deals with the problem at hand. For, as you shall see, each perspective offers valuable insights into human nature. The seven perspectives most prevalent today include the following:

1. The biological perspective

2. The psychodynamic perspective

3. The behaviorist perspective

4. The humanist perspective

5. The cognitive perspective

6. The sociocultural perspective

7. The evolutionary perspective

I Was Born This Way

Biological psychology enjoyed its most recent vogue during the 1990s when Congress declared it the "decade of the brain." And what a decade it was! Thanks to biological psychology, we have a much better understanding of the role our biological makeup plays in mental health and mental illness.

The biological perspective looks to the body to explain the mind. Biological psychologists look at the influence of hormones, genes, the brain, and the central nervous system on the way we think, feel, and act. How much of our personality is inherited? Is there a gene for suicide? Does mental stress cause physical illness? Do the brains of schizophrenics function differently than those of normal people? In the endless "nature versus nurture" debate of human behavior (see Chapter 3), biological psychology clearly sides with nature.

Brain Buster

Your genes may be causing your blues! We now know that depression runs in families, and that there are chemical changes in the brain that coincide with clinical depression. Medications, psychotherapy, and other treatments can adjust these changes and chase depression away.

Biological psychology has been instrumental in the development of medications that effectively treat depression, anxiety, bipolar disorder, and schizophrenia. It has reawakened our awareness of the mind/body connection and given us specific ways to measure, and conquer, stress. Through its identification of the physiological components of many mental illnesses, it has helped tear down the false dichotomy between illnesses of the mind and illnesses of the body. This has helped to remove the stigma associated with mental illness—a development that has been as beneficial to people's mental health as any technique developed in the last 20 years!

It's Only the Tip of the Iceberg

The psychoanalytic perspective (psychoanalysis is the technique, not the theory) views behavior as driven by powerful mental conflicts locked deep within the subconscious. Sigmund Freud, the father of psychoanalysis, thought most people were riddled with conflicts between their own needs and society's demands.

Freud thought that an adult's mind was like the tip of an iceberg: he believed that conflicts arise, and are pushed down, when we are children. Because of this, we have little insight into the motives that drive our behavior as adults. We do, however, get clues through dreams, *slips* of the tongue, or sudden, unexplainable behavior. Freud believed that unconscious conflicts were the source of his patients' pain and frequently led them to behave in an irrational manner.

def•i•ni•tion

A **Freudian slip** is a mistake or substitution of either spoken or written words. Freud believed that such "slips" come from unconscious wishes that pop up unexpectedly through unintentional words. By analyzing these "slips," a person might get some clues into his or her inner thoughts or "real" intent or wishes.

Freud also believed that children are naturally sexual and aggressive, but he believed that society was not willing to accept these natural urges in youngsters. He specifically pointed the finger at parents who, he claimed, often became upset when faced with a child's erection or natural interest in bodily functions, and often punished the child for expressing natural urges.

Thus Freud explained the beginnings of psychological and behavioral problems. To survive the threat of parental punishment, the child quickly learned to push these natural urges out of sight and out of mind. Freud attributed much of human discomfort to the ongoing battle between our own individual needs and desires and society's rules and norms, a battle that continues long after we pass through childhood.

Freud was perhaps the first to stress the influence of traumatic childhood events on shaping our personalities and worldviews. He was the first to recognize that human behavior is not always rational or easy to explain. He was also the first to use talking in a therapeutic setting as a cure for mental illness, and to see the healing that can occur when a client remembers, and works through, the trials and tribulations of childhood. Last but not least, Freud certainly had a way with words; he gave us many words that are now a common part of our lingo: Oedipal complex, penis envy, id, ego, and superego.

We're Just Rats Caught in a Maze

The behavioral perspective all started with rats. After spending many years watching rats race through mazes, a psychologist named John Watson realized he could accurately predict where a rat would run if he knew where it had found food on previous trials. He was impressed with the amount of information he could learn about rats just by watching their behavior and understanding the environment in which it occurred. And he could change the rat's behavior pretty quickly by putting the food in a different place.

Maybe, he thought, people aren't much different. Maybe we aren't as complicated as we think, and maybe all that mental mumbo jumbo like thoughts and feelings doesn't matter. Maybe, he proposed, human behavior is as simple as **ABC:**

Antecedent	The environmental trigger
Behavior	The behavioral response to the environmental trigger
Consequence	What happens next

Watson believed psychology should seek to understand people by studying what happens to them and how they respond. His focus was firmly on the bottom line: behavior. He theorized that behavior usually started as a response to an environmental event. From this he went on to reason that the consequences of that response would determine whether that behavior would increase over time or become less frequent.

Insight

You can (and probably already do, sometimes) use behaviorism in your daily life. Any time you use praise or rewards to get the kids to do their chores, you're acting like a behaviorist!

Let's say that every time the phone rings, your new love interest is on the line. Chances are you'll start racing for the phone at the first ring. On the other hand, if bill collectors often give you a jingle, you might ignore the telephone no matter how many times it rang.

Behaviorism ruled the psychological roost for almost 50 years, and it contributed many practical tools and ideas. For one thing, it shifted the focus of psychological research from generating insights onto behavior change. It gave us behavior modification, a process of shaping someone's behavior by consistently rewarding the desired actions, thus earning the eternal gratitude of countless parents, teachers, and savvy spouses! And it gave us some pretty powerful weapons against irrational fears and phobias (see Chapter 18).

I Think, Therefore I Am

Cognitive psychology is the study of people's ability to acquire, organize, remember, and use knowledge to guide their behavior. Cognitive psychologists think that we're much more than a bunch of rats. Yes, they say, we react to our environment, but we also act upon it: people solve problems, make decisions, and consider options and alternatives before we act.

The cognitive perspective assumes that there are connections between what people perceive, think, feel, and do. Unlike the behaviorists, cognitive psychologists think that what goes on inside someone's head is of critical importance. In fact, they believe that a lot of how we feel and what we do starts with what we're thinking, not with some impersonal stimulus from the environment. They would argue, for example, that someone who sees a cancer diagnosis as a meaningful personal challenge is likely to approach his or her treatment very differently than someone who views it as a death sentence.

Although the cognitive perspective focuses on the mind, it doesn't rely on introspection or intuition to study it. Cognitive psychologists study human behavior and then make inferences about the mind from their observations. For example, Swiss psychologist Jean Piaget gave children a series of problems to solve and then documented the mistakes they made and their reasons for their answers. After testing many children at varying ages, he formed his theory about how children develop their ability to reason.

Cognitive researchers develop theories about the mental processes that influence what we do. They test those theories by creating situations in which people would be expected to behave in one predictable way if the theory were true, or in another way if the theory were not true. Through the influence of cognitive psychology, we understand more about decision making, creativity, and problem solving than ever before. We've also learned how to do them better.

The influence of cognitive psychology is everywhere today. You see it in the numerous self-help books that proclaim the power of self-talk, and in the concept of attitude adjustment. If you've ever heard anyone say, "When life gives you lemons, make lemonade," he or she is speaking from a cognitive perspective.

It's a Dog-Eat-Dog World

You're probably familiar with Darwin's "survival of the fittest" idea. Darwin basically thought that the creatures whose inherited characteristics were best adapted to the environment were the ones that survived and reproduced. If a duck with a wide beak can get more food than narrow-beaked ducks, wide-beaked ducks will survive. Over time, all ducks will have wider beaks.

Evolutionary psychology applies that same principle of *natural selection* to human behavior. It holds that human beings, as a species, have acquired innate problem-solving tendencies that promote their survival and reproduction. Evolutionary psychologists study behaviors that are common among all humans and try to figure out how those behaviors helped us become top dog of the animal kingdom. They believe that a key to understanding human nature is in the behavior of our ancestors; if we can reconstruct the problems our ancestors dealt with, then we can understand the problem-solving tendencies that helped them survive and thus became a genetic part of being human.

For example, all human beings hate, love, and get angry. Evolutionary psychologists would say we inherited the ability to express our feelings from our ancestors because the ability to communicate feelings and intentions helped them survive. Once we know how our emotions evolved, we can be more aware of, and therefore control, these natural tendencies.

def•i•ni•tion

Natural selection is the Darwinian principle that says the best-adapted traits are the ones that will be passed along from one generation to another in a species. Creatures with less-well-adapted traits will die out before they can reproduce, so their poorly adapted traits will eventually disappear from the population.

Insight

Evolutionary psychologists have identified 26 behavior traits that all humans on our planet share. Here are a just a few of the more interesting ones: deception, detecting emotions, gossip, humor, perception of status/rank, and romantic love.

Of course, who, what, or when any one human being will love is a lot more complicated; we must also look at his or her culture, life experiences, genes, and personality. And we still have to contend with the here and now. A man might blame his having an affair on an ancestral legacy that called for men to ensure maximum reproduction by mating with multiple partners. He's still going to face his wife's wrath, and, possibly, the consequences of his behavior in court!

No Man Is an Island

Why do eating disorders only occur in countries like the United States, where "thin" is the beauty ideal? If aggression is a human instinct, why is the rate of violence so different from country to country? A sociocultural psychologist would tell you that if you want to understand such human behaviors, you must start with the culture in which people live.

All human beings have minds, but each culture produces a different version. The sociocultural perspective focuses on the differences among people living in various cultures as well as the ways by which people's thoughts, feelings, and behavior are influenced by their culture. From this perspective, our culture influences how we think, feel, and act. Culture teaches us about the roles we play and gives us informal rules about what is, and what is not, socially acceptable. If you've ever visited another country, you've encountered the sociocultural perspective up close; it can be quite a shock realizing that what's "normal" is suddenly different!

Even psychology has cultural biases. In the United States, a country that values self-sufficiency and individualism, the focus of therapy is often on individual behavior change. In many Asian countries, where fitting into the group is a highly valued trait, therapy would emphasize the understanding and acceptance of ourselves and the people around us. And in some Latin American cultures, where the family unit is *numero uno*, it would seem absurd to treat someone without including the whole family; behavior we would describe as healthy and independent might be viewed as selfish!

Looking on the Bright Side

Undoubtedly, the stereotype of the "touchy-feely" psychologist started with a humanist. As a backlash against the doom and gloom of the psychoanalytic perspective and the behaviorist's robotic view of humankind, the humanists looked on the bright side of human nature. People are naturally good, the humanists said, and if left to their own devices, they will strive to become the best they can be. Problems only come up when other people get in their way.

According to this view, a parent or teacher might criticize a child's natural attempt to grow. If this happens often enough, such criticized children begin to doubt their own thoughts and feelings. They begin to see themselves as incapable and, as a result, start mistrusting their own judgment. As adults, they may not take charge of their own lives because they no longer believe they are capable of doing so.

With this theoretical viewpoint, it's not surprising that regaining a positive self-concept is a major therapeutic goal. The self-esteem movement started with humanists; in addition to their emphasis on promoting positive self-concepts, the humanists encourage therapists to look at their clients' psychological reality—the way they perceive their experiences, rather than focusing on the experiences themselves. From the humanist perspective, a person's view of his or her life is much more important than what actually happened—understand her perspective and you'll know why she thinks, feels, and acts the way she does.

Psychology in Action

Different psychological perspectives offer different explanations for the same behavior. Take a look at how each perspective might try to explain this fictional scenario:

Janine, a straight-A college student and track star, lined up to compete at the NCAA 5,000-meter regional finals—held later on the same day that she had to take her MCAT. Having spent the night studying for that all-important exam, Janine was operating on three hours of sleep. As the runners took off, Janine got off to a slow start and fell behind. Suddenly, she veered off the track, scaled an 8-foot fence, and jumped off a 45-foot bridge. Her injuries ended her running career and indefinitely postponed her dream of medical school.

A Potpourri of Psychological Perspectives

Perspective	Burning Questions	Possible Answers
Psychoanalytic	What forces drove Janine so hard that she "snapped"?	Maybe her parents pushed her too much; perhaps she overcompensated for feelings of inadequacy by "winning" and panicked at the thought of failure.
Behaviorist	What have been the previous consequences for Janine when she lost a race? In the past, did she usually lose when she fell behind?	Maybe past losses were followed by painful consequences (criticism or derision) and Janine was trying to avoid experiencing them again.

continues

A Potpourri of Psychological Perspectives   (continued)

Perspective	Burning Questions	Possible Answers
Humanist	Was Janine's self-image such that she only felt loved and respected if she won?	Maybe she was trying to change the basis of her self-worth or trying to test her friends' and family's love for her.
Cognitive	What was Janine thinking during the race? How did these thoughts lead her to act the way she did?	Maybe her fear of failure interfered with her ability to think rationally and thus impaired her judgment.
Sociocultural	What has American culture taught Janine about winning and the price of failure? How would she expect others to treat her if she lost the race?	Maybe Janine's behavior was so desperate because of the social consequences she anticipated if she failed; maybe she took "winning isn't everything, it's the only thing" to the extreme.
Biological	Did Janine have an undetected medical condition that was aggravated by the running? Maybe she had a predisposition toward impulsive behavior?	Maybe Janine had an untreated chemical imbalance; maybe she had a brain tumor or some other physical problem that caused her to act out of character; maybe the physical effects of sleep deprivation were a factor.
Evolutionary	Was Janine's behavior an example of adaptive behavior gone awry?	Maybe Janine perceived her fear of failure like our ancestors perceived threatening predators and was trying to flee from them.

Each perspective approaches the scenario from a different set of assumptions (theoretical position) and therefore comes up with a different question to answer. Each question has a certain amount of validity, but it's clear that no single perspective asks, or answers, every question that the scenario raises. In the chapters that follow, we'll look more closely at how insights from all of these psychological perspectives have contributed to the development of the science of psychology as we know it today.

The Least You Need to Know

- Psychology is the scientific study of human behavior and mental processes.

- Psychologists wear a lot of different hats: they research why people think, feel, and act the way they do. They help people solve their problems, and they use their knowledge about human behavior to help courts, companies, schools, and sports teams run more efficiently.

- Because psychology is a science, the questions it raises must be objective and testable, and research must be theory based, systematic, and replicable.

- Predicting the behavior of groups is much easier than predicting the behavior of individuals. Applying statistical information about groups to one individual can be misleading and hurtful.

- There are seven major psychological perspectives in psychology today: biological, psychodynamic, sociocultural, evolutionary, cognitive, humanist, and behaviorist.

- Each of the perspectives employed by psychologists have contributed important insights into the how and why of human nature.

Chapter 2

Bio Psycho What?

In This Chapter

- ◆ The biology of psychology
- ◆ The best communication system ever invented
- ◆ What "getting on your nerves" really means
- ◆ Left brain or right?
- ◆ Why the brain doesn't always mind

"Let's brainstorm." "Watch it, you pea brain." "She's the brains behind it." When we listen to the words we use, it's clear that we know who rules the roost when it comes to human behavior. But we're still mystified by how it doesn't always listen to what we think we're telling it.

By the end of this chapter, you'll be up to speed on the biological hardware that programs human behavior. We'll explore the parts of the brain that cause us to think, feel, and do the things we do. We'll also explore how they do it; how different parts of the brain communicate with each other, how the brain gets along with the rest of the body, and how hormones and other chemicals influence human behavior. So let's get started at the real beginning of psychology—why we have the brains we have.

You Are What You Think

For hundreds of years, the Greeks thought the heart and blood were the head honchos of human beings. Who can blame them? Weighing in at around 3 pounds, the human brain looks like a wrinkled, gray cantaloupe. Even in the most vibrant human being, it appears to be sitting around doing nothing. When you contrast this with a fiery red, pulsing, beating heart, you'll understand why the Greeks made the heart our chief executive organ.

def•i•ni•tion

Phrenology was a pseudo-science in the nineteenth century that tried to use bumps on the skull as indications of intelligence and character. No wonder Ambrose Bierce defined phrenology as "the science of picking the pocket through the scalp!"

No, you can't tell a book by its cover, and you can't tell the marvels of the human brain by looking at it. If we want to understand human nature, we must first understand the nature of the brain because, in essence, psychology is the study of what the brain does. There's a biological counterpart to every thought or feeling we have. And, as you'll see, changes in the brain can dramatically change human behavior.

It's Evolutionary, My Dear Watson

We're all winners from an evolutionary perspective. The very fact that we're alive means our ancestors possessed favorable characteristics that enabled them to adapt and flourish in their natural environment. They passed these advantageous traits on to the next generation, who passed them on to their children, and so on, until here we are. We're the "fittest" in the "survival of the fittest."

Adapting to Changes

Ever feel like you finally figured out the rules of life and then someone changed them? So did our ancestors. Here they were, trying to adapt to their environment as best they could, and suddenly nature decided to play a joke or two. Resources became scarcer or the average temperature suddenly dropped. These environmental shifts could dramatically change which organisms were favored.

A dramatic rise in temperature, for example, might select against the animals with the heaviest fur. In addition, scarcity of resources sharpens the competitive edge and speeds up the natural selection process. Think about the scores needed to get into medical school or a competitive corporate environment and you'll know what I mean!

In terms of human evolution, two environmental adaptations assured us the highest place on the totem pole, and, of course, these are things all humans share today. These adaptations were *bipedalism*, the ability to walk upright, and *encephalization*, the development of a larger brain.

On Your Feet, Big Head!

Bipedalism, which occurred between 5 and 10 million years ago, freed our hands for grasping and tool use. It made us better able to explore and relocate than other species. When the going got tough, human beings were the first who were able to get going.

Human evolution really took off a couple of million years ago, when our brains got bigger. Encephalization gave us more "head room" for thinking and ultimately led to our increased ability to reason, remember, and plan.

From a psychological standpoint, though, we're more interested in what our evolutionary path means for brains living here and now. How do our brains help each one of us adapt to our environment today? How do they help us solve our problems, remember birthdays, and plan our future? To answer these questions, let's take a look at the human brain and what it does.

The Brains Behind the Research

A neuropsychologist is a psychologist specially trained in identification, assessment, and possible rehabilitation of brain damage. Neuropsychological assessment includes observation, personal history of the patient, and many specialized tests for memory, intelligence, and other functions. If a CT (computerized tomography) or an MRI (magnetic resonance image) gives us a picture of what the brain *looks* like, a neuropsychological assessment tells us what a person *can do* after injury or disease strikes.

Psychobabble

If you doubt there's a link between our brains and our behaviors, meet railroad manager Phineas Gage. In 1848, a construction explosion blasted an iron rod through his face and head. Astonishingly, he recovered from this injury and lived for another 12 years—but friends and family consistently said that he had changed from an efficient, capable manager to an irresponsible, moody, and, at times, vulgar human being. Phineas's altered brain created a changed man.

The Headquarters of Human Behavior

The brain contains more cells than there are stars in the universe. More than 100 billion of them, to be exact. And each part works together to produce, direct, and choreograph what we think, feel, and do.

A Living Record of Time Travel

One of the stories our brain tells us is the story of human evolution. From the neck up, it's structured in the order in which it evolved. The brain stem, the bulb where the brain meets the spine, is the oldest part of the brain; the midbrain and higher brain evolved on top of it in much the same way newer buildings are constructed on the old foundations of an ancient city.

As with your brain's structure, so developed the behavior each part of your brain controls. They, too, go from primitive to most sophisticated. The lower brain is responsible for aggression, territoriality, and rituals. The midbrain holds the limbic system, the seat of powerful emotions, sexual instincts, and the sense of smell. Over the top arches the cerebral cortex, the part of the brain that regulates higher levels of cognitive and emotional functioning. This is the site of reasoning, planning, creating, and problem solving, and it is the part that makes us human.

Insight

We share the lower part of our brain with all reptiles. Now you know where the expression "giving in to your baser instincts" comes from.

Hello Central!

The bottom-up approach is a useful way to organize the brain because it enables us to see the human brain's structural evolution inside each of us. We can also see how human behavior evolved from base instincts to thoughtful planning. From a psychological standpoint, you can see why it can be challenging to use your reasoning and self-control to keep from acting on powerful feelings or strong desires. After all, those desires have been around a lot longer than your logic!

If the brain is the headquarters of human behavior, the cerebral cortex is unquestionably the commander in chief. Not only does it make up two thirds of your brain, its job is to coordinate all the brain's units and strategically channel your resources in ways that will give you the best chance to survive and flourish in your environment. When we say "use your brain," the cerebrum is the part we're talking about.

Getting Your Brain Organized

When psychologists talk about the brain, they're almost always talking about the cerebral cortex, primarily because it's the part of our brain that makes us uniquely human. The lower and middle portions of the brain often get overlooked. However, these more primitive parts of the brain are the foundation on which our mental houses are built. You couldn't survive long without them.

A quick rundown of the parts of the brain will give you a good sense of the way cognitive tasks are parceled out. Each part is a specialist:

brain stem   Regulates the internal physiological state of the body

medulla   Regulates breathing and the beating of the heart

pons   Regulates brain activity during sleep

reticular formation   Arouses the brain to attend to new stimuli even during sleep

thalamus   The relay station between senses and the cerebral cortex

cerebellum   Organizes physical balance and movement

limbic system   Regulates motives, drives, feelings, and some aspects of memory

hippocampus   The key player in long-term memory

amygdala   The tough guy, with roles in aggression, memory, emotion, and basic motives

hypothalamus   Regulates eating, drinking, sexual arousal, body temperature

cerebrum   Regulates higher levels of thinking and feeling

cerebral hemispheres   Each half mediates different cognition and emotions

Left Brain, Right Brain

Do you prefer geometry or English? Would you rather be a painter or a writer? Are you creative or logical? Depending on how you answered, popular psychology would classify you as "right-brained" or "left-brained."

Insight _____

This "left brain/right brain" craze started with the discovery that the two sides of the cerebrum are not created equal. The two halves of the brain have different processing styles: the right half sees things holistically, while the left is more logical. In addition, they divide up the work. Some functions are more under the control of the right hemisphere and some are more under the control of the left.

Left-Leaning or a Rightward Slant?

For most people, the left brain is more involved in language and logic. The right half of the brain handles visual patterns and spatial relationships. Hence, painters are thought to be more "right-brained" and writers are thought to be more "left-brained." Sports psychologists have put the "right brain/left brain" concept to good use. By teaching athletes to use both sides of the brain, they help them improve their performance.

Insight _____

Many people think of visualization as imagining themselves on a movie screen watching themselves performing. The key to effective visualization, however, is to actively imagine yourself doing the desired event, using as many of your senses as you can (taste, touch, smell, hearing, and so on), and following this image with an image of a positive consequence for your improved performance.

For example, tennis players naturally exercise their left brain every time they swing their tennis racket. The series of steps that form a backhanded swing is a left-brain activity. However, players can also use their right brain to play tennis: lying awake at night, they can mentally practice their game. Tennis players who visualize the perfect swing in their mind's eye and practice it are making creative use of the right hemisphere's holistic processing. And it works!

This division of labor holds true for our feelings as well. The left hemisphere is associated primarily with positive emotions while the right hemisphere is responsible for negative emotions like anxiety and depression. Given that painters and sculptors use their right hemisphere so much, maybe there's something to the idea of a tortured artist!

Partners for Life

In reality, though, the popular left brain/right brain distinction is overly simplistic. These two halves of your brain are partners; they constantly talk to each other through a huge bundle of axons that connect the two hemispheres, the *corpus callosum.*

They also work in sync. For example, when you run into an acquaintance, your left hemisphere remembers his name and your right hemisphere recalls his face.

Oddly enough, the left cerebral hemisphere controls the movement on the right side of the body and the right hemisphere controls the left. When you write your name with your right hand, your left hemisphere is actually doing the work. Specifically, your left parietal lobe is busy—which brings me to the next topic of conversation: the four lobes that make up each hemisphere.

Meet the Mother Lobes

You have more lobes than the ones you hang your earrings on. Each half of your brain has four lobes—a parietal lobe, a temporal lobe, a frontal lobe, and an occipital lobe. You might not know them, but they know you. In fact, they make up a lot of who you are.

Front and Center

The frontal lobes, which sit just behind your forehead, are the newest additions to the human brain. They are considered the "executive" part of the brain. They are the seat of purposeful behavior: they plan, make decisions, and pursue goals. In addition, one of their most important functions may be to inhibit or override more primitive behavior. This is the part of the brain that keeps you from calling your boss an idiot—even when he deserves it!

Temporally Speaking

Your temporal lobes sit directly behind your ears—a convenient place for them, given that a primary job is to make sense of what you hear. The left temporal lobe enables you to understand speech. Your right temporal lobe helps you to understand music, the ringing of the telephone, and other nonverbal sounds. In neuropsychological terms, telling someone that she has an ear for music translates into excellent right temporal lobe functioning.

Parietals Rule

Your parietal lobes sit at the top of your head and integrate sensory information from the opposite sides of your body: your left parietal lobe makes sense of information coming in from the right side of the body and your right parietal lobe takes care of the left side. These lobes help you to understand what you're touching. When you reach into your purse or pocket, for example, your parietal lobes help you tell the difference between a quarter and a dime just by the way they feel.

Psychobabble

Oliver Sacks's *The Man Who Mistook His Wife for a Hat* gives you a close look at the impact of brain disorders on everyday life. The title of this book comes from one of Dr. Sacks's patients, who exhibited a condition known as facial agnosia (an inability to recognize faces). Mistaking his wife's head for a hat, he tried to pick it up off her shoulders and place it on a hat rack.

An Occipital Complex?

Last but not least, if you cup your hand on the back of your head, you are hugging your occipital lobes. Your occipital lobes make sense of what you see; their primary job is to process visual information. The left occipital lobe controls the right visual field in both your eyes, while the right occipital lobe controls the left visual field. Contrary to popular belief, you do have eyes in the back of your head!

Here's how the occipital lobes divide your vision: hold your hands out in front of your face so that your palms are facing you. Now, draw an imaginary vertical line down the middle of each hand. The right visual field is the right half of each hand; the left visual field is the left half of each hand.

Ever had double vision? New research suggests that we all do! In fact, new brain-imaging studies provide evidence that your brain has two completely separate visual systems. The visual system that shows you a coffee cup sitting on your desk isn't the same one that guides your hand to pick it up. The first system, called vision-for-perception, enables you to recognize objects and build up a "database" about the world. This is the system that gives you your conscious visual experience and enables you to see and appreciate the visual world. The other, less-studied, vision-in-action system provides the visual control you need to move about and interact with objects.

Brain scans have located the vision-for-perception system, deep in the cerebral cortex near the memory and language areas. This system is more interested in the identity of an object than in the object's orientation in space. In contrast, the vision-for-action system, located toward the top of the cerebral cortex near the motor and touch areas, is more interested in the object's orientation than its identity. Patients with damage to the perception system have no conscious visual experience of the form and shape of objects but can reach out and grasp them accurately. Conversely, patients with damage to the action system can't use vision to guide their movements even though they can still "see" the objects.

Working with Half a Brain

Once psychologists realized that different hemispheres did different jobs, they started wondering what one would do without the other. What would happen if the two halves couldn't communicate back and forth? Would they fight with each other? Would they get along?

Two researchers by the name of Roger Sperry and Michael Gazzaniga found some amazing answers to these questions. They studied patients whose corpus callosum (which connects the two hemispheres of the brain) had been cut in order to reduce the severity and frequency of their epileptic seizures. On the surface, these patients seemed fine; they walked normally, had no drop in their I.Q., and could carry on a good conversation. When information was presented to just one visual field, though, they behaved as if they had two separate minds.

Psychobabble

Could you really live with just half a brain? More than 50 epileptic children are successfully doing so. These children had severe, uncontrollable seizures confined to only one hemisphere; as a last-ditch measure, a hemispherectomy—the removal of one half of the brain—was performed. All are expected to lead normal lives.

In their experiments, Sperry and Gazzaniga flashed pictures of common objects on a screen and asked the subject to identify them. When the objects were flashed to the right, the person would look at the researchers as if they were complete idiots and say, "It's an apple." However, when the picture was flashed to the left, the subject would either deny that an object had appeared or would make a random guess.

When subjects were next asked to reach under a barrier and touch the object that had just been flashed, they could reliably identify the object with the left hand but not the right! The right hemisphere could remember the feel and shape of the apple but couldn't get the word for it. If you never forget a face and never remember a name, you can relate!

What was going on? Remember that the right hemisphere controls sensation and movement from the left half of the body, and vice versa. Remember, also, that input from the right visual field goes first to the left hemisphere, and vice versa. And recall that, in most people, language is controlled by the left hemisphere, and spatial perception (faces, pictures, geometry) is dominated by the right.

No matter how "smart" your brain is, if the different parts aren't communicating effectively, they don't work as well. And in the experimental subjects, the connection that let the hemispheres communicate had been cut. The information simply couldn't get where it had to go to be processed!

In a way, you might say that the brain's parts are like relationships—they need communication in order to thrive. Unlike relationships, however, the brain can call upon some superpowered equipment that virtually guarantees good communication. Let me introduce you to the fastest communication system in the world—your nervous system.

You've Got a Lot of Nerve

The brain is a truly complex organ, with all parts working together to produce everything you think, feel, and do. Your nervous system is the choreographer; it constantly sends and receives messages that coordinate the stage show of human behavior.

The Internet has nothing on your nervous system—it's a huge network of more than 100 billion nerve cells that rapidly relays messages to and from the brain. These *nerve* cells, called *neurons*, are specialized cells that receive, process, or relay information to other cells within the body. The fastest of these messengers can send electrical impulses at a rate of up to 250 miles per hour; with 100 billion cells to coordinate, they have to.

def•i•ni•tion

A **nerve** is bundle of sensory or motor neurons that exist anywhere outside the central nervous system. When someone is getting on your nerves, you only have 43 pairs for the person to get on—12 pairs from the brain and 31 pairs from the spinal cord. A **neuron** is a nerve that specializes in information processing.

The nervous system has two substations: the central nervous system (CNS) and the peripheral nervous system (PNS). The CNS is made up of all the neurons in the brain and the spinal cord, whereas the PNS is made up of all the neurons forming the nerve fibers that connect the CNS to the rest of the body.

Think of the body as an army—the brain would be the general, synthesizing and coordinating all bodily functions, interpreting all the messages coming in from the body, and sending strategic commands appropriate to the environmental situation. The spinal cord, a trunk line of neurons that connects the brain to the PNS, would be the lieutenant.

All the messages directed to the CNS are sent and received through the spinal cord. Damage to the spinal cord disrupts the brain's ability to send and receive messages and, if the spinal cord is severed, the brain can no longer receive important messages from its limbs about what they are experiencing. So, for instance, you wouldn't feel pain even if a toe was roasting in the fireplace. Without the lieutenant, the general can't send commands for the body to protect itself. Your foot soldiers—your sense organs—would be completely disabled.

No Pain, No Gain

I became painfully reacquainted with the efficiency of the body's communication system when my husband and I started salsa lessons. Mistakes are a natural part of acquiring any new skill, and when two beginners are dancing, this involves a lot of stepping on each other's toes. Over and over again, the nerves in my toes sent the painful message that 200 pounds of dancing male was standing on them. Time and time again, my brain prompted me to push him off and step aside. And, of course, my frontal lobes were busy reviewing the wisdom of my decision to take up salsa.

Psychobabble

It's hard to believe that wisdom comes with age when you realize that you lose almost 200,000 neurons each day. Fortunately, you start out with so many that even after 70 years you've still got more than 98 percent of your original supply. Besides, it's not the quantity that matters—it's the connections between the neurons that count. Albert Einstein had no more brain cells than you or me, but allegedly had incredibly dense connections between the various parts of his brain.

Speedy Delivery

Neurons are the basic unit of the nervous system. There are three types: sensory neurons, motor neurons, and interneurons. Sensory neurons carry information in from the senses toward the central nervous system. When my spouse stepped on my toes, it was the sensory neurons that got excited and sent the scoop to the brain.

Motor neurons carry messages from the central nervous system back to the muscles and glands. When they got the toe-stepping news, they probably said something like, "Get out of the way, you dummy. Move those feet and tell your partner to watch it." Since sensory neurons rarely communicate directly with motor neurons, the interneurons act as brokers. They relay messages back and forth between the two and, occasionally, communicate with other interneurons. I'm sure they were quite busy during my dance lessons!

Doing the Neuron Dance

So how do neurons do their thing? All neurons have a soma, dendrites, and an axon. The soma contains the nucleus of the cell and the cytoplasm that supports it. At one end of the soma are the dendrites, a bunch of branched fibers that receive messages from other neurons or sense receptors. The soma integrates the information from the dendrites and passes it on to a single, extended fiber called an axon. Still with me?

The parts of a neuron.

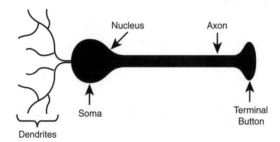

Neurotransmitters are biochemical substances that stimulate other neurons. More than 60 substances have been identified as neurotransmitters. Among these are dopamine and norepinephrine, both involved in schizophrenia, and serotonin, which, along with norepinephrine, has been associated with clinical depression.

The axon's job is to carry electrical impulses, called action potentials, away from the cell body to other cells. A neuron's message lies in the number of action potentials that move down the axon. In Morse code, the message lies in the number and sequence of taps; with neurons, it lies in the speed with which electrical impulses are produced. The axon conducts these electrical impulses along its length until they literally reach the end of their rope—swollen, bulblike structures called terminal buttons that lie at the end of the axons. Action potentials trigger the release of chemical substances called *neurotransmitters* from each terminal button.

When a neuron is stimulated by another neuron's impulses or by sensory stimulation, it fires off its own electrical impulse. The neural impulse travels the length of the neuron along the axon, finally arriving at the terminal buttons.

Synaptically Speaking

Here's where it gets a little tricky. There is no direct physical contact between a terminal button and the impulse's next destination. Instead, there's a gap at the near junction of two nerve cells—we call this gap a *synapse*. When an impulse is ready to leap the gap from a terminal button to the next stage in its journey, a small packet holding neurotransmitters (it's called a *synaptic vesicle*) moves to the inner membrane of the terminal buttons.

The vesicle ruptures, spilling its neurotransmitters into the synaptic gap, and they attach themselves to the neurons on the other side of the gap. If the neurotransmitter inputs are sufficiently stimulating, the receiving neuron will change—it'll either fire or be prevented from firing, depending on what it was doing before the inputs arrived. That's how the impulse message is relayed from cell to cell, for as far as the strength of the relayed impulse can carry it. And when your toes are hurting as bad as mine were, that's pretty darned far.

Blame It on Your Hormones

Remember all the weirdness you went through in your teens? Hair sprouting in different places and body parts growing at different speeds? How about those mood swings? Blame it all on your hormones.

Your nervous system gets most of the press, but there's another communication system that can pack a powerful punch in terms of what you think, feel, and do. It is your endocrine system, and its messengers are your hormones.

When Good Hormones Go Bad

You've heard of road rage, but how about 'roid rage? We all need our natural hormones, but abuse of anabolic steroids, the human-made version, can have scary consequences. Many athletes use these illegally in an attempt to enhance performance, but some side effects can be irreversible.

Teens who use steroids may have their growth stopped suddenly and permanently. Males can end up with shrunken testicles, infertility, and baldness. Females can grow facial hair and end up with a deepened voice. And then there are the cancer risks, and the possibility of steroid ('roid) rage—extreme mood swings that can lead to violence. Overall verdict is this: the possible medals aren't worth the health risks. If you have teens engaged in sports, keep an eye out for warning signs.

Midbrain Magic

The endocrine system, controlled by the hypothalamus in the midsection of the brain, produces and secretes hormones into the bloodstream. These chemicals are involved in a lot of different bodily functions, from your sexual development to your arousal, mood, and metabolism.

Not only does your endocrine communication system help you regulate everyday alertness and mood, it also helps you respond to emergencies. The most famous hormone is *adrenaline*, an energizer that responds to emergencies by preparing you for "fight or flight."

Adrenaline Alert!

Do you remember a time when you were driving and had a near miss with another car? Or any other close call? Then you probably remember your pounding heart, tensed muscles, maybe even a cold sweat.

Each of these "symptoms" is an example of your endocrine system preparing you to respond to a life-threatening situation. In fact, long after the danger had passed, you could probably still feel your endocrine system doing its job. As uncomfortable as it might feel, your ancestors wouldn't have survived without it.

The Brain Doesn't Mind

So you've got the basics of how the brain works, but as a budding psychologist, you want to know about the *mind*. Learning about lobes, hemispheres, and neurons may be interesting, but you're probably itching to learn more about thoughts, feelings, and deeds.

Unfortunately, from a scientific standpoint, the mind is a much slipperier concept than the brain. You can't just go to the doctor and get her to take a picture of your mind, and since you can't see it, it's hard to define it. That's where neuropsychologists step into the picture.

The Make-up of a Mind

Let's start by defining the mind as the sum total of all the thoughts, feelings, and sensations of which we are aware. It's the brain's consciousness. But the meaning of consciousness is subject to debate. Common sense says your mind rules as your brain, but science says there is strong reason to believe that your mind doesn't even understand a lot of what's happening in there.

Some research suggests that the mind's real job has been highly overrated—that, instead of controlling what we do, the mind may just interpret what the brain has already done. Experimenter Benjamin Libet wired subjects with electrodes that measure brain activity; he then seated them in full view of a rapidly rotating clock and repeatedly asked them to flex one finger. Each time they flexed, he instructed them to tell him the exact time they "ordered" their finger to flex. He kept track of three events:

1. The onset of increased brain activity recorded by electrodes

2. The actual flexing of the finger

3. The point at which each subject said he or she had "told" the finger to flex

What You Think Ain't What You Get

Libet found that a flurry of brain activity took place *before* the order to flex the finger was dispatched by his subjects' conscious minds. Their neurons were firing a third of a second before they were even conscious of the desire to act. The brain had started moving before the mind had "decided" to do anything.

Maybe, thought Libet, the mind only gives us the illusion of control. In his experiment, another brain mechanism seemed to delay the sensation of the finger moving long enough for the conscious mind to think that it had commanded the action and then felt the muscles act. Time and again, the conscious order and the actual flexing of the finger took place at virtually the same time. But the brain activity showed that by the time the mind ordered the finger to flex, the impulse had already been dispatched. All the mind got was a last-second opportunity to veto the decision!

Brain Booboos and What They Do

Imagine that your spouse is diagnosed with a brain tumor. After the initial shock, you and he discover that the tumor is nonmalignant and, although large, quite operable.

During surgery, the tumor is removed, recovery goes well, and your spouse is pronounced completely cured.

Except that he's not. Ever since his surgery, you feel like you've been living with a different person. Your sweet, patient, adoring spouse now seems moody, impatient, and short-tempered. Although your well-meaning friends and family are telling you both how lucky you are, inside you feel increasingly confused, frustrated, guilty, and scared. And you're no longer sure you want to stay married to the person your spouse has become.

Given the interlink between our minds and our brains, it's not surprising that injuries to our brains can do a number on our psyches. The severity and type of personality change usually depends on the part of the brain that's been injured. For example, because the frontal lobes often serve as "the brakes" in controlling our emotions, impulses, and instincts, a person with frontal lobe damage may have difficulty inhibiting inappropriate behavior. This person may be particularly prone to saying and doing things that may appear insensitive or irritable.

The survivor of a brain injury may become a more exaggerated type of the person he or she was before the trauma. My great-aunt Bess, who died from Alzheimer's disease, was a quiet, rather pessimistic person for as long as I knew her. As her dementia progressed, she would go for days without talking and developed considerable suspicions about the people around her. This exaggeration of pre-existing personality traits can make a progressive neurological illness difficult to diagnose, especially in the absence of physical symptoms.

Insight

Boost your brain—and help ward off Alzheimer's—with exercise! Researchers have found that regular exercise controls the expression of genes in an area of the brain important for memory and maintaining healthy cells in the brain; this maintenance breaks down in cases of Alzheimer's.

Now you can see why we've spent so much time on biopsychology. The mind may act as if it's running the show. We may think it is. But, from research like Libet's, we can see that much of what goes on in our brain is outside of our conscious awareness. The mind may be more of an interpreter than a leader; although it gives us rational explanations for our behavior, it's not in the driver's seat. In the next chapter, we'll explore two areas that influence how well we drive: nature and nurture.

The Least You Need to Know

- ◆ The human brain evolved into its present form because it contained features that enabled our ancestors to thrive.

- ◆ The brain's structure reflects our evolutionary history: the old brain governs the most primitive human behavior, the midbrain is the seat of human drives and emotions, and the newer cerebral cortex guides the most complex thinking and feeling.

- ◆ The cerebral cortex—divided into two hemispheres and eight lobes—is the headquarters of human behavior.

- ◆ The human nervous system, which sends messages to and from the brain through electrical impulses, is the best communication system in the world.

- ◆ Medical tests can define damaged areas of the brain, but a neuropsychologist can assess how well a person is able to function after an injury or disease.

- ◆ Natural hormones keep our bodies and brains in balance, but abuse of steroids (human-made versions) can result in irreversible physical harm.

- ◆ The mind is the part of the brain that we are conscious of; its main job may be to make sense of decisions that the brain has already made.

3

The Chicken or the Egg?

In This Chapter

◆ Refereeing the nature-nurture debate

◆ Let's get typical

◆ Getting into your genes

◆ Just what *are* you born with?

◆ You're *so* mature

Are you the way you are because of your genes or because of your life experiences? This nature-nurture debate has a long, tedious, and politically influenced history.

In the nineteenth century, for example, educated people widely believed that "biology is destiny"; Sir Francis Galton did a study showing that eminent people (of which, not coincidentally, he was one) produced eminent heirs while a study of the infamous Jukes family revealed that seven generations of family members had cost the state $1.5 million dollars through various types of crimes. In the twentieth century, many psychologists considered infants to be blank slates, waiting to be written on by their parents and teachers.

> **Brain Buster**
>
> There's danger in overly simplistic explanations for something as complex as human behavior. Over-reliance on "nature" explanations has led to justifications of racism. Over-reliance on the "nurture" side can lead to neglect of real, physical causes of arrested mental development, such as insufficient diet, lead poisoning (from paint chips), and other environmental hazards.

Today we know it's not so cut and dried. Whether they're studying personality, intelligence, or our susceptibility to mental disorders, psychologists are still trying to tease out how much our genes contribute to who we are and how much we're molded by our environment. In this chapter, we'll take a look at this "chicken or egg" debate, at why we have the genes we have, and at the role our environment plays in nurturing our nature.

Dancing with Wolves

In 1801, a 12-year-old boy was discovered in the woods outside of Aveyron, France. He had apparently been raised by wolves; no one knew where he came from and he acted more like a wolf than a human being. A French doctor named Jean-Marie Itard renamed the boy "Victor" and took on the challenge of teaching him to be human.

Taming the Wild Child

Jean-Marie began an intensive training program with Victor. Initial results seemed promising. Fairly quickly, Victor became affectionate and well mannered and could utter a few words. After five years, however, Victor could learn no more. Although he lived to age 40, Victor never became a fully functioning human being. From Jean-Marie's perspective, his experiment had failed.

Looking Beneath the Surface

But was it nature or nurture that failed? The good doctor had no information about Victor's genetic makeup; perhaps the boy had been abandoned because he was developmentally disabled to begin with. Perhaps no training program would have worked. Alternatively, maybe Jean-Marie's training program was off the mark and Victor could have whizzed through a different one. Or maybe Victor could have learned the lessons of human nature at one time, but had outgrown his receptivity to language by age 12.

Nature or Nurture

Are you the product of genetic Russian roulette, or have your life's experiences made you the person you are? For the past 200 years, scholars have argued over whether we are the product of genetic Russian roulette or our environment. It all started with a debate between two philosophers: John Locke and Jean-Jacques Rousseau.

The Great Debate, Philosophically Speaking

British philosopher John Locke formed the nurture camp. Babies, he argued, are born without knowledge or skills. We enter the world as blank slates upon which experience writes. Human development is directed by the stimulation received through experience and education.

"Hogwash," said French philosopher Jean-Jacques Rousseau. Human beings, he argued, are hardwired from birth with all our predispositions and abilities. Sure, we're unsophisticated when we enter the world, but we're also innocent and good. We're born noble savages.

When it comes to nature versus nurture, the issue is often more complex than it seems. Take Victor the wolf boy, for example. If his training program had produced a fully functioning, "normal" human being, it would have offered strong evidence that nurture is powerful. The fact that it didn't, however, doesn't prove the opposite. Since we have no information about Victor's genes, we can't say that Victor's stunted growth potential was due to nature *or* nurture.

Psychobabble

Probably the earliest experiment to address the nature-nurture issue was conducted by Fredrick II, King of Germany, in the thirteenth century C.E. To determine what language a child would speak if she were not spoken to by her parents in her early years, the King ordered the foster mothers of several babies to care for the babies but not to speak to or play with them. This experiment failed because all of the babies died due to a lack of attention, proving at least that all natures need to be nurtured.

Taking the Middle Road

In reality, complex skills are shaped by both our biological inheritance and our life experiences. Your heredity gives you your potential, but it is your experience that determines how, and how much of, that potential is realized.

Take language, for example. We appear to inherit a predisposition for language; it's programmed in our genes. However, there is evidence that environmental stimulation must occur during early childhood for maximum language development. If, like Victor, that optimal period is missed, our ability to learn language will be impaired. We can learn a little, but we'll never be the chatterbox we might have been if we'd had our environmental boost!

Asking the Right Questions

A common mistake made in the nature-nurture debate is in asking the wrong questions. For example, asking how much of your intelligence was a gift from your parents and how much was acquired by the sweat of your brow is, if taken literally, silly. In some respects, both nature and nurture contribute 100 percent. After all, if you didn't have any genes at all, you wouldn't be alive. And your mother's womb was your first environment—you wouldn't be alive without that, either. No environment, no person—no person, no intelligence.

Psychobabble

Politics and genetics make dangerous bedfellows. Biological views of behavior have been used to justify horrible deeds, from the six million Jews, Gypsies, homosexuals, and others put to death in the name of "racial impurity" in Nazi Germany to the inaccurate views of heredity that fueled the Rwanda-Burundi and Bosnian civil wars.

The real nature-nurture question is whether differences in a trait among a *group* of individuals are due more to differences in their genes or to their environment. In other words, why are some people smarter than others? Why do some people graduate from high school and others drop out? The nature-nurture question helps us look at groups of people and explain or predict their differences; it's not very good at helping us predict why individuals do the things they do.

Differences in intelligence may be due to genes for one set of people and environment for another. If you were raised in a loving family and I in solitary confinement,

I.Q. differences are more likely to be due to environment. If we were raised in similar homes, though, differences in our genes might have more influence.

What Twins Tell Us

When scientists try to tease out the relative influence of nature and nurture, they are essentially trying to figure out how much of human nature is inherited. *Heritability* is the degree to which variation in a particular trait within a certain group stems from genetic differences among those members as opposed to stemming from environmental differences.

If a trait can be passed down from parent to child, we would expect relatives to be more similar in that trait than people who are not related. So, if we have smart parents, we should see smart kids, and, assuming that our kids don't marry any dummies, smart grandkids.

The catch, of course, is that relatives often live together. The fact that brothers and sisters have more similar I.Q.s than unrelated people does not, by itself, tell us whether it's the egg (the genes) or the chicken (the home) that's responsible. Here's where the twins come in.

Identical twins have identical genes; they are the only human beings who truly have the same genetic nature. Fraternal twins and other siblings share only about 50 percent of their genes. In their journey through the nature-nurture tunnel, scientists have found that studying the natural differences between twins helps them see the light at the end.

For example, comparing the I.Q. scores between identical twins reared in the same home and identical twins adopted by different families at birth enables us to look at the influence of environment on intelligence. Since identical twins have exactly the same genes, we can feel pretty confident attributing any I.Q. difference to the different environments in which they were reared. On the other hand, if identical twins reared miles apart from each other have more similar I.Q. scores than fraternal twins who shared a bedroom since birth, nature pretty much wins the debate.

Insight

Ever wondered how much you were related to other relatives? You're 100 percent related to your parents as a team (50 percent to each). You're 50 percent related to your sibling, 25 percent related to your grandparents, 12.5 percent related to half-siblings and first cousins, and 6.25 percent related to second cousins.

And with regard to intelligence, nature has come out the winner. Identical twins consistently have more similar I.Q. scores than fraternal twins *regardless of the environment in which they are raised.* Anatomy, however, is not destiny. There's a surprisingly small relationship between intelligence and success, suggesting that smart genes may give us a jump start in life, but they won't carry us over the long haul. Like our muscles, our intelligence can't help us that much if we don't use it.

Family Genes and Other Heirlooms

Research with twins does seem to tell us that smart parents make bright children and dumb parents don't have many children in graduate school. But how does all this genetic passing down work?

When dad's sperm and mom's egg unite, the new cell it creates is a *zygote.* This zygote contains the full human complement of 23 paired chromosomes, with one member of each pair coming from each parent. The zygote grows up and becomes you. Because each sperm cell is different from each egg cell, each zygote is different from each other.

The fact that genes come in pairs helps geneticists calculate *percent relatedness,* the amount of genes you share with another human being. You may be the spitting image of your dad, but you have 50 percent of your genes from your mom and 50 percent from your dad. Genetically, you are 50 percent related to each of them.

The difference between the actual amount of genetic material you share and the way you physically look illustrates the difference between your *genotype* and your *phenotype.* *Genotype* refers to the entire set of genes you inherit, your biological potential. *Phenotype* refers to the observable properties of your body and your behavioral traits. Your phenotype might look just like your dad, but your genotype comes from both your parents in a 50–50 split.

Dominating Genes

Your genotype is predetermined—50 percent of your genetic makeup comes from Dad, 50 percent from Mom. Your phenotype, on the other hand, is a battle for control between your genes. And just as the most aggressive warriors often win their battles, the most dominant genes dictate your phenotype.

Gregor Mendel was the first person to realize that some genes are dominant over others. A *dominant gene* is one that will produce its observable effects if it is present in either parent; a *recessive gene* will show up only if both parents possess it.

Jeepers, Creepers, Where'd You Get Those Peepers?

The reason there are more brown-eyed people than blue-eyed ones is because the gene for brown eyes is dominant: if one parent contributes blue-eyed genes and the other contributes brown-eyed ones, the child will have brown eyes. But we all know a few blue-eyed children whose parents are both brown-eyed. How can that be? Simple—sometimes brown-eyed parents have a recessive gene for blue eyes lurking in the background, and those are the ones that got passed along to form the blue-eyed child's zygote. (Because blue eyes are recessive, both parents must have contributed blue-eyed genes in order for them to show up in their offspring.)

You Can't Get Lost with This Map

A *genome* is an organism's complete set of DNA (deoxyribonucleic acid), the chemical compound that contains the genetic instructions to make that organism. Thanks to the Human Genome Project (HGP), we now have the complete mapping and under-standing of all human genes. The full sequence was completed and published in 2003.

We learned some pretty interesting things from this international research project. For one thing, we humans have about 30,000 distinct genes residing on our 23 chromosome pairs. We're a lot like chimpanzees, sharing about 98.7 percent of our genetic code with these adorable creatures. And the difference between me and Albert Einstein, genetically speaking, is less than 1 percent!

def•i•ni•tion

The term **genome** refers to the full complement of an organism's genetic material, in other words, a blueprint for building all the structures and directing all the processes for the lifetime of that organism.

Too Much Information?

Having the HGP completed is like having a basic owner's manual. The good news is that this manual may help us find and fix faulty parts before they cause us problems; we've already started identifying specific genes that contribute to cystic fibrosis, mental retardation, and some forms of cancer.

But we will also face new ethical dilemmas and, for some of us, some tough personal choices. What will health insurers do if they know a person has a high likelihood of developing cancer? Would you still get pregnant if you knew your child would have a 25 percent chance of developing Parkinson's disease?

Would you want to have genetic testing to find out if you were likely to develop Alzheimer's disease? Anatomy is not destiny, and yet knowing that we were at high risk for a debilitating illness could literally rob us of a quality life long before we had the chance to see if our grim genetic potential became a reality.

Psychobabble

Want to get your personal genome mapped? You can, for a mere $2,200,000. Harvard Medical School, though, hopes to bring the cost down to $1,000 sometime in the next few years. Before you take advantage of this, though, you might want to watch the movie *Gattaca* and ask yourself this: do I really want to know *everything* I could be at risk for?

Don't Blame Your Genes

If you were a smart kid, thank your parents for your good genes. If you dropped out of school to flip burgers, and now regret that you never lived up to your potential, blame yourself. Your genes aren't responsible for your behavior.

The influence of our genes on our behavior is indirect. Their main task is building and organizing the physical structures of the body, including the brain. These structures interact with the environment to produce behavior. Good genes give us resources for coping with our environment, but a bad environment can challenge even the most resilient genes.

Insight

When we discuss environment, it's important to remember that the environment is affected by *culture*. Culture is a system of shared ideas about the nature of the world and how to behave in it. These ideas shape how we learn and behave. You may be genetically hard-wired to be able to learn language, but the fact that you're reading this sentence in English is a direct result of your culture, not your genes.

Growing Up on the Wild Side

Take, for example, a child growing up in an extremely violent neighborhood. Evidence suggests that the stress of living under these conditions may stimulate the development of the part of the brain that responds to threatening stimuli and organizes aggression. The child may, as a result, be more aggressive, because the environment in which he or she lives encourages the aggression centers of the brain to become more developed.

Over time, a high-crime environment might naturally select more aggressive individuals and, as a result, genes that promote the development of the brain's aggression center could be passed down to future generations. But be careful about the conclusions you draw from this: there's a big leap between inheriting a predisposition for aggression and actually committing a crime. We might be predisposed toward violence to help us survive a bad neighborhood, but our genes don't pick up a gun and shoot it.

The same is true for all human behavior. Natural selection has bred us to be better at doing whatever we needed to do to survive and thrive in our environment. As a result, certain behavioral mechanisms have evolved, including our capacity for language, our ability to learn and remember, and our problem-solving skills.

What About the Suicide Gene?

A couple of years ago, I was driving on my way to a meeting and I overheard a radio announcer proclaim the discovery of "the suicide gene." To hear him talk, you would have thought that some of us had a time-bomb lurking in our DNA that would, without warning, manifest itself via a jump out of a high window or the uncontrollable chugging of our roommate's sleeping pills.

No disrespect to Mr. Mendel, but we aren't peas in pods just waiting to be manipulated by a single gene. Common, complex disorders are genetically influenced but not genetically determined. Many genes are involved in complex psychiatric disorders. Genes work like risk factors, slightly increasing or decreasing risk for a disorder. They're not like master puppets pulling our strings.

Genetic information can help us take more control over our lives by helping us identify our individual susceptibility to certain problems. By doing so, it could clarify the specific factors that interact with this susceptibility to produce certain behaviors or diseases.

Insight

Genetic information may also provide guidance for targeted screening efforts; for example, people who have a first-degree relative with a history of depression are more likely to develop an affective disorder themselves, particularly in response to an environmental stressor. Screening these individuals for major depression six months after the loss of a loved one is likely to be much more effective than screening all bereaved people.

Typical Human Behavior

Understanding our genes can help us to understand our own behavior. *Functional* psychology tries to explain behaviors in terms of the purposes they serve for the individual. *Evolutionary* psychologists look at the bigger picture and try to understand why human beings, as a species, act the way they do. In essence, they study universal human behaviors and try to figure out what caused these behaviors to evolve. Their questions are generally functionalist in nature, such as …

- Is it possible that some human behaviors evolved because ancestors who did those things had an environmental edge?

- What might that edge have been?

- How, for example, did talking help human beings get along better in the world?

Similarity Can Breed Content

Evolutionary psychologists are particularly interested in *species-typical behavior*— behaviors that are so common among the members of a species that they can be used as identifying characteristics. Barking, four-legged walking, and pooping on front lawns pretty much sums it up for dogs. Two-legged walking and talking are species-typical for humans.

Insight

There appear to be seven basic emotions that are universal among human beings: surprise, fear, disgust, anger, happiness, contempt, and sadness. When you're feeling sad, it can be comforting to know that every other human being has felt this way, too.

So are human emotions. From an evolutionary perspective, human emotions may have motivated our ancestors to do the things they needed to do to survive. Perhaps ancestors who felt angry were more likely to protect themselves or defend their turf!

Not only do we all feel the same feelings, but human beings are also pretty darned good at knowing what others are feeling, too. Researchers showed photographs of American people expressing the seven basic emotions to people in many different cultures, including a preliterate, geographically isolated tribe in New Guinea. In every culture, people were remarkably accurate at detecting the emotion expressed. You don't have to be Charles Darwin to see the survival benefits of recognizing the face of an enemy!

But *Vive la Différence!*

Species-typical behavior does not mean that human beings are all alike. Not all human beings feel happy eating chocolate ice cream, nor do all of us cry when we're afraid. In humans, species-typical behavior means that we are biologically prepared for that behavior. But exactly when, how, and why each human experiences and expresses his or her unique feelings is a complicated jumble of biology, life experience, and cultural legacy. Species-typical behaviors identified by psychologists include …

- ◆ Living in communities
- ◆ Male violence
- ◆ Nepotism (favoring kin)
- ◆ Marriage contracts

Evolutionary Theory Gone Awry

The application of evolutionary theory to psychology has stirred up a jumble of emotions, not to mention some pretty dark ulterior motives. Instead of explaining behavior through evolution, evolutionary psychology has, at times, been used to justify it.

Mother Nature's Morality

One misuse of evolutionary psychology is the *naturalistic fallacy*. According to this error in logic, nature is guided by a moral force that favors what is good or right. If male mammals in the wild dominate females through force, well, that's the way it "should be." British philosopher Herbert Spencer, a contemporary of Darwin, used this argument many times to justify the most extreme abuses of nineteenth-century capitalism. Of course, his biggest fans were those in power at the top of the industrialist ladder.

I Just Couldn't Help Myself!

A second misuse of evolutionary psychology is known as the *deterministic fallacy*. It's the genetic version of "the devil made me do it." According to this viewpoint, our genes control our behavior and there's nothing we can do about it. If natural selection teaches me to fight for my territory, can I help it if I slugged the man who took my parking space? It's genetic!

Or maybe it's cultural. No matter how aggressive my nature, if I grew up among the Amish, I may be less likely to react violently because of the cultural taboo in my environment. On the other hand, if I was raised by gang members in a tough part of town, I may slug the man over a parking place just to fit in with the crowd.

In reality, neither genes nor social pressure influence our behavior in a way that's beyond our control. We can control—or rebel against—our environment and we can learn to control ourselves.

Home, Sweet Home

We've talked a lot about nature in this chapter—from genetics and species-typical behavior to evolution. As we've seen, though, even the clearest examples of nature's influence can be changed by nurture.

> **Insight**
>
> Ever marvel at how differently you and your sibling feel about experiences in the same family? Each child growing up in the same family can *experience* that environment differently; for example, a baby with an irritable temperament may elicit different reactions from the people around him or her than one blessed with an easygoing nature.

For example, common sense would lead you to expect that siblings growing up in the same family would have a lot in common. They have the same parents. They play in the same neighborhoods. They go to the same schools. In fact, they pretty much share the same learning opportunities. Even if siblings have no genetic relationship, as is the case with adopted siblings, you'd think all those shared childhood experiences would have an impact.

It should come as no surprise, then, to discover that family environment has a strong early influence on children's I.Q. scores. Adopted siblings living in the same home have more similar I.Q. scores than siblings who live apart. However, this similarity fades as the siblings grow up and begin to create their own environment. The intellectual advantage or disadvantage of being raised in a particular home fades by early adulthood.

How does this happen? Early environmental influences disappear in adulthood because, when they're grown, siblings choose different environments to live in. We can choose an environment that encourages us to either use our brain or lose our marbles!

Baby Builds on Blueprints

But even after taking into account the genes that your parents gave you and the environment you're born into, there's still something more to be reckoned. And that "something more" is the unique, the individual, the personal *you*. You came into the world prepared to take your inheritance and grow with it and, from birth, you've been hard at work.

Babies come into this world with some pretty sophisticated equipment and some pretty strong preferences. Even while they're still in the womb they're moving around, listening to their mother talk, and preparing for their grand entrance into the world. When they're born, they are already biologically prepared to seek food, protection, and care.

For example, from birth, babies establish a relationship with people who can take care of them. They start out preferring female voices and, after just a few weeks on the outside, they can recognize their caregiver's voice. By seven weeks, they've learned to scan their caregiver's face and start to make eye contact when he or she talks. If Locke and Rousseau had spent any time around babies, they would have quickly given up the "blank slate" or "noble savage" descriptions. Pre-programmed "friendly" computers is a better description of newborns.

Insight

Our early years are very important. Our brains grow 50 percent larger in the first 12 months after birth, and by our second birthday, our brains are 80 percent larger than the brains we were born with. This growth eventually tapers off, and, by age 12, we're pretty much stuck with the brains we have.

As early as 12 hours after birth, babies show distinct signs of pleasure at the taste of sugar water or vanilla, and show aversion to the taste of lemon or the smell of rotten eggs. Days-old infants quickly learned to anticipate dessert when researchers stroked their foreheads and then fed them sugar water. Not only did babies turn their heads in the direction of sugar, but they also cried when the goods weren't delivered. From birth, it seems, we feel pain when a reliable relationship breaks down.

Is "Normal" Just a Setting on the Clothes Drier?

Genetic inheritance gives a baby a jump start on life, but he or she still has a lot of growing to do. After birth, a child's physical growth and abilities follow a genetically based timetable. This genetic blueprint is responsible for the appearance of certain behaviors at roughly the same time for all human beings, taking into allowance cultural variations. And, as you're about to see, it is the following of this timetable that, from a maturation standpoint, makes us "normal."

Oh, Grow Up!

If anyone has ever said that to you, they were giving you a clear message that you weren't living up to their expectations of how a person your age should behave. But how do we know how we're supposed to behave at what age? We know by looking at the human process of *maturation*, the timely and orderly sequence of developmental changes that takes place as a person gets older.

def•i•ni•tion

Maturation refers to the process of growth typical of all members of a species who are reared in the usual environment of that species.

For example, by four months, most babies sit with support. Between five and six months, they stand holding on to something, and at about a year they start walking. If a baby can't do these things, parents start worrying.

Walking follows a fixed, time-ordered sequence that is typical of all physically capable members of our species. In cultures where there is more physical stimulation, children begin to walk sooner. However, contrary to many parents' beliefs, babies do not require any special training to learn to walk.

The Parental Part of the Equation

While baby's doing his developmental thing, part of a parent's emotional growth is learning to relax and trust her baby to develop at his own pace. That's because the parent's role in the process is to provide the emotional security that is necessary for her child's physical growth. For, as you're about to see, physical and emotional development go hand in hand.

What's Your Attachment Style?

The way we attach to our earliest caregivers can set the pattern for our relationships for the rest of our lives. To see how you tend to relate to others, put a check beside the self-descriptions that you most agree with:

1. ____ I am somewhat uncomfortable being close to others; I find it difficult to trust them completely, difficult to allow myself to depend on them. I am nervous when anyone gets too close, and often love partners who want me to be more intimate than I feel comfortable being.

2. ____ I find it relatively easy to get close to others and am comfortable depending on them. I don't often worry about being abandoned or about someone getting too close to me.

3. ____ I find that other people are reluctant to get as close as I would like them to. I often worry that my partner doesn't really love me or won't want to stay with me. I want to get very close to my partner, and this sometimes scares people away.

If you selected (1), you're expressing an avoidant, insecure attachment style. About 25 percent of us have this attachment pattern. Twenty percent of us will choose answer (3), which represents an anxious-ambivalent, insecure style. Fifty-five percent of us are lucky enough to answer (2), which suggests that we attached securely to our parents and are secure in our attachment to others.

Growing Up Emotionally

Watch a baby learn to walk and you aren't just witnessing physical development. You're witnessing emotional growth, too. From birth, our minds and bodies are intertwined.

Insight

While there may be "sensitive periods" during which children need nurturing in order to be able to form attachments, the upper age limit for these sensitive periods may be much older than the previously believed first year of life. Studies show that children adopted before age four tend to bond well with their parents, while children adopted after age four are more likely to experience problems attaching to their caretakers.

As babies begin to physically explore their worlds, they depend on their parents to make them feel safe. Time and time again, toddlers go back and forth between venturing out into the world and returning to check in and make sure Mom or Dad is still around should things move a little too fast. What does this pattern mean for a child's development? Children who don't trust their parents to be there when they get back often don't venture out to explore.

Studies of infants reared in institutions have clearly demonstrated the criticalness of the parent-child attachment to social and physical development. Infants who were isolated for the first eight months of life rarely tried to approach adults later on, either to hug or caress them or to get reassurance when in distress. And, not surprising, this social impairment led to other developmental delays—such children failed to utter a single word by the first year of life.

Fortunately, few babies ever face the trauma of living in isolation for the first few months of life. However, relationships between parents and children are complicated, and all of us have experienced at least one occasion when a parent couldn't be there for us. What impact does this have?

Psychologist Mary Ainsworth studied young children and their relationships with their primary caregivers. By placing them in novel situations where they were briefly separated from their parent, she identified three different attachment styles—one secure style and two insecure styles. And each of these attachment styles influenced the child's physical development.

Ainsworth discovered that securely attached children felt closer to and safer with their caregivers. As a result, they were more willing to explore or tolerate novel experiences. They were confident they could cry out for help or reunite with a caregiver if needed.

Insecurely attached children, on the other hand, reacted to separation and new situations with avoidance, anxiety, or ambivalence. Anxious or ambivalent children sought contact with their caregivers but were fearful and angry when separated from them. These children were also difficult to console when reunited with their parents.

Children with an avoidant attachment style, on the other hand, didn't seem to care whether their primary caregivers left, and they showed little emotion when they returned. Dr. Ainsworth hypothesized that these children were victims of long-term rejection and had given up on their efforts to have a consistent, caring caregiver. In reaction to an abusive or neglectful environment, these children developed an unhealthy protective shell around their hearts. In extreme cases, they became adults with little concern for anyone but themselves.

Nature? Nurture? It's Both!

In some respects, we're back where we started at the beginning of this chapter—in between nature and nurture. Children who aren't loved don't grow. Children who have irritable natures may be harder to nurture. Intelligence is in our nature, but success depends on nurture. When it comes to human beings, nature and nurture are inseparable. Given the amazing ways children develop, which we'll discuss in Chapter 4, perhaps that's the way it should be.

The Least You Need to Know

- We're the product of both nature and nurture: our genes give us our biological potential; our environment, including our culture, determines how we express it.

- Every human being inherits certain behavioral tendencies that helped our human ancestors survive and thrive, but what triggers these tendencies and how often they are expressed varies across cultures and individuals.

- The Human Genome Project gave us a map of all of the human genes. Future work may lead to genetic treatments for illnesses and raise some challenging ethical dilemmas.

- Genes never directly control behavior. None of us is born a killer or a saint.

- Emotional and physical development are inseparable. Children need emotional security to grow physically, and one source of that security is a healthy attachment to their parents.

Chapter 4

It's Only a Stage

In This Chapter

- From boredom to brain scans in baby research
- Learning the lingo
- Natural-born psychologists
- Exploring the mind of a child
- Lurching from crisis to crisis

Human beings have historically had some pretty strange ideas about children. Maybe that's why the field of developmental psychology is still a baby; it wasn't born until the first half of the twentieth century. Since then, what we've learned is that children are pretty impressive. And it's constantly changing! Research in this area has exploded in the past few years, as we've evolved new techniques for finding out what's happening in the minds of even the smallest infants.

In this chapter, you'll learn how children's thoughts and language develop. You'll learn about a lot of different stages children go through, and how each stage prepares a child to deal more effectively with the world around him or her.

You'll also learn a lot about yourself. Understanding how children develop speech will not only teach you some healthy respect for children's built-in desires to communicate, but it will also give you valuable insight into yourself. As you learn how children learn, take time to reassess your life. As you'll see, children seem to intuitively seek out experiences and create adventures that help them make the most of their biological potential. Do you?

It's a Dog's Life

Do you know that at one time there were laws in England that protected animals from mistreatment—but there were no laws protecting children from similar abuse? Under English common law, children were considered property.

Fortunately, one far-seeing judge refused to go strictly by the book. When an abused child was reported by an animal shelter worker, the judge creatively declared the child "inhuman," thus protecting her under the animal laws and allowing her to be removed from the home. Soon after, the first child abuse law was passed.

The Development of Child Development

The field of child development was born in the first half of the twentieth century. Sigmund Freud had begun talking about the influence of childhood on adult mental health, and scientists suddenly became curious about the life and experiences of children. Before that, people had some pretty strange ideas about child development.

Period	Prevailing Attitude About Children
1500	Children over six are small adults and should behave accordingly.
1500–1700	Children are family property and contribute to household income.
1800s	Decreased need for cheap labor; childhood extended to adolescence; beginning to be seen as valuable and vulnerable, children are "potential persons"; rise of child-oriented families, juvenile courts, and field of developmental psychology.
1950–present	Children have legal rights, including the rights to due process in legal courts and to self-determination.

Studying Bored Babes

Studying child development means studying babies. After all, the most rapid part of child development is in the first 18 to 24 months of life. But how do we do it? Babies aren't exactly giving speeches during these first few years. How do we know what babies know and how they know it? We used to rely primarily on human nature's built-in tendency to become easily bored. Researchers call this *habituation*, and babies do it as much as grownups do.

More recent studies often rely on more sophisticated instruments and tests. EEGs (electroencephalograms) and other direct measurements of brain waves look like they will be the "waves" of the future in baby research.

Hundreds of experiments have shown that babies look longer at new things than at familiar ones. When shown a pattern, for example, babies show a lot of interest at first and then, over the course of a few minutes, look at it less and less. They become habituated to it. This aspect of baby nature is so reliable that developmental psychologists use it to assess infants' abilities to perceive and remember. Brain-wave studies and laser eye tracking let us look even closer at the tiniest responses babies have.

And one of the things we've discovered while studying babies is that babies are constantly studying, and they're naturally drawn to studying things that provide them the most efficient opportunity to learn. For example, not only do babies waste little energy restudying objects they've already seen, they show a strong preference for objects in their environment that they can control.

Two-month-old infants show much more interest in a mobile that moves when they touch it as compared to a motor-driven one. And they get pretty mad when this self-controlled device is disconnected.

That would make it sound as if Rousseau's idea that all children are born innocent and good is out the window. But not so fast! The work of psychologist Martin Hoffman indicates that one of the first emotions infants display is empathy—concern for others. Of course, other studies show that another early emotion babies exhibit is jealousy, so let's not give Rousseau *too* much credit.

Fast Learners and Good Teachers

Babies are fast learners, and some surprising studies are showing that they learn faster and earlier than we thought. For instance, up until about three months of age, a baby can recognize a scrambled photo of her mother just as quickly as a photo in which everything is in place. And six-month-old babies can tell one chimp from another just as easily as they can recognize individual faces. By nine months, their focus shifts more to their own species; they lose their chimp-separating ability but gain a greater ability to distinguish between subtle differences in human faces.

Perhaps they're such good learners because they have some pretty good study habits. Infants across cultures engage in a sophisticated exploration called *examining*. When they encounter an interesting object, they hold it up in front of their eyes, turn it from side to side, pass it from one hand to the other, squeeze it, mouth it, and generally do whatever they can to figure it out. And they pay attention to detail: they look more at colorful objects; they feel objects with different textures; and they shake, rattle, and roll objects that make sounds.

Insight

Recent studies suggest that how well children imitate their mothers at age one can predict which children will show a well-developed conscience as preschoolers. Children who, when asked, eagerly imitated their mothers' simple actions at 12 months were, by age 3½ to 4, more likely to follow the rules and show guilt when breaking them.

Teenagers may not respect their elders, but babies do. They recognize the value of experience as a teacher and they start cashing in on the wisdom of their parents. Six-month-olds, for example, will look at their parents' eyes, follow their gaze, and then look at what the adult is viewing. The baby will then check back and forth periodically to see if the parent is still looking.

Babies, it seems, are born students, and their biggest teachers are Mom and Dad. From emotions to language, they practice what they see, hear, and feel every day.

I Second That Emotion

We used to believe that babies younger than six months didn't recognize emotions. Newer research, though, indicates that infants just a few months old can recognize and react to other people's happiness, anger, and sadness. Some studies suggest that babies themselves feel empathy even sooner—perhaps when they are only days or weeks old. By age two, most children will label themselves as sad, mad, or glad depending upon the circumstances they are reporting.

Why is this important? From an early age, babies use emotions to gather information and make decisions; by watching the actions and reactions of others, they gain important clues about what's important and what's not, what to avoid and what to seek out.

A baby who does not reach certain key "emotional milestones" may have trouble learning to speak, read, or do well in school later. Learning more about emotional development and recognizing problems early on may identify at-risk children before they even start school, allowing a chance for early intervention.

Learning Baby Talk

Walking upright and growing bigger brains may be our two biggest evolutionary accomplishments, but language runs a close third. Not only is vocal communication useful for a group, but it is also immediately useful and necessary for individual survival. As any parent can tell you, young children use sounds and gestures to show that they are hungry, tired, or unhappy.

I've spent seven years trying to learn Spanish and failed, so it depresses me to think I could have spoken any one (or more) of 3,000 languages, if only I'd started early enough. No matter what their native language, children have pretty much mastered it by the time they are three or four years old. In fact, between 18 months and 6 years of age, the average child learns about one word per waking hour!

Babies begin practicing cooing sounds at about two months, and progress to babbling at about four to six months. These early sounds appear to be wired in; deaf infants coo and babble at the same age and manner as hearing infants, and early babblers are as likely to contain foreign language sounds as native-language sounds. By 10 months, though, children start babbling in sounds that imitate their parents. If a deaf infant is exposed to sign language, she will start babbling with her hands.

Insight

Unfortunately, you can't play CDs or DVDs in a foreign language and hope Junior will pick up the lingo. The research of Patricia Kuhl shows that while infants learn any language easily when exposed to it in person, they apparently tune it out as background noise if it's only presented electronically.

Children learn language in three initial stages—one word, two words, and telegraphic speech. They start out by naming things that are present and then begin asking for things. At around 18 months, a naming explosion occurs and children begin to learn words at an astonishing rate. In the early two-word stage, children can use combinations of words to make meanings, although they stick to the bare necessities.

In their early two- and three-word sentences, children's speech is *telegraphic*, mainly consisting of nouns and verbs that get the message across. "Zachary eat" wouldn't make Zachary's third-grade grammar teacher very happy, but it's pretty effective at getting his mommy to head for the refrigerator.

When it comes to getting their message across, children are downright geniuses. Parents certainly help by talking to them and providing them with plenty of opportunities. And, as you're about to see, lads and lasses may be born with some of their language talent built in.

Psychobabble

What nonhuman creature can correctly name objects, colors, and materials—in English, not sign language? He may even be the first nonhuman to show an understanding of the concept of zero. Give up? It's a bird, it's a plane ... okay, it's a bird. Alex the African gray parrot, protégé of biologist Irene Pepperberg. She believes that gray parrots may have cognitive abilities similar to a four- or five-year-old child.

LADS and LASSes

Language researchers have been so impressed with children's knack for languages that they began wondering if human beings were born linguists. Many theorists believe we have an innate, biologically based mental program for language acquisition. These theorists believe that we don't just repeat what we hear, but that we follow a preprogrammed set of instructions to acquire language and vocabulary. Noam Chomsky, a pioneer in this area of linguistics, called these speech-enabling structures *language acquisition devices*, or *LADs*.

def•i•ni•tion

Language acquisition devices (LADs) are the preprogrammed instructions for learning a language that some linguists believe all infants are born with. Language acquisition support systems (LASSes) are the circumstances that facilitate the efficient acquisition of language.

Other researchers agree that human beings have a genetic predisposition for language, but that this built-in capacity is not a rigid device but rather a set of lessons and "listening rules" that helps us perceive and learn language. For example, babies pay attention to the sounds and rhythm of the sounds they hear others speak, especially the beginnings, endings, and stressed syllables.

In addition, children seem to be born using certain grammar rules. They come into the world with some natural biases in how to use and apply new words. For example, children have natural tendencies …

♦ To link new words to objects for which children do not already have a name (if a child has three objects and already knows the names of two, he'll assign any new name he learns to the as-yet-unnamed object rather than wonder if it is a synonym for either of the named ones).

♦ To assume that all nouns are common nouns (for instance, calling all men "Daddy").

♦ To overextend common nouns to things that are similar (calling all round objects "balls").

Sure, these assumptions lead to some pretty funny talk, but think how efficient they are. If you're learning a new language, it's a lot better to group similar objects together and give them similar names than to assume every new item is a world unto itself. And think how confusing it would be if we wondered if every new word was merely a synonym of something we already knew. These built-in language teachers help speed up our early language development.

The jury is still out for LADs but not for *LASSes, language acquisition support systems*. In order for our language potential to blossom, we must grow up in a responsive environment with plenty of opportunity to practice. Without it, we miss the opportunity to fully express ourselves.

Insight

A 2005 study found that immigrant children still mastering the English language can be misdiagnosed as speech impaired (and shuffled into special education) because the normal errors made while acquiring a new language often resemble those made by language-impaired, monolingual children. To guard against this, speech assessment test scores of non-native English-speaking students should be compared to other youngsters who are learning a second language, not monolingual English-speaking children.

Remember Victor, the wolf boy from Aveyron (Chapter 3)? Undoubtedly, one of the reasons his language skills never caught up is the fact that he was deprived of a language acquisition support system in childhood; he missed the critical period for language development. In every known case in which children are deprived of early language opportunities, their language skills are permanently impaired. When it comes to LASSes, we either use them or lose them.

Listen and Learn

Of course, there's another big influence that helps children talk faster: parents. If you're a parent, then you're bilingual. You speak your native tongue and also *parentese*, a lingo that involves speaking in an exaggerated, high-pitched tone of voice, emphasizing and repeating important words, and using short, staccato bursts ("uh-oh") to signal taboos. Most of us call this "baby talk" and it just happens to be the language babies learn best.

In fact, just as babies are amazingly skilled language learners, caregivers are incredibly gifted speech teachers. Not only do we speak in parentese, we also engage our infants in training dialogues. From birth, we talk to our newborns and then wait for a reply. Early on, we'll accept just about anything as a valid reply before continuing—a burp, a sneeze, a yawn. Like any good teacher, though, we make more demands as our children grow, matching our expectations to their abilities.

> **Insight**
>
> The time to start monitoring your child's television exposure starts at 12 months! New research found that one-year-old infants can pick up emotional information they see on television and use that information to guide their behavior.

Evolution must have thought talking was a pretty nifty ability to have, considering all the help it has given us in learning how to do it. Babies come programmed for speech and they're given parents who are natural language teachers. No wonder children have such a hard time being quiet; it's against their nature!

The Child Psychologist

Language is one area that children are fascinated with; psychology is another. They may start out exploring the outer world, but they pretty quickly show a fascination with their inner world as well. They also begin to use words like *dream, forget, pretend, believe,* and *hope* as they talk about internal states.

And not just their own. As early as 15 months of age, children can understand the concept of false beliefs and how actions can follow them. For example, imagine a scenario in which two brothers hide a batch of cookies together in the cabinet. The older brother, Vincent, goes out to play, while the younger boy, Josh, eats all the cookies. Does the older brother, Vincent, come back to look for the cookies? Research showed that even a 15-month-old child could understand that Vincent would look for cookies even though there are none left. In fact, by the time children have learned the words to say it, usually between two and a half and three and a half, they routinely begin to attribute thoughts, feelings, and motives to the things people do. A four-year-old soap opera fan will assure you that the heroine of *As the World Turns* is crying because she's sad, or that Daddy is getting a beer because he's thirsty. Luckily for parents, an understanding of some of the ulterior motives that drive human behavior come later!

As we've seen, even two-year-olds know the difference between make-believe and reality. This early distinction between make-believe and reality may be a necessary survival tool—a child who understands the difference has the foundation for understanding that beliefs can differ from reality and that people can fool others by manipulating their beliefs. By age four, children become pretty skilled at detecting deception in others—and using it for their own advantage as well. And by age seven, children are able to recognize and discount statements that are clearly aligned with the self-interests of the speaker.

> **Insight**
>
> Fifteen percent of the U.S. population has a learning disability. A common disability is dyslexia, characterized by problems in expressing or understanding language. The person with dyslexia has problems either translating language to thought (as in listening or reading) or thought to language (as in writing or speaking). It has nothing to do with intelligence.

All this worrying about the motives and intentions of other people can take its toll. Wouldn't it be wonderful if we were oblivious to the minds of other people? No more self-consciousness or worrying about making a good impression? Believe me, there have been plenty of times in my life when I would happily have subscribed to the "ignorance is bliss" school of thought.

As wonderful as it might be to imagine, our lives would be much more difficult if we were so blissfully oblivious. It would be like living among aliens. We might be able to study them and fit in by copying their behavior, but we would never truly feel at home. Autistic children may know exactly what this feels like. Autism is a disorder characterized by severe deficits in social interaction and language acquisition, a tendency toward repetitive actions, and a narrow focus of interest, and it can result in a complete inability to relate to, or understand, people.

Putting Our Thinking Caps On

The minds of my preschoolers fascinate me. "Is Doc Ock real?" they wonder again after watching Spider-Man for the ninety-seventh time. When I tell Zane, my four-year-old son, that chewable Tylenols are for his headache, he immediately puts the pills on his forehead. When my soon-to-be five-year-old daughter gets scared, she feels safe when I tell her about "nice" monsters but thinks I'm pulling a fast one if I try to convince her they aren't real. No matter how grown-up our children try to be, their minds work differently from ours.

The Curious Child

Jean Piaget, the child-mind pioneer, was also fascinated by the minds of children. Watching his own three children develop sparked an interest in children's minds that lasted more than 50 years. What he concluded was that children are scientists who begin to experiment and explore their world from the moment they're born. Mental development, he believed, naturally arises out of this exploration.

Of course, infants start with what they can see, feel, taste, touch, hear, and smell. Before long, children start putting two and two together and realizing that certain actions go best with certain objects. Sucking goes best with nipples. Banging goes best with rattles. Smiling goes best with Mommy's face. Piaget called this ability to develop mental blueprints linking actions and objects the development of *schemes*.

As soon as the baby develops a sucking scheme for nipples, no more effort is wasted in trying to squeeze milk out of a rattle or a teddy bear. Not only do these schemes save time, they are the foundation upon which babies learn more sophisticated lessons, through what Piaget calls *assimilations* and *accommodations*.

Coping with Curveballs

One of the things we learn early on is that life is constantly throwing us curveballs and we have to find ways to hit them. Sometimes we can fit that curveball into our current environment with just a minor tweak (assimilation), and sometimes we have to adjust our way of thinking (accommodation). A baby who's a champion nipple sucker might easily be able to incorporate cups or bottles into her sucking scheme. Eating from a spoon, however, is a whole new challenge.

Piaget considered the assimilation of new experiences similar to the digestion of food. Two people might eat the same food, but the food will be assimilated into the body differently depending upon that person's digestive system, metabolism, and so forth. Moreover, just as wolfing down crayons or dirt will not help our bodies grow, new experiences that are too different from existing schemes can't be mentally digested, and will not result in growth. Give a toddler your hand calculator and you might get a stellar display of his banging scheme, but you won't teach him arithmetic.

Insight

In Piagetian terms, life is a series of assimilations and accommodations. Children either fit new info into their current schemes or make room for entirely new ones. And they're usually a lot more willing to consider new schemes than their older, supposedly wiser, elders—that's what people mean when they refer to "childlike wonder."

Performing on Stage

Piaget was interested in more than how children think. He was also interested in *what* and *why* they think. Over and over, he watched children solve problems and asked them to explain their reasoning behind their solutions.

Not surprisingly, he found that four-year-olds thought differently than fourteen-year-olds. He also found that four-year-olds often came up with similar solutions to the same problems. Putting two and two together, he proposed that most children develop their thinking in stages, going from a concrete, here-and-now focus to a more abstract, future-oriented approach. He came up with four stages of cognitive development, each of which roughly correlated to a child's chronological age:

- Sensorimotor stage (birth to 2 years old)

- Preoperational stage (2 to 7 years old)

- Concrete operations (7 to 11 years old)

- Formal operations (12 years old and up)

Sensorimotor Stage

In the sensorimotor stage, thoughts and behaviors are pretty much one and the same. Infants spend their time examining their environment and placing objects into schemes for sucking, shaking, banging, twisting, dropping, and other categories that cause general mayhem for their parents.

Babies take a giant leap forward when they begin to understand the concept of *object permanence*—that objects still exist even though they're out of baby's sight.

Piaget and other early researchers thought that babies didn't grasp object permanence until about nine months. Newer research by psychologist Su-hua Wang shows that babies may understand the concept as early as 10 weeks. Of course, they still want the concept confirmed by endless games of peek-a-boo.

General theme: monkey see, monkey do.

Preoperational Stage

To you and me, a skillet is a cooking utensil. The only creative energy we spend on a skillet is in deciding what to cook in it. Give a preschooler a skillet and, alakazaam, you have the lead guitar from the newest band or the only Star Wars gun that will kill Darth Vader. Children in this stage have a well-developed ability to magically transform everyday items into symbols and to re-create events that they have seen. However, while their thinking is no longer bound by the here and now, it is very much bound by appearances—witness my son's insistence that the taller cup has more water, no matter how often I showed him otherwise.

> **Insight**
>
> Marilyn Shatz found that even four-year-olds modify their speech to two-year-old siblings to take into account their younger brother's and sister's language abilities, suggesting that preoperational kids may not be as completely self-centered as we once thought.

This is also an age of profound self-centeredness. If a child falls off a chair, it's a "bad" chair and needs to be punished—after all, *something* made him fall, and it certainly wasn't *his* fault. Ask a four-year-old to tell you another person's point of view, and she'll tell you her own thoughts and feelings, because she hasn't developed the cognitive ability to do otherwise.

General theme: it's all about me!

Concrete Operations

By the time they reach the age of seven, children are starting to realize that appearances can be deceiving. They have, for instance, developed the concept of *conservation*: they realize that no matter how much outward appearances change, physical properties don't change unless something is added or taken away.

Much of the problem solving done by children in this age group consists of what Piaget called *operations*, mentally reversing the consequences of an action to figure out cause and effect. Ask a 10-year-old bicyclist whether the chain or the fender is crucial to his cycling and he won't have to take apart his bicycle to tell you. By mentally removing each part, he'll know that the chain is connected to the pedals and the pedals move the wheels and, therefore, the chain is critical but the fender is not.

General theme: take things literally.

def•i•ni•tion

Conservation is the awareness that appearances can be deceiving and that unless something is added or taken away, an object is the same no matter how it looks on the outside. Mommy in a mask and costume is still, recognizably, Mommy (unless that costume is *very* good).

Formal Operations

Remember the game "20 Questions," where the winner is the person who guesses the right answer by asking the fewest yes/no questions? You have to enter formal operations to be really good at it, which is why children have trouble playing the game until they reach this stage, around the age of 12.

Children still in the concrete operations stage tend to limit their questions to specifics. If the correct answer is some kind of animal, a child might ask questions like, "Is it a dog?" or "Is it a monkey?" A formal thinker, on the other hand, might ask questions like, "Does it fly?" or "Does it have hair?" before moving to more specific questions. Formal operations enable us to see the "big picture"; in this stage, we develop general principles that we can apply to hypothetical situations.

General theme: think ahead.

Recent research suggests that Piaget might have been behind the curve in realizing the true learning potential of children. Researchers have found, for example, that toddlers between two and a half to three and a half years old begin to move from the ability to distinguish amounts to the ability to distinguish between numbers of discrete objects. As early as three years, some children exhibit nonverbal math skills, comprehending quantity and performing simple addition and subtraction using groups of objects. We can't blame Piaget too much; because a preschoolers' verbal understanding of conventional math terms is limited, their ability to comprehend quantitative concepts is often overlooked.

From a practical standpoint, parents can tap into this ability by giving children the language to express it. Playing counting games can help children begin to label quantity. Setting the table together can include counting out the number of forks— one … two … three—and teach your child an even harder concept: responsibility!

The Human Computer

In the cognitive development arena, a quality versus quantity debate is being waged. Piaget believed that the quality of a child's thinking was different as it moved through each developmental stage. The five-year-old who assumes that a taller glass holds more water thinks differently than a ten-year-old who understands that appearances can be deceiving.

Or does she? One perspective of cognitive development would argue that the difference in thinking isn't a matter of quality. Both the five-year-old and the ten-year-old are doing the same kind of thinking, but the ten-year-old is doing it at greater capacity. This is the information-processing perspective, which views a child's mind as something like a computer. It is wired like an adult's, but during childhood it is handicapped by limited memory capacity.

Insight

Most professional magicians hate performing in front of small children, unless they have developed special routines for kids. Why? Because magicians generally work on the principle of misdirection, distracting you from something they don't want you to notice. Children before the formal operational stage can be tough to fool because they think differently and aren't easily misdirected.

The information-processing model holds that the mind's basic machinery consists of attention devices for bringing information in, working memory for actively thinking about information, and long-term memory for holding that information so that it can be used again in the future. In this view, cognitive development is a gradual increase in the capacity of working memory.

From this perspective, the five-year-old's inability to understand that the same amount of liquid can look different depending upon the shape of the glass is not due to poor quality. It's because their minds can't yet hold the information long enough for them to mentally reproduce the experiment and solve the riddle. As a result, their attention gets stuck on first impressions, the different sizes of the glasses.

Speak Before You Think—or Vice Versa

You still might not want to sit next to one on an airplane, but you've got to have a healthy respect for children by now. After all, what adult do you know who can learn any one of 3,000 languages, turn any household device into a lethal weapon, and train grownups to be at his or her beck and call? Kind of makes you wonder what happens when we grow up, doesn't it?

Children are linguists. They're psychologists. They're scientists. And according to a psychologist by the name of Lev Vygotsky, they're apprentices as well. In fact, Vygotsky thought children learn much more through their relationships than through their solo adventures in the world. According to this view, we speak first and think second.

Piaget considered language to be a side effect of children's development of thought. Vygotsky argued that language is the foundation for the development of higher thought. He believed that words not only provide the building blocks for advanced thinking, but they actually direct our thinking in ways that reflect the activities and values of our culture. Thus, children who grow up in cultures where counting is important develop an efficient set of number words. Some Eskimo cultures have several different words for *snow* because differentiating between different types of snow is critical to their survival.

According to Vygotsky, children first learn words to communicate with others, but then they begin to use those same words as symbols for thinking. In fact, he thought that much of our cognitive development is a matter of internalizing the symbols, ideas, and modes of reasoning that have evolved over the course of history and make up the culture into which we are born. A Vygotskyan would say that all human beings share the same brain, but our individual minds are a reflection of our culture!

The Moral of the Story

"Those are bad thoughts." "I think it's the right thing to do." "She made the wrong decision." From an early age, we do a lot more than think our thoughts. We evaluate them. In fact, by the time we're adults, rarely a thought goes by without us attaching some moral weight to it. But how do we learn to make these value judgments?

Lawrence Kohlberg was intrigued with how people develop their sense of *morality:* concepts of what is right and what is wrong. His curiosity eventually led him to develop the best-known psychological explanation for moral development. Similar to Piaget's thoughts on cognitive growth, Kohlberg believed people

def•i•ni•tion

> **Morality** is a system of beliefs, values, and underlying judgments about the rightness of human acts.

acquired their morals in stages and that individuals in all cultures went through them in the same order. Kohlberg thought that our moral development went from a self-centered focus to a higher level that focused on the good of society. Here's how he thought that human moral development plays out for most of us:

The Morality Play

The Stage	The Plot	The Motive
Stage 1	Seek pleasure, avoid pain	Avoid pain or getting caught
Stage 2	Weigh the costs and benefits	Achieve the most rewards
Stage 3	Be a good kid	Be popular and avoid disapproval
Stage 4	Be a law-abiding citizen	Stay out of jail, avoid penalties
Stage 5	Make win-win deals	Do what's good for society
Stage 6	Live by your ethics	Be just, don't disappoint yourself
Stage 7	Be in tune with the cosmos	Think about what's best for the universe

As you look at Kohlberg's stages, it may have occurred to you that when it comes to developing morals, a lot of people you know seem to be developmentally delayed. Well, it's true. In reality, many adults never reach stage 5 and few go beyond it. I, personally, still wonder what the heck stage 7 really means!

> ### Psychobabble
>
> Kohlberg realized that his stages were more idealistic than realistic. His own virtues, however, apparently didn't include an appreciation for diversity. Not only are some of these stages limited to Western culture, but he had the nerve to propose that women's morality is less fully developed than men's!

Empathetically Yours

In addition, there is a big difference between moral beliefs and moral acts. If you want to predict whether someone will behave morally, skip right over these stages and measure his ability to empathize with others. *Empathy*, the ability to feel another person's feelings, is what motivates a child to behave morally. By age 13 to 15 months, a baby will try to comfort a crying playmate. She may even enlist Mom's help by grabbing her hand and pulling her in the direction of the bawling baby. A baby like this may not be high up on Kohlberg's moral ladder, but she's well on her way to making good moral decisions.

Growing a Happy Child

Whew! As grownups, it's easy to think that childhood is a piece of cake; how many times did *your* parents tell you that the carefree days of childhood would be the happiest time of your life? Hearing this can be pretty darn depressing to a kid, especially when her major crush won't give her the time of day. Fortunately, all it takes is a little child-development research and—presto—we remember that all that thinking, speaking, and figuring out makes growing up pretty hard work.

Of course, parenting is hard work, too, which is probably why it's easy to forget that the hills of childhood all seem like mountains at the time. There's no magic formula when it comes to raising a happy child. However, parents who help their children develop resilience are arming them with the tools that will enable them to take life's knocks, weather the storms, and feel good about themselves despite it all.

It can be helpful to think of resilience as a set of life skills that enables a person to bounce back from setbacks. These skills translate into certain thoughts, feelings, and behaviors, such as the following:

- **Behavioral resilience**   The ability to interact successfully with others and to solve problems.
  Building blocks   Teaching your child how to respond to teasing, how to stand up for herself, etc.

- **Cognitive resilience**   The ability to talk to yourself in an empowering way and to have an optimistic outlook about the future.
  Building blocks   Teaching your child how to use self-talk in a positive way, how to rethink a problem to find a solution, giving her an emotional vocabulary, etc.

- **Emotional resilience**   The ability to feel good about yourself regardless of what is going on around you.
  Building blocks   Nurturing a child's natural talents, interests, and abilities, giving permission to make mistakes, etc.

Midlife Isn't the First Crisis

If your life is one crisis after the next, welcome to the club. Psychologist Erik Erikson's life was like that, too. As a middle-aged immigrant to America, he faced a lot of conflicts as he adjusted to his new life. He must have noticed that a lot of other people had crises in their lives, because he developed the theory that we all have conflicts and challenges at different stages in our lives. In his view, our emotional and social development depends upon how we deal with these crises.

> **Insight**
>
> The age of onset for most psychiatric disorders is between 18 and 24. This fact, along with the stresses of college, dating, entering the work world, and becoming an adult, makes a good case for building a strong support system and having access to at least a few trusted elders during this tumultuous time.

Erickson coined the term *psychosocial crises* to describe successive turning points or choices that influence personality growth across the life span. Each crisis requires a new level of social interaction; if we turn in the right direction, we build up a sense of trust, security, and confidence in ourselves. If we don't, life keeps getting harder and harder; we may have ongoing feelings of insecurity, low self-worth, and a lack of self-confidence. Personal crises aside, here are the eight developmental crises we all have to go through:

Eight Human Crises and How They Turn Out

Age	Crisis	Good Ending	Bad Ending
0–1½	Trust vs. mistrust	I can rely on others	Insecurity, anxiety
1½–3	Autonomy vs. self-doubt, lack of control, feelings of inadequacy	I am my own person	Helpless to change things
3–6 years	Initiative vs. guilt	I can make things happen	Lack of self-worth
6 years– puberty	Competence vs. inferiority	I can lead	Lack of self-confidence

Age	Crisis	Good Ending	Bad Ending
Adolescence	Identity vs. role confusion	I know who I am	Unclear sense of self
Early adulthood	Intimacy vs. isolation	I can be close to others	Feeling alone, denial of need for closeness
Middle adulthood	Generativity vs. stagnation	I can see beyond myself	Self-indulgent concerns
Late adulthood	Ego-integrity vs. despair	I have contributed	Disappointment

A Self-Help Psych-Up

Want to boost your self-confidence? Try the same four strategies that preschool teachers use to boost their students' sense of initiatives:

1. Encourage yourself to make choices and follow through with them.

2. Make sure that at least some of your goals are small enough that you are bound to reach them.

3. Expand your horizons by trying lots of new and different things.

4. Be tolerant of your accidents and mistakes, especially when you are trying something new.

The theme of this chapter has been child development. As you've seen, however, the way children grow teaches us a lot about human nature in general. First of all, we come into the world with a lot of neat equipment, and our environment is prepared to help us learn how to use it. Second, there is a time and place for everything; our language, our thought, our sense of morality, and our emotional development all take place in stages that can be influenced by our environment, but not necessarily altered by it. And, finally, there are few shortcuts in life; not resolving one of Erickson's stages is likely to come back to haunt us.

The Least You Need to Know

◆ Babies come into this world programmed to explore and conquer. Their natural interest in novel experiences and low tolerance for boredom helps us understand infants' inborn ability to learn.

◆ Babies are as busy learning about the internal world of emotion as they are absorbing information about the outside world.

◆ Children have a knack for languages. With the help of a responsive environment and plenty of opportunities to practice, they have a pretty good understanding of grammar by the time they are six years old.

◆ By the time they're two, children understand that people have reasons for what they do; by the time they're four, they know people's motives aren't always honorable; and by the time they're seven, they have a healthy dose of cynicism.

◆ Psychologist Jean Piaget discovered that children mentally grow in stages, moving from a clumsy exploration of the immediate environment to the ability to hypothesize and think ahead.

◆ Morally speaking, children's understanding of what is right and wrong evolves as they get older, but their moral actions are more likely to be guided by their ability to feel empathy for others.

◆ Life is a series of turning points, and how we handle them will either move us forward or hold us back.

Part 2

Wake Up and Smell the Coffee

Is what you see the same as what's out there to be seen? Humans have some pretty miraculous sensory mechanisms—and an even more impressive data-processing center, better known as the brain. In this part, you'll learn all about how you take information in from the world around you, and how your mind makes sense of all that data. From learning to memory, from remembering to organizing, your mind is a marvelous tool—here's where you'll learn all about its inner workings.

Chapter 5

Come to Your Senses

In This Chapter

◆ Making sense out of things

◆ When the pain is "all in your head"

◆ Coming to attention

◆ Discovering why you're more organized than you think

◆ Life is but a dream

Conventional wisdom tries to have it both ways: "Seeing is believing" and "Life is but an illusion" are equally considered commonsense descriptions of how the world works. And in a very real sense, conventional wisdom is right. Our senses *do* provide us with reasonably reliable information—but the representations they give us of the world aren't as literally accurate as we tend to believe.

Without much conscious effort, we are constantly taking in information about the world and sending it on to our brains to make sense of it. In this chapter, we'll explore sensation and perception: how our senses process information, and how our first perceptions set the stage for how we think, feel, and interact with our world. In short, perception is the foreplay to the rest of psychology.

Creating a Sensation

We use our senses to guide us through life. Sometimes, they signal danger: a friend of mine recently commented that a blind date "made the hairs on the back of her neck stand up." She "sensed" that he wasn't trustworthy, and if she's smart, she'll trust herself and steer clear of him.

Our senses also give us pleasure—the feel of our boyfriend's lips, the sight of Van Gogh's paintings, or the taste of a double helping of tiramisu.

But for all the good they do us, our senses never get the credit. Human nature seems to hold fast to the belief that the joys of life are "out there"; we rarely recognize that without our senses we wouldn't have much joy at all. Instead of applauding the chef for a good meal, perhaps we should be thanking our taste buds!

In reality, it is your physiological response to these things that makes you feel good, not the things themselves. When you have a bad cold and can't smell for a few days, the sweetest perfume loses its allure. Your perception of things is even more complicated; you'll smell the same perfume, but perceive it differently depending on the circumstances: the same scent that had you drooling with lust can become nauseating after you've fallen out of love.

The discovery that our perceptions of the world differ from physical reality led scientists to ponder the relationship between our mental world and the physical world in which we live. And this journey led them to another discovery.

On the Threshold of Discovery

The earliest psychologists were fascinated by the relationship between physical stimuli and the behavior or mental experiences that they evoked. In fact, *psychophysics*, the study of psychological reactions to physical stimuli, is the oldest field of psychology.

The goal of psychophysicists was to map physical reality onto psychological reality. At what point, they wondered, does physical reality become human reality? To answer this question, pioneers began tracking the point at which physical differences in sound or light became mental distinctions. How bright does a light have to be in order for us to see it glowing? What's the softest sound we can still hear? It depends, they discovered, on the individual. People have different sensitivities to environmental stimuli.

Star Light, Star Bright

Let's say you and a friend are stargazing and you point out a faint star. Your friend says he can't see it. Thinking it's because he's not looking in the right place, you spend several frustrating minutes giving him the exact location of the star and pointing out brighter stars nearby. If he still can't see it, it may be because his *absolute threshold* for light is different from yours. An absolute threshold is the smallest, weakest amount of a stimulus that a person can detect. If you can see the star and he cannot, the star's light is above your absolute threshold and below your friend's.

Psychophysicists are also interested in our *difference threshold*, the smallest physical difference between two stimuli that can be recognized. Let's say you do your best studying with Nirvana blasting in the background. Your roommate, on the other hand, prefers a study atmosphere similar to a funeral parlor. Your

def•i•ni•tion

Psychophysics is the study of psychological reactions to physical stimuli.

earphones are broken and it's the night before a major exam. Your roommate asks you to turn down the radio; you want to be considerate but you also don't really want to turn the radio down. The least amount you can lower the volume to prove your good intentions while still keeping the volume audible would be the *just-noticeable difference*.

Crossing the Threshold

Absolute and difference thresholds are constantly in use to guide safety regulations. For example, when warning lights are built into cars, safety engineers must make sure that they're bright enough to take your attention away from other dashboard lights. Without psychology, there'd be a lot more car accidents!

We may not be faster than the speed of sound or able to stop a speeding bullet, but our senses are pretty good at tuning in to our environment. The average person can …

   ◆ See a candle flame at 30 miles on a dark, clear night.

   ◆ Hear the tick of a watch under quiet conditions at 20 feet.

   ◆ Taste 1 teaspoon of sugar in 2 gallons of water.

   ◆ Smell one drop of perfume diffused into a three-bedroom apartment.

   ◆ Feel the movement of a wing of a bee near his or her cheek at a distance of 1 centimeter.

Get Your Signals Straight

The work of psychophysicists would be easier if perceptual differences between people were always due to physical reasons—if they were due to better hearing, sight, touch, smell, or taste. However, early psychophysicists failed to realize that differences in thresholds could be due to psychological reasons. And one of the biggest psychological reasons they overlooked was human bias. They did not recognize that our responses to environmental stimuli are biased by our past experiences as well as our expectations of the current situation.

That's where signal detection theory comes in. This theory recognizes that our ability to perceive stimuli in the environment is influenced by psychological as well as physical factors. Perceiving sensory stimulation requires more than just responding to it; it requires making a judgment about its presence or absence as well. Just as jurors can be predisposed to vote innocent or guilty, our experience and expectations might lead us to be too ready to say we heard something or we didn't.

Insight

Certain situations obviously pull for one bias over another; a doctor who feels a lump under a woman's breast knows she has much more to lose if he misses a dangerous condition than if he raises a false alarm. When it comes to medical problems, give me a doctor with a liberal bias!

Here's a story any new mother can relate to. My sister doesn't have any kids, while I have four. Time and again, she'd come over to visit when one of my babies was down for a nap. There we'd sit, both yakking away, with the television on in the background and the periodic blare of a train tunneling along the tracks across the street from our house. "There's the baby," I'd say, jumping up to rescue our wailing bundle of joy from his or her crib. My sister, however, didn't hear a peep, attesting to the fact that a) I have more emotionally invested in tuning in to the sound of a baby's cry, and b) yes, it's true, you'll never relax the same again once your baby rocks your world.

Common Senses

Signal detection theory helps us understand all the things that influence our ability to make sense of our environment. But what are the "signals" that we detect? How do things "out there" (light waves) become things "in here" (the perception of a beautiful painting)? Through energy.

The study of sensation is a study of energy. Whether it's sound waves or light waves, physical energy from a stimulus in the environment stimulates our sensory neurons, which, in turn, convert this energy into electrochemical signals that the nervous system carries to the brain. This process is known as *transduction*. These neural messages are the language through which our sense organs talk to our brains.

Your senses have a lot more in common than you might think. They all use transduction to communicate sensory input to the brain. They also tune out stimulation that does not change in intensity or some other quality, a process known as sensory adaptation. When you first put on your shoes, you are aware of how they feel on your feet. Wear them a short time and, unless they're pinching your toes or rubbing your heels, you forget about them.

Sensory adaptation enables us to make the most of our senses by encouraging them to focus on novelty. From a survival standpoint, it was critical for us to be able to focus on sudden changes in our environment; abrupt changes most often signaled danger to our ancestors. If, for example, they had been too busy focusing on the constant sense of discomfort that comes from sitting on rocks, they might have missed real danger, like a large predatory animal emerging from the bushes.

Psychobabble

Viva la aromatherapy? Maybe. Researchers have recently found that certain smells can actually stimulate the other senses, making them either more or less vigilant. Bad smells, for example, may trigger our brain's danger center, signaling our other senses to be on the lookout for possible danger and causing us to pay more attention to visual cues in our environment.

What Stimulates You?

Life is a stimulating experience. What stimulates us at any given moment depends upon the part of the body we're talking about. Take a look at what really stimulates us—and what really gets stimulated.

Sense	What Stimulates Us	What Gets Stimulated
Hearing	Sound waves	Pressure-sensitive hair cells in cochlea of inner ear
Vision	Light waves	Light-sensitive rods and cones in retina of eye
Touch	Pressure on skin	Sensitive ends of touch neurons in skin
Pain	Potentially harmful stimuli	Sensitive ends of pain neurons in skin and other tissue
Taste	Molecules dissolved in fluid	Taste cells in taste buds on the tongue
Smell	Molecules dissolved in fluid	Sensitive ends of olfactory neurons in the mucous membranes

The Big Five

We've already talked about some of the things our senses have in common. On a daily basis, though, we're much more aware of their differences. Seeing is different from hearing. We use our sense of sight to feast our eyes upon our loved ones and our sense of touch to enjoy the pleasure of human contact. Let's look at the unique contribution each of our senses makes to understanding our world—starting with the "big five": vision, hearing, smell, taste, and touch.

Vision

Most people say they would rather lose their hearing than their sight. Our ancestors would agree—from an evolutionary perspective, vision has been our most important sense.

Photoreceptors in our eyes gather light, convert its physical energy into neural messages, and send it on to the occipital lobe in the brain for decoding and analyzing. Transduction happens in the retina, which is composed of light-sensitive layers of cells at the back of the eyes.

Those cells in the retina are called *rods* and *cones*. Rods are receptor cells that permit vision in dim light; they are highly sensitive to the perception of light but can't distinguish colors or details. Cones, on the other hand, operate best in bright light, where they permit sharply focused color vision. With their help, we can visually discriminate among five million different colors—but we only have the language to identify 150 to 200 of them.

Brain Buster

All of us have a *blind spot*, a small part of the retina that is not coated with photoreceptors, which creates a small gap in our visual field. We aren't aware of our blind spot because our eyes compensate for each other, and our brains "fill in" the spot with information that matches the background.

Hearing

"If a tree falls in the forest and no one's there, does it make a sound?" This Zen riddle plays upon the fact that "sound" refers both to the physical stimulus we hear and to the sensation the stimulus produces. If we were using the term *sound* to refer to the physical stimulus, our answer would be yes. If we were referring to the sensation and no one was around to experience it, the right answer would be no.

Sounds are created when actions, like banging, cause objects, like drums, to vibrate. These vibrating objects push air molecules back and forth and, as a result, change the air pressure. These changes in air pressure travel in *sine waves*. Picture ocean waves breaking on the shoreline. How *fast* the waves crash determines the frequency we hear. High frequencies produce high sounds and low frequencies produce low sounds. How *high* the waves are at the crest dictates their amplitude. Sound waves with large amplitudes are loud and those with small amplitudes are soft.

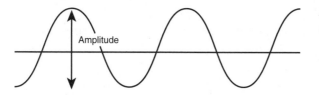

Amplitude

A simple example of a sine wave.

Hearing is made possible when the ear and the brain convert sine waves into the experience of sound. Sound waves travel into the ear, transfer from tissue to bones in the middle ear, and are transformed into fluid waves in the inner ear. The vibrations of these fluid waves stimulate tiny hair cells to generate nerve impulses to the auditory part of the brain. And, of course, our brain analyzes these sounds and responds appropriately, such as telling us to cover our ears when we hear fingernails scratching on a chalkboard!

Smell

Smell is our most primitive sense, which may be why we take it for granted. It's a real bummer, though, when we lose it; not only does the world seem bland, but it tastes bland, too. Our sense of smell probably developed as a system for finding food, and anyone with a cold can tell you that our taste buds get a lot of the credit that our nose really deserves.

Odors are chemical molecules. When they hit the membranes of tiny hairs in our noses, the receptors there translate them into nerve impulses, which are relayed to the olfactory bulb, the part of the brain that decodes and interprets smells.

Our sense of smell may also be the one most linked to memory. To this day, the smell of peanuts reminds me of my childhood home in Alabama; a certain men's cologne takes me back to the frat house of a hot-n-heavy college romance. New mothers who wear the same perfume every day are likely to create a strong olfactory memory bond with their baby; in fact, sharing that scent with a babysitter may also help keep the baby calm while Mom's away.

Taste

A taste bud is no galloping gourmet. It can tell whether foods are sweet, sour, bitter, or salty, and that's just about it. Food critics rely on their sense of smell to distinguish between subtle food flavors more than on their ability to taste them.

Your taste receptors, located on the upper side of your tongue, transduct chemical molecules dissolved in saliva to the taste center of your brain. If you've ever burned your tongue on hot soup, you may have noticed that your sense of taste was temporarily disrupted. But never fear! Those buds are amazingly resilient; they are replaced every few days. In fact, your sense of taste is the most resistant to damage of all your senses.

Touch

Food lovers aside, touch is the most pleasurable of all the senses. Not only is it the main avenue to sexual arousal, but it is also critical for healthy development. Children who are deprived of touch can develop *psychosocial dwarfism*, a condition whereby their physical development is stunted.

Your skin contains nerve endings that, when stimulated by physical contact with outside objects, produce sensations of pressure, warmth, and cold. These sensations are the skin senses, and you could not survive without them. Not surprisingly, your sensitivity to touch is greatest where you need it the most: on your face, tongue, and hands.

The Sixth Sense?

While we've discussed that there really are more than five senses, when most people talk about "the sixth sense," they are talking about one of two things: either ESP (extrasensory perception), or a really good movie with Bruce Willis.

ESP is the term collectively used for such things as telepathy (reading another person's mind), precognition (predicting the future), and other abilities considered outside the norm of physical senses ("I see dead people"). But does it exist?

The answer is an absolute, resounding "Maybe." Do many people report such experiences? Yes. Can these experiences be reliably, scientifically reproduced under the strict experimental conditions we discussed in Chapter 1? No. Studies suggesting that ESP exists have been criticized for either the way that they have been conducted or the way that the results have been interpreted. And oddly enough, the same studies do not yield the same results when different people conduct them. So for now, the jury is still out and the debate continues.

Pain in the What?

Although not included in the favored five, pain is a body sense that warns us of potential harm and helps us cope with sickness and injury. In the fight to survive, it's one of our best defenses. It is also one of our most puzzling senses, because our experience of pain is influenced by a number of psychological and social factors.

Nobody likes to be told that a pain is "all in your head," but in truth, it often is. The way we experience our pain, the way we communicate about it to others, and even the way we respond to pain-relieving treatment, may reveal more about our psychological state than the actual intensity of the pain stimulus. Stomachaches hurt; however, someone who's unhappy at work may find the discomfort unbearable, while someone energized at work may feel that it's merely annoying.

Think of pain as your emotional experience of a physically distressing sensation. Things that intensify your emotions, like upsetting thoughts or catastrophic events, can magnify your experience of pain. Cultural attitudes and gender roles also play a role in our relationship with pain. For instance, early studies reported a consistent gender difference in pain perception—in the laboratory, women had a 20 percent lower pain tolerance than men. While these findings were initially attributed to biologically different pain thresholds, recent research suggests that the gender difference in pain tolerance may be in the *expression* of pain, not the *perception* of it.

> **Psychobabble**
>
> We all have a built-in mechanism that temporarily prevents us from feeling pain when, for survival purposes, it is best to ignore our injuries. This phenomenon, *stress-induced analgesia,* has helped hundreds of firefighters and police officers perform heroic deeds in the face of extreme trauma and in spite of personal injury.

In the lab, men tended to endure temporary discomfort rather than risk losing face by showing vulnerability to the researcher. Women, on the other hand, may be more accurate reporters because they feel less social pressure to endure unnecessary pain and are likely to speak up when something hurts. When it comes to your expression of pain, it's not all a function of biology; it's also your willingness to say "Ow!"

The Placebo Effect

The fact that pain is as much about what we perceive as it is about actual physical experience has both advantages and disadvantages. On the down side, researchers just about pull their hair out when one of their control groups—a group that gets no real treatment and so is supposed to stay the same—actually gets better. That's because the control group is supposed to be the yardstick; by comparing the treatment group to the control group, we can hypothetically see if our treatment or manipulation actually worked. And yet some people who participate in research studies and take inactive medications called placebos do see health improvements; people taking placebos have experienced reduced pain, healed ulcers, and eased nausea, and even had warts disappear.

However, solving the mystery behind the placebo effect may give us clues as to how to use our minds to help our bodies in everyday life, whether it's having positive expectations about our medical treatment, receiving support, or developing a supportive and positive relationship with a physician. In addition, the mind-body pain link enables us to use mental procedures to alleviate physical pain. Hypnosis can be a powerful pain reliever; the physical cause of the pain is still affecting the nerves, but you actually use mind over matter to control your experience of it. People have used hypnosis for pain control in dentistry, childbirth, and even in having surgery with no anesthesia or pain medications!

> **Psychobabble**
>
> Phantom pain is pain in a limb or body part that is no longer there, such as a leg that has been surgically removed. The feelings of pain, itching, or pressure feel just as real to the person as any other physical feelings. If someone has phantom pain, trying to "talk him out of it" won't work; he'll need help from a specialist in this area for relief.

Starting from the Top Down and the Bottom Up

If you think your senses are complicated, you ain't seen nothing yet. After your senses take in all that stimulation, your brain still has to make sense out of it. What is that round thing? Have we ever seen it—or anything like it—before? Is it a ball, an orange, or the moon? And, once we figure out what it is, we've got to figure out what to do with it.

If you've never been particularly proud of your organizing skills, your self-esteem is about to get a boost. Your brain has an amazing ability to automatically sort objects by size, distance, proportion, color, and many other categories. It solves mysteries hundreds of times a day by taking clues (sensory information from the environment) and using them to solve the puzzle by identifying the object. The "detective skills" you use are of two types—top-down processing and bottom-up processing.

Bottoms Up

Bottom-up processing is *data driven*—it starts with independent information from the outside and works its way inward to an interpretation of that information. When we process this way, we start with the environment; our eyes, for example, pick up colors or other visual cues as they look around. Using this data, our brain instantly tries to put together a visual image.

Interestingly, you are more likely to notice the "big picture" before you see details because your brain is so attuned to figuring out the whole landscape. For instance, you'll know that the shape coming toward you is a human being before you'll detect the color of her hair or eyes, or even her gender.

Of course, your brain doesn't just rely on information from your immediate environment to make sense of the world. It also makes use of your past experiences, knowledge, cultural background, motivations, expectations, and memories. This part of perceptual processing is known as *top-down processing* because your brain is comparing what you're currently seeing, hearing, or touching with your ideas, expectations, and memories of similar objects.

Watch Out! Reality Under Construction

The interaction of top-down and bottom-up processing means that our perceptions of reality are never truly objective. We are constantly constructing reality to fit in with our assumptions about how we think reality is, or ought to be. Because of our unique backgrounds, it really is true that no two people ever "see" the same thing.

Not only are we "topping down" and "bottoming up" at the same time; ideally, these processes are constantly balancing out. Consider what would happen if we relied exclusively on the current sensory stimuli of bottom-up processing to make sense of our world. We'd register experiences, but we wouldn't be able to learn from them.

Similarly, if you're relying too much on top-down processing, you might be caught up in a fantasy world of hopes and expectations, and overlook the reality staring you in the face. If you've ever stayed in a bad relationship because you kept pretending it was better than it was, maybe your perceptual processing was top heavy!

Life Is an Illusion

Do you ever wear dark clothes or vertical stripes to make yourself look thinner? If so, you're making use of illusion through your choice of clothing. By taking advantage of perceptual distortions, like dark colors appearing smaller than bright ones, we can artfully steer others into seeing us in a certain light.

Deceptive Appearances

We experience a perceptual illusion when our senses deceive us into perceiving an event or an object in a manner that is demonstrably incorrect. You might *look* thinner in vertical stripes than horizontal ones, but the tape measure or scale will clearly show that you aren't.

Illusions take advantage of our natural tendency to perceive objects in certain ways; in effect, they trick our senses. For example, from an early age, we learn cues that tell us about the relationship between size and distance. We learn that most objects that we see near the earth's horizon are farther away than objects we see near the zenith (straight up)—so birds or clouds seen near the horizon are usually farther away than those that are directly overhead.

Up, Down, Near, and Far

There are, however, exceptions to this rule. You may have noticed that the moon looks much larger when it is near the earth's horizon than when it's above us. When asked whether the horizon moon is farther or closer than usual, most people say closer. In this case, our perceptual systems apparently ignore the relative appearance of size, considering the fact that the moon does not change sizes, and our perception imposes the interpretation that, because the moon appears larger at the horizon, it must be nearer to us. In reality, the moon is the same distance away from us at either position.

Typically, illusions are more common when the sensory stimulus is ambiguous. When information is missing, elements are combined in unusual ways, or familiar patterns are not apparent, our senses are much more vulnerable to deception.

Meet Ponzo the Western Illusion

In the following figure, which line is longer, the one on top or the one on bottom? People from the United States often say that the top line is longer, but not everybody sees it that way. The Ponzo illusion is an example of our cultural background influencing our perception of ambiguous information and, alas, leading us astray.

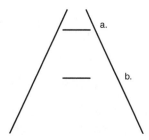

If you grew up in the United States, you are used to seeing long, flat highways or train tracks winding off in the distance. You've probably noticed that, if you look at them, the lines seem to come closer together off in the distance. People who grow up with these experiences learn to interpret perspective and distance involving lines and edges; in this case, they use converging lines as a cue for distance.

In the drawing, the top line appears to be longer because its higher position implies it is farther along the converging tracks. On the other hand, people who live in countries that provide little exposure to wide open spaces or, for that matter, tall, right-angled buildings, have fewer opportunities to learn the perceptual cue that converging lines imply distance. People in Guam, for example, are much less likely to fall for this illusion and will report that the lines are the same length.

Pay Attention When I'm Talking to You

Great illusionists have the gift of commanding our *attention*. Through their smoke and mirrors, they focus our attention on one thing while they're doing something else in the background. Great illusionists know that attention is the first step in sensation and perception.

def•i•ni•tion

Attention is a state of focused awareness coupled with a readiness to respond.

As we go about our daily activities, hundreds of things compete for our attention. Most of the time, we have a lot of conscious control over what we attend to. In fact, when our elementary school teacher told us to quit goofing off and "pay attention," she was relying on us to exert voluntary control over ourselves and tune in to our schoolwork.

If we are to fully understand anything, we have to focus on one source of information at a time. When we "pay attention," we are selectively attending to one source of information and blocking out others. Attention basically does three jobs:

◆ It helps us screen out irrelevant stimuli and focus on relevant information.

◆ It helps us consider the most appropriate response.

◆ It chooses the information that will enter in, and stay in, our awareness. If you don't pay attention to something, it can't be stored in your memory.

Here's an example of how attention works. Have you ever been at a party and suddenly heard your name? You might have been standing in the same place for half an hour, aware that conversation was going on around you but clueless as to what was actually being said. The minute the person says your name, though, you find your head whipping around and tuning in to his or her words. It's almost as if the person said your name in a louder voice, although you know this isn't true.

It seems louder to you because your name rings an internal bell. Imagine that your brain is a radio scanner and your attention is the station you're listening to. Personally interesting or perceptually meaningful information can grab your attention and cause you to suddenly tune in to a channel, just like a scanner picks up a strong signal.

But, you're probably wondering, how can you tell that another station is broadcasting if it's not the one you're listening to? Because even ignored information gets processed at some level. Subjects who had separate messages playing in each ear were told to ignore one message and tune in to another. While they failed to recognize words in the unattended message even after it had been played 35 times, these same subjects instantly recognized their own name when it turned up in that message about one third of the time.

The sounds that babies make have the same attention-grabbing impact on parents that hearing our name does on partygoers. Any new parent can tell you that the minute his or her baby cries, it is useless to try to pay attention to anything else. You could be immersed in your last chance to cram for the GREs or glued to your favorite soap opera, but the faintest cry will grab your attention as strongly as if the baby had walked up and slapped you upside the head. Whatever skills babies lack, commanding attention isn't one of them.

Working Smarter, Not Harder

Your closet might not be organized, but your brain is. Not only is it organized, it's also efficient—it looks for organizational strategies that require the least amount of effort. This brain trait is often referred to as the *law of Pragnanz*. Simply put, this law states that the simplest organization requiring the least amount of effort will always emerge.

For example, your brain automatically assumes that objects having something in common go together. If, for example, you see three ducks sitting beside each other, your brain will assume that, since they're close to each other, they must go together. Similarly, objects that look alike are lumped together. And objects that are moving in the same direction and at the same rate are assumed to share a common fate.

So, at a minimum, your brain saves time and conserves energy by processing things in groups. Another natural organizational strategy is your brain's tendency to create maps. Using changes in color and texture as cues, your brain divides the world into meaningful regions. The fact that my shirt is blue and my pants are yellow helps you know that I'm not wearing a one-piece jumpsuit. Hair has a different texture than skin does and our brain instantly recognizes it as a different feature.

Insight

Do you believe that washing your car is a surefire way to make it rain? Are you a gambler who is confident that a dry stretch without a lucky seven means a seven is due? Scientists think that much of our superstitious behavior may be our brain's tendency to look for patterns—even when they're not there!

Two other perceptual strategies for organizing information have interesting parallels in human behavior. First, we have a tendency to fill in the gaps—our need for perceptual closure is so strong that our brain will often fill in the missing edges, making us see incomplete figures as complete. The fact that we aren't aware of our visual blind spot is one example of our brain's automatic ability to fill in the gaps. As a psychological parallel, our psyches tend to fill in the gaps, too. How many hours have you spent trying to fill in the gaps left by someone's inexplicable or hurtful behavior?

The second organizational strategy, our tendency to see a figure against a background, has similarly profound effects. Our brains naturally look for ways to categorize information into foreground (the primary object of interest) and background (the backdrop against which the figure stands out). Colors and textures create regions, and our brains naturally place some in front of others. And, of course, we do this psychologically as well; when we go to a party, a striking member of the opposite sex may quickly become the foreground and everyone else become the backdrop.

Insight

How you feel about the war in Iraq is likely to be a good predictor of how likely you are to continue believing a news story that supports the war effort—even if it is later discredited. In the March 2005 issue of *Psychological Science*, researchers reported that repetition of inaccurate news stories tends to create false memories, and that corrected information does not change Americans' beliefs unless they were skeptical of the information to begin with.

In everyday life, our tendency to try to lump things into groups can lead to a real problem called stereotypes. "Well, you know women drivers ..."; "All black people have rhythm"; "He's a blond, what do you expect?" In stereotyping people, we do two things: we learn to regard people as either "us or them" and exclude those who are different, and we miss out on treating people as true individuals who have something unique to offer. Sometimes we have to use those frontal lobes we discussed in Chapter 2 to keep ourselves from getting carried away with trying to overly organize the world!

Psychobabble

What letters would you replace the asterisk with in the following two word series?

Sheep, goat, horse, cow, b*ll

Nickel, dime, quarter, dollar b*ll

The four words before the one with the fill-in-the-blank letter create a certain *perceptual set;* they encourage you to see stimuli in a certain way. In this case, you were perceptually set to read "bull" for the first group of words and "bill" for the second.

Don't Take It out of Context

The last stage of perception is identification and recognition—how the brain adds meaning to the facts it perceives. It takes all that sensory data and finds the appropriate context in which it belongs. We rely on context in our environment to help us make sense of things—so much so that if we encounter people or things that are out of their usual context, it can throw us for a perceptual loop.

When we encounter things out of their normal context, it can be confusing. Identification and recognition relies on our memory, expectations, motivation, personality, and social experience to help us understand what is being perceived. If you always see a business associate in business meetings, you expect to see him in that context. When you see him at the beach, you may not recognize him right away—he's out of his usual context so it takes you longer to adjust.

Context? Which Context?

But your idea of a proper context is likely to be different from mine. Each of us works from what are known as *perceptual sets*, conditions that determine one's readiness to detect a particular stimulus in a given context—and the specific conditions that make up one person's perceptual sets can be very different from the conditions that make up somebody else's.

One of the most fascinating things about psychology is how complicated human beings are. A famous saying in psychology is "Don't confuse the map with the territory," meaning that our view of the world—our map—is just one of many possible interpretations of our environment. In the next chapter, we'll take a look at how we become aware of our map—through consciousness.

The Least You Need to Know

- Sensation makes us aware of conditions inside or outside our body; perception makes sense of them.

- Our senses convert physical energy from our environment into neurochemical signals, which they send up to the brain to be analyzed and interpreted.

- Our experience of pain is as much a product of our mind as it is of our body. In some circumstances, we can use our minds to overcome pain.

- While our ability to pay attention is often under voluntary control, we're programmed to tune in to information that is personally meaningful or relevant.

- Our ability to make sense of our world requires the matching of information from our current environment with our prior experiences, memories, and expectations.

Chapter 6

It's Consciousness-Raising Time!

In This Chapter

- Getting the scoop on sleep
- We're all dreamers at heart
- Four paths to an altered consciousness
- The pharmaceutical problem

Imagine how you would feel if, in the middle of a breast exam, your doctor blurted out, "Oh, my God, I feel a lump in your breast! It could be cancerous." The fear that this unprofessional remark would cause could be traumatic even if he turned out to be wrong. For good reason, doctors are trained to keep unfounded suspicions to themselves.

Doctors who'd never do this in an exam room have unintentionally terrorized patients with similar remarks in the operating room. Because the patient is under anesthesia, doctors assume that the patient is unaware of what's being said. Not necessarily. Surgery patients under anesthesia may still hear what is going on around them. Even casual remarks in the operating room can be hazardous to our health!

How can we remember things that happened when we're unconscious? In this chapter, you'll learn that the line between consciousness and unconsciousness is blurrier than you might think. We'll take a look at how our brains produce consciousness, how our behavior interacts with our various states of mind, and why there appears to be a human need to alter our consciousness.

Are You Self-Conscious?

The word *consciousness* gets a bad rap these days, probably because it was overused in the 1960s. Unless you're in California, you're likely to view anyone who talks of a "higher consciousness" with some degree of suspicion. However, to the extent that a "higher consciousness" is greater self-awareness, it is the ultimate goal of most psychologists.

def•i•ni•tion

Consciousness refers to our awareness of ourselves and all the things we think, feel, and do.

As you learned in Chapter 5, we sense much more than we pay attention to. If you think of your consciousness as the front page of your mental newspaper, attention is the lead story that you can't resist reading. And your senses tell you that the story is in the newspaper to begin with.

On the Wings of Fantasy

On a basic level, you're conscious that you are constantly perceiving and reacting to information in your environment. While you're gazing out your office window at the beautiful grass below, you can imagine yourself lying on the grass and taking a nap. You can wonder why the grass is so green outside and wonder what kind of fertilizer the groundskeeper uses. And, on a higher level, you are aware that you're sitting at your office desk daydreaming about being outside and you can feel guilty that you aren't getting your work done.

Consciousness is pretty complicated and, as a result, you aren't always aware of what's going on in your head. By the time you're grown up, you're so used to certain thoughts that entire conversations can be going on in your head without your even noticing them. But even though you don't notice them, they're still having an impact.

You Are What You Think

Ever felt sad or angry but didn't know why? If you traced the origin of these feelings, chances are you'd discover that they were caused by self-defeating or negative thoughts. "I must be a loser going to another get-together by myself" is a surefire bummer of a thought, even if you're headed to the shindig of the year. If you let those thoughts stir around in the background of your consciousness long enough, you might decide to skip the party and go home and drown yourself in chocolate ice cream.

Being aware of your consciousness, on the other hand, gives you the power to understand your thoughts and feelings, evaluate their usefulness, and decide how much you'll let them influence your behavior. And the first step in raising your consciousness is to understand how your consciousness works.

Unconscious, Higher Conscious, and Everything in Between

For Freud, consciousness is just the tip of the iceberg. The stuff that crosses your mind lies on the surface, but underneath lurks a whole lot of murky activity that is completely outside of your awareness. In reality, consciousness is more like an elevator building. It has different levels, and information travels back and forth between them. Let's take a brief look at the four other levels of consciousness:

◆ Nonconscious

◆ Preconscious

◆ Subconscious

◆ Unconscious

Automatic Pilot

Your nonconscious handles information that is never represented in consciousness or memory but is critical to bodily and mental activity, such as information needed in controlling your heartbeat or regulating your blood pressure. With considerable practice, through methods like biofeedback or meditation, some people can even learn to partially control these automatic processes.

The File Cabinet

Your preconscious stores all the information that you don't need right now but that you can readily access if something calls your attention to it. If I ask you what you had for dinner last night, your preconscious opens that file and transfers it to your conscious. You aren't aware of that information until it is asked for.

The Secret Service

Subconscious awareness involves information that is not currently in your conscious but can be retrieved by special recall or attention-getting devices. Information stored in your preconscious, such as what you had for dinner last night, was once conscious; however, you may be completely unaware of information stored in your subconscious. For example, under hypnosis, former surgery patients have recalled detailed operating room conversations that they were completely unaware of overhearing.

The Clearinghouse

According to Freud, your unconscious handles memories, ideas, and emotions that are just too darned scary to face. Outside his school of thought, however, there has been little support for the existence of an unconscious. New research that studies unconscious thought processes suggests that your unconscious may act as a clearinghouse for sorting through and storing all the data you encounter but don't attend to.

Insight

Daydreaming, a mild form of altered consciousness, occurs when attention shifts away from your immediate surroundings to other thoughts. Daydreams are most likely to occur when you're alone, relaxed, or bored. On average, people spend about 10 percent of their time day-dreaming.

The various levels of consciousness work together to run a pretty organized outfit. While your conscious mind is busy focusing on day-to-day operations, other parts are in the background making sure the office is running smoothly. Of course, even the hardest workers need a break to recharge their batteries. Let's take a look at a "vacation" your consciousness gets every day: sleep.

Alpha, Beta, Delta—the Sleep Fraternity

What is sleep really for? Evolutionary psychologists think that sleep evolved to restore your body from the wear and tear of the day and to help keep you out of trouble. Animals that eat low-calorie foods and thus need to spend a lot of time eating don't snooze much; animals that eat high-calorie foods sleep longer. Sleep is nature's way to keep idle animals from going astray!

In human terms, the sleep club is definitely one in which you want to be an active participant. Sadly, we seem to be getting less sleep than our ancestors did—about 100 years ago, our great-great-grandparents were sleeping about an hour and a half more per night than we are now.

New research suggests that poor sleep habits are as influential as poor nutrition and lack of physical activity in the development of chronic illness. The potential danger arising from sleep deprivation is obviously greater in some occupations than in others; according to NASA, one in seven pilots nods off at the cockpit, and pilot fatigue contributes to one third of all aviation accidents. And if that isn't bad enough, preliminary studies indicate that, as counterintuitive as it seems, if you lose enough sleep, the disruption in your hormonal system may actually cause you to gain weight!

In particular, if you're getting six and a half hours of sleep a night or less on a regular basis, your body is more likely to undergo potentially harmful metabolic, hormonal, and immune system changes. You can't cheat and still get the benefit of regular sleep, either, by engaging in "sleep bulimia," a slang term used to describe weekday under-sleepers who try to catch up by sleeping late on the weekend. On a positive note, it might be easier to burn the candles at both end as you get older; by age 80, six hours or less of sleep per night is normal.

When it comes to consciousness, sleep is a paradox. On the one hand, we talk about "walking around in our sleep," when we're so tired we can barely hold our heads up. We talk about being "knocked out" when our head hits the pillow after a hard day. At the same time, we can feel more "conscious" and alert in the middle of a dream than we do after a big meal in the middle of the day.

All the World's a Stage

Until the *electroencephalograph* (*EEG*) came along, scientists pretty much thought that sleep was a mindless activity. The EEG enabled us to record the electrical activity of the brain at any stage of alertness and quickly put this assumption to rest. The EEG soon made it clear that when you fall asleep, your brain goes through four predictable stages, indicating four distinct cycles of sleep.

Stage one is the brief transition stage that occurs when you're first falling asleep. On an EEG, your brain waves slow down and become large and regular *alpha waves*. Stages two through four are successively deeper stages of true sleep. They show up on the EEG as an increasingly large number of slow, irregular, high-amplitude waves called *delta waves*.

def•i•ni•tion

REM sleep is characterized by rapid eye movement, brain activity close to that of wakefulness, and a complete absence of muscle tone. Most dreaming takes place during REM sleep; research now shows that REM sleep activates the limbic system, the most ancient part of the brain, which controls our emotions.

It takes about 90 minutes to move through the first four stages of sleep. After that, you move through the entire sleep cycle four to five more times during the night. After the first full cycle, however, you start going backward through stages three and two. You don't repeat stage one, however; in its place you enter the most exciting period of the night: *REM sleep.*

REM is the acronym for *rapid eye movement,* the condition that characterizes this stage of sleep. A lot goes on during REM sleep; in fact, if you couldn't see the person laid out in front of you, the EEG would convince you that he or she is wide awake. The EEG would show *beta waves,* the same irregular waves that your brain makes when you're solving problems in the middle of the day. During your first sleep cycle, you spend about 10 minutes in REM sleep; in your last, you may spend up to an hour.

No one knows exactly why, but we need our REM sleep. If we are deprived of REM sleep one night, our brain waves play catch-up the next. It may be that REM sleep plays a role in stabilizing our emotions and cataloging and storing memories. One product of REM has captured the imaginations of amateur and professional psychologists all over the world: dreams.

Brain Buster

Working too hard? Learning a new sport? Take a nap and catch a few extra winks in the morning. Recent research shows that a midday snooze can prevent burnout, and that late-stage (early morning) sleep boosts motor skill performance by 20 percent. Overall, studies suggest that the brain uses a night's sleep to consolidate the memories of habits, actions, and skills learned during the day.

I Must Be Dreaming

What do your dreams mean? The answer to that question depends on whom you're talking to. According to Native American tradition, dreams are messengers from the spirit world. Dreamcatchers, wooden hoops filled with a web made from nettle-stalk cord, were hung over the baby's cradle to bestow pleasant dreams and harmony. The good spirit dreams found their way through the tiny center hole and floated down the sacred feathers to the baby. The bad spirit dreams got caught in the web and disappeared in the morning light.

Freudian psychologists think that dreams serve two purposes. One, they guard sleep by disguising disruptive thoughts with symbols. Two, they provide harmless ways for people to fulfill their darkest desires without suffering the social consequences.

Hard-core scientists suggest that a dream's major job is to provide regular group exercise for the brain's neurons. According to this somewhat skeptical view, dreams are simply an accidental by-product of random electrical discharges, and the only reason they have any meaning is because the brain tries to add meaning after these discharges happen.

The fact is, we don't know who has the right answer. But it's kind of depressing to think that dreams might be random and meaningless, especially since some of our dreams seem to have fairly obvious relevance to what's going on in our lives. Almost everyone has had a dream that helped solve a problem or tough situation.

Actually, there is some scientific evidence that your psyche and your dreams are connected. Mental problems tend to extend REM sleep; it's as if our psyches need more time to work things out. And people who are going through similar life transitions often have dreams with similar themes; pregnant women often dream of having deformed children or strange births, while soon-to-be-newlyweds may dream of being late to the church or having a last fling with a former flame. People who have survived a traumatic event often relive the experience in dreams.

Ever had a dream in which you were falling off a cliff or showed up at an important event without your clothes on? Join the universal dream club. A study of dream content in 175 countries found that the majority of dreamers had had similar dreams at least once. Cross-cultural studies also show, though, that people from different cultures report dream content consistent with their unique culture and environment; while being chased seems to be a universal dream theme, in India you are more likely to dream of being chased by vultures. In Canada, bears are more likely to be your fantasy pursuers.

The Ticking of Your Biological Clock

All of us have biological clocks that affect our arousal and energy levels throughout the day. If your clock is set to be a night person, and you have to get up at 6 A.M. every day, then you're in a difficult situation.

Your biological clock—or, more properly, your *circadian rhythm*—is pretty sophisticated; it is a set of physiological activities that coordinate your hormones, metabolism, body temperature, heart rate, and, of course, level of arousal. While biological clocks vary from person to person, they are amazingly consistent within the individual.

If you could rise at any time you choose and retire any time you like at night, how would your day differ from your present routine? Would you be up at dawn or snoozing

def•i•ni•tion

Circadian rhythm means "about a day"—it's the clock that regulates your sleep-wake cycle. When it's disrupted by flying across several time zones, you get **jet lag,** which can involve fatigue, sleepiness, and subsequent unusual sleep and wake schedules.

till noon? Biological clocks are pretty resistant to change, so it can help to find a schedule that matches your natural biorhythms as closely as possible. And you can certainly cut down on relationship quarrels if your partner's clock ticks like yours; it can be pretty frustrating if the time you most feel like snuggling is the time your partner feels like snoozing.

Ticking clocks aside, human snoozers have more in common than you might think. Whether we're night owls or early birds, we're all tuned in to circadian rhythms, bodily patterns that repeat approximately every 24 hours. We all spend about one third of our lives sleeping. And, as you're about to see, few things throw your consciousness for a loop like a lack of sleep!

Insight

Of all groups in Western culture, teens may be most likely to go for long periods of time without enough sleep, mostly due to early class schedules. To combat this, some schools are making changes. High schools in Minneapolis now start classes an hour and a half later than previously—and have been rewarded with kids who miss fewer classes and make better grades!

Doc, I Just Can't Sleep

There's an epidemic in the United States, and it's caused by lack of sleep. As many as 100 million Americans don't get enough sleep every night, and it costs the United States billions of dollars in lost productivity each year. More than half of all night shift workers nod off at least once a week on the job. It may be no accident that disasters such as the Exxon oil spill and the Chernobyl nuclear power plant accident happened during the late evening hours, when key personnel were likely to be less alert due to insufficient sleep. The average person needs six to eight hours of sleep a night; if we don't get it, the only thing that will wake us up is enough sleep.

If there's one thing worse than not getting enough sleep, it's not getting any sleep. *Insomnia* is a condition in which you have a normal desire for sleep, put in your seven or eight hours in bed, but, for some reason, you can't go to sleep. Even if you lie perfectly still for seven or eight hours, you're likely to feel tired all day as a result of not sleeping.

Insomnia can be caused by a variety of psychological, environmental, and biological factors, including the following:

- Anxiety or depression

- Noisy next-door neighbors

- Exercise too close to bedtime

- The use of stimulants (such as caffeine) prior to bedtime

- Changes in work shifts

- Physical illness or discomfort

Insight

While insomnia has long been recognized as a symptom of depression, recent research suggests that a lack of sleep can actually trigger it. A person who experiences insomnia for longer than five days should call a physician to see if a short-term treatment is warranted.

Insomnia can take different forms. You can have trouble falling asleep, wake up off and on during the night, or crash immediately and wake up at 3 A.M. and be unable to get back to sleep. The "cure" for insomnia can be as simple as earplugs or as complex as psychiatric medication or surgery.

Another form of insomnia is *excessive daytime sleepiness*. This disorder, which afflicts about 4 percent to 5 percent of the population, might sound hokey; after all, most of us would say that we're sleepy during the day. However, sufferers of this disorder would argue otherwise. True daytime sleepiness is a persistent problem that can actually prevent you from functioning normally. Before doctors make this diagnosis, they have to rule out a number of medical problems, because chronic fatigue is a symptom of a number of serious medical conditions.

Brain Buster

The new generation of sleep medications, such as Ambien, Sonata, and Lunestra, seem to have fewer and less-severe side effects than other sleep medications, and show potential for long-term use. However, the safety of long-term treatment has not been proven.

Last and most serious of the sleep disorders is sleep apnea, a potentially life-threatening condition most commonly found in overweight, older men. Sleep apnea is an upper-respiratory sleep disorder that causes a person to quit breathing while asleep. When the blood's oxygen level drops low enough, emergency hormones are secreted and wake the person up. He starts breathing again and falls back asleep. This cycle can literally happen hundreds of times each night. Not only is this exhausting, but without treatment, the sufferer runs the risk of literally dying in his sleep.

To make the most of your need to sleep, try a little self-help for the sleep-deprived:

♦ Give up the sheep-counting. Recent research suggests that listening to soothing music for 45 minutes while lying quietly in bed may be the most effective sleep strategy.

♦ Go to bed and get up at the same time every day (yes, even on the weekends).

♦ Get regular physical exercise, but not within three hours of bedtime.

♦ If these don't work, consider seeing a professional. Relaxation training combined with therapy targeting anxiety-producing beliefs about sleep loss has been shown to be an effective treatment for insomnia.

Altered Consciousness

Sleep (and dreaming) is one form of altered consciousness. Human beings have invented thousands of others. There are roller coasters, Ferris wheels, and merry-go-rounds. Young children spin around and around until they get dizzy. There's meditation and yoga, and there are drugs and alcohol. These are all ways of expanding or altering our state of mind, and they seem to be a universal part of human nature.

Albert Einstein once said that a problem can't be solved at the same level in which it occurs. The fact that we have to use our mind to solve our mind's problems is one of psychology's biggest challenges. One benefit of altering our consciousness is that it shifts us out of our normal way of looking at things. By changing our focus, we can get a different perspective on ourselves and our problems.

People also alter their consciousness to avoid their problems or escape from reality. When it comes to mind-altering drugs, there can be a fine line between using them for relaxation, for fun, or as an escape. Let's take a look at four primary ways we can alter our consciousness, and the pros and cons of each:

♦ Hypnosis

♦ Meditation

♦ Hallucinations

♦ Drugs

Look Deeply into My Eyes

It is truly amusing to see old movies that include hypnosis as part of the plot. Inevitably, there is a Svengali look-alike waving a gold watch in front of an innocent and naïve young woman, chanting, "Keep your eyes on the watch as it moves back and forth … back and forth …." His voice gets deeper and we see her eyelids droop lower. She falls completely under his spell and the audience spends the rest of the movie watching her try to get out of the spell.

That's not the way hypnosis really works. If you've ever been hypnotized, you deserve much more credit than your hypnotist. The single-most important factor in hypnosis is the degree to which a participant has a "talent" for becoming hypnotized. Clinical hypnotists call this talent *hypnotizability*.

def•i•ni•tion

Your **hypnotizability** is a measure of how susceptible you are to entering a hypnotic state.

You're Getting Very, Very Sleepy

Your hypnotizability is the degree to which you respond to hypnotic suggestions. Hypnosis is *not* the result of gullibility or a deep-seated need to conform to social pressure. It has much to do with a unique expression of human imagination. Are you the kind of person who gets so involved in a book or a movie that it feels like you're a part of it? If so, you're probably a good candidate for hypnosis. A hypnotizable person is one who is able to truly immerse himself in the imagination and feeling of life experiences.

Since the inception of hypnosis more than 200 years ago, it has been impossible to find agreement among professionals about what it is. But even though "hypnosis" is still clouded in mystery and confusion, there are some key elements that can be used when talking about hypnosis and hypnotic states. In a general sense, *hypnosis* is an induced state of awareness characterized by deep relaxation and increased suggestibility.

And When I Snap My Fingers, You'll Remember Nothing

A subject under hypnosis is highly responsive to the hypnotist's suggestion; however, it is not a form of mind control. No one under hypnosis can be made to do something against his or her will. The person under hypnosis is fully in control of him- or herself at all times. And you can't get "stuck" under hypnosis.

Psychobabble

In 1897, a California murder defendant was hypnotized on the stand and swore he was innocent. Witnesses to the murder swore otherwise. Apparently, the jury was not in a trance; they recognized that a person could lie under hypnosis, believed the eyewitnesses, and convicted the defendant.

Researchers may disagree about the psychological mechanisms involved in hypnosis, but they agree about the powerful therapeutic influence hypnosis can have in reducing the psychological component of pain. Children undergoing cancer treatment, for example, have successfully been taught to use their imagination to distract themselves from painful procedures. Watching a parent and child take a hypnosis-induced trip to Disneyland in the middle of an oncology ward is not only a powerful testament to the science of psychology, it's also a testament to the human spirit.

For people who are hypnotizable, research supports the use of hypnosis in the treatment of headache pain, asthma, and a variety of dermatological symptoms. Unfortunately, for most people, hypnosis doesn't seem to help with smoking cessation, weight loss, or alcohol abuse. So if you were counting on a hypnotherapist to help you shed a few extra pounds, you'll be a lot better off investing your money in a good book on motivation techniques—or a gym!

Don't Bother Me, I'm Meditating

Meditation is another way of altering consciousness. It took a while before it caught on in the Western part of the world, perhaps because its "sit still and listen" focus can be a little hard for those of us who grew up in a "get up and get ahead" culture. But although meditation got off to a slow start, it is now one of the fastest-growing practices in the United States, and with good reason. If you're looking for a way to alter your consciousness, meditation may be the way to go.

First of all, anyone can learn it. *Transcendental Meditation*, the form of meditation that has received the most scientific investigation, basically involves sitting comfortably with your eyes closed and focusing on a mantra. A mantra is a word or phrase that you repeat silently to yourself. Practiced 15 to 20 minutes twice daily, it apparently enables your mental activity to settle down naturally while alertness is maintained and enhanced.

I Must Be Hallucinating

If you like having friends, hallucinations might not be the best way to alter your consciousness. Western culture has little tolerance for unusual perceptual experiences.

We tend to be afraid of people who have them. This attitude is not universal; in some cultures, people who hallucinate are viewed as spiritual leaders with a direct connection to the spirit world.

We're Not Talking Beads and Lava Lamps Here

It's easy to confuse hallucinations with illusions—we *all* see illusions. When you look at the flashing lights on a movie marquee, you see the illusion of a single light zooming around the edge of the sign. The appearance of movement in stationary lights is common; they look that way to most of us. Most of us don't, however, "see" lights around the heads of the people selling tickets in the box office. If you do, then you're having a hallucination. An illusion is a distortion of something that's there; a hallucination is seeing something that isn't there.

In general, hallucinations occur when your brain metabolism is altered from its normal level. They can be a symptom of many different diseases or conditions: high fever, an adverse reaction or side effect from a drug, ingestion of a hallucinogen, renal failure, migraines, or epilepsy.

> **Insight**
>
> Not only is meditation easy to learn, but it also has tremendous health benefits. Over a five-year study, practitioners of Transcendental Meditation got sick less often (doctor visits decreased by more than 50 percent), drank less alcohol, felt less anxious, and felt more resilient and emotionally mature.

Is This a Dagger I See Before Me?

Most of us, though, associate hallucinations with mental illness and, in particular, with schizophrenia. People with schizophrenia often hear voices inside their head, but truly believe that the voices are coming from outside themselves. Imagine how frightening it would be to hear a voice saying mean things about you, but not knowing who was talking or where the voice was coming from.

Fortunately, even Western culture is becoming more tolerant of different perceptions of reality, as overwhelming evidence points to schizophrenia being as much a physical disorder as diabetes or cancer. In addition, under certain conditions, we might all see reality differently. Trauma can cause just about anyone to hallucinate; some Vietnam vets, for example, were bombarded with "flashbacks," visual and auditory replays of traumatic combat scenes. And a significant number of ordinary people actually "see" or "hear" a deceased loved one within six weeks of his or her death.

Operating Under the Influence

And now, ladies and gentlemen, for the winner in the Most Popular Way to Alter Your Consciousness Contest: drugs and alcohol. Given the risks involved in this particular form of consciousness altering, it makes you wonder about the judges. Regular use of drugs and alcohol is so darned bad for you that it's hard for me to talk about it without sounding like the poster child for the "Just say no" campaign.

However, drug use does not always lead to drug addiction. Most teenagers try drugs and alcohol and the vast majority of them never become serious users. And yes, there are studies that suggest that one to two drinks a week can be good for your physical health, although if you have a strong family history of substance abuse, it's probably not worth the risk.

Some Pills Make You Larger

Psychoactive drugs—the ones that work on your brain and change your mood—are the ones most likely to become addictive. They attach themselves to synaptic receptors in the brain, and block or stimulate certain chemical reactions. It is these chemical reactions that you experience as increased relaxation, lowered inhibition, or greater self-confidence. Psychoactive drugs affect your mental processes and behavior by changing your conscious awareness. Let's take a look at the five classes of major mood changers:

- ◆ Hallucinogens
- ◆ Marijuana
- ◆ Opiates
- ◆ Depressants
- ◆ Stimulants

Hallucinogens, also known as psychedelics, distort your senses and alter your perceptions. They can also temporarily blur the boundaries between you and the things around you. Someone on an acid trip, for example, may feel as if she is a physical part of the guitar she is playing, or she can "see" the musical notes floating around her.

Marijuana is often classified as a hallucinogen, although it has some distinct properties of its own. The experience depends on the dose; small doses create mild, pleasurable highs, and larger doses result in long, hallucinogenic reactions. The positive effects include a sense of euphoria and well-being, and distortions of time and space. The effects, however, can also be negative, such as fear, anxiety, and confusion. Marijuana impairs motor coordination, making it risky to smoke and drive.

Opiates are highly addictive drugs that suppress your ability to feel and respond to sensations. Prescription versions are routinely used as painkillers. The most popular street version is heroin—users typically report a "rush" of euphoria when they first use it, followed by a trancelike state of relaxation (known as a "nod").

Depressants and stimulants are the most widely abused substances, although they tend to have opposite effects. Depressants, including alcohol, slow down the mental and physical activities of the body. They can temporarily relieve anxiety and stress but also quickly impair physical coordination and judgment. Someone who drinks too much is likely to slow down to the point of passing out.

On the other hand, stimulants like cocaine are "uppers." They speed up mental and physical activity. Cocaine and amphetamine users report increased confidence and higher energy when they first start out. An overdose of amphetamines can cause frightening hallucinations, dramatic mood swings, and paranoid delusions.

Do you use any psychoactive drugs? Well, do you drink coffee? Smoke cigarettes? Have a few beers now and then? If any of the above apply to you, then you're a psychoactive drug user. Of course, just because you rely on caffeine to get those peepers open or have an occasional drink at happy hour doesn't mean that you're a psychoactive drug *abuser*. That determination depends upon a lot of different factors, including the genetic die you were cast.

Brain Buster

Self-medicating for stress with alcohol or drugs is generally not a good idea. You risk trading off one problem for another. Don't believe me? Try volunteering a few hours at the local detox center. You may never chug another Sam Adams again.

Risking Addiction

Your risk for addiction depends on lots of things—your personality, your genetic makeup, your coping skills, and your family history of drug and alcohol abuse. It also depends on your drug of choice.

Mood Alterer	Most Popular Drug	Risk of Dependence
Hallucinogens	LSD	No psychological, unknown physical
Cannabis	Marijuana	Unknown psychological, moderate physical
Opiates	Heroin	High psychological and physical
Depressants	Alcohol, Valium	Moderate to high psychological and physical
Stimulants	Cocaine, speed	High psychological and physical

Lethal Weapons

Besides looking at addiction, one way to look at the dangers of a psychoactive drug is to compare the amount of the drug it takes to get the desired results (the effective dose, or ED) to the dose that will kill you (the lethal dose, or LD). For example, many people don't realize that they can literally die from a single drinking binge. Fifteen drinks in an hour can do it for many people, as the families of some college students have unfortunately found out. That's because, during a hard-drinking party, the usual social dose and the lethal dose are too close for comfort.

On the other hand, it is almost impossible to die of a lethal dose of marijuana; the ED and LD are very far apart. You might die of smoke inhalation first!

Does that make marijuana a great idea? Not exactly. New research shows that learning and memory problems caused by marijuana smoking persist for at least a week after you've smoked. And, while the brain seems to physically recover from heavy use after a month of abstinence, heavy marijuana users consistently have significantly lower income and educational levels than nonusers. And, of course, if the authorities find a bale of marijuana in the garage, you can find yourself in the local lockup. There are many risks and rewards you have to weigh before deciding to put something in your body—or garage.

The Monkey on Your Back

Being addicted to drugs has been called "having a monkey on your back." And for good reason! The harder you try to shake it off, the harder it clings to you. It demands to be fed at all hours of the day and night. It screams louder when you try to ignore it. No matter where you go, it's always there.

It All Sneaks Up on You

Continued use of certain psychoactive drugs lessens their effect over time, so that more of the drug is needed to achieve the same effect. The body develops a tolerance to the substance. To make matters worse, physiological dependence often goes hand in hand with tolerance. So at the same time that a user needs more of the drug to get the desired mental effects, he or she needs more of the drug for physical reasons, too.

After a while, addicts only feel "normal" when using. When they try to cut back or quit, they go through a process called withdrawal. Unpleasant physical and mental symptoms occur when a physically addicted substance abuser discontinues the drug.

The Addictive Mind

Psychological dependence can take place with or without physical dependence. When cocaine use became popular in the early 1980s, common wisdom held that it was not physically addictive, but that it was highly addictive psychologically. It was easy for people to become emotionally dependent on the "pseudo-confidence" that cocaine generated. A little closer to home is the panic that you may feel when you run out of coffee. While the physical dependency potential of caffeine is unknown, many of us experience the psychological addiction to coffee on a daily basis!

The "psychology" of drug use is amazingly complex. Even the immediate effects of drugs on your consciousness may be influenced more by your psychological factors than by the physical properties of the drug. The mood that you're in before taking the drug, your expectations of what will happen, and your history of prior drug use all play a crucial role. If you've ever had a few drinks when you were down in the dumps, and then wound up feeling more depressed, you know what I mean.

The Least You Need to Know

- Consciousness is the awareness of who we are and all the things we think, feel, and do.

- Sleep is a form of altered consciousness that probably evolved to restore our bodies after all the wear and tear of the day, and to keep our ancestors from having too much idle time on their hands.

◆ REM sleep is the most important of the four sleep stages. It's the time we dream, and it seems to help stabilize our mood and store our memories.

◆ Sleep disorders (including insomnia, excessive daytime sleepiness, and sleep apnea) are caused by a complex combination of psychological and physical factors.

◆ Four ways that people have purposefully altered their consciousness are meditation, hypnosis, hallucinations, and psychoactive drugs.

◆ Use of any psychoactive drugs requires close attention, as the line between desire and dependence can be hard to recognize.

Get *That* Through Your Thick Skull!

In This Chapter

- Learning which associations we're all members of
- Learning and our love life
- Thorndike's cats and Pavlov's dogs
- Facing irrational fears
- Banishing bad habits

This chapter is all about learning: *how* we learn, *what* we learn, and *when* we learn. As you read, you'll meet some interesting psychologists who, through their work with animals, pioneered our understanding of learning. You'll learn about the power of association and how our interpretation of the consequences of our actions influences our learning curve. And you'll learn how to apply the magical principles of learning to get rid of irrational fears, alter bad habits, and maybe even improve your love life!

Helpless

"I can't do it," four-year-old Sabrina whines as she hands you the magazine and scissors. "You do it for me." "But Sabrina," you argue. "You haven't even tried. I know you can cut out that picture yourself." Inwardly, you sigh, frustrated and confused by Sabrina's constant clinging and refusal to attempt new things.

What's going on with Sabrina? Why is she constantly demanding assistance from you while other children her age are eager to do things for themselves? Doesn't she want to learn to do things for herself?

We all need a little help now and then, but if we need it all the time, then we may have learned helplessness. Children as young as four can develop the belief that they lack the ability to impact their environment, and, as a result, they give up and stop attempting new tasks. Not only does learned helplessness interfere with our ability to take charge of our lives, but many psychologists believe it causes depression. *Learning* obviously isn't just about developing new skills; it's also about believing that we can.

def•i•ni•tion

The term **learning** refers to any process through which experience at one time can change our behavior at another.

Learning About Learning

We've all heard the saying "Experience is the best teacher." Learning theorists would say it's the *only* teacher. By definition, learning involves changing our behavior in response to experience. And, since much of psychology deals with the effects of experiences on our behavior, learning about learning is important.

Learning is one of those psychological concepts that's easy to understand but hard to see. Since learning is something that happens inside us, it can never be observed directly. Teachers give us tests because they are looking for evidence, or lack thereof, that we are learning the material in their class. Similarly, learning researchers have to depend on measurable improvements in performance when they're studying learning. Whether it's a grade on a calculus test or the number of trials it takes a rat to find food in a maze, behavior is the ultimate evidence of learning.

But the benefit you get from learning is not confined to behavioral change. Learning also expands your options. For example, even if you decide not to quit smoking right now, by learning effective smoking cessation strategies you can increase your ability to quit in the future. Similarly, an inspiring book, perhaps like the one you are reading, can increase your appreciation for its subject, motivate you to learn more, and affect your attitudes and choices for years to come. Now wasn't that money well spent?

Does the Name Pavlov Ring a Bell?

Association is the key to learning. I come from a long line of teachers and, believe me, the joys of learning were preached and the benefits of education drilled into my head. On the reverence ladder, school was right up there with church, and studying was considered as important as praying. I probably hid out in graduate school for so many years because my associations with hard work weren't nearly so pleasant!

A man by the name of Ivan Pavlov first discovered the power of positive associations, and he used it to teach old dogs new tricks. As a scientist, he had spent many years studying the digestive processes in dogs. To speed along his studies, he frequently asked his assistants to put powdered meat in the dogs' mouths so they would salivate. One day, he noticed a strange thing; his dogs were drooling before the meat powder even touched their tongues. The sight of the food, or the sound of food being poured into the dish, sent these dogs into a frenzy of anticipation.

def•i•ni•tion

In **classical conditioning**, two stimuli become so closely associated that one of them can elicit the same reactive behavior as the other.

Pavlov began deliberately controlling the signals that preceded the food. In one famous experiment, he sounded a bell just before placing the food in the dog's mouth. After several pairings of a bell with food, the dogs would drool in response to the bell sound alone. Pavlov was so fascinated with these events that he abandoned his original work on digestion, discovered *classical conditioning*, and changed the course of psychology forever.

If you're a pet owner, you're probably wondering what all the fuss was about. After all, within a week after getting your pet, you probably observed your little darling drooling to the sound of an electric can opener or the sound of food being poured into a dish. At the time, however, Pavlov's discovery was revolutionary.

For the first time, scientists could systematically study human learning by varying the associations between two stimuli and charting out what affect this had on a subject's response. Not only did Pavlov's research help us understand and use the power of positive association, but it ultimately paved the way for understanding the role that negative associations can play in the development of irrational fears and phobias.

On a gloomier note, classical conditioning has also given advertisers a lot of effective ammo. Every time they pair sex with their products, they're betting that the association between the two will have you drooling just like Pavlov's dog!

Learning the Classics

You, my friend, have been conditioned—and I'm not talking about your hair. Maybe you've formed an association between a certain piece of music and a relationship breakup, and now you feel sad every time you hear that song. Maybe you came down with a stomach virus after eating poached salmon, and now every time you even smell fish, you feel nauseated. Maybe you've been in a recent car accident; now, even though you know it wasn't your fault, you're a little nervous about getting behind the wheel. Whether you know it or not, you have thousands of associations living in your head and many of them got there through classical conditioning.

Psychobabble
Remember the old *Gong Show?* John B. Watson and his assistant, Rosalie Raynor, invented a different version. They quickly taught an infant named Little Albert to fear a white rat by banging a loud gong just behind the tot whenever the rat appeared. After just seven gongs, Little Albert was scared to death of the same rat he had played with before the training began. His fear was so great that it generalized to other furry objects, including a Santa Claus mask.

Coming In on Cue

Here's how these associations happen: human beings are biologically programmed to respond certain ways to certain things in the environment. We salivate when we eat food. We jump if we hear a sudden, loud noise. We jerk our hands away if we touch something hot. These natural reactions are unconditioned responses; we don't have to learn them.

Over time, though, we start noticing that certain cues might help us predict when an environmental stimulus (food, noises, burning) is about to appear. From an evolutionary standpoint, such cues signaling danger or benefits would be highly adaptive. Learning that a grizzly bear makes a certain noise in the bushes would be pretty useful information, especially if it keeps you from having to wait for physical confirmation of his presence! Similarly, the smell of something burning is a pretty good clue that fire is near, and it gives you the chance to respond to the smell in the same way you would to a fire—take it seriously and investigate immediately, before you get burned.

Where There's Smoke

In the fire example, the smell of smoke is the conditioned stimulus, and fire is the unconditioned stimulus. You'll naturally avoid fire—it's your unconditioned response to the unconditioned stimulus signaling danger. But over time, you'll associate that smoke smell with danger and respond to it as if the smell were the same as an actual fire. What separates unconditioned responses from conditioned ones is learning—you have to *learn* conditioned responses. The urge to avoid or escape is an unconditioned response to fire, but it's a conditioned response to the burning smell, because you had to learn it.

Here's another example:

Unconditioned Stimulus	Intimate body contact (heavy petting)
Unconditioned Response	Physiological arousal (getting "turned on")
Environmental Cue	Chanel No. 5

At first you get this sequence of behaviors:

Unconditioned Stimulus (petting)

+Environmental Cue (the scent of Chanel)

Unconditioned Response (getting turned on)

After several repetitions, you can cut directly to the chase, so to speak:

the scent of Chanel = getting turned on

In this example, intimate bodily contact is a natural stimulus for physiological arousal. On the other hand, contrary to what advertisers may say, you have not been biologically programmed to respond to the perfume Chanel No. 5. But if you've had enough pairings of this perfume and sexual arousal in, say, the back seat of your car on Friday nights, you can bet that even a whiff of Chanel will send those hormones flying!

Learning Isn't Always Fun

It would be great if all our classical conditioning were built on positive associations. Unfortunately, life doesn't work that way; negative stimuli also conditions us. Sometimes, in fact, learning can be downright aversive.

Brain Buster

Agoraphobia is an example of classically conditioned fear. People who have panic attacks often associate their physical symptoms with the environment in which they occur. In an attempt to ward off future attacks, they'll restrict their activities until they're literally unable to venture out of the house.

If the door to your office has a lot of static electricity and you get a jolt every time you touch it, the shock is an example of painful unconditioned stimuli. Your unconditioned response is avoidance. Over time, you may start approaching this innocent door with dread. You may begin to devise all kinds of quirky strategies for avoiding the shock—using a handkerchief to open to the door, always going in after someone else, or rubbing your feet on the floor to ground yourself. This kind of learning is called *aversive conditioning:* you learn an aversion to something that was previously perceived as harmless.

Aversive conditioning can be very powerful because of the fear associated with it. Not only do you want to avoid the object of your aversion, but you also become afraid of it. Fear is a hard emotion to unlearn—in fact, when strong fear is involved, conditioning can take place after only a single pairing between a neutral stimulus and an unconditioned stimulus. And it can last a lifetime.

During World War II, the signal used to call sailors to battle stations aboard U.S. Navy ships was a gong. To personnel on board, this sound was quickly associated with danger. Researchers found that even 15 years later, the sound of the old "call to battle stations" struck fear in the hearts of the navy veterans who had been aboard these ships.

If you find yourself having an "irrational" reaction to something, chances are you're the victim of negative classical conditioning. For this to happen, though, certain conditions have to be met.

Learning About Meaningful Relationships

Timing is as critical in classical conditioning as it is in good joke telling. During your lifetime, you'll form thousands of associations among the situations and events in your life. Not all of these become classically conditioned. For example, that song might give you the blues because it was playing on your car radio during a relationship breakup, but you probably aren't heartbroken every time you drive your car.

That's because not all associations are created equal. In a child's early years, just about anything resembling the conditioned stimuli will prompt a similar response. A child who has been bitten by a large dog will initially regard all dogs with suspicion. This is called *stimulus generalization*. It seems that evolution first teaches us that it's better to be safe than sorry.

Developing Discrimination

Over time, though, we become more discriminating. We learn to distinguish between the conditioned stimuli and its relatives. The child begins to realize that one bad dog does not spoil the whole bunch, and that she doesn't have to spend the rest of her life fearful of *all* dogs. When Little Albert realizes that the rat causes the gong to ring, while Santa Claus brings toys, he is engaging in *stimulus discrimination*.

Classical conditioning is a lot like dating; it's a balancing act between discriminating too much and responding the same way to too many stimuli! To find the proper balance, we rely on certain clues to help us figure out which associations are worth learning and which ones are not. There are three stimulating qualities that are most likely to result in classical conditioning:

- Contrast
- Contingency
- Information

> **Insight**
>
> Some apparently meaningful associations are just the result of an accidental pairing between two stimuli. These accidents can cause superstitious behavior, like the athletes who believe their "lucky" socks will help them win the championship!

Contrast

The smell of your mother's favorite perfume is more likely to stir up fond memories of her if you smell it in the middle of a business meeting than if you get your whiff of it at a perfume counter. You are more likely to notice stimuli that stand out from others around them. At the perfume counter, her perfume may get swamped by competing fragrances and lose its power over your associations.

Contingency

The most powerful associations occur when the conditioned stimulus *reliably* predicts the unconditioned stimuli. If you wear a certain perfume every time you and your boyfriend get together, he will be more likely to associate that fragrance with you.

Information

Conditioned stimuli are most likely to be conditioned if they provide *unique* information about the unconditioned stimulus. Where there's smoke, there isn't always fire, but the smell of something burning generally means there is. That's why you're likely to immediately investigate the smell of something burning; the smell provides important, generally reliable information about danger.

Think of the Consequences

Classical conditioning is a powerful form of learning. From an early age, we learn to associate good feelings with certain things in our environment and bad things with others. These feelings affect what we do. But there's a much more direct way that the environment shapes our behavior, and it's one that parents rely on every day when they interact with their child. It's the fact that every act has consequences, and the method of teaching that uses this principle is called *operant conditioning*.

def•i•ni•tion

Operant conditioning encourages us to behave in ways that exert influence or control over our environment. When a rat learns that pressing a lever gets more food, it has been **operant conditioned** to push the lever. When a child screams and gets her way, she's been conditioned the same way.

Parents know the power of rewarding a child for good behavior and punishing him or her for bad. Children do, too. They quickly learn that, no matter how good it might feel to punch a brother's lights out, the consequences can be pretty painful. They also learn to do things that have negative associations, like homework, if there's a big enough reward at the end.

Kitty in a Box

Psychologist Edward Thorndike was the first to get us thinking along these lines. While Pavlov was preoccupied with drooling dogs, Edward Thorndike was into cats. He spent a lot of time watching them try to escape from puzzle boxes. At first the cats tried a number of things that didn't work. Sooner or later, though, they would accidentally do something that enabled them to escape.

Escape was the reward for their efforts—and when Thorndike put them back in the box, they usually found the escape route a little sooner than the last time. After several trips to the box, the cats would immediately trip the lever or push the button that let them out.

Thorndike coined the term *law of effect* to explain his observation that consistently rewarded responses are strengthened, and those that aren't are gradually weakened, or "stamped out." Just like natural selection favored the evolution of characteristics that enabled the human species to survive, the law of effect says that behavior that gives rise to good consequences will be selected again in the future. From an operant perspective, you might say that learning is your own personal evolution!

Teaching Old Dogs New Tricks

What about behaviors that would never occur if animals were left to their own devices? In Thorndike's box, even the dumbest cat could eventually figure out the right answer. On the other hand, consider assistance animals for people with disabilities. These dogs are trained to act as the arms and the legs for their disabled partners. These dogs are taught to open doors, pull wheelchairs, and dial 911 in case of an emergency. We'd be hard-pressed to find an animal that spontaneously turns the light off and on. Trainers in this situation use a form of learning called *shaping*.

Shaping is a process of reinforcing the small steps that lead in the direction of the desired behavior. Here's how it works: let's say the trainers want Spot to learn to dial 911 in an emergency (and yes, many animals have saved their owners' lives by doing just this!). First, they look for a natural behavior—say, Spot wanders over by the telephone on his own. The trainers then start rewarding Spot with a treat every time he walks a little closer to the phone. Soon, he clues in and starts wandering over there more often.

> **Insight**
>
> Shaping has been successfully used to help mentally impaired adults learn complex behaviors like getting dressed by themselves. Every small step in the right direction, such as pulling a shirt over the top of the person's head, is rewarded by a token that the dog can exchange for food or another treat.

But then the trainers up the stakes. Soon Spot only gets the treat if he actually touches the phone. This progresses with more training until Spot actually learns how and when to pick up the receiver and dial the number. It's a long, difficult process, and not every animal can learn to do it, but it may mean the difference between life and death for Spot's owner.

There's More Than One Way to Skinner a Cat

Thorndike may have gotten the operant conditioning ball rolling, but it was B. F. Skinner who really invented the game. Not only did he invent much of the lingo we use to talk about the process, but his views came to dominate much of psychology for almost 50 years. According to Skinner, understanding another person was simply a matter of understanding the consequences that he or she experienced during a lifetime. To Skinner, operant conditioning and psychology were one and the same.

If you're trying to understand why your boss does the things she does, Skinner would tell you to evaluate the consequences of her actions. For example, what do other employees do when the boss yells at them? Do they snap to attention or get their work done more quickly? And don't forget to take a look at the boss's reinforcement history; maybe that habit of yelling was begun because yelling was the only way your boss could get attention at home. One thing is certain—somewhere along the line, your boss was rewarded for yelling and, as a result, you suffer the consequences.

Calling in Reinforcements

Skinner called this phenomenon *reinforcement*, any consequence that increases a particular behavior over time. A smile, a pat on the back, and a gold star are all examples of positive reinforcers (as we get older, we might prefer a raise or a vacation). Reinforcers can also be negative: if you take out the garbage because you don't want your mom to nag you, then her nagging is a negative reinforcer for your garbage duty. As moms know all too well, if those potential consequences weren't there, kids might be tempted to slack off.

Insight

If you speak softly, you don't have to carry a big stick: soft reprimands spoken only to the misbehaver are more effective than loud scoldings in front of others. And physical punishment must be immediate and consistent to be effective. However, keep in mind that even when physical punishment works, it sends the message that physical aggression is okay if you're big enough to get away with it.

Oddly enough, constantly rewarding someone is less effective rewarding him only occasionally. Say that Tommy, age three, begs for a toy once in a while when you're at the grocery store. You always say no, but once, tired and not in the mood for whining, you get Tommy the toy. Bad idea! Tommy got reinforced for the wrong behavior. Now *every* time you're at the store, he'll whine for a toy—just in case. Chances are, it may take months of "no" before he'll go back to just asking occasionally.

Consequentially

In fact, understanding consequences can be risky business. It's not always easy to tease out all the reinforcers for the things we do, and what is reinforcing to one person can be punishing to another. And negative consequences don't always work. Bad habits, like drinking too much or overeating, have negative consequences, yet we keep doing them!

The Terminators

Reinforcers explain how we learn new behaviors and why we keep doing them. But if you want to unlearn a behavior, you have only two choices: extinguish it or punish it.

"Just ignore it." "Don't pay any attention to him." Children throughout time have been given this advice from parents and teachers alike. Withhold the reinforcers for a certain behavior and, over time, the behavior is likely to stop. If you're a child, though, the time it takes to extinguish your classmate's torture can feel like a lifetime, which is why kids routinely reject this advice.

Nipping Bad Behaviors in the Bud

And kids aren't fools—trying to extinguish behaviors rarely works outside of a laboratory because it's difficult to remove all the reinforcers for a particular behavior. You may give your classmate the silent treatment for a year, but if other classmates are giggling every time your teaser calls you "four-eyes," he or she is still getting *plenty* of reinforcement. In the real world, extinction is much more likely to work if it is paired with *positive* reinforcement of the desired behavior.

"Spare the rod and spoil the child" refers to the other way to correct behavior—by punishing it. Like extinction, punishing a behavior reduces its frequency over time. Spanking, time-outs, grounding, taking away privileges, and yelling are all examples of punishment. The purpose of punishment is to reduce pleasure, either by taking away something the person likes (dessert, attention, TV privileges) or by giving the person something he doesn't like (a swat on the behind, a parking ticket).

Of Carrots and Sticks

But punishment works best in conjunction with positive reinforcement. All companies have disciplinary procedures for unacceptable behavior, but in recent years, one of the most popular recommendations to managers seeking to build employee morale has been for the manager to "catch them doing something *right*." Managers are encouraged to pay attention to examples of effective employee behavior, like getting to work on time, meeting project deadlines, or building teams. When they see it, they are encouraged to call attention to that employee, point out the stellar behavior, and praise, praise, praise.

The theory is this: a manager can move employees in the right direction with praise, while the disciplinary policies are the "big stick" for behavior that gets out of line.

Oh, Those Thumb-Sucking, Nose-Picking Kids!

My name is Joni and I'm a recovering nail biter. From the time I was about four years old, I chewed on my nails in spite of icky potions, stern admonishments, and dire threats. No matter what my parents tried, I gnawed my nails down to the quick for years. Gradually, this habit disappeared, seemingly on its own.

Childhood habits seem to start out as coping strategies. Children may resort to these behaviors when they are stressed, bored, tired, frustrated, unhappy, insecure, or falling asleep. The habit may be calming and soothing to the child. Most of the time, behaviors like thumb sucking, hair twirling, and nail biting are just part of a phase that the child will outgrow, not a serious medical problem.

In general, parents are better off ignoring their child's bad habits. No matter how annoying the behavior, yelling, calling attention to the habit, and punishment do not usually work to stop the behavior (and may even increase it!); but praise, positive rewards, and patience are likely to help. Instead of beating your head against a stubborn wall, try the following strategies:

- First try ignoring the behavior. Giving a lot of attention (even though it's negative) may actually encourage the behavior. Many kids prefer negative attention to no attention at all.

- Praise your child for good behavior. Catch your child being good, and tell her you noticed. For example, tell her you noticed that she wasn't chewing her nails, and mention how nice she looks.

- Be realistic. It is nearly impossible for a parent to stop a child's behavior until the child becomes interested in stopping. For example, a little girl may actually get enough "benefit" out of biting her nails that she will not be willing to stop until she's older and more interested in personal appearance.

- If there are lots of behaviors you want to change, then start by focusing on one or two of the most bothersome or dangerous ones. Don't try to make too many changes all at once.

- Try to figure out what may be making your child stressed. Give your child chances to talk to you about things that might be worrying him—and make eye contact and listen.

- Let your child make decisions by giving him acceptable choices. For example, "Would you rather have toast or cereal for breakfast?" This will help your child feel in control of some aspects of his life, and reduce stress and frustration.

- Redirect your child and help her find a better place, or a better way, to do what she is trying to do. For example, if her nose is irritated, have her clean it with a tissue, apply petroleum jelly, and then wash her hands. If she simply must go "digging," have her do it in the bathroom, not in public, and wash her hands afterward.

- Use natural and logical consequences for problem behavior. The purpose here is to get kids to make the right decision, not to bend them to your will. Be patient—it may take time for you to see results.

- Be firm and kind. Follow through every time on the natural and logical consequences.

- Have a few positively stated rules, and explain the reasons behind them.

- Make sure your child understands the results of breaking the rule.

- Here is the golden rule on this one: both parents need to agree to the same rules and enforce them. If Mom says "No" but Dad says "Who cares?" it's a losing battle.

The Behavior Police

It's easy to confuse negative reinforcement with punishment because they both involve negative or unpleasant experiences. However, they have opposite effects on our behavior; punishment always decreases behavior while reinforcers increase it.

If you treat your significant other well to avoid getting jilted, the possibility of getting dumped is a negative reinforcer. However, if, in spite of your good behavior, your significant other is dumb enough to dump you, you might feel punished for all of your good deeds. And, as you know if you've been the rebound in a rebound relationship, you might not be so inclined to make such an effort in the next one!

Terminators and Reinforcers

Kind of Stimulus That Follows Response	Do More of the Same (Reinforcer)	Cease and Desist (Punisher)
Positive	Reward, food, prize, praise, thanks	Criticism, disapproval, pain
Negative	Easing pain or discomfort	Privileges, ignoring, grounding

---

Psychobabble

Recent research indicates that thoughts and feelings don't influence only human behavior. Chimps can also be motivated by their feelings. In one dispute among chimpanzees, one chimp backed up another, which then failed to return the favor. In response, she chased and hit him. Apparently, even in the animal kingdom one good turn deserves another, and a bad turn can lead to revenge.

Learning on the Liberal Side

Some of Skinner's followers thought that his strict emphasis on behavior was too conservative. They took a second look at all that mental stuff Skinner had discarded and concluded that the thoughts and feelings we have about the consequences of our behavior play a key role in the way we learn. They realized, for example, that we don't all feel the same way about what happens to us—a reward for one person might feel like punishment to another.

This is the view held by cognitive psychologists, who say that the way you interpret the world has a big impact on how you feel and what you do. In other words, the meaning you give to the things that happen to you might be more important than the actual events themselves.

Attitudes and Expectations

Cognitive psychologists believe that classical conditioning occurs because the conditioned stimulus creates an expectation that the unconditioned stimulus is about to appear. When your cat hears the clanging of his food dish, he has come to expect that it's dinnertime, and he'll run to his dining spot.

Cognitive psychologists also think operant conditioning is much more complicated than the simple history of our rewards and punishments. The cognitivists believe that learning involves understanding the means to the end in addition to any thoughts and feelings we have about those means and ends. Whether you eat depends much more on how hungry you are than it does on your knowledge that opening the refrigerator will give you access to food. That knowledge gives you options; it doesn't force you to use them.

Experience and Interpretation

It doesn't take a rocket scientist to know that your interpretation of things has a lot of influence over what you do. One factor that influences your present "take" on things is your past experience—you're likely to compare current consequences with past ones and be either happy or sad about the results.

My mom's savvy dating advice clearly took this into account: "Don't ever start out doing things for a man that you don't plan on continuing." Mom was warning me of the *negative contrast effect*, the well-documented tendency for people to compare rewards and to be highly dissatisfied with any drop in reinforcement. We're much better off capitalizing on the *positive contrast effect* in our love lives, starting out slowly and then being kinder and more generous as time goes by. Sometimes, Mom really does know best!

The same thing happens at the office. As a list of office "rules" on a coffee cup says, "Do a job three times and it's yours." When a manager asks for a volunteer note taker at your next meeting, think carefully before you raise your hand. Raise it a couple of times and, before you know it, taking notes will become part of your job, whether you wanted it or not.

> **Brain Buster**
>
> A side effect of television violence is *psychic numbing*, a reduction in emotional arousal while witnessing violence. In situations where people are getting hurt, reducing the emotional distress of witnesses is a risky social outcome.

Attention, Please!

We also learn by what we choose to pay attention to and people seem to pay attention to more emotionally charged events. For instance, you may spend weeks trying to teach baby to say "ball," only to have her ignore you. But then, when she's in the car and someone cuts you off in traffic, she may happily parrot you yelling "*&@*#!!" in a heartbeat! On the positive side, we can use our emotions to motivate us, such as when we put the swimsuit picture on the refrigerator to help us stick to a diet or when we list all the payoffs for getting out of debt.

Studies are now showing what many good teachers have known for years: a good dose of humor can help you pay attention to information that might otherwise be too boring to bother with. It's not that humor itself causes us to learn more; it's that humor makes us more interested in learning. Of course, given the crucial role motivation plays in learning, we might argue that *wanting* to learn more is, well, more than half the battle.

Modeling Behavior

Thank goodness you don't always have to learn from your own mistakes. You learn a lot about getting along in the world by observing those around you. You can climb the corporate ladder by imitating your boss, you can learn from your parents' mistakes, and you can set a good example for your children. All of these are examples of *observational learning*.

The positive version of this is known as *modeling*. Children really do model what their parents do much more than what their parents say. Not only do they imitate their parents' behavior, but they also learn general rules about what is acceptable and what is not by watching others. Grownups also use modeling—if you're going to a party and aren't sure of the protocol, you may spend a few minutes watching the people around you to get the lay of the land.

Unfortunately, modeling doesn't always influence us in a positive direction. Albert Bandura found that children who first watched adults beat up a large inflated Bobo doll were much more aggressive in their play with the doll than children who had watched a gentle adult or no adult at all. Not only did the children imitate the adults' behaviors, but they were also amazingly creative at devising torture strategies of their own. Obviously, they were learning more than certain punches and kicks: they were getting the message that aggressive behavior in general is okay.

Insight

More attention is being paid to social aggression, the hurtful but more subtle ways that bullying girls wield power over their peers—through ostracism, public humiliation, criticism, and so on. New research suggests that social aggression (unlike physical aggression) is more a reflection of parental influence and peer environment than genetic makeup, and may be more easily channeled into positive behavior.

Don't Be So Scared

Fear is easy to learn and hard to unlearn. Classical conditioning helps us understand irrational fears as links between our emotions and certain stimuli in the environment. You might fear heights, for example, because you have associated them with falling, or you might fear public speaking because you associate all that attention with rejection or humiliation.

One powerful way of unlearning fear is called *systematic desensitization*.

Systematic desensitization is a therapeutic process that involves three steps:

◆ Listing the stressful situation in order of scariness

◆ Developing an emotion that is incompatible with fear

◆ Gradually confronting the situation, starting with a very mildly stressful one

You don't have to have a full-blown phobia to benefit from systematic desensitization. Learning the three steps will help in any situation, like asking someone on a date. Let's say you've been wanting to ask your next-door neighbor out for a date but just haven't got up the nerve to do it. Take the following steps:

1. **Write down several situations related to your fear, ranging from least scary to most scary.** Before you declare your undying love to your neighbor, or die from the fear that the thought of this evokes, think of several baby steps that would get you where you want to go—on a date. You might ask a friend's advice about approaching this person, ask a friend to role-play your date request, and then start making small talk with your neighbor. The key is to break down your fear into 10 to 15 small, progressive steps. No matter what your fear is, or how strong it is, there is always a first step that is acceptable to you.

2. **Relax.** There are numerous relaxation resources that will teach you the relaxation response (check Appendix B for a few). Relaxation is a powerful weapon against fear, and there are others. Assertiveness can also help. As a last resort, you might try running a couple of miles before you knock on your neighbor's door: it's hard to get all worked up about anything when you're tired!

3. **Just do it—gradually.** Sooner or later, you've got to enter the lion's den. Here's where systematic desensitization really earns brownie points. If you've listed your 15 scenarios, and role-played with your friend through the first 14, the toughest one isn't going to be all that tough.

Insight

Children with obsessive compulsive disorder develop irrational fears (fear of germs or dirt, getting sick, and so on) and develop obsessive behaviors (repetitive handwashing, avoiding doorknobs, etc.) to cope with those fears. New research shows that cognitive behavior therapy that helps these children practice gradually confronting those fears (for example, practicing touching a doorknob) is twice as effective as medication.

Getting Rid of Bad Habits

Bad habits are often a combination of classical and operant conditioning. Take smoking, for example. There's the classical conditioning component—over time, you associate smoking with a lot of other things you do. You reach for a cigarette after a good meal, you smoke in the morning when you're drinking coffee, and you light up when you're angry or stressed. These activities and conditions become deeply ingrained triggers for smoking.

Then there are the reinforcements. Inhaling smoke causes a temporary relaxation response, so smoking "feels good." If you're physically addicted, your body is rewarded by the nicotine entering your bloodstream. If you use smoking to handle strong feelings or stress, smoking gives you a "time-out" to regroup and think through the situation. You're caught in a conundrum—you have all these cues and triggers that remind you to smoke, and the reinforcements that encourage you to keep smoking.

That's why bad habits can be so persistent—in the short term, they're so gratifying. I might know that eating a chocolate cake will probably add a few pounds, but man, does that chocolate taste good!

Getting rid of bad habits is more than a matter of willpower; you must systematically disarm your triggers, get rid of your reinforcers, and gradually replace your behavior with healthier alternatives. Here are a few tips for starters:

- **Avoid the triggering situation.** If you smoke with your coffee, then switch to tea. If you can't go to the mall without buying a new outfit, don't go window shopping. If you scarf down potato chips whenever they're around, don't keep them in the house.

- **Change the situation.** Sit in the nonsmoking section of the restaurant. Put your clothes purchases on hold for a few hours, and then decide whether you will go back and buy them. Don't eat with the television on or standing at the kitchen counter.

♦ **Substitute.** Keep a journal of your thoughts and feelings that lead up to your habit and find other ways to fill these needs. If you shop in response to stress, take a bubble bath instead. If you eat when you're emotionally hungry, get a massage or talk on the phone to a friend. The next time you get angry and feel the urge to light up, try a short power walk first.

Chances are, you came into this chapter with some bad habits; whether it's overeating, smoking, or overspending, most of us have at least a few. And in spite of the negative consequences, we keep doing them over and over. I hope, however, this chapter has given you some insight into breaking them; if you've decided to move from insight to action, be patient with yourself, expect some slip-ups, and remind yourself it takes time. In the next chapter, we'll shed some more light on why we keep doing things that aren't in our best interest.

The Least You Need to Know

♦ Learning is the ability to profit from experience.

♦ Much of what we learn is the result of either classical or operant conditioning.

♦ Classical conditioning occurs when we realize that a previously neutral stimulus predicts an unconditioned stimulus. If this happens often enough, we start responding to the neutral stimulus alone.

♦ If you're rewarded for a temper tantrum, chances are you'll do it again; if you don't get what you want, you'll eventually stop—this is called operant conditioning.

♦ It's not just the consequences that influence your behavior, it's also how you interpret the consequences—a reward for one person can be perceived as a punishment for another.

♦ Understanding how you learn can help you to unlearn fear or get rid of bad habits.

Chapter 8

Coming to Terms with Your Memory

In This Chapter

- The court jester of the brain

- Understanding how your memories are made

- How to remember what you learn about memory

- The truth about false memories

- Exploring the mystery of repressed memory

For a while it seemed as if stories about recovering repressed memories were all over the news. Then there were all those stories about how those recovered memories were false. How is it possible to remember something that never happened? And how does a repressed memory happen, anyway? Memory distortion research has clearly shown that information that happens after the event, such as stories other people tell us about what happened, can actually be incorporated into our memory. And studies have given us lots of insights into the process by which the mind buries memories we find difficult or painful.

In this chapter, we'll take a look at the myths and realities of memory, how memory normally works, and when and why it doesn't. We'll look at some ways to improve memory, and how research into false memory and repressed memory has improved our understanding of both of these phenomena. As you read through this chapter, keep in mind one thing about memory: it's a lot trickier than you might think!

Kidnapped!

Until he was 15, child psychologist Jean Piaget believed that his earliest memory was of nearly being kidnapped at the age of two. He remembered vivid details of the event, such as sitting in his baby carriage and watching his nurse defend herself against the kidnapper. He remembered the scratches on his nurse's face, and the short cloak and white baton the police officer was wearing as he chased the kidnapper away.

However, the kidnapping never happened. When Piaget was in his midteens, his parents received a remorseful letter from his former nurse, confessing that she had made the whole story up and returning the watch she had been given as a reward. Piaget's memories were false.

But the nurse's confession raised a whole new mystery: how did Piaget remember something that never happened? Obviously, Piaget heard many accounts of this story as a child, imagined what he thought had actually happened, and projected this information into the past in the form of a visual memory.

The Court Jester

Your brain can store 100 trillion bits of information, so why can't you remember the name of the person you sat next to in homeroom during high school? If your brain is a kingdom, surely your memory is the court jester. It's always playing tricks. You can, for example, instantly recall things you never tried to learn (like popular song lyrics), and you can easily forget things you spent hours memorizing (like material you've studied for an exam).

And has anyone ever told you to "just forget" something that happened? Tell *him* to forget it; your memory doesn't work on command.

Whether you want it to or not, your brain stores all kinds of information. *Implicit memory* holds all those trivial facts, song lyrics, and general nonsense that

def•i•ni•tion

Implicit memory is your ability to remember information that you haven't deliberately tried to learn. **Explicit memory** is your ability to retain information that you've put real effort into learning.

your brain files away while you're concentrating on something else. Most of the time, however, researchers are more interested in studying *explicit memory*, which contains the information that people consciously spend energy processing.

Learning About Remembering from Forgetting

When it comes to memory, the proverbial elephant is way ahead of human beings—members of our species constantly forget, misremember, and make mistakes. These mistakes offer valuable clues about how memory normally works. For example, researchers have found that people forget for one of three reasons:

1. They don't get it to begin with.

2. They had it but they lost it.

3. They have it but they can't find it.

These mistakes reflect a failure in one of the three mental operations necessary for memory: encoding, storage, and retrieval.

For instance, I simply can't seem to remember my high school classmate's name, even though I sat next to her for years. Chances are, my memory failure is due to a retrieval problem—I have her name filed someplace but can't seem to open the right filing cabinet. If someone gave me a hint, I could probably come up with it. This "hint" would be a retrieval cue—information that will help me find and open the right cabinet.

On the other hand, if I was so self-absorbed in high school that I never learned my classmate's name in the first place, my inability to come up with it now would be an encoding problem. One clue that a memory failure is due to encoding is the ineffectiveness of hints or clues to prompt memory. If I never knew that my classmate's name was Denise Johnson, she could tell me her nickname, her initials, and her astrological sign—and I still wouldn't have a clue.

Alternatively, maybe during my high school years I was a conniving social climber and Denise didn't fit my idea of the popular crowd.

def•i•ni•tion

Amnesia is the partial or complete loss of memory, and can be caused by physical or psychological factors. Psychologically based amnesia can be triggered by a traumatic event; memory almost always returns after a few days. Soap operas aside, very rarely does a person lose her memory for large portions of her life.

Maybe I learned Denise's name long enough to ask her for a favor a few times, but then didn't think it was important to remember on a regular basis. In this case, my failure to remember her name today would be due to a *storage* problem.

Memory Tests

When teachers give us tests, they aren't just measuring our capacity for learning. They're also measuring our ability to remember what we've learned. Common sense might tell us that we either know something or we don't, so that any method of testing will give us the same results. Not so. The way we're tested can have a lot of influence over the results, because different types of tests engage our retrieval system differently.

For instance, keeping your eyes on this line, tell me the three mental operations that are required for memory. No peeking! Did you remember them? If not, see if you can recognize them from this multiple choice:

retrieval

categorization

storage

encoding

filing

Encoding, storage, and retrieval are the three mental operations required for memory. If you couldn't recall all three, but you recognized them in the multiple-choice question, your recognition is better than your recall. Recall questions give fewer cues than recognition questions and thus seem "harder" to those taking the test. It is possible to learn information but to have trouble retrieving it without those cues, although try telling that to your teacher after you've bombed an essay test!

The Long and Short of It

Think of memory in terms of threes. We've already gone over the three mental processes necessary for memory—encoding, storage, and retrieval. Each of these mental processes happens at least three times as the information makes its way through the three memory systems: sensory memory, working memory, and long-term memory.

Photographer at Work

Ever notice how you can still hear the sound of the television right after you turn it off? That's your sensory memory. Sensory memory holds an impression a split second longer than it's actually present, to make sure that you have time to register it. Its goal is to hold information long enough to give you a sense of continuity but short enough that it doesn't interfere with new information coming in.

Sensory memories capture impressions from all our senses. If the impression is a sound, the memory is called an *echo*, while a visual sensory memory is called an *icon*. At the most, your sensory memory works for only a second or two, but what it lacks in stamina, it makes up for in volume. For example, if I showed you a picture with a bunch of words on it for only a fraction of a second, you could only say about four of the words before you started forgetting the rest. However, you'd be able to pick out as many as nine. It seems we can remember words faster than we can say them!

> **Insight**
>
> Only about 5 percent of people truly have photographic memories, known technically as *eidetic imagery*. Such individuals can envision a previously viewed scene in their minds, as if they were experiencing the scene directly rather than scanning memory for traces or details. Apparently, such people are able to directly transfer their sensory impressions into long-term memory.

The Organic Data Processor

Working memory has more stamina than sensory memory, but it's no marathon runner; it only lasts for about 20 seconds. It works pretty hard for those 20 seconds, working through and sorting out information that has been transferred from either long-term or sensory memory. When information enters your working memory, it has already been reorganized into meaningful and familiar patterns. For example, when subjects are asked to recall lists of letters they have just seen, they are much more likely to confuse letters that sound similar—like B and T—than letters that look familiar. Yet another example of how misremembering teaches us about remembering!

Working memory deals exclusively with the here and now, preserving recent experiences or events. Because it is short term, its capacity is limited. When the items are unrelated, like the digits of a telephone number, you can hold between five and nine bits of information in your working memory. There are, however, strategies that expand your working memory and you use at least one of them all the time. When you look up a phone number and repeat it before you dial, you're using a rehearsal strategy to enhance your working memory.

The Curious Curator

Ever see the movie *Dreamcatcher?* There are many scenes showing one man's memory as a museum, with him searching through files and choosing to burn some "boxes" of information to make room for new information. And those images may not be too far from reality.

Just as a museum curator takes care of historical artifacts, your long-term memory collects and stores all the experiences, events, facts, emotions, skills, and so forth that have been transferred from your sensory and short-term memory. The information ranges from your mom's birthday to calculus equations. Essentially, the information in long-term memory is your library of knowledge of the world; without it, you'd be lost.

Long-term memory stores words and concepts according to their meaning, and files them next to similar words and concepts already in your memory.

Brain Buster

Use it or lose it? New research suggests that five minutes of math a day can help ward off the negative mental effects of aging. Don't like math? Okay, try some crossword puzzles or read a few pages out loud.

The smallest unit of meaning that you can store is a *proposition:* an idea that expresses the relationship between ideas, objects, or events. "Men are from Mars, women are from Venus" is a proposition about men and women. "Trees have green leaves" is another proposition. Some psychologists believe that these propositions are the building blocks of long-term memory, while others believe that we store verbal information in propositions and visual information in images.

Visiting the Museum

We all have different "artifacts" in our mental museum, but the structure of the "building" looks remarkably similar for each of us. It can be helpful to think of your memory museum as having two wings, with each holding different kinds of information. These wings are actually two types of long-term memory—*procedural* and *declarative*.

I Was Only Following Procedure

The procedural "wing" of your memory museum stores information about how things are done. Remembering how to ride a bicycle, tie your shoelaces, and put on your makeup are all stored in your procedural memory. All of the skills you learn consist of small action sequences, and it is these skill memories that get implanted in your long-term memory.

Skill memories are amazingly hardy. Even if you haven't ridden a bike in 30 years, the memory comes back amazingly fast once you have your behind on the seat and your feet on the pedals. The frustrating thing about skill memories, though, is that they are difficult to communicate to others. Ask a gold-medal gymnast to tell you exactly how she does her stuff on the balance beam, and she can't. And if she tries to consciously think it through while she's doing it, chances are her performance won't be as good.

Well, I Declare!

Declarative memory, on the other hand, deals with the facts. It is the part of our memory that enables us to survive school, win at Trivial Pursuit, and win friends and influence people. Unlike procedural memory, declarative memory requires conscious effort, as evidenced by all the eye rolling and facial grimaces that you see on the faces of people taking their SATs. Remembering the directions to the dance studio is an example of declarative memory; remembering how to dance is procedural.

The declarative wing of your memory museum has two rooms, one for *episodic memory*, the other for *semantic memory*. Episodic memory stores autobiographical information, such as thoughts, feelings, and things that happen to us. Semantic memory is more like an encyclopedia; it stores the basic meaning of words and concepts.

One way we know that episodic memory is different from procedural memory is the way it is organized. For example, when autobiographical information enters long-term memory, it is tagged with the time it happened and the

> **Insight**
>
> Research indicates that all of us have some degree of amnesia. Most of us can accurately recall what has happened in the last half of our lives. If you're 20 years old, you can remember the past 10 years. If you're 60, your memory's good for the last 30. Your 10-year-old child can recall the last 5. For most of us, the rest is a blur.

context in which it took place—a kind of marking that doesn't appear to happen with information stored in procedural memory.

On the other hand, you probably can't remember exactly when or where you learned your multiplication tables. When you do remember when or where you learned factual information, it is often because an emotional experience was attached to it. My brother remembers when and where he learned his multiplication tables because he was rapped on the knuckles several times for not practicing them as part of his third-grade homework. As in my brother's case, sometimes episodic memory can greatly assist semantic recall!

def•i•ni•tion

Retrieval cues are mental or environmental aids that help us retrieve information from long-term memory.

You've Got Rhythm

Some researchers have suggested that memories occur when different regions of the brain unite. For example, the memory of a dog might unite smell, sound, appearance, and name.

By measuring the electrical rhythms that parts of the brain use to communicate with each other, a team of researchers at the University of Arkansas for Medical Sciences and Johns Hopkins University showed that when someone has a memory of a dog, the thalamus, an important region of the brain that connects areas together, actually regulates the rhythms that connect brain regions. Now that's a pretty sweet move!

Now, *Where* Did I Put That Thought?

It happens to most of us about once a week. You see someone you've known for years, yet his name suddenly eludes you. You remember other things about this person, like where you met or past conversations you've had. But, temporarily, his name escapes you. Frustrated, you exclaim, "But it's right on the tip of my tongue!"

The tip-of-the-tongue experience has intrigued psychologists since the 1800s. Long-term memory preserves information for retrieval at any later time; a tip-of-the-tongue experience appears to be a breakdown in this retrieval process. Putting information into memory is half the battle, but you still have to find it when you need it.

Retrieval failure demonstrates an important concept in long-term memory—the difference between accessibility and availability. Your relationship with long-term memory is kind of like a crush; just because the object of your affection is single (available) doesn't mean she is interested in you (accessible). Sometimes, long-term memories are available somewhere in your mental filing cabinet, but you can't access them.

Generally, when you're trying to retrieve a memory, you'll simply use *retrieval cues*. These are prompts to help you recover information from memory. An example of such prompts would be the options presented on a multiple-choice test—they help you recognize the material you learned the night before.

Another retrieval aid is something most of us do frequently: when you're trying to remember where you put your car keys, you'll probably try to retrace your steps from the time you last saw them. Or you might think about where you've found those darned keys all the other times you've misplaced them. In either case, your internal retrieval cues help you remember.

Retrieval cues are helpful because they capitalize on your memory's natural tendency to organize and store related concepts and experiences together. Of course, if you'd just put the keys in the same place every time, you wouldn't be having this trouble to begin with! And, as you're about to see, you wouldn't have so many retrieval failures if you encoded it right in the first place.

Will You Gain Wisdom or Grow Senile?

If I had a dime for every joke I've heard about "old" people and memory problems, I'd be sipping piña coladas in Tahiti right now! For years, physicians believed that forgetfulness was an inevitable part of growing old. Many elderly people still do; they consistently list memory problems among the most critical ones they face. But are these beliefs accurate?

It depends on what kind of memory you're talking about. For example, aging has relatively little effect on short-term memory. Young adults and seniors differ, on the average, by less than one digit in the number of numbers they can hold in short-term memory.

Coming to (Memory) Terms

Some information in short-term memory is transferred and stored in long-term memory. It is this kind of memory that elderly adults have in mind when they complain about forgetfulness. Their most prominent complaint is remembering the names of people they met recently. Laboratory tests (using lists of words to be remembered)

Insight

Alzheimer's disease causes brain deterioration in middle or later life, usually after age 65. Family history plays a role in about 40 percent of people with early-onset Alzheimer's. While we still haven't solved the mystery of Alzheimer's, new studies suggest that quinolinic acid, a neurotoxin, may play a key role in speeding the onset and progression of the disease.

Brain Buster

Bad at names? Use the person's name out loud three times in the first few minutes after meeting, and you are much more likely to remember it later.

reveal that a moderate decline in memory for recent events accompanies normal aging. Some elderly adults remember as well as many young adults, indicating that this decline is a general pattern and not the inevitable fate for every person over 60.

Long-term memory for remote events (things that happened years ago) is pretty consistent over time. All of us forget personal information at some point during the first five to six years after it's been acquired. What's left after that usually sticks around. In general, elderly adults do have more trouble remembering some things—like when pain medication was last taken (temporal memory) and where they left their umbrella (spatial memory)—but if they use cues as reminders of things that need to be done, they are no more absent-minded than the rest of us. However, if an elderly person seems to show true memory problems, it is important to get an evaluation by a physician. Many medical conditions can mimic Alzheimer's: vitamin deficiency, small strokes, even depression. And many of these conditions are treatable.

You Can Always Make a List

What does all this mean? While I can't promise you that you'll gain wisdom in your golden years, you can rest assured that your memory doesn't have to trip you up as you age. When memory problems do exist, the use of written reminders and visual cues is highly effective at minimizing their impact. So quit worrying about losing your marbles and concentrate on putting more marbles in there!

Get It Right in the First Place

The way we put information in has a lot to do with how easily we can get it out. Have you ever studied for a multiple-choice test and then been ambushed by an essay exam? It's not a good feeling. No matter how prepared you were for multiple choice, chances are you didn't do so well with the essays. If you're smart, the way you prepare for an essay test is by memorizing the "big picture"—general information about the topic, broad concepts, and an overall analysis of the material. On the other hand, concrete facts and specific distinctions are most easily translated into multiple-choice tests.

Since long-term memory stores information logically and meaningfully, it makes sense to organize information when you first encode it in memory. Let's say you're really interested in the psychology of memory and want to maximize the chances that you'll remember the information in this chapter. One of the best encoding strategies was developed by Francis Robinson in 1970. It's the SQ3R method: Survey, Question, and Read, Recite, and Review.

How does it work? Let's use this book chapter as an example. First, *survey* the chapter—take a quick look and get an idea how it is organized. Second, develop some *questions* about each subheading.

Then *read* the chapter, and write down the answers to the questions you had. After that, without looking, *recite* out loud those answers you wrote down. Now, *review* all the material again, and keep *reciting* information aloud.

The SQ3R method makes the most of your long-term memory's natural organizer. *Surveying* helps your brain get organized. *Questioning* assists in breaking the information down into manageable chunks, and also makes

> **Insight**
>
> Think getting older is a bummer? Nip that attitude in the bud. According to a study by a Miami University researcher, keeping a positive attitude about aging can extend a person's life by seven and a half years, which is longer than gains made by not smoking and exercising regularly.

it more meaningful to you. *Reading, reciting, and rehearsing* all work to store the information. And, of course, taking the time to use these encoding strategies helps you overcome one of the biggest personality traits that leads to forgetfulness—plain, old-fashioned laziness!

Hooked on Mnemonics

"Use *i* before *e* except after *c*." "Thirty days hath September, April, June, and November." "In 1492, Columbus sailed the ocean blue." No, I haven't regressed to the third grade. I'm giving you examples of *mnemonics:* short, verbal devices that encode a long series of facts by associating them with familiar and previously encoded information.

In the world of grownups, acronyms and jingles are commonly used mnemonics. AT&T is a lot easier to remember than American Telephone and Telegraph.

Marketers weren't born yesterday; they regularly use jingles and rhymes to build product recognition and keep that annoying commercial playing in your head long after you've changed the channel.

Mnemonics are very effective memory aids. They not only help us encode the information in a creative and distinctive way, but they also make it much easier for us to recall it when we need it. Psychological research has studied three types of mnemonic strategies:

1. Natural language mediators

2. The method of loci

3. Visual imagery

Using *natural language mediators* involves associating new information with already stored meanings or spellings of words. Creating a story to link items together is an example of using natural language mediators. For instance, to remember the three stages of memory, you might say to yourself, "It doesn't make sense (sensory memory) that she's working (working memory) so long (long-term memory)."

Insight

Getting ready for a high-school reunion? Get out that yearbook and you're sure to be "Most Popular." Forty-eight years after graduation, students were only able to recall 20 percent of their schoolmates' names. After looking at old photos, though, they could name them 90 percent of the time.

The *method of loci* could help you remember a grocery list. Imagine a familiar place, like your office or bedroom, and mentally place the items on various objects around the room. When you need to recall them, you take a trip around the room and retrieve them.

Visual imagery is a third mnemonic device. In this method, you just create vivid mental pictures of your grocery items. Mentally picturing a cat mixing *shampoo* and *eggs* to make *cat food* would certainly create a lasting impression on your memory.

Mnemonics Boosters

When it comes to mnemonics, all images are not created equal. Here are five tips for boosting the power of your mnemonics:

1. Use positive, pleasant images. The brain often blocks out unpleasant ones.

2. Use humor. Funny or peculiar things are easier to remember than normal ones. (Yes, rude or sexual rhymes or images work, too.)

3. Vivid, colorful images are easier to remember than dull ones.

4. Use all the senses. Give your visual images voices, smells, touch, taste, and feelings.

5. Give your images movement.

And while it may not be a mnemonic, take a tip from Chapter 6 and get enough sleep. Sleep appears to play an extremely important role in the memory process.

Brain Buster

Having trouble remembering difficult information? Don't say it, sing it! Many medical schools teach their students songs with familiar tunes but new words to help them memorize anatomy, diseases, and so on. Don't believe me? Ask your doctor to sing the "Supercallifragalistic" song—it probably won't be the words you learned!

Warning: Under Construction

Your memories are often under construction. They can change with time and are influenced by your past history, current values, and future expectations. In addition, they can be strengthened, or even built, by social influence.

Were you watching television the morning of September 11, 2001? If so, do you remember seeing images of the first plane, and then the second plane, hitting the towers? If you do, you are one of the majority of Americans who has a false memory about this! Only the video of the *second* plane hitting a tower was shown on that day. The video of the *first* plane striking the other tower was not shown until the following day—September 12. But almost three out of four of us remember it incorrectly.

How accurate and reliable is memory? It's a hard worker, but it gets easily confused. Memory studies show that we often construct our memories after the fact, and that we are susceptible to suggestions from others that help us fill in any gaps. One way a police officer can screw up a victim's identification of an assailant is by showing a photograph of the suspect in advance of the lineup. When this happens, the lineup is contaminated by the photograph—it is impossible to know whether the victim recognizes the suspect from the crime scene or the photograph.

And don't rely on your gut instincts to improve your memory. Studies have clearly shown that a feeling of certainty about a memory means nothing about whether your memory is accurate. If you really want to be sure your memory is accurate, your best bet is to do some detective work and look for corroborating evidence!

The Truth About False Memories

In 1990, teenager Donna Smith began therapy with Cathy M., a private social worker who specialized in child abuse. Although Donna had entered treatment reporting that she had been sexually abused by a neighbor at age three, Cathy M. repeatedly interrogated Donna about her father. After several months of pressured questioning by her therapist, Donna lied and said her father had "touched" her. When her therapist reported her father to the authorities, Donna tried to set the record straight, only to be told by her therapist that all abuse victims tried to recant their stories.

def•i•ni•tion

The **false memory syndrome** is a pattern of thoughts, feelings, and actions based on a mistaken or inaccurate memory of traumatic experiences that the person claims to have previously repressed.

Donna was confused but continued to work with Cathy M., who continued to make suggestions and reinforce any suggestion of incest. Over the course of several months, Donna came to believe that her father had been a chronic sexual abuser. She began "remembering" him practicing ritual satanic abuse on her younger brothers. Only after she was placed in foster care away from her therapist did Donna regain her perspective and the courage to tell the truth. By this time, her family was emotionally and financially devastated.

Insight

When three- and four-year-old children are questioned about an event by a neutral person, they recall with 90 percent accuracy. However, when children are repeatedly interviewed with misleading suggestions, they may come to believe that the suggested events happened and persist in their belief even when told otherwise. And research suggests that even professionals can't tell the difference between what really happened and what the child believes.

Sorting the True from the False

Unfortunately, Donna's experience is not an isolated incident. There are similar stories of adults who enter therapy to resolve some conflict or gain happiness and, with the therapist's "support," suddenly start remembering traumatic abuse or incest. As these "repressed" memories are unleashed, the person may take long-delayed action such as criminal prosecution or public denouncement.

But while false memories do occur, by no means are most memories of child sexual abuse false. Given that studies estimate that one out of every four girls will be sexually exploited before the age of 18, odds are that anyone who remembers child sexual abuse is telling the truth. The rare occurrence of false memory is likely to happen when a vulnerable person hooks up with a therapist who, intentionally or not, implants false memories through hypnotic suggestion, by asking leading questions, or by defining "abuse" and "incest" so broadly that, in retrospect, innocent actions suddenly take on menacing meaning.

The Political Problems

As you might imagine, the false memory syndrome is a political hot potato. On the one hand, survivors of sexual abuse have fought a long and hard battle to gain credibility, protection, and help. On the other hand, the concern remains that there is no scientific evidence for repression of multiple traumatic events that happen over an extended period of time. Still, there is the very real fear that a few misguided therapists and their clients could undermine the true stories of thousands of others. Whatever is the outcome of this heated controversy, we can all agree that our society will not benefit from having more victims—neither victims of sexual abuse nor victims of false memory.

Exploring Repressed Memories

I vividly remember the exact moment the Columbia space shuttle exploded on February 1, 2003. I had just pulled in to the Party Store to shop for my kids' Valentine's cards when I heard a news bulletin on the radio. My mom could vividly remember where she was and what she was doing when she heard that John F. Kennedy had been assassinated. Nineteenth-century researchers discovered the same phenomenon when they asked people what they were doing when they heard that Abraham Lincoln had been shot.

These memories are called *flashbulb memories*, long-lasting and deep memories that occur in response to traumatic events. Not everyone has flashbulb memories and not every tragic situation causes them. Recent research, in fact, has questioned the validity of the flashbulb effect, but what it does support is our tendency to remember upsetting or traumatic events.

However, what may be most remembered during times of extreme stress or trauma is the emotional distress. Memory research shows that, during times of extreme stress or trauma, we can store the emotional experience separately from the personal facts of what actually happened. Studies show that under conditions of extreme stress, the hippocampus (the part of our brain that records personal facts) may dysfunction, causing the details of the traumatic event to be poorly stored. On the other hand, the amygdala, that part of our cortex that stores emotional memories, often becomes overactive when under stress, enhancing the emotional memory of a trauma. As a result, a 25-year-old might be terrified of flying because of a traumatic plane ride as a child and yet not remember the childhood experience that triggered the fear.

Real-life traumas in children and adults—such as school ground shootings or natural disasters—are generally well remembered. Complete amnesia for these terrifying episodes is virtually nonexistent. People who have repeated war traumas, and even children, generally remember their experiences. In fact, many of them report having great difficulty getting the events out of their dreams or minds; they can't repress them even though they want to.

def•i•ni•tion

A **repressed memory** is the memory of a traumatic event retained in the unconscious mind, where it is said to affect conscious thoughts, feelings, and behaviors even though there is no conscious memory of the alleged trauma.

We know that people forget things. We know that people later remember things that they had forgotten earlier. And psychologists generally agree that it is quite common to consciously repress unpleasant experiences, even sexual abuse, and to spontaneously remember such events long afterward.

Intuitively, the ability to block out repeated childhood trauma seems like a pretty good survival strategy; if you can't get away from it physically, at least you can in your mind. However, until we have more evidence, Sigmund Freud's idea that we might store the memory of traumatic events in a place outside of our unconscious will stay up in the air.

I can tell you that I've had therapy clients who were victims of documented incest (the perpetrator had confessed and been sent to prison), and yet siblings who were also victims claimed to have no memory at all that abuse had occurred.

The Least You Need to Know

◆ Your memory doesn't mind very well—it often misremembers, forgets, and makes mistakes.

◆ The three mental operations required for memory are encoding (putting information in), storage (filing it away), and retrieval (finding it). Forgetting is a failure in one of these areas.

◆ While elderly adults seem to have more problems remembering recent events, using written reminders and other memory strategies can minimize their impact.

◆ Mnemonics are very effective memory aids that help us store information in a way that we can easily recall it later on.

◆ False memories can fool us and they can fool professionals. Although not likely, it is possible to remember serious childhood trauma that never happened. It is also possible to forget details of a traumatic event but have strong emotions associated with things that remind us of it.

◆ The truth about repression is still up in the air. Most people remember ongoing traumatic events.

Part 3

The Forces Are with You

What's the most important thing that a detective looks for when solving a crime? Elementary, my dear Watson: it's motivation. Almost all of human behavior is driven by motives, whether or not we're conscious of them at the time. Here's where you'll get the scoop on the major motives that drive us to do the things we do, and how we can harness our motivations to make our lives better.

Chapter 9

What's Your Motive?

In This Chapter

- The body's balancing act
- The dieter's dilemma
- Sex is a state of mind
- The roots of sexual orientation
- The thirst for power and the drive to achievement

On July 24, 2005, Lance Armstrong won the Tour de France for an unprecedented seventh consecutive time. During post-race interviews, he attributed his motivation during his last race as showing his five- and three-year-old kids—there to cheer him on—who he is and what he does. However, Lance's driving ambition ever since he was diagnosed with cancer on October 1, 1996, has been to change the way the world looks at the disease and show other cancer victims that the impossible can become possible.

Motivation is what makes us do what we do. But where does motivation come from? How do we stick to our diet, study when we feel like sleeping, and keep going when life tries to knock us down?

In this chapter, we'll explore the drives that power human behavior. We'll explore juicy motives like hunger and sex; you'll see why you need them and what you'll do to get them. We'll explore the mind-motive connection, and the pluses and minuses of having a brain that can influence our base instincts. And we'll visit some of the "higher" motives, such as the need for achievement, and give you a chance to find out what motives drive you to work every day.

It's a Jungle in Here

How are you feeling right now? Hungry? Sleepy? Angry? How you feel will affect your ability to focus on this chapter. If you're hungry, then fantasies of home cooking may get sandwiched in between these appetizing paragraphs. If you're sleepy, you might respond to my wittiest comments with, "Oh hmmm … zzzzzz."

Your mental state will also cause you to pay attention to some things over others. If you're feeling down, you might have started out reading the chapter on mood disorders. If you're trying to diet but are having a little problem keeping the refrigerator closed, this chapter might have caught your eye. Clearly, your mental state affects your thoughts and your actions.

But what makes you hungry, or sleepy, or angry? What causes you to behave in a certain way at a particular time? When we look at the complexity of human motivation, one thing becomes clear: it isn't just a jungle out *there*. It's a jungle in *here*, too.

Let's Get Motivatin'

When psychologists use the term *motivation*, they're talking about all of the factors, inside us and in the world around us, that cause us to behave in a particular way at a particular time. Lots of things, like our genes, our learning histories, our personalities, and our social experiences, all contribute to motivation. Internal conditions that push us toward a goal are called *drives*. External motivations are called *incentives*.

def·i·ni·tion

Motivation is the physical and psychological process that drives us toward a certain goal. If the "push" comes from within, we call it a **drive**; if it comes from an external source, we call it an **incentive**.

Motivated behavior is always directed toward an incentive—the sought-after object or result that will satisfy a drive. My hunger drive sends me heading toward the refrigerator, and the mint chocolate-chip ice cream in the freezer is an incentive for me to walk a little faster.

Hungry Like a Wolf

Drives and incentives always complement each other. If one is weak, the other must be strong enough to motivate the goal-directed behavior. If the only thing in the fridge is cottage cheese, I've got to be pretty darned hungry to traipse to the refrigerator. Of course, if I'm hungry enough, even cottage cheese can look pretty tasty. So not only can drives and incentives influence one another, they can also influence each other's strength; hypothetically, at least, I could be full enough so that even mint chocolate-chip ice cream wouldn't be very appealing.

Professors wonder whether students who fail exams "aren't motivated enough." Coaches speculate that winning teams were "hungrier" and "more motivated" than their opponents. Detectives seek to establish the motive for crimes. Clients come to therapy looking for the motivation to quit bingeing. Not only is motivation one of the most commonly used psychological terms, it's something we never seem to have enough of!

What Drives Your Body?

If you were attracted to psychology because of all the big words, you'll like this one: *homeostasis*. Homeostasis is the equilibrium our bodies must maintain to keep us alive. For example, body temperature, oxygen, minerals, and water must be kept within a certain range, going neither too high nor too low. When our equilibrium is off, our bodies encourage us to take action to regain our balance. When you chug a quart of water after running a few miles, your motivation to drink is an upset in homeostatic balance, and your behavior is designed to correct it. You can even blame your high air-conditioning bills on homeostasis; when you're too hot, your body signals you to find cooler temperatures!

Homeostasis is helpful in understanding thirst, hunger, and our need for oxygen, salt, and temperature control. But many things that motivate us aren't necessary for our immediate survival. Take sex. Most of us are pretty motivated by it, but despite what an overly amorous paramour may have told you, nobody can die from lack of sex.

Psychologists have puzzled over this glitch in the homeostasis theory until their puzzlers were sore. To solve this dilemma, they distinguished between *regulatory* drives that are necessary for physiological equilibrium, and *nonregulatory drives*, like sex, that serve some other purpose. Although as you're about to see, even regulatory drives like hunger can have hidden motives.

Investigating Motives

Psychologists must always infer motives from behaviors—after all, you can't *observe* motives directly. If you're eating, you're hungry. If you're drinking (water, at least), you must be thirsty. Psychologists are constantly looking for links between the stimuli (including conditions and situations) that lead to motivation, and the responses (behaviors) that are produced by motivational states.

Psychologists also look for the "whodunit" in your behavior, which, in this case, refers to the brain. In the early 1950s, scientists began poking around in the brains of animals to see which parts controlled what drives. They'd either create lesions to remove any stimulation from reaching that part of the brain, or they'd plant electrodes that would provide more stimulation. Then they'd watch to see what happened. What they observed formed the basis of a lot of what we know today about human drives, particularly hunger.

The Mystery of Hunger

In the 1950s, scientists discovered the hunger-hypothalamus connection. They found that animals with lesions to the lateral area of the hypothalamus were completely disinterested in food. These animals would literally starve to death if they weren't force-fed through a tube. On the other hand, if the lateral part of the hypothalamus was stimulated, the animals would gorge themselves. Excited, these researchers quickly proclaimed the lateral hypothalamus as the "hunger center" of the brain.

Inside the Pleasure Dome

If you're looking for a scapegoat to blame those few extra pounds on, don't jump the gun. Later experiments showed that the hypothalamus was interested in a lot more than food. When researchers presented these same overly stimulated animals with other incentives, like sexual partners, access to water, or nest-building materials, these animals engaged in a frenzy of behavior that matched whatever incentive was provided. If sexual partners were available, they had an orgy. If water was handy, they drank it until they were about to explode!

While stimulation to the lateral part of the hypothalamus causes bingeing, manipulating another part of the hypothalamus, the ventromedial part, has the opposite effect. Stimulation here can cause an animal to stop eating altogether.

Is Your Hunger in Your Head?

We've come a long way in understanding the roots of the hunger drive. It's now believed that a tract of neurons running through the hypothalamus was responsible for the initial research findings. This bunch of neurons isn't actually part of the hypothalamus; they just travel through it on their journey from the brain stem to the basal ganglia. Also, as previously noted by the frenzy of activity, this tract seems to be part of a general activation system—stimulation seems to give the message, "You've got to do something." What that "something" is depends upon the available incentives.

We're All Picky Eaters

When it comes to hunger, the hypothalamus isn't completely innocent. It has neurons that, at the very least, can modify your appetite. When researchers destroy parts of the lateral hypothalamus, lab animals cut back on their eating but don't completely quit. They eat enough to survive, but remain at a lower-than-normal weight, and most of their other drives are normal. No, this procedure isn't available in humans!

To see whether the lateral hypothalamus did indeed play a role in hunger and wasn't just a thoroughfare for that tract of hungry neurons, researchers implanted tiny electrodes in this part of a monkey's brain. What they found is that the hypothalamus is a picky eater.

First of all, the monkey would only become excited by food if it was hungry and food was available. The cells would become active when the hungry monkey saw or smelled food, but not when the monkey was exposed to stimuli that had never been associated with food. In addition, the hypothalamus would get "tired" of certain foods; if the monkey had eaten several bananas, the cells would stop responding to that food but would continue to respond to peanuts and oranges!

> **Insight**
>
> Apparently, the beginning of a new year is not enough motivation for most of us to shed extra pounds. At the stroke of midnight every New Year's Eve, more than 130 million Americans resolve to lose weight but only 14 percent will keep those resolutions.

What all this means to us, then, is that the hunger motive involves a part of the brain that is programmed to respond to food cues when we're hungry. When we're not hungry, those same food cues would leave us cold, at least from a physiological perspective. If you've ever been on a diet and found yourself drooling over every food commercial, your response is literally "all in your head"! It's in your brain.

The Dieter's Dilemma

Let's get a few things straight. Your weight has little to do with willpower. Studies show that thin people have no more willpower than fat people do. Skinny people are not more conscientious, or less anxious. They are not morally superior. In fact, fat people and thin people do not differ on any personality characteristics.

But don't obese people eat more than people of normal weight? Maybe. Research indicates that while most people of normal weight generally eat only when hungry, most overweight people frequently eat for emotional, rather than physical, reasons. And the same neurochemical imbalance that leads to depression can also tempt us to consume excessive amounts of carbohydrate-rich foods, raising the possibility that some people who chronically overeat may, in fact, be depressed.

Brain Buster

Want to lose weight? Strike the word *diet* from your vocabulary forever. Instead, exercise five times a week (for at least 30 minutes); don't dip below 1,200 calories per day, or try to cut fat out completely; quit depriving yourself of favorite foods; and get reacquainted with your body's hunger and fullness cues.

Of course, the relationship between food and feelings is complex for many of us. All dieters, regardless of their weight, are more likely to eat in response to stress; the weight difference between stress eaters and nonstress eaters may be that overweight people are more likely to be on a diet. Stress can make all of us vulnerable to the munchies, but if we've been fighting hunger cues already, we're more likely to give in to temptation.

Mmmmmm, It's So Appetizing!

Another challenge for dieters is our culture's *appetizer effect*, which tricks our bodies' normal methods of food-regulation. Here's how this works: all of us have built-in bodily signals for hunger and fullness. When we're hungry, our stomachs growl; when we're full, our stomachs send signals to the brain, telling us to stop eating. The amount of sugar (glucose) in the blood also cues our bodies to start, or stop, eating; high blood sugar says stop, and low blood sugar says go. And our fat cells secrete a hormone, *leptin*, at a rate that is proportional to the amount of fat being stored in our cells. The greater the amount of leptin, the less our hunger drive is stimulated.

Insight

The average American consumes 3,800 calories a day, more than twice the daily requirement for most adults.

The problem is that our hunger isn't just dictated by the amount of food in the stomach, blood, or fat cells. Our environment can have a powerful influence. Any stimulus in our environment that reminds us of good food can increase our hunger drive—and that's where the *appetizer effect* kicks in.

Anyone who's ever had a second slice of pecan pie can attest to the fact that the appetizer effect, plus the availability of yummy foods, can easily overwhelm the body's fullness signals. In addition, the appetizer effect can actually stimulate physical hunger. Just the smell of McDonald's french fries can cause our insulin to drop and cause us to head to the drive-through.

My Genes Made Me Do It!

Just in case you aren't completely bummed out by now, there's yet another reason why dieting is so hard. We each inherit a certain weight range, and it is difficult, without a major life change, to get below it. If your genetic weight range is between 120 and 140, you can comfortably maintain a weight of 120 through a healthy diet and regular exercise. If, however, you wouldn't be caught dead in a bathing suit until you're below 110 and are constantly dieting to reach this goal, you're setting yourself up for failure.

Even if you starve yourself down to this weight, you'll have a lot of trouble maintaining it. And losing and regaining weight, known as *yo-yo dieting*, tends to make you fatter over time. In fact, while dieting is often promoted as a solution for weight loss, it is often what causes average-size people to gain weight in the first place!

Insight

Obesity sleuths have found clues to at least 20 of the most chronic and deadly medical disorders (breast cancer, cardiovascular disease, Type II diabetes, and so on) in the conflict between our sedentary lifestyle and our built-in genome for physical activity. Apparently, we inherited our need for exercise from our Paleolithic ancestors; when we don't engage in regular physical exercise, it can lead to an altered protein expression of this genome that leads to chronic illness.

Come On, Baby, Light My Fire

Enough about food. Let's talk about sex. First of all, how interested are you in it? How much do you know about it? Interest and knowledge are not the same thing, and interest without knowledge can cause serious problems. Here's a little quiz to assess your knowledge about male and female sexuality.

Answer true or false to the following questions:

1. Men and women go through the same sequences and phases of sexual response. ____True ____False

2. Many women can have multiple orgasms, while men rarely do in a comparable time frame. ____True ____False

3. Penis size is generally unrelated to any aspect of sexual performance. ____True ____False

4. Women tend to get aroused more slowly, but often remain aroused much longer. ____True ____False

If you answered true for all of them, go to the head of the class. Masters and Johnson shocked the nation when, in the 1960s, they began studying human sexuality by observing and recording what people actually did when they had sex. Surveys about American sexual behavior had been done before, but Masters and Johnson were well aware that people aren't always honest about what does or doesn't happen in the bedroom. Perhaps they had overheard one too many locker-room bragging sessions and decided to see the truth with their own eyes.

What they saw were men and women exhibiting remarkably similar patterns of sexual arousal and response. Differences that did exist had to do with timing and stamina. Women were slower on the uptake, but once they got going, they could last longer than the Energizer Bunny. Men, on the other hand, got off to a faster start, but fizzled out sooner.

Penis size had nothing to do with any aspect of sexual performance, with one exception. Men who thought it mattered were less secure about their sexual prowess, leading the researchers to conclude that a man's attitude about his penis size could have a big impact on his sexuality even when his actual penis size doesn't. On the other hand, a big attitude can quickly make up for a small penis.

As it turns out, the same is true for a woman's feelings about her body. You don't have to be built like Angelina Jolie to enjoy a roll in the hay. And if you believe it, your sexual confidence alone will turn a few heads!

Ready, Set, Blast Off

Physically, both men and women go through four stages of sexual response. Hopefully you've experienced them for yourself. Just in case you haven't, or you want to see if your experience matches everybody else's, they are …

1. **Excitement.** This is the beginning of arousal. Everything heats up; blood rushes to your pelvis, and your sex organs enlarge.

2. **Plateau.** This is the peak of arousal. You breathe faster, your heartbeat speeds up, and you get ready for the climax.

3. **Orgasm.** This is the release of sexual tension. Men ejaculate and women experience genital contractions.

4. **Resolution.** This is the letdown. The body gradually returns to normal.

Driving the Sex Machine

I hate to burst your bubble, but calling someone "an animal" in bed is not a compliment. When it comes to sex, we humans are much wilder and have a lot more fun. A lot of female animals, for example, only have intercourse at certain times of the month, whereas women are liberated from the control of their menstrual cycle. We can, and do, get turned on at any time during the month. Among animals, intercourse occurs in a stereotyped way. Among humans, sexual positions are limited only by our imagination. It'd be much more flattering for a rat to playfully paw her sexual partner and call him "a sexual human."

> **Brain Buster**
>
> If you're getting ready for a hot date, don't skimp on the fragrance. A recent study found that a few whiffs of men's cologne actually increased physiological arousal in women. And another study found that men guessed a woman's weight as being lower when she wore perfume than when she didn't!

Those Sexy Hormones!

We do have some things in common with our less sexually evolved friends, however, and one of those things is hormones. In all mammals, including humans, the production of sex hormones speeds up at the onset of puberty. Men get jolted with testosterone and women get an estrogen charge. However, these famous hormones have a silent partner that gives us a head start in the sex department. This less-known helper, produced by our adrenal glands, is called *droepiandrosterone*, or *DHEA*.

Before we enter that tumultuous time called puberty, DHEA is already behind the scenes stirring things up. Boys and girls begin to secrete DHEA at about age six, and the amount rises until the midteens, when it stabilizes at adult levels. Most men and women recall their earliest clear feelings of sexual attraction as occurring at about 10 years of age, well before the physical changes brought on by estrogen or testosterone. Research suggests that these feelings are brought on by DHEA.

Tanking Up on Testosterone

Once things get stirred up, though, testosterone keeps us stirred up—yes, even for women. Testosterone maintains a man's sexual drive during adulthood by stimulating his desire; this hormone has little to do with sexual performance. Men castrated in accidents almost always experience a decline in their sex drive and behavior, and testosterone injections bring it back. Similarly, men with unusually low levels of testosterone show a dramatic increase in sex after a few booster shots. However, a couple of extra testosterone doses won't turn a man into a sex maniac; if his testosterone is within normal limits, any additional amount doesn't seem to have any effect. In fact, taking unneeded testosterone can affect a man's body's ability to produce it naturally.

In women, ovarian hormones, like estrogen, play a role in our sex drive. Our adrenal glands also play one; they produce DHEA and, believe it or not, testosterone. Women who've had a hysterectomy and women whose adrenal glands have been removed often report a plummeting libido. Like with men, testorone treatment can give a low libido a much-needed jolt; while it hasn't yet received FDA approval, a testosterone patch has been developed to reverse sexual apathy. However, let's not forget that, for women, much of our sexual desire is based on interpersonal and contextual—not physical—factors. If we're trying to restore our sexual flames, improving the intimacy in our romantic relationships, having plenty of time and energy to give, and eliminating stressors like the fear of getting pregnant may be much more effective (and less expensive) than a trip to the doctor's office.

Sex in Low Gear

Fabulous orgasms aside, sex is mainly in your head. Unlike other animals, what turns humans on has less to do with physiological need than with cognitive desires. We fantasize, we interpret sexual experiences, and we have sexual beliefs and values. Even the subjective experience of an orgasm can depend on interpersonal factors (feeling safe or liking a person) as well as physical stimulation. For humans, the real sex organ is the brain.

I Love You for Your Mind

The complexity of human sexuality is wonderful, but the rewards have their risks. Because human sexuality is as influenced by the mind as it is by the body, a number of physical and psychological factors can throw your sex drive out of gear. Traumatic sexual experiences, fears of pregnancy or disease, relationship conflict, performance pressure, and shameful messages about sexuality can reduce sexual desire and can even prevent your body from functioning normally. Physical causes include various drugs, medications, and chronic medical conditions. The causes of sexual difficulties are as varied and unique as the problems that result from them.

When a person has ongoing difficulties, he or she may have a *sexual dysfunction*— a frequently occurring impairment during any stage of the sexual response cycle that prevents satisfaction from sexual activity. These disorders generally fall into four categories: sexual desire disorders, sexual arousal disorders, orgasm disorders, and sexual pain disorders. Interestingly, sexual dysfunctions are more common in the early adult years, with the majority of people seeking treatment during their late 20s and early 30s. The two most widely publicized disorders have been sexual arousal disorder in women and impotence (erectile dysfunction) in men.

> **Insight**
>
> While the most common sexual dysfunction is premature ejaculation, half of all men experience occasional impotence, and, for one out of every eight men, it's a chronic problem. While drugs for erectile dysfunction (like Viagra and others) can be helpful if the cause is purely physical or related to confidence alone, the drugs can't heal relationship problems or underlying psychological issues.

Dealing with Dysfunction

The most effective treatment, of course, depends upon the nature of the sexual dysfunction. Some sexual dysfunctions, like arousal problems, tend to be psychological in nature, while others, like sexual pain disorder and impotence, can have numerous causes. In many situations, a combination of physical and psychological treatments is most effective.

Oriented Toward Sex

Clearly, human sexuality is pretty complicated. Even your most primitive sexual urges are often at the whim of your thoughts and feelings. And, while these thoughts and feelings can certainly add spark to your sex life, they can also dampen your ardor. Your sex drive can go up or down depending on a lot of physical and psychological factors.

Sexual orientation, however, is not a matter of "getting up" or "lying down." It's a different ballpark altogether, and its causes have been a matter of political debate and scientific inquiry. In fact, so many theories have been thrown around, so many political agendas mixed in with science, and so much misinformation distributed that it's hard to tease out truth from fiction. Psychologists haven't exactly been at the forefront of the tolerance movement; in the 1980s, homosexuality was still classified as a mental disorder.

Birds Do It, Bees Do It; Fruit Flies, Too?

In the past, most psychologists argued that sexual orientation was learned. Some still do. However, there are a few problems with this explanation.

First, if sexual orientation is learned, why is it that the vast number of children who are raised by two homosexual parents are heterosexual? Why does homosexuality exist in other species—are they learning it from the dog next door or the monkey in the next tree?

Between 1 percent and 5 percent of men and women are homosexual in every culture, in countries where homosexuality is accepted and in countries where it's outlawed. Further support has come from an unexpected source—the nose. Scientists trying to sniff out biological differences between gay and straight men have found that sniffing a chemical from testosterone, the male sex hormone, causes a response in the sexual area of both gay men's and straight women's brains—not, however, in the brains of straight men. And, finally, scientists have located a gene in fruit flies that, when altered, completely changes the sexual orientation of the insect. While all the evidence isn't in, the pendulum seems to be swinging toward a biological basis for sexual orientation.

It's Just the Way It Is

We know genetic differences play some role in determining sexual orientation. Roughly 50 percent of identical twins share the same sexual orientation. In contrast, if you have a gay sibling, your chances of also being gay are about 15 percent, compared to the 1 percent to 5 percent of the general population.

Recent studies suggest that sexual orientation is something we discover about ourselves, not something that we choose. Think about your own sexual orientation.

When did you first know you were attracted to men or women? Homosexuals and heterosexuals alike say that their sexual orientation was present in their childhood thoughts and fantasies, typically by age 10 or 11.

Did you consider all the alternatives and then consciously choose the one that felt right to you? Did you ever think you made a mistake or that you should give a different sexual orientation "a chance"? Chances are, at some point you just knew your sexual orientation, probably long before you understood it. Whatever its cause or causes, sexual orientation is a deeply rooted and early emerging aspect of our self.

> **Insight**
>
> It seems that our politics are catching up with our research. As of 2005, 15 states have laws that prohibit discrimination because of a person's sexual orientation, and bills to add this demographic to the national civil rights laws are cropping up in our nation's capital regularly.

In Search of Higher Ground

Sex is a lot of fun, but we can't spend all of our time doing it. In fact, in the late 1960s Abraham Maslow proposed the revolutionary idea that people are ultimately motivated to grow and reach their potential. At a time when most psychologists thought motivation was driven by a need to make up for some physical or psychological deficit, Maslow's optimistic view of human motivation was a breath of fresh air.

Beginning with Basics

Maslow would certainly agree that we have to put first things first—basic needs have to be met before we search for higher ground. If we're starving, worries about our self-esteem take a back seat. That fight you had with your best friend pales in comparison to the rumblies in your tummy. If you're hungry enough, even concern over whether you reset the house alarm might be forgotten in your race to the refrigerator. In wartime and other times of starvation, people have been known to kill family members or sell children for food.

While no one would condone those actions, Maslow would understand them. It's hard to even think about anything else when our basic hunger drive is not being met. Missionaries around the world often feed and clothe people before they try to convert them. They may not be licensed psychologists, but they understand at least one thing about human nature: the need for knowledge and understanding is not a priority until we're fed and clothed. It's impossible to climb to higher ground when we're stuck at the bottom of the ladder.

Brain Buster

Believe it or not, it's possible to be too motivated. While motivation energizes us on simple tasks, it can quickly disrupt our performance on difficult or more complex ones, because the high need to achieve gets consumed by pressure-induced anxiety. A highly motivated (and, of course, prepared) student may be better off exercising for an hour before a test than cramming up to the last minute.

Moving on Up

Maslow believed that our basic needs naturally formed a hierarchy, from primitive to more advanced goals. At the very bottom are our most basic biological needs, like hunger and thirst. The next rung up the ladder is our need for safety and security. In the middle are our needs for knowledge and a sense of belonging, and at the very top are the spiritual needs that enable us to identify with all of humankind.

Of course, not all of us get to the top of the ladder before our time on earth runs out. If you were raised in the ambitious United States, chances are you got far enough up to reach a need for achievement. Let's take a look at a motive that, for better or worse, has made our country what it is today.

The Need to Achieve

If you had to predict who would be a success in life, would you take the person with the highest I.Q. score, the best grades, or the strongest need to achieve? Personally, I'd pick the person motivated to do well. We all know bright people who chronically underachieve. And we also know some high school graduates who tanked the SATs and could now afford to buy the company that publishes them. In the long run, desire and perseverance exceeds talent or brains.

Brain Buster

Children who enjoyed reading were given gold stars as an added incentive, and the experiment backfired! Being handed external rewards for doing something we genuinely like shifts the motivation outside of ourselves; instead, reinforce the internal rewards by asking the child to tell you about the stories he or she reads, read together, or join a parent/child bookclub.

The "need for achievement," first identified by Harvard psychologist David Murray, refers to differences between individuals in their drive to meet a variety of goals. When your need for achievement is high, you're energized and focused toward success, and motivated to continually evaluate and improve your performance. When channeled properly, this can be an organizing force in linking your thoughts, feelings, and actions. Taken to an extreme, it can be a monkey on your back. Perfectionism is a need for achievement that has gone haywire.

One of the most interesting ways that the need for achievement influences you is in the way you approach a challenge. For instance, a group of subjects were presented with an impossible task that could not be solved. When people were told that the task was difficult, those who had a high need to achieve kept trying longer than those who had a low need to achieve. Low-need achievers also kept at it, but only when they were told that the task was easy. When the low-need achievers were told that the task was difficult, they either didn't think it was worth the effort or weren't willing to spend it.

> **Brain Buster**
>
> When trying to reach a goal, it can be helpful to periodically view your progress through the eyes of someone else—by either talking to a friend or writing down your progress as though you were an objective party. Individuals trying to reach a goal tend often to focus on what has not been, or what has yet to be, accomplished while an objective viewpoint tends to reveal both the progress that has been made and the work ahead.

What Motive Works for You?

All of us work better when our jobs match our personal motivation. Psychologists David McClellan and John Atkinson studied motives that drive people in work situations. They found that all people have three motivational characteristics, and that their behavior is likely to be determined by the degree to which each is present. These three motives are …

- A need to achieve
- A need for power
- A need for affiliation

Let's take a brief look at each of these three in action. See whether your motives would most likely steer you into politics, business, or nonprofit work.

Achievement in Action

At work, you appreciate a supervisor who gets down to business and lets you work independently. You hate for people to waste your time, and prefer to focus on the "bottom line" of what needs to be done. When you daydream, you are most likely to think about how to do a better job, how to advance your career, or how you can overcome the obstacles you are facing. You can motivate yourself well and like to succeed in situations that require outstanding performance.

The Thirst for Power

You want a supervisor who's a mover and shaker and can serve as a role model. You are good at office politics and know that the best way to get to the top is by who you know and who they know. You have strong feelings about status and prestige and are good at influencing others and getting them to change their minds or behavior. When you daydream, you are most likely to think about how you can use your influence to win arguments or improve your status or authority. You like public speaking and negotiating.

The Team Player

You are a "people" person. You want a supervisor who is also your friend and who values who you are and what you do. You are excellent at establishing rapport with others and enjoy assignments that allow you to work within a group. You are very loyal and get many of your social needs met in your job. You are well liked; people may come to you with their problems and value your advice. You are great at planning company social functions and are often recruited to serve on the hospitality or banquet committee.

> **Insight**
>
> Not sure what your work motives are? Check out this website to discover your work personality and land the job of your dreams: www.allthetests.com/personality.php3?katb=0470.

Human motives are fascinating, ranging from basic, universal needs for shelter, food, and clothing to complex, unique drives for self-esteem and achievement. Richard Nixon and Mother Theresa may have both needed to eat, but their "higher" motives led them down vastly different career paths. Whether you're a born Richard Nixon or Mother Theresa, though, there's one motivator that lights a fire under all of us. In the next chapter, we'll take a look at the motivational power of emotions.

The Least You Need to Know

- Our bodies seek to maintain homeostasis, or balance—if our equilibrium is off, our body signals us to take action to fix it.

- The hunger drive is a strong part of our body's balancing act, but not all hunger is based on bodily needs—strong food cues from the environment can cause physical hunger even if we don't need food.

- Human beings are the sexiest creatures on the planet, with a wider sexual repertoire and an ability to respond to a number of physical and psychological stimuli.

- Sexual orientation is much more of a discovery about oneself than a conscious choice. It is determined early and is very rarely changed.

- Until we meet our basic survival needs, it's hard to be concerned with love, self-improvement, or spirituality.

- At work, people may be motivated by a need for power, achievement, or affiliation, or a combination of the three.

Emotions in Motion

In This Chapter

- Finding the source of your feelings
- Tuning in to your body
- Who's in charge here?
- What's your emotional I.Q.?
- Managing your everyday moods

The powerful love between Romeo and Juliet. The bitter rivalry between Caesar and Mark Anthony. The passion of Martin Luther King Jr. When it comes to human beings, emotions move us.

How do couples maintain their love in the face of constant danger? How do the spouses of firefighters and police officers kiss them good-bye every day, knowing each time that this could be the last time they see them? In the face of stress, do we learn to ration our emotions? Do we gradually lose our ability to feel? This chapter explores the psychology of emotions; how we feel and express them, how our culture influences them, what purpose they serve, and how we can handle our own moods more effectively.

Hooked on a Feeling

Whether we admit it or not, our emotions guide much of what we do; they focus our attention, help us record experiences more strongly in our memory, and arouse us.

Most of us equate emotions with feelings. We feel angry, sad, afraid, or happy. But, in reality, emotions are much more complicated. When we feel an emotion, we experience a complex pattern of physical arousal, feelings, and thoughts in response to a personally significant situation. Imagine your boss humiliating you in front of your co-workers. Not only would you feel angry, you would think angry thoughts. You might find yourself plotting revenge or obsessing over why he did that. And, although your blood wouldn't literally boil, your heart would beat faster and your blood pressure would rise.

Your emotions would stimulate you to take action. You might yell or cry in the privacy of your office. You might spit in his coffee cup when he wasn't looking. If it happened often enough, you might quit your job. Or you might decide to reframe your boss's rude behavior as his problem, and not take it so personally. No matter what you do, you are responding to your emotions; they have signaled danger and geared you for action.

How angry you get about your boss's rude behavior will depend on how personally significant the situation is to you. Situations that are perceived as highly threatening or highly rewarding will be highly emotional. If your boss's opinion is important to you, or if his comments challenge your sense of self-worth, you'll feel much angrier than if you discount what he says or refuse to take it personally. Similarly, if you had a great time on a first date, you're going to be much more disappointed if she never calls you again. You've had a taste of the rewards, and now they've been taken away!

Insight

Think you can hide your feelings from your children? Think again. By age five, children can recognize surprise, disgust, happiness, sadness, anger, and fear about as well as most college students.

Adjust Your Attitude and Improve Your Love Life!

For many of us, adjusting our attitudes about emotions would greatly enhance our relationships. For example, one of the easiest mistakes to make in your interactions with other people is assuming that there's a "right" amount of emotional intensity for any situation—that the only "right" amount is the amount you personally feel. So it's easy to think that someone who feels more strongly than you do is "overreacting."

And of course, when you try to "help" him by pointing this out, he blows a fuse!

Certainly, some people are hotheads and some people are unusually sensitive. However, most of the time, people have emotional reactions that are consistent with the importance of the topic. You might not mind being called "Baldy," but to someone who invests a lot of self-esteem in his physical appearance, that teasing comment can be highly threatening and provoke strong feelings. So the next time someone "overreacts," don't waste your energy trying to change his feelings. Try changing your *own* attitude!

> **Insight**
>
> Romantic love is about a lot more than lust. In fact, brain images of newly-in-love young men and women showed neurons firing in the areas of the brain associated with motivation and reward, which may be why we feel "driven" to win the affection of our loved one. Sex and love involve quite different brain systems.

Where Did These Feelings Come From?

Let's face it. Love may not make the world go 'round, but it sure helps people put up with each other. It gives us rose-colored glasses in the beginning of a relationship. It gets us through the hassles of meeting someone, courting them, getting married, and fighting over the remote control. Could parents put up with all the sleepless nights, poopy diapers, and Barney videos without that incredible emotional bond with their child? Apparently, evolution thought not.

Ever notice how cute babies are, whether they are baby humans, baby kittens, or baby chimps? Of course you do—you're hardwired to notice it and respond protectively! You're genetically programmed to respond to "neonatal (baby) features"—especially those big eyes. As children grow up, their features become more proportionate and adult, and you stop feeling quite as protective toward them (unless they're your own).

Our emotional capacity may have been naturally selected. Ancestors with the strongest feelings may have been more motivated to defend their turf, protect their young, and impress their mate than those who were less passionate. Emotions aren't just feelings; they are feelings associated with tendencies to behave in certain

> **Psychobabble**
>
> Researchers have found that 70 percent of the outcomes of recent political races could be predicted based on the candidates' babyfacedness! Apparently, the same facial features that endear us to newborns cause us to question the competency and maturity of babyfaced adults.

ways. They are inherited, specialized mental states designed to deal with recurring situations in the world.

From an evolutionary perspective, sexual jealousy can be viewed as a special switch that is "turned on" to deal with an unfaithful mate. When a partner is unfaithful, this emotion energizes us for possible conflict. It may have motivated our ancestors to either eliminate the rival or punish or leave the mate. In modern times, it often triggers memories that cause us to reassess the relationship. Luckily for all of us, evolution also gave us some "control" buttons that prevent us from acting impulsively on our feelings!

> **Psychobabble**
>
> Furious at a loved one? Before approaching her, do something physical (jog, exercise) to reduce the physical arousal, and then think about it. Don't let yourself plot revenge strategies or relive what's happened; instead, channel your thoughts into a goal that will help you maintain self-control (for example, "I want to get this resolved before our party tonight").

Seen this way, emotions evolved to stimulate whatever biological or psychological processes were needed to deal with a given situation. They may also help us use our energy most effectively. For example, happiness and sadness are moods that regulate your energy in opposite directions. When you're "on a roll" and things are going well, you feel happy. When you're happy, you're more optimistic, active, and energetic, which, of course, helps *keep* you on that roll.

Sometimes, though, the best thing to do is nothing. When you lose a loved one, there's not much you can do to change it. Emotions like sadness are passive; they tend to slow you down and enable you to conserve your energy—which may be why they evolved in the first place.

Body Feelings

Your emotions aren't all in your head—they're whole-body experiences. People who are anxious say their heart is racing, they can't breathe, they feel jittery, and they can't sit still. People suffering from depression lose their appetite and can't sleep. Your body and your mind are constantly interacting with each other, and the messages your body sends can either magnify or inhibit your emotions.

This emotional connection between your "mind" and your body is formed in your brain. While certain parts of your body respond to different emotions, your brain is the matchmaker that coordinates these bodily changes and emotional feelings. Specifically, the amygdala in the limbic system and the frontal lobes in the cerebral cortex act as your emotional regulators.

Are you a quick judge of character? Can you leap tall buildings at the first sign of danger? Thank your amygdala—your own, personal crisis manager. It does a quick survival check by assessing the emotional significance of a situation and generating some of your immediate responses. Through connections to the hypothalamus, your amygdala gears your body for action by stimulating the hormones that produce the physical responses (like increasing your heart rate and blood pressure) that accompany strong emotions.

> **Psychobabble**
>
> Think animals don't have emotions? Think twice before you tease one. A young killer whale in captivity pushed an oceanarium worker to the floor of the tank and briefly held him there. When aquarium managers investigated, they learned that this particular worker had a history of secretly teasing the killer whale.

Animals become pretty whacked out when their amygdalas are removed. For example, monkeys whose amygdalas have been removed demonstrate a fascinating phenomenon known as *psychic blindness*. They can still see objects, but they seem to be completely indifferent to the psychological significance of them. Nothing scares them. Nothing angers them. And they become pretty indiscriminate in their search for pleasure; some of them attempted to eat or have sex with just about anything—alive or not!

Humans aren't quite that indiscriminate, even without their amygdalas. Among humans, the amygdala keeps us from getting suckered by enabling us to interpret the emotions of others. People who have suffered brain damage to the amygdala lose that ability. It's a subtle version of psychic blindness in which they lose the ability to detect fear or anger in the voices or faces of others.

You can't blame (or credit) *all* your emotions on your amygdala, however. Your frontal lobes are also critical in your conscious experience of feelings, and they help you get a grip on the way you express them. Your frontal lobes help you plan, and initiate, your responses to your feelings. You probably don't have fewer emotions than your most primitive ancestors; you've just developed the brakes—your frontal lobes—to help control them. Without our frontal lobes, we'd still be bopping each other over the head with clubs!

What We Think About Feelings

In Chapter 3, we talked about the nature-versus-nurture debate in child development. Here's another chicken-or-egg argument, and this is an emotional one: which comes first, your emotional feelings or your bodily sensations? In other words, does your body react to your feelings or are your feelings an interpretation of your bodily sensations?

Insight

If you're about to fall on your head, you might want to turn to your right. Damage to the left frontal lobe typically lowers positive emotions (like happiness), while damage to your right frontal lobe produces a decline in negative ones (like anger).

Common sense argues for the first explanation. First you get angry and then your body responds to that anger by getting all fired up. However, William James, the father of American psychology, was never one to succumb to common sense. He thought the reverse was true. In his view, we don't cry because we're sad; we're sad because we cry.

James's beliefs arose from a single research subject: himself. When he analyzed his own feelings, he concluded that they really began as sensations in his body. For instance, when he really stopped to think about what "fear" was to him, he concluded that it was the sensation of pounding heart, shallow breathing, and shaky limbs. Anger, he believed, came from the physical jolt of temperature and blood pressure rising.

James thought there were predictable bodily changes for each emotion and that, without these bodily changes, there would be no feeling. Interestingly, people throughout the world report amazingly consistent bodily changes with different emotions.

The essence of James's theory is that our initial assessment of a situation (that a snake is poisonous) and the subsequent physical arousal occurs quickly, automatically, and without conscious thought. Since, in James's view, emotion was always a conscious experience, it could not be part of the initial process. Instead, the emotions came later, as a result of the physical sensations. The sequence went like this:

1. You get punched.

2. Your body responds to the punch automatically.

3. Your mind registers your bodily response and interprets it to mean that you're angry.

Once again, it was up to the cognitive psychologists to shed some light on things. Stanley Schachter recognized that emotions are dependent on more than feedback from the body. In his view, our perceptions and thoughts about what's happening influence what kind of emotion we feel (anger, fear, joy), and sensory feedback from the body influences how intensely we feel it (very joyful or mildly happy). If you see a snake, for instance, your belief that snakes are dangerous will cause you to feel fear, and if your body gets all fired up (you start sweating, your heart starts pounding), your fear might turn to terror.

Unfortunately, what we think isn't always right. For example, children who have been physically abused are much more likely to think that others are angry—even when they're not. When shown pictures of faces, these children were able to accurately recognize the pictures, but categorized them differently; they were much more sensitive to anger. Experience apparently can shift where a person draws the boundary of a particular emotion, and this idea runs counter to claims that boundaries for emotions are innate.

Psychobabble

When are emotions "real"? In one study that measured brain waves, the auditory hallucinations of schizophrenics actually stimulated the parts of the brain that involve motivation and emotion. In addition, there was no corresponding activity in the part of the brain that checks out reality. This brain pattern suggested that there would be no way of knowing whether these voices were real or whether an emotional response to them was reasonable.

While the neural processes that the brain uses to perceive and categorize emotion might be innate, how people actually perceive and understand expressions of emotion can be shaped by experience. It may be the case that physically abused children develop a broader category of anger because it's adaptive for them to notice when adults are angry. But while this sensitivity could be protective in a threatening environment, it could be disadvantageous in others. An abused child might over-interpret a social cue, such as an accidental ball toss during recess, to be hostile. As a result, the child might try to protect herself by lashing out, calling names, or exhibiting other inappropriate behaviors.

Schachter came to his conclusions after playing around with people's emotions. He injected some of his subjects with adrenaline and then exposed them to emotion-eliciting stimuli, like a sad movie or an angry story. Adrenaline itself did not produce any particular emotion; the subjects might have felt jittery or jazzed up, but they didn't associate it with a feeling. When the drug was combined with an emotional situation, however, their emotions were stronger. They felt angrier in response to the angry story and sadder over the tear-jerking movie. I wonder if a little coffee drinking with a new flame would make the love bug bite a little harder?

Touchy-Feely Psychology

Adrenaline isn't the only thing that can jumble up your feelings. Apparently, so can wishful thinking. Listen to this: a few years ago, a friend of mine told me he was attracted to a new co-worker, Linda. He was convinced she felt the same way. "She's so cute. Whenever I go into her office, she seems so nervous. She gets so distracted when I talk to her; she stumbles over her words, and yesterday, she dropped her pencil. I know she likes me."

Recently, at a dinner celebrating their wedding anniversary, Linda was talking about their early courtship. "I don't know why Rob was attracted to me. I was a nervous wreck over having my first job. I was so preoccupied with doing well, I barely even noticed Rob's existence until he asked me out." What Rob had optimistically interpreted as a sign of Linda's interest in him was a bad case of first-job jitters!

Unfortunately, these kind of emotional misinterpretations can lead to tragedy. In many date-rape situations, the male thinks, "Well, if she really wanted me to stop, she'd scream, or hit me, or run away" while the female freezes, thinking, "If I scream, or hit him, or try to run, he might hurt me even worse. Maybe if I just don't respond he'll realize how scared I am and stop."

Emotions—our own or others—can be hard to figure out. The physical arousal that accompanies different emotional states can be similar. For example, your heartbeat will speed up and your blood pressure will climb whether you're feeling angry or afraid. Our mental processes go far beyond fitting a label of "sad, mad, or glad" onto our feelings. We also try to figure out why we feel a certain way and what our reaction means.

The Mind and Body, Working Together

Because of the strong link between physical arousal and emotional arousal, we sometimes misinterpret physical cues as emotions. Being overheated can be interpreted as feeling anxious. Being tired can feel like depression. And being physically charged can be misinterpreted as sexual arousal.

This has some practical utility. First of all, it suggests that taking care of your body is one of the best paths to good mental health—being tired or hungry, for example, makes you much more vulnerable to mood swings.

Are You Cultured?

All human beings are remarkably similar with regard to the kinds of emotions we feel. We also speak and understand the same emotional language; the facial expression of a sad New Guinean is similar to your sad face. But if you've ever traveled in another country, you'll have noticed that culture sets the standard for when to show certain emotions and for the social appropriateness of various emotional displays, and those standards vary from one place to the next.

Cross-Cultural Confusion

I've done quite a bit of work with a Finnish-owned company that has a huge headquarters in the United States. The communication glitches that occur between the Finns and the Americans are quite amusing. One of the biggest cultural differences is in the expression of emotion. In fact, early on, I was given a cartoon that was titled "The Finnish Expression of Emotions." Underneath it was a list of numerous emotions— sad, happy, afraid, surprised, angry—and above each emotion was a picture of the exact same stone face!

From an American perspective, the Finnish culture seems to breed a bunch of Mr. Spock clones. From a Finnish perspective, Americans probably seem like a bunch of impulsive, irrational children! While Americans and Finns feel the same feelings, their culture sends very different messages about what you can do and say about them.

Guilt Trippin'

In addition to the cultural influence on emotional expression, some feelings may have a social motive behind them. Guilt, for example, may have evolved as a form of social control that motivates people to be nice to each other. For example, to avoid guilt, we're likely to act in ways that enhance our relationships with others. If someone has ever laid a guilt trip on you, you know that it can be a powerful social influence; when I miss a lunch date with my son, the guilt he can induce suddenly gives this four-year-old a tremendous amount of power!

And, last but not least, guilt is a way for partners to restore justice in their relationship. If you lie to a friend, you might benefit in the short run, but you'll feel bad about the consequences to the relationship. One hopes you'll feel bad enough to regret your mistake, 'fess up, and make amends.

Coding and Decoding

I once watched a *60 Minutes* episode featuring a woman who was conned out of thousands of dollars by a man pretending to love her. This brave woman went public with a humiliating tale of a con artist who not only manipulated her feelings, but who did a remarkable job of disguising his own. Experiencing your own feelings is one important survival skill, but communicating them is another. And, as this woman learned the hard way, decoding the way others are feeling can help us more accurately predict whom to approach and whom to avoid.

Apparently, evolution thought that human beings would benefit more from the ability to hide their emotions than from the ability to detect a lying salesperson or a con artist. Most people I know, though, think they can have it both ways. Most of us think we are good judges of character, and we're sure that we'd never have been as gullible or naïve as that woman on *60 Minutes*. If that's what you think, it's time to be honest with yourself.

Insight

Evolution programmed us to respond emotionally to threats in our environment, and we're still doing it. The percentage of airline travelers who felt nervous about flying jumped from 60 percent to 81 percent in the six months following the 9/11 hijackings.

Most of us are poor lie detectors. The key to detecting deception rests in perceiving patterns of the liar's behavior and facial expressions over time. Once you've established a baseline of how she normally behaves, you're more likely to smell a rat. Without the chance to observe that person in different situations over time, you're unlikely to accurately judge her honesty.

Smart Feelings

Eleanor Roosevelt was known as "First Lady of the World" decades after her husband, President Franklin D. Roosevelt, died. Biographers, determined to uncover how this plain, modest housewife became one of the world's most influential women, spent years interviewing her closest friends and family. What they discovered was that Eleanor possessed an uncanny understanding of people, an endless compassion for the underdog, and an incredible ability to motivate and channel her emotions into purposeful goals. In pop-psychology terms, Eleanor Roosevelt was a genius of emotional intelligence.

Emotional intelligence teaches us that, in the contest of life, we're much better off being Miss Congeniality than Miss America. Interpersonal relationships, we're finding, hold the keys to much of what life has to offer, and our ability to understand ourselves and others are the skills that get us the key. In his groundbreaking book *Emotional Intelligence*, psychologist Daniel Goleman outlines interpersonal skills that he believes greatly enhance, or hurt, our quality of life:

- **Self-awareness**   knowing what you're feeling when you feel it

- **Managing your emotions**   knowing what to do with your feelings

- **Motivating yourself**   channeling your feelings in the right direction without acting impulsively

- **Empathy**   feeling for others and accepting their feelings, too

- **Handling relationships**   having good interpersonal skills so that others feel good about you

The phrase *emotional intelligence* was first coined by Yale psychologist Peter Salovey and the University of New Hampshire's John Mayer to describe qualities like understanding one's own feelings, empathy for the feelings of others, and the ability to use one's emotions in a helpful way. An *emotional quotient (E.Q.)* is not the opposite of I.Q.; some of us are blessed with a lot of both, while some with little of either. Researchers are now trying to understand how the two complement each other—how our smarts about our feelings help us put our intelligence to better use.

We already have some clues. Students who are depressed or angry literally cannot learn. Children who have trouble being accepted by their classmates are two to eight times more likely to drop out. And the manager who answers his e-mails and is a good collaborator with colleagues is far more likely to be successful than the lone-wolf genius.

Brain Buster

If you want an emotionally intelligent physician, research suggests that you choose a female general practitioner and (if you're a woman) a male gynecologist. By searching databases of patient communication between 1967 and 2001, a team from Johns Hopkins found these two groups spent more time listening to their patients, treating them like treatment-decision partners, and engaging in more emotionally focused tasks.

Why are some people more "emotionally intelligent" than others? Emotions might be built-in, but they can be shaped by experience. Even very young children develop a repertoire of sensitive responses when they see others acting compassionately.

If, on the other hand, the feelings that a child expresses are not recognized and reinforced by the adults in her life, the child will gradually become less able to recognize them in herself or in others. Not only will this cause problems in her relationships, but she will also have lifelong trouble with something we all struggle with now and then—managing her everyday moods.

Managing Your Everyday Moods

Do you ever wake up on the wrong side of the bed? Do you sometimes get in a bad mood for no reason? Do you have a temper that's hotter than a jalapeño? If you answered yes to all three questions, here's your diagnosis: you're moody!

Moods aren't the same as emotions, although they do have a great deal in common with them. First of all, moods are often less intense and longer lasting than emotions, although this isn't true in the case of clinical depression. And, unlike most emotions, moods don't seem to have an identifiable cause; we can't pinpoint the reason why we are in a bad or a good mood.

So where do moods come from? Many people think that your routine activities, relationships, successes, and failures create your moods. But, as it turns out, that's only partly correct. Your health, sleep, food, amount of recent exercise, and even the time of day are contributors to your mood, too. In fact, moods are crucial indicators of your physiological functioning and your psychological experience at any given moment. Your mood is like a clinical thermometer, reflecting all the inner and outer events that affect you.

Meet the Mood Managers

Whether you're consciously aware of it or not, you continually sense your moods and try to improve them. In fact, you spend more time than you might think trying to regulate your moods.

However, there's a caveat. People with low self-esteem are less motivated than people with high self-esteem to improve a negative mood, even when they are offered an activity that will change their frame of mind, a team of American and Canadian psychologists has found. Many people with low self-esteem believe that sadness is part of life and that they shouldn't try to get rid of it, whereas people with high self-esteem believe in doing something to feel better if they have a negative experience or get in a bad mood. If your self-esteem has been feeling a little shaky, you may need to give yourself a little kick in the booty to shake yourself out of the doldrums.

What are some ways you try to change your moods? Do you listen to music? Exercise? Watch T.V.? Have sex? Eat? Call someone? Or do you try to stay away from people, or avoid what's upsetting you?

If you use physical exercise as one of your mood-management strategies, go to the head of the class. Studies show that regular physical exercise is one of the most effective mood regulators you have. Even a 10-minute walk can beat the blues and raise your energy level.

Other effective mood managers are listening to music, relaxation techniques, challenging negative thoughts, using humor, and getting lost in a hobby or productive activity. Expressing your feelings through writing (such as keeping a diary or journaling) may actually help not only your emotional health, but your physical health as well! And as any psychologist will tell you, focusing on others can be amazingly effective at taking the focus off yourself and gaining some emotional perspective!

On the other hand, avoidance, isolating yourself from others, and behaviors such as eating, smoking, and drinking reduce tension in the short run, but may increase tension over time. Yes, eating chocolate can change your serotonin levels temporarily and make you feel happier for a little while—probably until the next time you see your backside in the mirror.

Talking things over with a friend is a good strategy as long as you end your conversation with an action plan and don't get stuck wallowing in your emotions! And if coming up with action plans is a problem, no sweat! You'll learn all about them in the Chapter 11, when we talk about problem solving.

Psychobabble

Believe it or not, your problems seem different at different times during the day, depending on your mood and your energy level. See for yourself: write down a personal problem you're having and then make a journal entry about it at four separate times during the day. Don't be surprised if the same problem that looked so grim late at night seems less troublesome at midmorning.

Drugs and Emotions

Drugs, whether legal or illegal, affect not only our judgment but also our emotions. It's no coincidence that most cases of sexual assault and domestic violence occur when the perpetrator is under the influence of a drug—usually alcohol. Drugs can heighten our own sense of emotion and make us care less about the other person's feelings, or lead us to feel that the other person "deserves" punishment. Then we can be left sobering up later, in a jail cell, not believing what we've done.

Use of some drugs, such as PCP or ketamine ("Special K"), has been associated with some especially horrific episodes of violence. Despite the old "Reefer Madness"–type movies, though, this is not an effect of marijuana.

Does that mean we can't even have a glass of wine with dinner? Of course not. But it's a good idea to keep away from all drugs—including alcohol—when you're already angry. Remember, alcohol can *feel* like a stimulant at times, but in reality, it's a depressant.

There is even some evidence that years of heavy drug or alcohol abuse can stunt emotional growth. Ever met a 30-year-old alcoholic who still seemed like a teenager emotionally? That may have been true in a way. If he spent 15 years drinking every time he was upset instead of learning to cope with his emotions, he may still react like he's 15 instead of 30.

Ground to Trauma Control: Do You Read Me?

Rape. A devastating earthquake. The murder of a child. These are experiences that, thankfully, most of us will never encounter. And not surprising, our emotional reaction to these forms of extreme trauma can feel like out-of-body experiences when, in reality, they are our body's amazing way of helping us cope with a horrible situation at a pace and in a way we can handle.

Physiologically, many people report initially feeling numb, disoriented, or shocked. Unfortunately, a response that can be easily misinterpreted by loved ones as either an inappropriate lack of feeling (why isn't she crying about what happened?) or a lack of emotional impact (she's such a strong person; maybe she just didn't let it get to her). This physical and emotional numbing is often short-lived, followed by a flood of emotions including terror, rage, grief, and physiological arousal.

There may be a physiological "loop" that we get caught up in, between the amygdala, where we process emotions, and the hippocampus, the main memory-processing center. The emotion triggers the memory, the memory triggers the feelings again more intensely, and we get caught up in a painful circle that we can't seem to escape. Understanding this loop and learning how to break it may lead to new treatments for *posttraumatic stress disorder (PTSD)*.

The "recovery" time from a trauma varies from person to person; for many people, "normal" healing time can take up to two years. Recovery, of course, does not mean that the person is the same—there may be spasms of grief or periods of emotional fallout for years. Social support appears to be a critical factor in helping people recover from trauma; many personal testimonies of trauma survivors indicate that not being supported by the people they counted on, and being blamed for bringing horrendous experiences upon themselves, have left deeper scars than the traumatic event itself.

def•i•ni•tion

Posttraumatic stress disorder, or PTSD, is a psychiatric disorder that can occur following the experience or witnessing of life-threatening events such as military combat, natural disasters, serious accidents, or violent personal assaults like rape. People who suffer from PTSD often relive the experience through nightmares and flash-backs, have difficulty sleeping, and feel detached or estranged; these symptoms can be severe and impair the person's daily life.

Don't Do Me Any Favors

Social support following a trauma, however, does not necessarily mean counseling. Counseling sessions, known as "debriefings," are often given to survivors immediately following disaster. These sessions generally involve providing a format in which emergency personnel and survivors can discuss their feelings and reactions, thus reducing the stress that results from exposure to traumatic events.

However, two studies after 9/11 suggest that this method may do nothing to prevent psychiatric disorders and may even be harmful. A comprehensive review of psychological debriefings found that one-shot individual debriefings did not reduce psychological distress nor prevent the onset of PTSD. Those who received the intervention showed no significant short-term (three to five months) reduction in the risk of PTSD. At one year, one trial reported that there was a significantly increased risk of PTSD in those receiving debriefing. According to a Dutch study of debriefing in multiple situations, there is little evidence that recipients' long-term mental health is better than people who get no counseling, or those who just talk to friends and family. While the research jury is still out, a better initial approach to trauma may be to hand out a list of symptoms, discuss practical strategies for boosting resilience, and make sure survivors know how to find support systems. Alternatively, intervention could be delayed a few weeks to separate the majority of resilient people who are recovering on their own from those who are not getting better. Special attention could be paid to survivors, families of victims, and first responders such as firefighters, who are at higher risk for long-term problems. At that point, administering intensive treatments such as cognitive behavioral therapy to specific individuals has a much better chance of reducing the risk of long-term trauma.

No one knows how long clinicians should wait after a traumatic event to evaluate individuals to see whether they are getting better on their own. One school of thought is to keep help available whenever people seek it. Gee, what a concept!

The Least You Need to Know

- Evolution apparently gave us emotions to motivate us to take care of ourselves and to stick with the people we love.

- Emotions are whole-body experiences, combining feelings, thoughts, and bodily sensations.

- Emotional intelligence is the ability to be aware of, and effectively use, our own feelings and the emotions of those around us.

- Our moods are like clinical thermometers that tell us how we're doing physically and psychologically. Physical exercise is perhaps the best way to regulate them.

- Drugs, including alcohol, can intensify emotions—often in a negative or dangerous way.

Chapter 11

Think Before You Speak

In This Chapter

- ◆ Meeting the mind detectives
- ◆ Putting together your prototypes
- ◆ Seeing how your culture changes your mind
- ◆ Examining the evidence
- ◆ Investigating the Sherlock Holmes in your head

Long before serial killer Wayne Williams was caught, psychologist John Douglas described him as a 20-something black male and a police buff. He described another serial killer, known as the Trailside Murderer, as a stutterer. And he pegged the Unabomber as a highly intelligent white male with an obsessive-compulsive personality and a previous university affiliation. In all three instances, he was right.

How can someone like Douglas come up with accurate profiles of murderers he's never even met? In this chapter, you'll find out.

Get ready to explore the way people think—how we form our thoughts. Along the way you'll learn how people use mental scripts and schemata to figure out the mysteries of daily life. You'll learn about common problem-solving strategies, and how mental shortcuts can help you solve problems more efficiently (and, sometimes, lead you astray).

Getting Into Another's Mind

People like John Douglas aren't psychic. They just understand the criminal mind. Douglas spent 25 years working as a behavioral profiler with the investigative support unit for the FBI, spending hundreds of hours in prisons getting inside the minds of convicted serial killers. Using what he learned there, he has developed behavior profiles of criminal offenders. John Douglas may have more insight into the thoughts that drive criminal behavior than anyone else.

Mind Detectives

When I was 16, I took one of those high school vocational tests. When mine came back, the advised career was "private investigator." Given that I had never met a private investigator and grew up at a time when it wouldn't have been the kind of career advice my guidance counselor would have given a female, this was not the most useful psychological test I've ever taken. My only consolation was that my best friend was advised to become a funeral director!

Years later, I realized that my high school vocational test was smarter than I thought. I did become a private investigator—of the mind. Psychologists are, in essence, mind detectives. They are constantly looking for clues about human nature by examining thoughts, feelings, and behaviors. When I am doing therapy, my client and I are trying to solve the mystery that brought him or her to my office.

The human mind is uniquely suited to solving mysteries, and going beyond the evidence to find a solution that seizes new insights, opportunities, and interpretations. Sometimes the results are as impressive as Douglas's profiles of killers he never met. Other times the mysteries the mind solves are more mundane. In every case, the tools the mind uses in problem solving are called *cognitive processes*.

def•i•ni•tion

> **Cognitive processes** are the mental abilities that enable you to know and understand the things around you. They include attending, thinking, remembering, and reasoning.

Solving problems is what we all do, every day. Our ability to go beyond the surface of things—to make sense of clues and solve mysteries—are the gifts of our cognitive processes. Our thoughts enable us to carry around mental representations of our physical and social worlds wherever we go. They enable us to look back and investigate why we behaved in a certain way, and they enable us to look ahead to predict what might happen. Our cognitive processes are our detective tools; we use them to explore and improve the world around us.

Some of our cognitive processes mentally represent the world around us. They classify information and interpret our experiences. These are like the evidence files that detectives gather, organize, and review when they're working on a case. And just as a detective might have a map of the scenes of a series of crimes, we have a mental map of how to get to work every day. Other cognitive processes, like our dreams and fantasies, are internally focused; they help us solve your future mysteries more effectively.

Models of the Mind

Cognitive psychology is the "science of the mind." It all started in 1945, when a mathematician named John von Neumann compared the electronic circuits of a new digital computer to the brain's neurons and the computer program to the brain's memory, introducing the human computer analogy for the first time. Psychological researchers Herbert Simon and Allen Newell continued von Neumann's research. They were able to develop computer programs that mimicked human problem solving, thereby giving us new ways to study mental processes.

The idea of creating models of the mind caught on. Today, researchers build conceptual models to help them understand the processes involved in information processing. These *cognitive models* are metaphors to explain how information is detected, stored, and used. The most popular model for years has been the information-processing model.

def•i•ni•tion

A **cognitive model** is a hypothetical representation of how thought processes work. Just as a model airplane is a small replica of a real one, cognitive psychologists build cognitive models to explain how the human mind takes in and uses information.

Information Overload!

The information-processing model hypothesizes that thinking can be broken down into component parts that work together to create a system of information flow. According to this model, the key to understanding cognition is to examine these parts and to see how they work together. In this model, thoughts are either "on" or "off," and they are in a static (still) state until moving on.

But there's a new model in town. A recent study at Cornell University suggests that our thoughts may act less like a computer and more like a living organism, flowing back and forth in a continuous stream. This is the *dynamical-systems* approach.

According to this model, it may be possible to be between two or more thoughts. For example, let's say you're in a study where you're asked to click on the computer image that matches the experimenter's spoken word. If you're asked to click on a "candle," and the two images are of a jacket and a candle, the mouse would immediately move to the candle. However, if the images are of "candy" and "candle," your mouse is likely to move in a curve, as if your brain starts processing the "can" part first and, as a result, hovers between the two (keeping both options open) until the rest of the word is said. It's as if your brain is hovering between two thoughts before one finally wins out.

Insight

No matter how impressive our cognitive abilities are, we just aren't programmed for multi-tasking—at least when it comes to sights and sounds. New research indicates that both talking and listening while driving impair our ability to navigate safely. Turn off those cell phones when on the road and keep heated driver-to-passenger conversations to a minimum.

Investigating Thoughts

Cognition is an active process: you aren't just taking information in; you're also simultaneously sorting through it, making sense of it, and transforming it. This transformation of basic input into news you can use involves a number of sophisticated tasks—judging, problem solving, planning, reasoning, imagining, and, sometimes, creativity.

As complex as it is, though, thinking is also practical. If you think about it, you'll realize thinking is *always* some form of problem solving. Just about everything you think is directed toward making things clearer, better, or different. It's your built-in self-improvement program!

You might be wondering how we know so much about thoughts, since they can't be observed directly. Cognitive psychologists had a few problems to solve themselves when they began studying human cognition. Undaunted, they came up with some pretty clever investigative tools to measure the mind. Let's take a look at some of the most popular mind measures:

- Introspection
- Behavioral observation
- Error analysis
- Brain scanning

Introspection

In the late 1800s, psychologist Wilhelm Wundt taught people to study their own minds. Using a self-report method called *introspection*, he encouraged them to write down their sensations, images, and feelings *as they were having them.* By getting people to record their mental processes as they were occurring, Wundt hoped to break them down into their smallest unit.

Wundt thought that through this process, we should begin to see patterns of sensations, images, and feelings emerge. Over time, we should be able to present various individuals with certain stimuli and generate the same images, thoughts, and feelings in all of them, just as in classically conditioned behavior. Wundt optimistically believed that if we could understand human thought, then we could predict it and, when our thoughts weren't working properly, we could change them.

Alas, he was dead wrong. People are much more complicated than Wundt thought, which makes them much more interesting, unpredictable, and, bummer, much harder to study. Introspection is a great individual pastime but a poor research tool.

> **Insight**
>
> Cognitive psychotherapy is the fastest-growing kind of talk therapy in the world. It focuses on helping clients change negative thinking patterns that lead to depression, anxiety, and other mental problems.

Behavioral Observations

Ever noticed how your thoughts and actions don't always match up? You can be thinking about strangling your boss at the same time you're smiling and nodding in response to her inane comments. Nevertheless, observing what a person is doing, and the situation in which it occurs, can help us figure out the thoughts, feelings, and motivations guiding them. If we see someone crying, we know to interpret it differently depending upon whether we see it at a funeral (probably grief) versus a wedding (happiness—we hope!).

Although Wundt's thoughts were off the mark in terms of how thoughts develop, he did solve a few research problems. One useful contribution was his observation that reaction time is a useful measure of the complexity of thinking required for any given task; the longer it takes to perform a task, the more complex its solution is likely to be. Today, cognitive psychologists often use reaction-time tests to gauge mental flexibility and quickness.

def•i•ni•tion

Think-aloud protocols are a new twist on introspection studies. In these protocols, subjects are asked to describe the strategy they use to solve a problem as opposed to a description of the problem itself. These studies indicate that people's problem-solving strategies in action are much different than they think. For example, shoppers are much more opportunistic and impulsive in their trip-planning than they believe themselves to be. Of course, that's no great surprise to us impulse buyers!

Analyzing Errors

Ever make the same mistake over and over again? Well, we all do, and cognitive psychologists are pretty darned happy about it. It helps them get to know us better. In fact, cognitive psychologists study errors in thinking about as much as they do anything else.

What cognitivists have learned is that people don't just jump to the wrong conclusion, they often jump to the same wrong conclusion over and over again. This is why, as you'll see later in this chapter, there are some thinking errors that we all make, and some of them suggest that people make pretty poor jurors.

Brain Scanning

When Benjamin Franklin discovered electricity, he had no idea what he was doing for the human brain. Not only did his discovery enable us to see the light outside, but he ultimately enabled us to measure the light bulbs inside our heads. It has helped researchers see the different brain waves that we produce when we sleep (see Chapter 5), and to measure changes in activity related to a particular mental event—a pattern known as an *event-related potential* (*ERP*).

In fact, with electrical measurements, researchers can even tell which light bulbs are going off in what part of the brain. For example, while you're reading these pages, lights are going off in the part of your brain that perceives the words, the part that compares them to other words you've read, and the part that organizes their individual meanings into coherent thoughts. Even the sentences themselves can cause different ERPs; the part of the brain that gets excited over an unfamiliar word is different than the part of the brain that tries to untangle a confusing sentence structure.

Clearly, mind detectives use a variety of tools in their exploration of the mysterious human mind. But what are they looking for? What are these tools actually going to help them find? Let's take a look at how thoughts are structured. As you're about to see, it's a lot harder to get lost in thought than you might think.

Jeopardy of the Mind

If your brain were a game show, it would be *Jeopardy*. It loves categories—creating categories, putting information into categories, and fitting new stuff into old categories. Your brain is a categorizing machine.

It's also lazy. It would rather put information into existing categories than build new ones. As a result, your brain looks for similarities among individual experiences—it prefers to treat new information as instances of familiar, remembered categories. "Been there, done that" is a concept with which your brain is very familiar.

I'll Take "Building Blocks" for $200, Alex

The categories are the building blocks of thinking—we call them *concepts. Animal,* for example, is a concept that conjures up many related creatures that we have grouped together in a single category. *Dog* is another concept, although the category it refers to is a smaller one. Concepts can also represent activities (your idea of exercise may differ from mine), relationships (apples and bananas are both fruit), and abstract ideas (truth, justice).

In relationships, concepts can cause trouble. Here's an example. If, on our first date, I asked you if you thought honesty in a relationship is important, you'd probably say yes. Social pressure aside (who would go out with someone who said no?), you'd probably mean it. However, your understanding of the concept of *honesty* might be entirely different from mine, and the concepts *important* and *relationship* can muddy the waters even further. Your definition of honesty might mean that outright lying is off limits, but it's okay to leave a few things out. Or I might agree that honesty is important, but not as important as staying out of trouble!

The best way to understand a person's concept of a complex term like honesty is to see whether he acts in ways that are trustworthy. If there's a discrepancy between someone's words and actions, believe what he does, not what he says. Actions do "speak louder than words"!

Building the Building Blocks

Just as a good relationship involves finding someone with whom you have a lot in common, a basic task of thinking is concept formation—identifying what objects or ideas have in common and grouping them accordingly. "How are they the same?" is a fundamental question that your mind is always asking. Psychologists still aren't exactly sure, though, what features the mind considers when answering this question.

In other words, when your mind asks this question, what does "the same" mean? Do the objects need to look similar, do similar things, or what? Let's take a look at two schools of thought that attempt to solve this riddle—the *critical features theory* and the *prototype hypothesis*.

> **Insight**
>
> To understand the difference between *necessary* and *sufficient* features, think of the birds and the bees. Both have wings—a necessary feature to define either one. But wings alone are not sufficient to tell the two apart.

You're Just My Prototype

According to critical features theory, our brain stores mental lists of important characteristics that define concepts. If the concept were *bird*, then *feathers* and *beaks* would be critical features. These critical features are qualities or characteristics that are both necessary and sufficient for a concept to be included in a category. A concept is a member of the category if (and only if) it has every feature on the list.

The second school of thought, the prototype hypothesis, proposes that we build a mental model of our conceptual category—an ideal or representative example that all other members of the category must resemble. This ideal is called a prototype.

Lists or Likeness?

Here's how the two schools of thought differ. Let's say you're trying to define the concept "potential marriage candidate." According to critical-features theory, you'd make a list of characteristics: handsome, funny, intelligent, ambitious, generous, and empathic. Then you'd spend your time looking only for those individuals who meet all these criteria.

The prototype hypothesis, however, suggests that you would be more likely to build a mental model of your ideal mate. If you worship the ground your mom or dad walks on, you're likely to use him or her as the prototype of the perfect wife or husband, and date only those individuals who are similar to that parent in significant ways.

The critical-features approach is rigid. If a person doesn't live up to all the features on the list, he or she simply doesn't count as a member of the category. The prototype approach is a little more flexible; if a person does not exactly match the ideal model, he or she can still be classified as belonging to the same category. There will never be anyone just like Mom or Dad, so we settle for someone who is close enough.

One from Column A, One from Column B

Recent research suggests that these two schools of thought are both right—sometimes. When it comes to concepts such as mammals, the critical-features approach works well; all mammals are warm-blooded, have vertebrae, and nurse their young.

Other concepts—like birds—are harder to peg. *Wings*, *flies*, and *feathers* seem like pretty safe critical features, but what about penguins and ostriches? They're birds, but they don't fit neatly into our critical-features category. "Bird" is a blurry category; it has no clear boundaries between members of its class who fly and do not fly. To correct this fuzziness, we probably define our concept of bird not only by critical features (feathers) but also in relation to our ideas about typical members of the category— our prototype.

> **Insight**
>
> Police use prototypes all the time when they help witnesses identify criminal suspects. They prepare a prototype face made of plastic overlays of different facial features taken from a commercially prepared Identi-Kit, and then ask the witness to modify the prototype model until it is most similar to the suspect's face.

Great Expectations

Quick! Tell me 10 things you associate with having a picnic. Here are the 10 that come to my mind: sunshine, a blanket, a picnic basket, fried chicken, hard-boiled eggs, potato salad, salt, relaxation, sand, and ants. That's my schema for picnic; it's what I expect.

Schemas are packets of information that help us anticipate what we'll find when we encounter a certain concept, category, person, or situation. These expectations come from our understanding of, and experience with, this person, place, or thing. For example, I've certainly had my picnic rained out, but that's not what usually happens— so rain is not part of my picnic schema. On the other hand, I've never been able to prevent a certain number of ants from sharing my lunch.

New information is easier to handle when you can relate it to existing knowledge. If you ask me if I want to go on a picnic, I can quickly review my picnic schema and compare the costs (ants, sand) to the rewards (fried chicken!). But schemas do more than help you make quick decisions. They also help you fill in the gaps when something is missing.

Unfortunately, schemas can also help us fill in the blanks incorrectly. Ever see the man in the moon? Faces are overlearned, so it's not surprising that we can see shadows and think faces—even when they're not there.

Insight

By assigning a preconceived set of characteristics to a group, we then jump to conclusions about individual members of that group and ignore evidence to the contrary. Unconscious biases are especially likely under time pressure; for example, students were much more likely to misidentify a flashed picture of a "tool" as a "gun" when first flashed a picture of an African American and asked to respond within one second. When given more time to respond, the participants almost always corrected their error.

The Big Fish or the Whole Ocean?

Our mental schemas are, not surprisingly, greatly influenced by our culture. Richard Nisbett and his colleagues, for instance, showed American and Japanese students underwater scenes and asked them to describe what they saw. Most Japanese students started with the background and described the scene as a whole; we Americans started with the biggest, brightest, fastest fish!

These different emphases on contexts (the whole versus the biggest parts) carried over to social perceptions as well. Explanations for mother-daughter conflict, from the Japanese perspective, centered on a lack of understanding between the two (seeing both sides) while Americans sided with one or the other. And during group decision-making tasks, we Americans tended to think "win-lose," to focus on differences, and to hold out until one side won; Japanese students preferred compromise.

We can see how different mental schemas can foster radically different behaviors. We can also see how not understanding different schemas (or being unaware of our own) can lead us to assign personality labels to people or stereotypes to groups rather than try to understand the cultural assumptions guiding the behavior.

Danger, Danger, Danger

Your mind is constantly drawing on old information to make sense out of new data. If you find a discrepancy between new input and already-stored schemata, you adjust by either updating old information or ignoring the new input.

Unfortunately, if we approach new information with an already-formed idea of how it's supposed to fit into our grand conceptual schema, we are likely to tune in to information that confirms our expectations and tune out the information that doesn't fit. For example, people who are told that they are about to meet someone with schizophrenia often "see" these characteristics in their new acquaintance, even when the information is completely false. Our schemata may make it easier for us to understand information but, if we're not careful, our schemata can also distort it.

We're All Actors Following Scripts

Nicole Kidman may get $18 million a movie, but we're all pretty good actors. After all, we've been reading *scripts* since we were small. From a psychological standpoint, a script is a special name for a schema about how things are supposed to happen. And, as long as everyone knows (and plays) his or her part, everything is fine.

We follow scripts for just about every common experience in our lives. We have scripts for marriage proposals (bended knee, romance, diamond ring) and birthday celebrations (cake, jokes, gifts). We have expectations (scripts again) about how our boss should behave. These scripts help us know what actions and events are appropriate for a particular setting; they help us decide what to expect or how people should behave under certain circumstances.

When you and I are following similar scripts, we understand the "meaning" of that situation in the same way and have the same expectations of each other. This script may not always be good for our relationship; after all, if your script for romantic involvement includes violence and so does mine, our script may be familiar to both of us, but it's not healthy. We would both benefit from rewriting that script.

Also, when people follow different scripts, it can be pretty uncomfortable. If your script for a first date includes being wined and dined by someone eagerly picking up the tab, you are not going to be happy when your date asks you to split the check. Which is why most of us tend to stick with people who share common scripts.

At the same time, while it might be more comfortable for people to stick with what's familiar, it's also limiting. If you aren't exposed to new ways of being, you have less opportunity to reexamine old schemata or scripts to see if they're still relevant. And you have virtually no opportunity to learn new ones.

Many of us gripe about our parents' occasional tendency to forget that we've reached voting age; we complain that they're "stuck in the past" or "trying to keep us from growing up." However, as always, there's more than one side to this story. It may be that we haven't reexamined our own scripts for our parents, so that we're still relating to *them* in ways that were more appropriate to our more youthful selves. And dare I mention how easy it is, after a few days of this treatment, to start acting like a teenager again?

Be Reasonable

What do Sherlock Holmes, Albert Einstein, Marie Curie, and Jonas Salk have in common? Whether the task was solving a crime or finding a vaccine for polio, these people had incredible minds that enabled them to transform information in unique and revolutionary ways.

def•i•ni•tion

> **Reasoning** is a process of realistic, goal-directed thinking in which conclusions are drawn from a set of facts.

Now that we've examined the basics of thinking, let's take a look at the really fascinating, creative stuff our minds do with all these concepts, schemata, and scripts. Cognitive psychologists are fascinated by the way people use their mental building blocks to solve problems and achieve new insights. This creative process begins with *reasoning*. We are reasonable *before* we're creative.

There are two types of reasoning: inductive and deductive. Deductive reasoning starts from your ideas about the "big picture" and tries to apply it to the current situation. Let's say your theory is "all bosses are out to get their employees." What you're really trying to figure out is whether your boss is out to get you. If you were using deductive reasoning, you might generate several hypotheses that, once tested, should confirm or discount your somewhat paranoid theory about bosses.

First, you generate hypotheses about conniving bosses. Hypothesis 1: conniving bosses take credit for your work. (Uh-oh! Just last week, your boss got a pat on the back for the filing system *you* devised!) Hypothesis 2: conniving bosses say one thing and do another. (You just remembered that your boss promised you a raise a week ago, but your paycheck isn't any bigger!) Hypothesis 3: a conniving boss will give you a lower performance evaluation than you deserve. And so on. In this case, perhaps your conclusion is that there's enough evidence to support the validity of applying your general "conniving-boss theory" to your current boss.

But what if the evidence doesn't support your theory? You not only got credit for that filing system, you got a bonus in your paycheck and a rave review at evaluation time—hardly the behavior of a conniver. At first, you might cling to your general bosses-are-connivers theory, but then decide that your boss is that one-in-a-million exception to the rule. Over time, however, especially if you encounter several benevolent bosses, you will hopefully begin to reexamine your general theory. But there's no guarantee! Human beings are tricky; we hold fast to existing beliefs and are most likely to judge as true the conclusions with which we already agree!

Inductive reasoning, on the other hand, starts with *specific* observations and clues. For example, let's say your boss "forgets" to give you credit for an idea at a staff meeting. Being the generous person you are, you at first shrug it off as a mere oversight. Then it happens again. Later, your boss encourages you to apply for a higher position in another department, and then you learn he sabotaged your candidacy. With inductive reasoning, once you begin to detect patterns and regularities among those observations, you formulate some tentative hypotheses to explore, and end up developing some general conclusions or theories. In the conniving-boss scenario, you don't have to be psychic to see a pattern of deception emerging. If you're smart, you'll watch your back.

> **Insight**
>
> What really matters in a relationship? The same religious background, similar political beliefs, intellectual compatibility, in-laws you love? One answer may surprise you: the happiest couples often have similar problem-solving strategies. Looking at this may be a smart thing to do before saying "I do!"

Problem Solving

What's the fastest way to get to work in the morning traffic? How are we going to get a 24-hour project done in 8 hours? And how can we get that cute guy or girl in cubicle number 27 to acknowledge our existence? Problem solving is the space between what we know and what we need to know. Any time our thinking is directed toward solving specific challenges, we're doing it.

> **Insight**
>
> Which kind of logic would you use to find your lost keys? Most of us would use inductive reasoning to search our memory and review the evidence. By mentally replaying what was going on when you first came into the house, and retracing your steps, you'd eventually solve the mystery of the missing keys.

Try This at Home

Everybody can improve his or her skills at problem solving. Here are just a couple of ways you can hone your abilities:

◆ If you want to rev up your brainpower, play with toys. Adult puzzles and games encourage problem solving much like children's toys do. Don't get trapped by the rules of the game; after you've whipped your friend at backgammon, make up another game with the backgammon board and pieces.

◆ Engage in an activity that uses skills you don't normally use. If your job involves nothing but reading and writing all day, try playing chess on the computer or building a 3-D jigsaw puzzle to keep that visuo-spatial area in shape. If you engineer circuits all day, though, a crossword puzzle might be what you need.

◆ Having trouble finding a solution to a specific problem? Shift your perspective by asking yourself what someone you admire would do in your situation. And capitalize on the power of sleep; just before going to bed, think about your problem and the various choices you could make. Think about each choice clearly in your mind. Tell yourself you're going to make the decision while you're sleeping. You may not get the solution the next morning, but if you keep trying, within a few days you'll wake up with your mind made up.

Defining Your Puzzles

Sometimes it's hard to know what the problem really is. For example, an unhappily married friend of mine wanted to try to "fix" her marriage. However, when she tried to discuss it with her husband, he repeatedly said he was happy, nothing was wrong, and that they didn't need any professional help. When her communication strategy didn't work, she began to rethink the problem. Maybe her unhappiness was her problem alone. This started her wondering whether, rather than investing more energy in her marriage, she ought to find a way to be happy herself.

Once she identified her problem this way, she quit trying to arm wrestle her husband into couples' therapy. She decided to get some therapy on her own, and she made an appointment to get her own life back on track. Within a month, her husband was sitting on the couch right beside her. He later said he had been terrified to go to therapy, but more terrified of losing his wife. Sometimes, if we just can't come up with the right solution, it pays to take a second look at the problem.

Desperately Seeking Solutions

Of course, even when we know what the problem is, we still have to solve it. We all have a variety of search strategies we can use as we attempt to find our way through life's maze. Two such strategies are *algorithms* and *heuristics*.

An algorithmic approach to solving problems involves systematically thinking through every possible solution. A heuristic approach, on the other hand, adopts a "rule of thumb" that serves as a shortcut to solving complex problems. This rule of thumb is based on general strategies that have worked in similar situations in the past. Heuristic advice like "never go to bed when you're mad" has helped thousands of newlyweds.

Psychobabble

A 1991 national poll calculated that 31 percent of adult respondents said yes to at least one of these indicators of alien abduction: being lost for at least an hour without remembering why; flying through the air without knowing why or how; waking up paralyzed with the sense of a strange presence in the room; seeing unusual lights in a room without understanding what caused them; or discovering puzzling scars on one's body with no memory of what caused them. Strange beliefs might not be reasonable, but they sure are common.

Guilty Until Proven Innocent

Algorithms can be terrifically time-consuming, so it's no wonder that people use heuristics a lot of the time. Sometimes they're useful; it's probably hard to go wrong with the "never go to sleep mad at each other" heuristic. However, our use of mental shortcuts can also result in *cognitive bias*, leading to thinking errors that impact our judgment and impede our decision-making ability. In fact, we humans seem to have a number of built-in biases.

Remember that one of our natural biases seems to be our mind's need to find connections between events and concepts. This means that it will look for connections even between random events, and see events that occur together as somehow causing each other. Many medical professionals will tell you that a full moon "makes people crazy" and will give you erroneous anecdote after anecdote about ER statistics on full-moon weekends.

Another cognitive bias is our tendency to believe that we control our own fate. While this is generally a healthy belief, this bias can also lead us to make faulty *judgments*.

def•i•ni•tion

A **judgment** is the process of using available information to form opinions, draw conclusions, and evaluate people and situations. Judgments have a lot of influence over what we decide to do.

Brain Buster

Beef up your immunity to faulty logic by looking for these kinds of fallacies: the "slippery slope" (once someone drinks a beer, she's doomed to alcoholism), the "hasty generalization" (I know that women are inferior to men; my former coworker, Jane, always held our team back), and the "false alternative" (what doesn't kill you makes you stronger).

But faulty judgments, like blaming the victim, can be not only unfair but also dangerous. The "she asked for it" attitude toward rape victims is an extreme example of out-of-control human logic.

Strangely enough, though, faulty assessments can work in our favor if they promote a more favorable opinion of ourselves. A recent study shows that those of us who think we look younger than our age are more satisfied with life than those of us who think we look our age or older. And this seems to hold true regardless of whether other people (or the mirror) agree with us!

Another cognitive bias, the *availability heuristic*, encourages us to estimate probabilities based on our personal information or knowledge; if we've experienced it, we're likely to overestimate the frequency of its occurrence. The *representativeness heuristic* can also do some social damage. It is based on the idea that people and events can be grouped into categories. Once you've been categorized, the assumption is that you share all the features of other members in that category—and they share all your features, too.

For a person caught in the representativeness heuristic, an individual woman or man could easily be viewed as the official representative of his or her particular demographic. How would you like others to judge you as the official representative of your race or gender?

Fortunately, people, places, and things do not neatly fit into categories simply because we lazily assign them to certain groups. Which gives us another reason to celebrate the complexity and diversity of unique individuals.

Seven Strategies for Improving Your Decision-Making Batting Average

In many ways, we're a result of all of the decisions we've made in our lives to date. Recognizing this, here are some tips to enhance your decision-making batting average.

◆ Write down the pros and cons of a line of action. It clarifies your thinking and makes for a better decision.

◆ Consider those affected by your decision. Whenever feasible, get them involved to increase their commitment.

◆ Determine alternative courses of action before gathering data.

◆ Before implementing what appears to be the best choice, assess the risk by asking, "What can I think of that might go wrong with this alternative?"

◆ Mentally rehearse implementation of your choice and reflect in your imagination what outcomes will result.

◆ As part of your decision-making process, always consider how the decision is to be implemented.

◆ Once you have made the decision and have started what you are going to do, put the "what if"s aside and commit yourself to your plan of action.

◆ Recognize that you will make mistakes. For instance, many expert profilers thought that in the case of the Washington, D.C., sniper killings the sniper was one white male—instead, it was two African Americans working together!

Our cognitive processes have an impact upon every single aspect of our lives. Not only do they enable us to solve life's mysteries, but they strongly influence how we feel about them. "I think, therefore I am," may be somewhat of an overstatement, but not by much!

The Least You Need to Know

◆ Psychologists are detectives of the mind—by observing human behavior, analyzing errors, and scanning our brains, they gather clues about the way our minds work.

◆ Thinking is like a highly sophisticated assembly line made up of concepts, schemata, and scripts. What these conceptual parts look like is partly determined by our past experience and our culture.

◆ There are two types of reasoning: inductive (which moves from general principles to specific cases) and deductive (which moves from specific clues to general conclusions).

◆ All thinking is geared toward solving problems, and uses either algorithmic (considering all solutions) or heuristic (shortcuts based on prior information) strategies.

◆ Heuristics save time, but they can also lead to cognitive errors.

Don't Blow a Fuse!

In This Chapter

◆ Counting the many ways you can be stressed

◆ Finding out why stress is just a *GAS!*

◆ Discovering the difference between coping and moping

◆ Understanding how your mind controls your matter

◆ Learning the write way to reduce your stress

"Stress is when you wake up screaming and realize you haven't fallen asleep yet." "Hand over the chocolate and no one gets hurt." "If stress burned calories, I'd be a size 5." Even our t-shirts seem to admit that stress is a constant factor in our lives!

This chapter focuses on one of the greatest mental-health challenges facing Americans today: stress. You'll find out what stress is and what causes it. We'll also take a look at the psychological effects of physical illness, how psychological illnesses can cause physical symptoms, and the complex interaction between our brain, body, emotions, and immune system. Don't get stressed by all this, though—we have a whole chapter at the end of the book on positive psychology and coping!

Defining Stress

Public speaking. The GREs. Getting laid off. Reading these words may fill some of us with delight (at last, I don't have to go through that daily grind anymore!) and some of us with terror (I'll die if I have to get up in front of that group). While some life events are stressful for all of us, the fact that we feel differently about the same events confirms an important part of stress—to some extent, it's in the eyes of the beholder.

In fact, for something to be stressful, we must consider it threatening to us in some way—either physically or emotionally. Next, for stress to occur, we have to have some doubt or question about our ability to deal with the stressor effectively. Getting married or starting a new job is often stressful because we're treading on new ground and haven't yet proven to ourselves that we can handle it.

How Can I Be Stressed? Let Me Count the Ways ...

Psychologists Suzanne Segerstrom, Ph.D., and Gregory Miller, Ph.D., analyzed the results of nearly 300 studies and sorted stress into five different categories, including the following:

- *Acute time-limited stressors:* lab challenges such as public speaking or mental math.

- *Brief naturalistic stressors:* real-world challenges such as academic tests or job interviews.

- *Stressful event sequences:* a focal event such as loss of a spouse or a major natural disaster, such as Hurricane Katrina in September 2005. These events give rise to a series of related challenges (rebuilding a home, recovering from the fear) that people know at some point will end.

- *Chronic stressors:* pervasive demands that force people to restructure their identity or social roles, without any clear end point—such as injury resulting in permanent disability, caring for a spouse with severe dementia, or being a refugee forced from one's native country by war.

- *Distant stressors:* traumatic experiences that occurred in the distant past yet can have long-lasting emotional and cognitive consequences, such as child abuse, combat trauma, or having been a prisoner of war.

A sixth class of stressor not mentioned by our illustrious researchers is the *background stressors*, also known as daily hassles. You can probably list the ones you had today: the neighbor's car alarm that went off at 3 A.M., the ATM that was out of cash, the kitty that missed the litterbox again. As minor as these may seem, they add up; there is a clear relationship between those small, everyday irritations like time pressure, money problems, annoying neighbors, and health problems. If your life is filled with hassles, take care of them or, at the least, change your attitude toward them.

Stress Is All Around

Have you ever heard anyone say he needed *more* stress in his life? I haven't. There are literally hundreds of stress-management tapes, books, and courses on the market, and not one of them offers strategies for increasing it. In the high-powered era in which we live, stress reduction has become a part of the American dream.

Given that we're constantly trying to get rid of stress, wouldn't we all be better off without any? Not really. Without stress, we would have no problems to overcome, goals to reach, or inventions to create. Pretty soon, we'd wind up as lazy couch potatoes with dull wits and no motivation. Even if we didn't, life would be pretty boring, which can be pretty stressful itself!

def•i•ni•tion

Stress is a general term that includes all the physical, behavioral, emotional, and cognitive responses we make to a disruptive internal or external event. **Stressors** are the events that trigger a stress response.

Stress and the Individual

Stress is a part of being alive. Being stressed out, however, isn't. Stress becomes a problem for us when we have too much stress and not enough resources to cope with it. Yet what is "too much" stress?

We've all known people who bounce back from even the toughest challenges, while others seem to have trouble coping with life's daily hassles. People also respond differently to the same stressor; the next time you're stuck in traffic, take a look around. You'll see some people calmly bebopping to the radio while others are frantically pulling onto the shoulder and craning their necks to look for a break in the traffic.

The difference between the beboppers and the neck craners is how they interpret the stressor and the coping resources they rely on to deal with it.

What Determines Your Stress Level

Stress is uniquely personal. Our response to stress is a combination of bodily reactions, thoughts, feelings, and behaviors. Take a look at all the factors that determine a person's stress level, and you'll understand why one person's pleasure is another person's poison.

Factors Affecting Your Personal Stress Level

Internal Factors	External Factors
Physical health	Medical care
Genetic vulnerabilities	Finances
Mental health	Skills and training
Self-esteem	Support systems
Temperament	Counseling
Self-confidence	Predictability of stressor
Cultural expectations	Frequency of stressor's occurrence
Cultural definitions	Intensity of stressor's occurrence

Your unique combination of personal factors, externally available resources, and certain attributes of the stressor itself are what determine just how much stress (if any) you'll feel in response to a given stressor.

Your ability to cope with small to medium stressors right now is also affected by major stressful events in the past, especially if they're in the recent past; for example, you're going to get much more upset if you get into a fender-bender on the way home from your father's funeral than on the way back from the 7-11.

Making Change

Evolution gave us stress to keep us on our toes, and we're still trying to keep our balance. Historically, changes in food supply, weather, or safety were the stressors that our human ancestors faced. While today's challenges are more likely to involve our self-esteem than our physical safety, they still require coping with change.

When you think about it, change is the culprit in much of our stress. Whether it's the loss of a loved one or the birth of a baby, adjustment to a new situation requires a lot of energy and, sometimes, different coping strategies. Having a "good" change can be especially difficult because our expectations don't match reality.

For example, society tells expectant parents that the birth of a child is an utterly joyful event. When a new parent is less than thrilled with the reality of existing on two hours of sleep and changing diapers every 10 minutes, he or she can easily interpret the resulting stress as a sign of bad or incompetent parenting. This, of course, only adds more stress. If new parents can see their stress as a normal reaction to a dramatic lifestyle change, they might applaud themselves for surviving rather than berate themselves for feeling grouchy and tired!

Sometimes, stress appears before change even takes place. The "cold feet" many people get before their marriage is an example of the anticipatory stress of getting hitched. Change may put the spice in our life, but it also can also give us heartburn!

> **Insight**
>
> Too much change can be hazardous to your health. Recent widows and widowers are much more vulnerable to all types of disease in the six months following the death of a spouse. Losing someone close to you is a red flag to take extra good care of your mental and physical health.

> **Brain Buster**
>
> If possible, avoid major decisions when you're stressed out; stress distorts and clouds your thinking. In addition, since stress impairs your ability to hold your tongue, avoid people or situations in which it might not be in your best interest to blurt out the truth!

How Do You Know if You're Stressed Out?

"I'm stressed out," you tell your best friend. But how do you know? Since people experience stress differently, it is important to know what being "stressed out" feels like to you. What do you do, how do you feel, and what are you thinking? When you're stressed, write down what you do, how you feel, and what you're thinking—and use your responses to conduct regular stress checkups. To get you started, here are some of the most common symptoms of stress:

◆ Feeling on edge, frustrated, easily annoyed

◆ Having trouble concentrating or making decisions

◆ Finding even simple things to be burdensome or difficult

- Eating more or less than usual

- Experiencing mood swings

- Feeling distracted—having a hard time keeping track of little things

- Being irritable or impatient

- Overreacting with strong feelings to minor events

- Not getting as much pleasure out of things that you usually enjoy

- Drinking more to relax or feel less tense

Burning Out

I once read that the average career life of a therapist was seven years. After seven years, most psychotherapists who are on the "front lines" dealing with clients every day go AWOL. They quit. They change careers. They burn out.

Burnout is a combination of emotional exhaustion, personal detachment, and a reduced sense of accomplishment that most often plagues professionals in the service industries—doctors, lawyers, mental health professionals, teachers. Anyone who has high-intensity contact with other people on a daily basis is at risk for job burnout. Unfortunately, not only does the professional suffer, but inadequate or impersonal care may shortchange the person on the receiving end.

def•i•ni•tion

> **Burnout** is a unique pattern of emotional symptoms often found in professionals who have high-intensity contact with others on a daily basis. It is a form of emotional fatigue characterized by exhaustion, a sense of failure, and a tendency to relate to others in a depersonalized and detached manner.

The Fires of Burnout Build over Time

Burnout is the end result of chronic, interpersonal stress. And it can happen in our personal lives, too. Ever had a friend whose life was one crisis after the next? With the first crisis, you probably mobilized all your resources to help your buddy out. With the second, you also responded to the "fire alarm." By the tenth or eleventh, however, your attitude may have been a little more cynical and your offer to help a lot slower. Your friend has cried wolf one too many times and burned your caring right out of you!

Buffering Against Burnout!

Chronic stress can cause serious physical and mental problems. Most of these problems can be prevented, and burnout is one of them. Health-care professionals who regulate the amount of face-to-face patient contact, who take regular vacations and mental health days, who schedule in leisure activities, and who get support from work colleagues and family members, are much less likely to burn out.

But what kind of support do we need? While the old adage "Misery loves company" is well and good, new research suggests that equally stressed partners or friends aren't the best social buffers when we're trying to get a grip; it may be better to talk to someone who's in a better frame of reference. In other words, when you've gone over the side, it's best not to expect reinforcement from someone who's in the same lifeboat.

> **Insight**
>
> It's not the pressure, monotony, or danger in a job that stresses us the most. It's two things—either feeling we don't have the resources to do the job well, or having no sense of how it benefits others.

I Feel Like Fighting or Flying Away

You and a close friend are having lunch with a new work acquaintance. As you go through the normal get-acquainted chitchat, the conversation gradually turns to your love lives. While your friend is spilling her guts about her romantic history, she suddenly begins to tell your acquaintance about your recent breakup with a mutual work colleague. With you sitting right there, she goes on and on about your lingering feelings and your discomfort at seeing this person at work every day. Shocked at her breach of confidentiality, your blood pressure starts to rise and you're suddenly torn between punching your friend in the mouth or running out of the restaurant.

Punching out your friend might feel good for a few minutes, but you know it would only make matters worse. And running from the restaurant would not only make you feel foolish, it might confirm your new acquaintance's view of the emotional instability your friend's words seem to imply. So why do you feel like running away or striking out?

Remember the endocrine system from Chapter 2? This communication system helps regulate things like blood pressure, metabolism, and heart rate. As you sit there in the restaurant, clenching your fist and tightening your jaw, you are experiencing the *fight-or-flight syndrome*, a sequence of internal processes that are triggered by your endocrine system when it prepares for a threatening situation. This syndrome is not to be taken lightly; at least 15 bodily changes are triggered all at once.

> **Insight**
>
> Preliminary research findings suggest that stress and aggression may be intertwined at the biological level; stress lowers our brain's ability to inhibit aggression, and acting aggressively triggers more stress hormones (making it harder to stop). This stress-violence cycle may partially explain why a bad day at the office could prime someone for violence later in the day.

Unfortunately, it's very rare these days for your built-in ability to become an instant lean, mean, fighting machine to pay off. Certainly, when it comes to relationships, your best bet is to stay calm, listen, and respond rationally. For example, if you logically think through your friend's breach of confidence, you might interrupt tactfully and let her know you don't want to talk about these things. And you can make your boundaries clear for the future. This may not be as immediately gratifying as a kick in the pants, but it's a lot more effective in the long term!

It's a GAS, GAS, GAS

Of course, the long term isn't necessarily our strong suit. In some respects, human beings are better equipped for the short run than the long haul. We get tired of the same foods. We get bored with the same activities. We get burned out on our jobs and, yes, sometimes we do punch out our friends! Even our stress responses work better in the short term; if we have to fight or flee too much, our emergency response system breaks down.

> **def•i•ni•tion**
>
> The **general adaptation syndrome (GAS)** is a pattern of general physical responses that are triggered by any stressors, no matter what kind.

Hans Selye was a man with great endurance and a psychologist's interest in the effects of chronic, severe stress on the body. He started wondering what would happen if the body were in a constant state of alarm. He got his answer—nothing good. Over time, chronic stress can tear us down and wear us out.

GASsing Up

According to Selye, one of the reasons that life stressors have a cumulative effect is that our bodies can't distinguish between them. Instead of generating different physical reactions to different life events, our bodies have a general physical response to any stress. Selye called the pattern of bodily reactions to an ongoing, serious threat the *general adaptation syndrome (GAS)*, and identified three stages that make it up. Let's take a look at each stage:

1. Alarm

2. Resistance

3. Exhaustion

All Stations on Alert!

The alarm stage is the "fight-or-flight" response in action. The body mobilizes energy to deal with a specific stressor, such as a near car accident, making a public speech, or getting married. Adrenaline is released into the bloodstream, commonly causing sweaty palms, a pounding heart, rapid breathing, increased blood pressure, and slowed digestion. Although these symptoms can be uncomfortable, your body returns to normal fairly quickly once the stressor is alleviated. No harm done.

Insight

The number-one cause of posttraumatic stress disorder (PTSD) is motor-vehicle accidents. Accident survivors most at risk for PTSD are those who suffered a serious physical injury, witnessed the death or serious injury of a loved one, had reason to fear that they might die during the accident, and have limited social support during the recovery process.

Fighting Harder

If the stressor continues, however, the body tries to compensate by kicking into overdrive. Temporarily, it works harder to resist the stress—hormones continue to pump adrenaline, physical arousal remains high, and the immune system works harder. Of course, you might not feel any of these things. What you may feel, though, is anxiety and a sense of being pressured or driven. You may begin having problems remembering details and you may start to feel fatigued. If you find yourself drinking more coffee, smoking more cigarettes, or boozing more than normal, your body may be trying to cope with too much stress.

Ending in Exhaustion

Over time, chronic stress consumes more energy resources than your body can produce. Your hormones "burn out," leaving you with less resistance to emotional stress and physical illness. The emotional burnout that chronic stress produces is often known by another name: depression.

You'd save your body a lot of wear and tear if you could just switch your stress response on and off as needed, or if you could teach it the difference between a life-threatening event and a stressful, but happy, occasion. Unfortunately, you can't. What you *can* do is work with your stress response by building up your emotional "muscles" to handle stress more effectively.

Coping or Moping

I once had a client who was a young, single mother of two very active sons. One of her sons had been diagnosed with attention deficit disorder and a learning disability, and needed extra attention and support. This woman received no financial or emotional support from her ex-spouse, who had left her for a younger woman and quit his job. Week after week, she worked full time, juggled her bills, and did a pretty darned good job of single parenting.

Yet she often came into my office in tears, berating herself for being unable to "cope" with her situation. In her definition, occasionally losing her temper or feeling stressed out was "not coping." In my professional opinion, the fact that she got through each day was a miracle and was worthy of an Olympic gold medal in the coping department.

Developing a lifestyle that enhances your physical or mental well-being is a good strategy. Who could argue with advice such as exercise regularly, eat healthy food, and get plenty of sleep? But a good lifestyle can't keep bad things from happening. When they do, the way you cope with them can mean the difference between bouncing back and getting knocked on your behind.

Coping is any strategy you use to deal with a situation that strains or overwhelms your emotional or physical resources. For example, if you get laid off from your job, you might feel angry and hurt, fantasize about revenge, and then polish your resumé and hit the pavement. Different stressors require different coping strategies; grieving the loss of a child would require different coping strategies than putting up with a chronically nagging spouse.

Not All Coping Is Created Equal

Let's say you applied for your dream job three months ago. You believe you were qualified for the job and were sure you'd get it. However, six weeks ago, harsh reality knocked on your door—you found out someone else was hired. Now all you can think about is how it should have been. Even though you know you should pick yourself up and start job-hunting again, you find yourself daydreaming about what would have happened if you'd been hired. You spend hours plotting revenge on the company official whom you're sure gave you the thumbs down. Are you coping?

Therapists would say no. Instead, they'd say you're defending against the pain of rejection by escaping into fantasies. Coping, on the other hand, involves identifying and eliminating the source of your problem—your lack of a job and your disappointment over not getting the job of your dreams.

The difference between coping and defending can be tricky to understand and even harder to detect in our own lives. As a rule of thumb, defending ourselves merely lessens the symptoms of the problems, often only temporarily. Coping, on the other hand, gets to the root of the problem and focuses on changing what we can change and making peace with what we can't.

Psychobabble

The next time you find yourself worrying, channel your stress into anticipatory coping. Mentally review similar past experiences; these will reacquaint you with what mistakes to avoid repeating, what reactions to expect, how you will feel, and what resources can help. Plan what you will do to cope with this stressor more effectively than you have in the past. Whereas worrying can increase stress, anticipatory coping can help you prepare for a stressful event.

What Are You Coping With?

Life would be a lot easier if the perfect solution to every argument was to look your opponents in the eye and tell them your honest thoughts and feelings. This coping strategy might work well with your spouse, but there aren't many job supervisors who want to hear that you think they're incompetent boobs. Psychologists would agree that facing up to a stressful situation is always a pretty good idea, but finding the best way to face up to it depends on the situation.

Categories of Coping

In general, coping strategies fall into two categories—problem-focused coping and emotion-focused coping. Each has its strengths and weaknesses, and each is best suited to particular categories of stressors.

Insight

Avoidance coping strategies ultimately cause more stress. Common avoidance tactics include denial (hey, there's no problem), distraction (having an affair instead of dealing with marital problems), venting (yelling or worrying without taking any action), and sedation (numbing through drugs, alcohol, overeating, and so on).

Focusing on the Problem

With problem-focused coping, you deal directly with the stressor to change or eliminate it. You confront your teenager about running up your long-distance phone bill or, more realistically, you put on a block so that she can't dial out. You take a self-defense class to cope with your fear of being victimized. Problem-focused coping works best when the stressor is controllable—when you can actually do something to change it.

Gaining the Emotional Edge

With emotion-focused coping, the goal is to change the way you feel and think about whatever is stressing you. For example, unless you can afford to quit your job, it might not be a good idea to confront a critical or controlling boss. You can, however, get emotional support from co-workers in the same boat. You can also use self-talk that lessens your boss's impact on you: the next time he criticizes you, you can mentally remind yourself that it's your boss's problem and he is the one who should be embarrassed by such behavior, not you.

Insight

Men and women returning from combat in the Iraq war showed similar levels of—and reactions to—stress. Gender differences in coping, when present, are limited to what events are considered to be most stressful on a daily basis; women say that relationship hassles top the stress list, and men complain most about work-related problems.

Emotion-focused coping works best for stressors that you can't control. They don't eliminate the source of the stress, but they can change what the stressor means to you. It's a lot more stressful to think of divorce as a personal failure than to think of it as a painful learning experience.

In reality, of course, many stressors in our lives have both uncontrollable *and* controllable parts. A person who has cancer can seek the best medical care and take control of her illness. At the same time, however, that person can't change the diagnosis and will have to find ways to cope with the fear, anger, and sadness that accompany such a scary illness.

Identifying Your Stressors

If you frequently feel victimized by life's events, you may be using emotion-focused coping to deal with situations you can change. One of the complicated parts of coping is identifying which events are controllable and which are not. How many times have you heard a friend complain about her boyfriend over and over, yet she never tells him what is bothering or hurting her? It's fine that she's dealing with her emotions by complaining to her friends, but she should have an action plan in place before she hangs up the phone!

Stressful Thoughts

Oh, no, I have only seven more weeks to finish this book. That's not enough time! What if I miss my deadline? I've heard my publisher is really strict about deadlines; they will never ask me to write another book if I turn this one in late. Maybe they won't even publish this one!

Do those thoughts sound like a good general coping strategy to you? Probably not; in fact, you may have started getting nervous about my deadline, too. The way we think about the stressors in our lives influences both the emotions we have about them and the solutions we come up with. To some extent, they're the key to both emotion-focused *and* problem-focused coping.

For example, before you can decide what to do about whatever event is stressing you out, you have to identify it and evaluate its severity. This is called cognitive appraisal, a highly subjective

Brain Buster

People who procrastinate over school or work tasks are more likely to have health problems. Although procrastination itself is linked to stress, procrastinators are also more likely to behave in an unhealthy way (put off sleep, grab something to eat on the run) or delay medical treatment (canceling a doctor's appointment).

and amazingly powerful process. As you can see from my frantic thoughts about my deadline, the time pressure (the stressor) of writing this book sometimes became much greater because of the catastrophic thoughts (the cognitive appraisal) that went with it. Even psychologists have trouble coping sometimes!

Psychobabble

In 1974, bank employees in Stockholm, Sweden, were imprisoned in a bank vault for five days during a robbery. Upon their release, the employees expressed warmth—and even attraction—for the men who had taken them hostage. This bizarre emotional response became known as the Stockholm Syndrome, a coping pattern in which hostages and prisoners identify and sympathize with their captors. Sometimes, extreme situations trigger extreme forms of emotion-focused coping.

I Think I Can, I Think I Can, I Think I Can

And it helps to believe that you can cope with your stressors. People often underestimate their ability to cope with life's curveballs. Even though they've survived relationship breakups, career disappointments, physical illnesses, and many other stressors, the minute a new stressor comes along they start thinking that they can't cope with it.

One of the most powerful stress-busting strategies is to keep track of your coping history. Seeing your impressive track record helps you keep at bay any untrue negative self-statements like, "I'll never get this right" or "I just can't stand this."

Mind over Matter

The boundary between your mind and your body is so thin that it's practically non-existent. Psychological stress leads to bodily arousal. Depression lowers your immune system. And thinking more positively about a stressful event can actually help your body relax.

This shouldn't be all that surprising. After all, your brain is responsible for your thoughts and feelings as well as for the regulation of many of your bodily functions. No wonder experiences that have an impact on your thoughts and feelings can also affect your physical functioning.

In fact, sometimes the body expresses what the mind can't. One example of this is when a person experiences bodily ailments in the absence of any physical illness.

Psychologists call these *somatoform disorders*. The most dramatic of these disorders is *conversion disorder*, in which the person temporarily loses some bodily function in ways that cannot be explained by physical illness.

A less dramatic example is *somatization disorder*, which is characterized by a long history of vague and unverifiable medical complaints. Most typically, the person complains of symptoms of several disorders; so, for example, the person might complain of headaches, dizziness, heart palpitations, and nausea. While a certain percentage of people with these diagnoses turn out to have underlying medical conditions, a significant number have an underlying psychological condition—depression.

def•i•ni•tion

Somatoform disorders are mental disorders in which the person experiences symptoms of physical illness but has no medical disease that could cause them. **Conversion disorder** and **somatization disorder** are included in this category.

Culture and Stress

In many cultures, it's not acceptable to seek help for a psychological or emotional problem, but it *is* okay to go to the doctor for a physical issue. Physicians dealing with people from different cultures have to learn when a stomachache is probably an ulcer, and when it's probably a mother-in-law!

If you notice that your headaches only seem to flair up at work, or your stomach only cramps when your spouse walks in the door, your emotional stress may be talking to you through your body.

Seeking Immunity

The field of psychoneuroimmunology is the study of the interactions between the brain, the body, the emotions, and the immune system. We now have scientific confirmation that mental stress puts us at risk for physical illness; an increasing number of studies show that emotional distress shuts down some of the body's defenses against viruses and, in that way, makes us more vulnerable to infectious diseases.

It seems that evolution had to make a tradeoff. When the emergency stress response is triggered, the body mobilizes all of its resources for action. Functions that are not on the emergency team are temporarily shut down. While hormones are raging around preparing for battle, energy-consuming aspects of the immune system, like the production of white blood cells, are temporarily suppressed.

Insight

Short-term stress actually "revs up" the immune system, an adaptive response preparing for injury or infection, but long-term or chronic stress causes too much wear and tear, and the system breaks down. The immune systems of people who are older or already sick are especially prone to stress-related change.

The good news is that we can significantly impact our body's response to stress. Here's an example: one important part of your body's immune system is the natural killer cells (called T-cells). These amazing fighting units have the ability to recognize and selectively kill both cancer cells and virus-infected cells. Experimenters have actually measured variations in natural killer cell activity based on interactions between stress and attitude.

For example, Dr. Steven Locke at Harvard Medical School questioned subjects about stressful events in their lives and also about their psychiatric symptoms of distress. He then took blood samples and used them to measure their natural killer cell activity. The subjects were sorted into four equal-size groups according to the level of their stress and the degree of their symptoms.

The killer cell activity level of the group with high stress and low symptoms was *three times higher* than those with high stress and high symptoms. People under stress who know how to deal with it emotionally appear to have more immune activity than even unstressed people with poor mental habits.

Writing Your Way to Physical Well-Being

Recent studies completed by scientists at Southern Methodist University and Ohio State University College of Medicine have proven that writing contributes directly to your mental and physical health. Tests conducted by a team of clinical psychologists and immunologists demonstrated that subjects who wrote thoughtfully and emotionally about traumatic experiences achieved increased T-cell production, a drop in physician visits, fewer absentee days, and generally improved physical health.

Here are three ways to get you started:

◆ **Reflective writing.** Write about events that are happening to you or around you as if you are an outside observer. This strategy is especially effective when writing about life changes, whether in your job or career, relationships, or in physical and emotional health. Begin writing with the phrase, "It was a time when ..." and then describe the event in detail, using as many of your senses as possible. What were the sounds, smells, sights, feelings, and so on, that were present? Write about the event as though you were observing yourself. Use "she" and "he" rather than "I" in your sentences. Writing about events as an outside observer can help you gain perspective on an otherwise very personal experience.

◆ **Cathartic writing.** Write about your feelings, all of them. Put your pain, fear, anger, frustrations, and grief down on paper. Don't just write when you're feeling upset or sad—try it when you're feeling joy and gratitude, too. Begin with the phrase, "Right now I feel …" then let yourself write whatever comes out. If you run out of feelings, reread what you've just written and then write the next thing that comes to mind.

◆ **Unsent letters.** An unsent letter is a way to express your true feelings when you may not feel comfortable doing it more directly. This technique is especially helpful in dealing with death or divorce. These are situations in which you may not be able to talk with the person directly. Begin with a salutation, just as you would if you were writing a letter, "Dear …" Then let your pen and paper lead you. You may be surprised at the power and clarity that you experience from your writing. Your journal may be just a starting place for a whole new level of communication with others.

Playing Catch-Up

We started off this chapter looking at the evolution of our "fight-or-flight" response to emergencies. In some respects, our bodies have not caught up with the times. They're still using the same old emergency system that our ancestors used to fight off bears and defend their territory. Luckily for us, our brains have given us the ability to develop some nifty coping strategies to handle the stress in our lives. If we use them, we can help the evolution of our own body—that is, the aging process—go more smoothly.

The Least You Need to Know

◆ We feel stressed when we consider an event to be threatening and we aren't sure if we have the resources to cope with it. It is a normal response to overwhelming internal or external events.

◆ Common symptoms of stress include feeling irritable and on edge, overreacting to minor events, mood swings, and difficulty concentrating.

◆ While stress initially energizes the body to take action, over time it is physically exhausting and our immune system is weakened.

◆ We handle threatening situations by coping—either through changing the situation or by altering the ways we think and feel about it.

◆ Psychological difficulties can get channeled into physical symptoms; psychologists call these "somatization disorders."

Part 4

Self and Otherness

What is it that makes us feel as if we belong? And what makes us feel like outsiders? Each of us possesses a unique mix of personality traits, values, behavioral styles, and beliefs—a combination of elements that makes for the incredible diversity of humankind. Here's where you'll learn all about these building blocks of the individual personality, and about the factors that shape each of us as we experience our way through life. You'll learn what is meant by "intelligence" and how it's measured, and you'll explore the murky area between eccentricity and abnormal behavior.

Chapter 13

Me, Myself, and I

In This Chapter

- Discovering why we're *all* "material girls" (or guys)
- Understanding teenage angst and other postpubescent blues
- Getting in touch with your masculine and feminine sides
- Making your midlife crisis-free
- Seeing how far your gender bends
- Finding out what happens when identities get disturbed

Who are you? What are you? *How* are you? These are all aspects of a larger question: how is your identity formed?

In this chapter, we'll help you answer that question. We'll explore how people develop their self-concept, and straighten out that overused but frequently misunderstood thing called self-esteem. And last, but certainly not least, we'll talk about the ways we protect our good opinion of ourselves, and how we dissociate ourselves from bad experiences.

Gender and Selfhood

What if someone told you that you had to live the rest of your life as a member of the opposite sex? You'd still think of yourself as a man (or a woman) and have the same feelings and behaviors. Nothing about you would change, but from this day forward, the world would treat you as if you were of the opposite gender.

That's how Canadian Michelle Josef, born as Bohdan Hluszko, has felt all her life. Since the age of seven, Michelle thought of herself as a girl and was often mistaken for one. But Bohdan was biologically a boy. For years, he tried everything to cope with his ongoing sense of being a woman trapped in a man's body: drugs, therapy, marriage, and cross-dressing. Finally, he reached the end of his rope, called a friend, and said he was going to shoot himself.

> **Brain Buster** _____
>
> If you're female, get out there and play ball! Numerous studies show that girls who participate in competitive sports have higher self-esteem, score better on achievement tests, are more likely to attend college, and are less likely to get involved in drugs and alcohol.

That was the day Bohdan Hluszko died and Michelle Josef was born. Rescued from the brink of suicide, Michelle began years of psychotherapy and hormone treatments. She began living as a woman and is working toward sex-reassignment surgery. Bohdan/Michelle had a particularly difficult time figuring out who he/she was. After all, gender is the most fundamental characteristic of who we are. But it's not easy for many of us, either. And there are other important aspects of selfhood, beyond gender, that we need to consider.

Know Thyself

In ancient Greece, worshippers who wanted to know the future would consult the oracle at the Temple of Apollo in Delphi. At the Temple entrance, a stone inscription counseled visitors to "Know Thyself"—something psychologists counsel their clients about today. Apparently, good advice is timeless.

> **Insight** _____
>
> The only other animals beside ourselves who have passed the rouge test of self-recognition are the other great apes: chimpanzees, bonobos, orangutans, and at least one species of gorilla. Other animals continue to treat the mirror image as another animal and try to threaten or chase it away.

Self-awareness is one of the hallmarks of human nature, and it starts early. By about 15 months of age, infants understand that they are separate from other people and things in their lives. Around this time babies stop reacting to their image in a mirror as if it were another child and begin to see it as their own reflection. If a researcher places a bright red spot of rouge on an infant's nose while she's watching in a mirror, the 15-month-old responds by touching her own nose to feel or rub off the rouge. A younger child will touch the mirror or look behind it to find the funny-looking, red-nosed baby.

But Who Is Thyself?

Just who is the self and how do we know about it? If psychologist William James had known Madonna, he would have said she was right on when she sang about being a "material girl." James believed that we're all partly material girls or guys. In his view, the "material" self is an essential part of who we are; the other two parts are the social self and the spiritual self. Each of these is essential to the way we experience ourselves.

Our Toys "R" Us

For James, just about everything we came into contact with on a regular basis became part of our identity. For example, James believed that the "material me" is the part of the self that is concerned with the body and with material possessions. He wouldn't bat an eye at a car buff's need to wash and polish his new Jaguar every weekend. Why not? James would argue that the Jag is an extension of its owner's identity.

It's Who You Know

A second part of James's self, the "social me," revolves around our interactions and reputation with others. James believed that our relationships with other people were a strong part of our identity. If you got upset when someone hurt your feelings, your therapist might recommend that you read the book *Codependent No More*, but William James would say your feelings are perfectly normal. After all, when your family or friends are hurt, hasn't part of your "self" been threatened?

That's the Spirit!

The "spiritual me" is the one that holds your private thoughts and feelings. You don't have to go to church to get in touch with your spiritual side, but you do have to spend time alone getting to know yourself.

Reflections in a Looking Glass

Many years ago, sociologist Charles Cooley coined the phrase "looking-glass self" to describe the influence that others' opinions have on our self-concept, especially when we're young. He believed that we defined ourselves, in part, by what others "reflect" back in response to who we are and what we do. In Cooley's opinion, we use the inferences and images other people have of us to build our own self-concepts.

Mirror, Mirror on the Wall

If a child is treated lovingly, she believes she is lovable. If he is told he is handsome (and treated handsomely), he comes to believe that, too. To a child, the difference between being "good" and "bad" is not so much how he behaves, but how he is treated. What awesome power (and responsibility) grownups have!

The impact that your perceptions can have on a child's sense of self has been widely documented. Children really do live up to our expectations and opinions of them—for better or worse. The good news is that you can put your influence to good use. If you want a child to develop a certain quality, treating her as if that quality is already present can actually shape the child in that direction. Telling a child "you are" has a much greater impact than saying "you should be."

Reflections in a Golden Eye

Studies clearly illustrate that a child's self-concept changes in accordance with feedback from teachers and peers. In experiments where children were told they were a certain kind of person, they responded by behaving in a way that was consistent with this feedback. For example, one group of children was told they were neat and tidy, another was told they *should be* neat and tidy, and a third group was given no direction at all. Those who had been told they were neat and tidy became neater and tidier, while the others pretty much stayed the same.

Of course, most people aren't as easily manipulated as the children in this experiment. However, adults can be amazingly vulnerable to the whims and feedback of others if they haven't developed a strong sense of identity. If you don't know who you are, you may change your self-perceptions every time someone misperceives you; if your sense of self is strong, however, you're more likely to correct the misperceptions of others than to change your self-concept to fit them.

> **Brain Buster**
>
> Is your self-concept realistic? Here's a test to help you find out. Write down the top-10 adjectives that you believe most fully express who you are. Now, ask five of your closest friends or family members to do the same thing. (Make sure you're getting along with them when you ask.) How closely does your own description match up with the others'? Could you be wrong about yourself? Could your friends be wrong about you?

It's Like, You Know, a Teen Thing

Although our self-concept begins at birth, it's during the teen years that our identity really takes shape. According to psychologist Erik Erikson, between ages 12 and 18 we begin to discover who we are, and, as many parents know firsthand, who we don't want to be. In fact, much of adolescents' "rebellion" against parents and other authority figures is a healthy attempt to get some space and figure out the lay of the land for ourselves.

Adolescent Angst

While we often associate identity crises with midlife, Erikson believed that the first identity crisis happens in adolescence. This very necessary crisis involves discovering one's true identity among the many different roles we play for different audiences: parents, teachers, and friends.

In Erickson's opinion, resolving this crisis is both a uniquely personal process and a shared social experience. While teens are going through it, they're struggling to find themselves without losing the comfort of belonging with friends and family members. This can be a tough balance to achieve; 15 to 25 percent of adolescents report feeling very lonely as they search for the real "me" inside.

The Power of the Peer Group

Peers are especially important to a teen's identity formation. As teens move away from their parents, they spend less time at home and more time with peers. They also use peers to try out different social behaviors. One compromise between a teen's need for independence and desire for interdependence involves experimenting with different norms, such as clothing or hairstyle, within the security of a peer group, a clique, or a romantic partner.

Ironically, although new norms may establish a teen's separateness from the family, they simultaneously establish conformity with his or her peers. Teens who successfully navigate the new "rules" of cliquedom may have a heavy price to pay for their sense of belonging; teens rated as "popular" appear more likely to experiment with drugs and sex than their "average" peers—apparently in a desire to fit in and please everyone.

The Family Circle

Although a teenager's major source of approval and acceptance comes from the peer group, teens still rely on their families for structure and support. Teens spend a lot of time talking about their parents, even if that talk isn't very flattering. Trying to be different from your parents requires a lot of involvement and attention, because you have to consider what your parents are before you decide what you are not.

Going through an identity crisis can be painful at any age, and it's no fun for most teens. The rewards, however, are great. Teens who face identity issues head-on develop an identity that remains stable regardless of the setting or the social group in which they find themselves. They have a clearer sense of who they are and they're better able to make independent decisions and choices about their career, relationships, and life in general.

In Defense of the Midlife Identity Crisis

Surviving adolescence gives most of us a couple of peaceful decades before the next identity crisis hits. This is the one you've surely heard about: your friend turns 40, ditches her vice-presidency and six-figure salary, and buys a cabin in the backwoods of Montana. Or the straight-laced accountant suddenly starts wearing leather and espousing new age mysticism. The stable family man buys a red Porsche and finds a girlfriend half his age.

But is it real? Studies say yes, but not as often as we think. Only one in 10 midlifers goes through a true crisis, where their world suddenly turns upside down and they consider radically changing their lifestyle. However, many are likely to experience a midlife review of their accomplishments and make some adjustments to their expectations and goals.

> **Insight**
>
> Charles Dickens referred to a character in his 40s as a "dear old man," but baby boomers think midlife begins at 50. So you may still have a midlife crisis—just a decade or so after the age your parents had theirs!

When mortality rears its threatening head, many people find themselves thinking about spirituality as well as the legacy they'd like to leave behind. In fact, a midlife review may be the process by which people not only evaluate the first half of their lives, but also figure out the pleasures of the second.

Getting Older *and* Better?

For years, it was assumed that our personalities were pretty much formed by early adulthood. But more recent research suggests otherwise. And on the whole, the changes our personalities go through are good ones.

In our 20s, we're likely to become more conscientious, which helps us be more organized and committed at work. In our 30s, our relationships may blossom as we become more agreeable. We females, in particular, age as well as the finest wine; as we get older, we worry less and our moods level out. Sorry, guys; research suggests that unless you take some active steps to change, a worrier at age 20 will be a worrier at age 40.

Avoiding the Comparison Trap

You're ready for a night on the town. For once, when you look in the mirror, you feel pretty satisfied with what you see. Until you step out of your apartment. There, waiting in line for the elevator, is the clear winner of the Supermodel look-alike contest. Suddenly, you feel like running back into the apartment and pulling the covers over your head until the next eclipse of the moon.

Keeping Up with the Joneses

For better or worse, we all compare ourselves to the people around us. This cursed tendency probably has its origins in Cooley's "looking-glass self." While we're busy building models of ourselves from the feedback others give us, part of that work is comparing our models of ourselves to the models we observe of other people. As we grow older, this comparison becomes an internal frame of reference through which we see ourselves.

The evaluation part of such a *social comparison* can be very emotional. You feel good when you think you measure up to others, and bad when you don't. Some people might argue that every adjective we use to describe ourselves is secretly a comparison. If I describe myself as "tall," the implicit question is "tall in comparison to whom?" The answer to that question depends upon who is your *reference group*.

> **Insight**
>
> There's a difference between healthy self-esteem and narcissism. If your new beau tends to consistently think he's more attractive, smarter, and more unique than others, consider this a "red flag." Research shows that he is more likely to avoid intimacy, play emotional games, and cheat on you.

Referentially Speaking

The reference group is any group you use for social comparison. At work, it might be your coworkers or, if you have a competitive streak, your boss. For teenagers, it's almost always their peers. Sometimes a shift in your sense of self-worth can occur with a new job or a move to a new school; such a move entails a change of reference group that can have a dramatic impact on your self-esteem.

Beautiful teenage girls often see themselves as ugly, and the more often they read fashion magazines, the more likely they are to do so. Girls who compare themselves with airbrushed supermodels are bound to feel bad about themselves because they are comparing themselves to a fantasy reference group. Even the models themselves don't look like that when they wake up in the morning, so how can any normal teen hope to do so?

Hello, Your High Esteemness!

The number-one, most popular psychology buzzword today is *self-esteem*. I've heard the low self-esteem "diagnosis" used to explain everything from a car that won't run to a boyfriend who won't commit. Low self-esteem, it seems, is either a worldwide epidemic or a popular excuse for bratty behavior—maybe both!

Self-esteem is a particular way of experiencing the self. While we most frequently think of it as a feeling ("I don't feel good about myself," or "I need to feel better about myself"), it is much more. It is a way of thinking and acting and feeling. For example, self-esteem is your tendency to experience yourself as being capable of coping with life's challenges and of being worthy of happiness and love. The two components most often linked to self-esteem are self-confidence and self-respect.

Self-esteem is not the same as being conceited or having a "big ego." In fact, people you might call vain or selfish generally have low self-esteem. Here are a few other myths and realities of this important, but misunderstood, concept:

Myth: If your self-esteem is too high, you will be self-absorbed and selfish.

Reality: It is impossible to have too much self-esteem. Self-absorption comes from not having enough self-esteem.

Myth: If you want to raise your child's self-esteem, praise her for whatever she does.

Reality: Children quickly realize when parents' praise is not based on their efforts or accomplishments. Too much praise can feel like "pressure"; and unconditional praise (which is different than unconditional love) isn't credible. It can actually *lower* a child's self-concept.

Myth: If you want to solve your problems, raise your self-esteem.

Reality: The myth has it backward. Self-esteem is often raised by meeting your problems head-on and treating yourself with respect.

Myth: Your self-esteem is determined by your childhood.

Reality: Self-esteem is something that can be raised or lowered at any point in life. Your parents can give you a boost, or throw you some curveballs, as can your peers, teachers, and others.

Myth: If you have good self-esteem, nothing bothers you.

Reality: Struggle is a part of life, and sooner or later we all feel anxiety and sadness, and go through tough times. Self-esteem won't protect you from pain, but it can help you bounce back faster and help you believe that you'll make it through.

> **Insight**
>
> In mid- and later life, self-esteem and happiness don't always go together; we can be happy even if our self-esteem isn't up to par. Happy low self-esteemers are those who are more extro-verted, satisfied with their leisure time, have a sense of purpose, and are in good health. In con-trast, unhappy midlifers with high self-esteem aren't satisfied with their accomplishments; they know they've had "what it takes" but are dissatisfied with how they've used it.

"High self-esteem" is something you earn; it is an active process of treating yourself (and others) well, and replacing negative or self-critical thoughts with acceptance and realism. The good feelings you associate with self-esteem are often the result of hard work. Luckily, you have some built-in mechanisms that protect your self-esteem from your own misdeeds as well as your daily trials and tribulations. One of the most fasci-nating mechanisms is the self-serving bias—a tendency to accept credit when things turn out well, and to blame the situation or other people when things go badly.

Safeguarding Self-Esteem

You consider yourself a principled, loyal person who would never cheat on your spouse or loved one. Yet, at a recent work conference, you gave in to temptation and hit the sack with a colleague. Now what do you do?

Chances are, the first thing you'd do is try to get rid of the emotional turmoil your actions have created. We're uncomfortable when our actions don't match our self-perceptions, beliefs, and values. According to cognitive theorist Leon Festinger, we experience an internal tension he calls *cognitive dissonance*.

Festinger's theory of cognitive dissonance says that we all have a strong need to per-ceive a consistency between our thoughts, words, actions, and values. When we do something we think we "shouldn't" have, we search for some viable explanation that will make our emotional discomfort go away.

def•i•ni•tion

Cognitive dissonance is the inner conflict we experience when we do something that is counter to our prior values, beliefs, and feelings. To reduce our tension, we either change our beliefs or explain away our actions.

Cognitive dissonance motivates us to try to rationalize our contradictory behaviors so that they seem to follow naturally from personal beliefs and attitudes. For your conference fling, you might try denial ("It wasn't really sex"), or you might revise your attitudes to make them fit your actions ("As long as my spouse doesn't find out, no harm was done" or "I'll make it up to him in some way"). You then might internalize your attitude to make acceptable what otherwise appears to be irrational or wrong.

To some extent, this self-justification is the gentle art of verbal self-persuasion. You're actively using your communication skills to convince yourself that your actions were justified—or at least understandable. If this sounds like plain old excuse-making to you, it is—except that you're making convincing excuses to yourself!

Sex Roles and Designated Gender Drivers

When did pink and blue become the designated drivers of our gender identity? Why wasn't it yellow or green? I know women who hate pink for what it implies (and some who love it for the same reason). Even today, with more gender equality, we have trouble giving up our stereotypes. The helpful clerk in the toy store asks if you're buying for a girl or a boy. Unisex clothing is blurring the gender lines a bit, but there is still that holdover for "frilly" versus "rugged."

Insight

The issue of political correctness may have some merit, after all. Research suggests that referring to doctors, college professors, bankers, and executives by the generic "he" may contribute to the gender stereotyping of these professions as appropriate for men, but not for women. Peer pressure at its worst!

Puppy Dogs' Tails or Sugar and Spice?

One reason we may never settle the nature-nurture debate of male-female differences is that parents begin interacting differently from birth depending on the sex of the child. Parents tend to focus on different behaviors and interpret the same behavior differently. If you follow traditional thinking, you are much more likely to believe that your bawling six-month-old boy is angry but that your squalling six-month-old daughter is sad or afraid. Such gender imprinting shapes our identities from birth.

Insight

Forget Mars and Venus—we're both from Earth! While the popular media plays up men and women as psychologically different as two planets, a 2005 review of 46 studies found that these differences are vastly overestimated and that men and women are more similar in personality, communication, cognitive ability, and leadership than we've ever realized.

Gender, Worth, and Self-Worth

In many cultures there is great celebration at the arrival of a new son, while plans for the daughter include selling her off in marriage for a good price. Already in China, the "one-child" policy has resulted in many Chinese couples giving girls up for adoption in order to be able to have (and keep) a boy. But if this continues, who will all the boys in a generation marry? Imagine what these practices do to a girl's self-esteem from day one.

Gender is a fundamental part of your self-concept. From birth, a boy and a girl will have a dramatically different experience—just because they are of different sexes. And gender does more than shape who we are. It can have a profound influence on what we, and others, think we're worth. Luckily, gender identity is much more complicated than mere biological sex. And it's this fact that can even the odds for women.

Call It Gender, Not Sex

Your gender identity is your personal sense of maleness or femaleness, and it isn't fully established until you're about three years old. Until that age, gender reassignments can occur fairly easily; after that, children think of themselves as either permanently male or permanently female. Although your genes determine your sex, your gender identity may be like language—easily acquired, but only in a critical "window" during early childhood.

Your gender identity is much more complicated than your sexual identity—it's your total pattern of traits, tastes, and interests. In the past, masculinity and femininity were thought to be polar opposites (pink or blue, passive or aggressive). Men were thought to have instrumental qualities (to take action), and women were believed to have expressive qualities (nurturant, gentleness). There were often dire consequences for failing to conform to these gender norms.

Insight

Our sexual orientation (homosexual, bisexual, or heterosexual) is very resistant to change. Our sexual preferences (what turns us on) are more fluid. They generally develop in early adolescence; for boys, they are often wrapped around first sexual experiences and masturbation fantasies. Research shows that girls are more likely to get turned on by scenarios involving plot lines, intimacy, and characters. So, boys, get that erotic music playing and those fire logs burning.

There were two major forces in the twentieth century that spurred women to challenge traditional gender roles. Oddly enough, the first was World War II. Suddenly, traditionally "weak" women were operating heavy machinery, dealing with blood-and-guts injuries, and flying cargo planes. When the war ended, women were supposed to go back to their traditional roles, but many did not.

Next came the birth control pill. Women were freed to choose the number of children they had, and therefore could enter the workforce in greater numbers. Voilà! They got in touch with their "masculine side," and proved that sex roles could be transformed.

Gender Bending

Do you consider yourself feminine, masculine, or somewhere in between? How do you think others see you? What are your earliest memories of being aware that you were a boy or a girl? The answers to all of these questions provide clues about your gender identity.

Not so long ago, many people (including a fair number of psychologists) assumed that the "proper" personality for a man did not include nurturant behavior, and that women should be compliant and nurturing and essentially passive. In fact, if you asked a man if he was in touch with his feminine side he might have punched your lights out!

We now know that women who get in touch with their masculine side, and men who discover the "woman" within, are better off for doing so. Men and women with androgynous personalities are far more successful (and happier) than are people with stereotypically masculine and feminine personalities.

Meet Mr. and Ms. Androgyny

The androgynous personality incorporates both the positive feminine or expressive qualities of nurturing, kindness, and an ability to listen to others, with the positive qualities stereotypically associated with masculinity—such as self-assurance, decisiveness, and leadership ability.

It's a widespread phenomenon these days. We see it with the melding of roles in two-income families. Men travel around with baby carriers on their backs, or pushing strollers, and doing grocery shopping with the toddler sitting in the cart. And these men don't look any less masculine to me (and their wives look a whole lot happier). Another sign of progress is the increasing opportunity for women to play team sports; anyone watching the U.S. women's soccer team win the World Cup got a firsthand glimpse of female competitiveness and power.

> **Insight**
>
> Your definition of what is "masculine" and "feminine" depends largely on the culture you are reared in. While North American men are taught to shake hands or playfully "knock each other around" to show affection, in Thailand it is considered "masculine" for men to walk down the street holding hands; in Russia, men often kiss each other in greeting.

In other words, anyone can have the tastes, abilities, and temperaments of both a male and a female. The androgynous person has a healthy mix of masculine and feminine qualities—the best of both worlds.

Do you? See how androgynous you are. Rate the traits in the three columns with the number that best fits you according to the following scale, and see if your world needs to be expanded.

1 = never true

2 = rarely true

3 = sometimes true

4 = often true

5 = always or almost always true

Column 1	Column 2	Column 3
Loyal	Moody	Act as a leader
Cheerful	Happy	Forceful
Compassionate	Secretive	Assertive
Warm	Reliable	Independent
Shy	Tactful	Willing to take risks

Scoring: Add up your scores in each column. In column 1 are stereotypically feminine traits, in column 2 are neutral traits, and in column 3 are stereotypically masculine traits. Subtract column 1 from column 3; the higher the score, the more "masculine" you are; the lower the score (including negative numbers), the more feminine you are. The neutral column is neither stereotypically masculine nor feminine; it is there as a "control" to prevent expectations about which adjectives are masculine or feminine from completely dominating your scores.

The Big-Time Gender Blues

Remember Bohdan/Michelle at the beginning of the chapter? He/she is a transsexual, a condition technically referred to as *gender dysphoria.* While we don't know the exact prevalence of gender dysphoria, 1 out of every 30,000 males and 1 out of every 100,000 females seeks sex reassignment surgery in the United States, and each one has the biological makeup of one sex but the psychological makeup of the other. The transsexual truly feels trapped inside the wrong body.

Boys with gender dysphoria are typically preoccupied with traditionally feminine activities. They may prefer dressing in girls' or women's clothing or may improvise such items from available materials when clothes aren't available. They show a strong attraction for the stereotypical games and pastimes of girls, may express a strong wish to be a girl, and, when young, may express the belief that they will grow up to be a woman. Girls with gender dysphoria display intensely negative reactions to parental expectations or attempts to have them wear dresses or other feminine attire, have powerful male figures as fantasy heroes, and may dress and act like boys.

> **Psychobabble**
>
> More than one parent has sent a child to "reparative" or "conversion" therapy, a controversial treatment that attempts to convince someone to change his or her sexual orientation. There is no scientific evidence supporting this therapy and, in fact, according to the American Psychological Association, it can cause depression, anxiety, and self-destructive behavior.

Children do not "grow out of" gender dysphoria. Oftentimes, they become socially isolated and, like Bohdan/Michelle, spend years trying to come to terms with their gender dysphoria and confusion. Sex-change surgery, considered the best treatment for those who qualify, is a gradual and strict process. The individual must live as the other gender for one to two years before surgery, undergo a rigorous battery of psychological tests, and undergo a lot of hormone replacement treatment before the final decision is made. Although only a handful of patients qualify for sex-reassignment surgery each year, most transsexuals are much happier with their new lives.

Sacrificing Identity to Escape Pain

Your identity is, fundamentally, who you are. From birth, you struggle to define the boundaries between yourself and the people around you. You develop a sense of your gender, and work hard to decide what it will say about who you are. And you use built-in strategies to protect your "self" from your own behavioral errors and to buffer you from hurtful feedback from others. In short, you work hard to build, and then protect, your identity.

If your emotional pain is great enough, however, you might sacrifice parts of who you are to get away from the hurt you feel. This is what happens with *dissociative disorders*. A dissociative disorder is a psychological disorder characterized by a disturbance in the integration of identity, memory, or consciousness; some aspect of the person's personality seems separated from the rest.

In other words, people with these disorders escape from their conflicts by giving up parts of themselves, sacrificing a consistent and continuous identity to get away from intense psychic pain. Dissociative disorders are involuntary psychic tradeoffs. Let's take a look at three of them:

- Psychogenic amnesia
- Dissociative fugue states
- Depersonalization

Dissociative (Psychogenic) Amnesia

Psychogenic amnesia is a psychological disorder in which a person loses the memory of important (usually stressful or traumatic) personal experiences for no apparent physical reason. For example, an uninjured driver in a serious car crash in which a friend was killed may not recall anything that happened from the time of the accident until a few days later. Understandably, in that tragic situation, the psyche may decide that it's worth losing a few days of one's identity to avoid the pain of remembering such a sad experience.

Dissociative Fugue States

The fugue state is a fascinating and rare phenomenon in which someone suddenly leaves home but doesn't remember how or why, loses his or her identity, and sometimes actually develops a new identity. Often, the person's new identity contrasts sharply with his or her original identity. For example, a timid man might turn into a fast-talking hustler. While soap opera plots may try to convince you otherwise, most fugue states involve brief, apparently purposeful travel with only partial construction of a new identity. In fact, about half of all fugues last less than 24 hours.

Psychobabble
In 1980, a woman dubbed "Jane Doe" was found wandering in a park in Florida. She was emaciated and near death, and she had no memory of her name or her past. She even lacked the ability to read and write. After a national search, an Illinois couple recognized Jane Doe as their daughter. This girl had moved to Florida four years earlier and not contacted them again. They were confident that she was their daughter, but Jane Doe was never able to remember her past or what had happened to her.

Depersonalization

Ever feel like you're walking around in a dream? If you suffered from depersonalization you'd feel like that a lot. Depersonalization disorder is characterized by an ongoing and persistent sense of feeling detached from yourself. It's as if there's an invisible wall or shield that is between you and your feelings, thoughts, and experiences. "I feel like a robot walking around," or, "I feel like I'm just observing myself" are common complaints. Extreme stress can bring this feeling on for all of us, but for the clinically depersonalized individual, this is an ongoing, distressing part of everyday life.

Dissociative disorders are identity disorders; they disrupt our ongoing and stable sense of who we are and they break up our integration of thoughts, feelings, and behaviors. You've probably noticed, however, that I haven't mentioned the most famous dissociative disorder of them all—multiple personality disorder. Don't worry, we'll discuss it at length in Chapter 14.

Playing the Odds: Integrating Dissociative Disorders

So what's the best treatment for dissociative disorders? To some extent, the jury is still out. There are still no established practice guidelines for treating dissociative disorders.

Psychotherapy is the primary treatment, and often involves techniques that help the client remember and work through the trauma that triggered the dissociative symptoms. Creative-art therapy, including music, poetry, drama, art, and dance, can help clients who have difficulty expressing thoughts and feelings, while cognitive strategies can help the client gain mental mastery over traumatic events and undo negative or unhealthy ways of thinking. Bibliotherapy (learning about the disorders through read-ing) and graphotherapy (journaling or keeping a diary) are often recommended. Other possible treatments are hypnosis, relaxation, and behavior modification.

Medications don't seem to help with the dissociative symptoms, but because anxiety and depression often co-exist with dissociative disorders, medications can help with mood regulation. Helpful drugs can include antidepressants, benzodiazapines (anti-anxiety meds), and, occasionally, low doses of neuroleptics (usually used in psychotic disorders).

The Days of All Our Lives

When you think about it, you'll see that we're *all* multiples, in a way. I am a mother, a daughter, a sister, a writer, a psychologist, a friend, and a wife, and who "I" am differs a little in each role. I interact differently with my children than I do with my close friends.

If the raw material for self-understanding lies in our relationships, it seems like we have a tough row to hoe. I mean, how can we develop a stable self-concept when we play such different roles with such unique people? And, indeed, with all the different traits and attitudes that various roles require, to some extent we all develop multiple personalities.

The Many Faces of Me

Research has shown that you don't just have one self-concept—you have many, de-pending upon the social role in which you are engaged. Ask me what kind of mother I am, and I will say "playful, loving, and a student in the art of patience." As a writer, I define myself as "committed, passionate, and outspoken." In some respects, then, self-concept is like a spider web; some self-perceived traits are attached to specific roles (the knots in the web), whereas others are attached to several roles. These are the strands that tie our identities together.

You might think that juggling multiple self-concepts would be psychologically stress-ful. But the reverse is actually true. Having multiple roles seems to keep us from put-ting all of our emotional eggs in one basket. Having multiple roles and lots of traits provides a buffer against becoming depressed when one role is lost or diminished in importance. For example, when a woman's only role is the care of her family, then when the kids leave home she feels she has lost her identity and suffers what is known as the "empty nest syndrome." Role jugglers of the world, unite!

As you've seen throughout this chapter, self-concept gets set pretty early in life. While our identities are formed in our teen years, our self-esteem, and ability to play many roles, continues to evolve. By the time we're all grown up, most of us have a good idea of who we are. In the next chapter, we'll take a close look at a trait that, in the United States, has a lot of influence over our sense of identity—intelligence. You'll find out how smart human beings really are as we explore intelligent life (on this planet).

Brain Buster

Celebrate your ethnic heritage—it's good for you! Studies show that black children from home environments rich in African American culture had greater factual knowledge and better problem-solving skills—a finding that held true even when the researchers took family income into account. Also, racial pride was associated with fewer behavioral problems.

The Least You Need to Know

♦ We develop our self-concept, beginning at about age 15 months, by relating to the world and internalizing feedback from the people around us.

♦ Self-esteem has a lot to do with self-worth and self-respect. We can grow it by changing our attitudes and behaviors.

♦ Our gender has a strong influence on our identity formation. If we can develop both our masculine and our feminine traits, we're likely to be happier.

♦ A transsexual has the psychological identity of one sex and the body of the other.

♦ Dissociative disorders involve a disturbance in identity, memory, or consciousness. Treatment often centers around integrating these "split" parts of oneself.

♦ We all have multiple roles to play in our lifetime, and the more we have, the happier we'll be.

He's Got ... Personality!

In This Chapter

- ◆ How stable *are* you, really?
- ◆ Unlocking the secrets of your personality
- ◆ Why Minnesota is the personality state
- ◆ Discovering the state your traits are in
- ◆ Spotting the "sick" personality

Like many nurses in the early 1900s, Margaret Sanger saw some harsh realities. She watched countless women, desperate to avoid having yet another mouth to feed, die from illegal abortions. Unlike other nurses, Margaret Sanger decided to find an answer to her patients' pleas for safe contraception no matter what the cost. She left nursing and put her husband and three children in the background—and ultimately changed women's lives forever.

For 40 years, Margaret Sanger challenged the laws that made contraception a criminal act, insisting that women take control of, and responsibility for, their sexuality and childbearing. She lost her husband and was jailed several times for illegally distributing information about birth control. And she won! In 1960, the U.S. Food and Drug Administration approved the "pill," a contraceptive that Sanger co-sponsored.

What drove Sanger in her crusade? What personality qualities empowered her to endure such personal sacrifice and punishment? In this chapter, you'll find out what made Margaret Sanger the person she was—and what makes you the person you are. We'll explore all the ingredients that go into personalities, and how much depends upon genes, hormones, environment, or birth order. You'll see how psychologists test personalities, and how stable our personalities really are. And you'll learn the difference between an offbeat personality and a serious personality disorder.

Finding the Person in Personality

Are you fun-loving? Patient? Shy? When we describe ourselves, we tend to think of certain traits or qualities that have been around for a long time and hold true in a number of circumstances. For example, if you describe yourself as "patient," you might be remembering how you interact with your children, how you generally listen to others without interrupting them, and how you stick with a difficult task until it's finished.

def•i•ni•tion

Personality is the unique bundle of all the psychological qualities that consistently influence an individual's behavior across situations and time.

In the study of personality, psychologists try to study how individuals differ from each other yet are the same within themselves. They tend to focus on two qualities: uniqueness and consistency. *Personality* is the sum of all the unique psychological qualities that influence an individual's behavior across situations and time. Someone who is shy may blush easily, avoid parties, and wait for other people to take the initiative in conversation. On the other hand, a person who is reticent about public speaking but is the life of the party in other situations wouldn't be classified as having a shy personality.

Understanding personality traits gives us a sense of who we are, and it helps us (to some degree) predict the behavior of the people around us. And, through personality testing, it gives psychologists an x-ray of our psyches.

X-rays of the Psyche

Personality tests don't measure *how much* personality you have but rather *what kind.* There are two kinds of personality tests: objective and projective. Objective personality tests are paper-and-pencil "self-report" tests with true-or-false questions. You answer questions about your thoughts, feelings, and actions by checking *true* if the statement is generally or mostly true, and checking *false* if it is false most of the time. Projective tests, including the well-known "inkblots," are more subjective—they're subject to interpretation by the person giving them.

Personality testing scares a lot of people because they misunderstand what it can and can't do. First of all, personality testing is more like taking an x-ray than looking into a crystal ball: the results can suggest what's wrong, but they can't tell you how it got broken or to what extent it's affecting your life. The same test results that indicate antisocial behavior might show up in a politician *and* in a convicted felon!

Second, personality test results are practically useless when taken out of context. They must always be evaluated in terms of the test subject's current life situation. Someone who is usually reticent may become very effusive if she just won the lottery. And a person who's just lost a loved one might look seriously depressed on a personality test when, in fact, he or she is just experiencing the normal throes of grief.

I found this out the hard way when, as a psychology graduate student, I was blindly given the Rorschach inkblot test as part of my personality assessment class. What did I see in those inkblots? Well, let's just say I saw quite a few teddy bears. Imagine my humiliation when my professor casually commented that "seeing" furry animals suggested that someone was excessively needy! Okay, I had just broken up with the love of my life and moved 500 miles away from home!

> **Insight**
>
> People who score as extroverts on personality questionnaires choose to live and work with more people, prefer a wider range of sexual activities, and talk more in group meetings, when compared to introverted personalities.

Minnesota, the Personality State

Maybe Minnesota needs to consider changing their license plates to reflect their fame in psychology circles: the most popular objective personality test was developed at the University of Minnesota.

The Minnesota Multiphasic Personality Inventory, or MMPI, first appeared in the 1940s. It originally consisted of more than 500 true-and-false questions that asked about a person's mood, physical symptoms, current functioning, and a whole lot more. In the late 1980s, the original version underwent a significant revision (MMPI-2) because some questions were deemed inappropriate, politically insensitive, or outdated.

The MMPI-2 has 10 *clinical* scales, each designed to tell the difference between a special clinical group (like people suffering from major depression) and a normal group. These scales measure problems like paranoia, schizophrenia, depression, and antisocial personality traits. The higher a person scores on a clinical scale, the more likely it is that he or she belongs in the clinical group.

Brain Buster

Let's say you want to take a vacation from work and think that "depression" might be a good excuse for a little R-and-R. If you answer yes to every "depression" question on the MMPI-2, you'd certainly look depressed. In fact, you'd look so depressed that the results would indicate that you're exaggerating (or outright lying) about your level of emotional distress!

The MMPI-2 also has 15 *content* scales. These measure various mental health problems that aren't, in and of themselves, diagnosable psychiatric disorders. Some of the content scales measure low self-esteem, anger, family problems, and workaholism, among other problems. Low self-esteem is not a clinical diagnosis, but it certainly contributes to a number of psychological disorders, such as depression and anxiety (discussed in Chapter 19). The job of the content scales is to pinpoint specific problems that either contribute to, or put someone at risk for, a full-blown psychological disorder.

Can You Pull the Wool over Your Psychologist's Eyes?

Since objective tests like the MMPI-2 are self-reporting, you might think they'd be easy to fake. If, for example, you were faced with the choice of either going directly to jail or looking "crazy" and staying out, surely you'd fake the results, right? Well, you could, but the odds are you'll get caught!

That's because the MMPI-2 has built-in "lie detectors." Psychologists weren't born yesterday! The tests have safeguards that detect lying, carelessness, defensiveness, and evasiveness. So while you're free to answer "true" or "false" however you please, it's almost impossible to convince the test that you're answering honestly if you're not.

Projecting Your Personality

It'd be even harder to fake a projective test like the Rorschach, because there are thousands of possible answers. How could you know what answer would give the results you wanted? And even if you tried to second-guess the test, the answers you gave would still provide valuable clues about your true personality.

Projective personality tests are based on the theory that your inner feelings, motives, and conflicts color your perception of the world. The less structured your world, the more likely your psyche will spill over onto what you see. This is what happens when you look at clouds. The next time you're outside with a friend, look at the sky and tell each other what you see. You might see a dancing clown while your friend spies a rocket
poised for blastoff. Both of you are right—the
cloud shapes are ambiguous and open to several
interpretations.

In some respects, you and your friend have just
participated in a projective "test." You have
both used your senses and personalities to make
meaning out of relatively shapeless clouds.
Psychologists rely on this same process when
they give you those famous ink blots known as
Rorschach cards.

> **Psychobabble**
>
> Want a partner who'll be faithful and stay away from the booze? Rate your mate! Go to www.members.aol.com/HOON4VR/personality.html for a virtual bonanza of personality quizzes. Hint: You've struck gold if he or she scores high on the conscientious scale.

Ink Blots of the Mind

The Rorschach was developed by Swiss psychiatrist Hermann Rorschach (pronounced *raw-shock*). While working with teenagers in a psychiatric hospital, Hermann watched them playing a popular game called "Blotto." Certain children, he observed, gave different answers to questions posed by the game, and he surmised that these different answers might provide clues into the minds, and personalities, of the players. Using this premise, he fooled around with a bunch of ink blots, and published the Rorschach in 1921.

When you take the Rorschach test, the examiner gives you 10 cards, each with an inkblot on it, and asks you to describe what you see. You will be assured that there are no right or wrong answers and, if you're like most people, you will immediately think the examiner is pulling the wool over your eyes.

Such skepticism is partially valid—yes, there technically *are* "wrong" answers to the Rorschach (and no, I'm not going to tell you what they are!). However, there are literally hundreds of *right* answers, and a tremendous amount of room for creative responses as well, so your examiner is not pulling the wool over your eyes too much.

Is Your Personality Stable?

When I wrote the first edition of this book in 1999, personality research showed that most of us have remarkably stable personalities—that is, that the tennis buddy you partnered with in high school is likely to be the same funny free-spirit at your 25-year high school reunion.

However, as noted in Chapter 13, new studies have found that our personalities continue to change long after we reach age 30. Of course, the way we know if our personalities are stable or not is by measuring them. Some personality tests do a pretty good job at describing the individual qualities that make each of us unique. And while they're not perfect at predicting a person's behavior, the tests are certainly better than chance.

The Theories Behind the Tests

Odds are, you're already a seasoned personality theorist. I bet you choose your relationships based on a personal theory about what personalities make good friends, how you can tell who is untrustworthy, and what qualities would make a person a good role model. We all naturally assume that certain personality characteristics will lead to certain behaviors, and we try to associate with people who will do things that make us happy (and vice versa). In other words, every single one of us is a personality theorist.

Through observations, interviews, biographical information, and life events, researchers in personality theory have developed beliefs about the structure and functioning of individual personalities. Their goal is to understand the personality and to predict what a person will do based upon what is already known about him. The tricky part is in separating out the *traits* from the *states*; in other words, figuring out if people act in a certain way because of who they are or in response to a sticky situation in which they've landed.

def•i•ni•tion

A **trait** is a stable characteristic that influences your thoughts, feelings, and behavior. A **state** is a temporary emotional condition.

What State Are Your Traits In?

From a psychologist's point of view, a personality trait is a relatively stable tendency to act in a certain way. Generosity, shyness, aggressiveness—these are all examples of traits. Traits are considered to be ongoing parts of the person, not the environment; they follow us wherever we go.

That's not to say that the situation, for better or worse, doesn't influence your expression of the traits you have. Let's say you're hot-tempered by nature. If someone runs into your car in a parking lot, you're more likely to fight or yell than someone who doesn't have as much built-in aggression. However, in many other situations, such as sitting in a classroom, you'd probably be much less likely to get into a screaming match, even though you still have an aggressive temperament. For a hot-blooded temperament, then, the environment provides the spark that sets it afire.

When psychologists are trying to figure out personalities, a psychological state can throw a monkey wrench into the works. Unlike traits, states are temporary conditions. Hunger, for example, is a state; it can be powerful when it's there, but it goes away after we eat.

Often, our emotional responses to situations are temporary states and when we get away from the situation, or when circumstances change, our feelings do, too. If someone comes to therapy complaining of depression, a psychologist has to figure out whether that person is in a state of sadness or has a depressive personality trait. And, of course, there's some relationship between the two—an aggressive personality trait will lead to more angry states!

Psychologist Walter Mischel thinks there may be a "happy medium" between states and traits, which he calls situation-specific dispositions. He believes that people are likely to be highly consistent over time in response to the same situation, but that their behavior may not generalize across settings. For example, if you were a cheater on tests in high school, chances are that you'll also cheat on tests in graduate school. This doesn't necessarily mean, though, that you'd cheat on your taxes or on your spouse.

Allport's Search for Personality

The jury is still out on exactly how many personality traits we really have. If you checked the dictionary, you would find over 18,000 adjectives that could describe our characteristics! Psychologist Gordon Allport considered personality traits to be the building blocks of an individual's overall personality. He also thought that some traits were big building blocks, some were medium-size, and some were smaller. These three different-size blocks represented the varying degrees of influence that the trait had on a person's life.

According to Allport, a cardinal trait is a single giant-size trait around which someone organizes his or her life. Martin Luther King Jr. may have organized his life around social consciousness, seeking to improve the quality of life for African Americans. Not everyone has a cardinal trait.

The building blocks of personality.

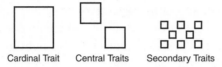

Cardinal Trait   Central Traits   Secondary Traits

A central trait represents a major characteristic of a person, such as honesty or optimism. Surely Gloria Steinem's outspokenness is a central trait that enables her to withstand criticism and controversy and speak before large audiences about women's rights. People can have more than one central trait.

A secondary trait is an enduring personality trait, but it doesn't explain general behavioral patterns. Personal styles (being a "sporty" dresser) and preferences (I like tall, blue-eyed men) might be examples of secondary traits. We all have a lot of secondary traits.

Apparently, patience was a central (if not cardinal) trait in Gordon Allport's personality—he spent his entire career working to make sense of personality traits. He began by boiling down all of the dictionary's 18,000 personality-related adjectives into 200 clusters of synonyms (groupings like easygoing, lighthearted, and carefree), and then formed two-ended trait dimensions. For example, on one such dimension, "responsible" might be at one end, and "irresponsible" would be at the other. In our daily lives, all of us would fall somewhere on the continuum between these two adjectives.

After having countless people rate themselves on these 200 dimensions, Allport looked at the relationships between the synonyms. To his astonishment, he found there were only five basic characteristics underlying all of the adjectives that people used to describe themselves. These became known as the "Big Five" dimensions of human personality—the five categories into which Allport organized all of our traits and behaviors. To help remember them, think of the acronym *OCEAN*:

- **Openness to experiences.** At one end would be individuals who are creative, intellectual, and open-minded versus people who are shallow, simple, and less intelligent.

- **Conscientiousness.** Here would be organized, responsible, and cautious persons as opposed to those who are irresponsible, careless, and frivolous.

◆ **Extroversion.** These people are assertive, outgoing, and energetic rather than quiet, reserved, and shy.

◆ **Agreeableness.** Here individuals who are sympathetic, kind, and affectionate are contrasted with those who are cold, argumentative, and cruel.

◆ **Neuroticism.** Here we contrast an anxious, unstable, and moody personality with one that is emotionally stable, calm, and content.

The Eysenck Alternative

Another psychologist, Professor Hans Eysenck of the University of London, used some different numbers to measure personality. On the basis of his research, he came to believe that there were 21 personality traits that were consistent with three major dimensions of personality. If you ever take his personality assessment, the Eysenck Personality Profiler, your scores will fit into three categories:

◆ **Extraversion.** Measures traits including activity level, sociability, expressiveness, assertiveness, ambition, dogmatism, and aggressiveness.

◆ **Neuroticism.** Measures traits like inferiority, unhappiness, anxiety, dependence, hypochondria, guilt, and obsessiveness.

◆ **Psychoticism.** Measures traits such as risk-taking, impulsivity, irresponsibility, manipulativeness, sensation-seeking, tough-mindedness, and practicality.

Insight

Did you have a favorite blanket or stuffed animal growing up? Object relations theorists would call this your "transitional object" and would interpret this as a symbol of comfort and security as a baby begins to emotionally separate from his or her parents and starts realizing that ultimately he or she will have to face this big bad world alone.

You've probably noticed some overlap in the two personality theories we've discussed. Each emphasizes the ability to get along with others, general emotional adjustment, and flexibility and open-mindedness as key parts of a person's personality. But how do people become more open-minded or outgoing? Are we born with pizzazz or do we have to go to charm school to get it?

The Personalities Behind the Theories

Before you buy into someone's analysis of your psyche, you need to be a sophisticated personality theory consumer. For example, it's important to understand the time within history that the theory was developed; each theory of personality was developed in a social and cultural context that influenced the theorist's thinking. In addition, the personality of the theorist inevitably crept in; just as your personality theories are based on your life experience, so have the trials and tribulations of the theorist contributed significantly to his or her theoretical views.

So, when you read about the latest or greatest personality theory, pay particularly close attention to the following:

◆ Whether the theory focuses or normal or abnormal behavior, or both

◆ How much scientific method versus clinical intuition has contributed to the theory

◆ Whether the theory explains how personality develops or focuses on the adult personality

In addition, look for the assumptions behind the theory. Does the theorist believe that we have free choice or that forces over which we have no control determine our behavior? Does she or he think that our behavior is more influenced by past events or future goals and aspirations? Does the theorist think personalities can grow and change or does he or she think that we're stuck with the personalities we have? Neither side of these questions is necessarily right or wrong, although my personal theory is that some of these sure do give us more options than others. When it comes to my personality development, I want some room to grow!

Miss Congeniality or Misunderstood?

Who in your school was voted "Best Personality"? Who was most popular? What do we mean when we say someone has "personality plus"?

These questions bring us right back to the "nature-versus-nurture" debate you learned about in Chapter 3. When it comes to personality, most people vote for nurture as the primary influence—we tend to credit, or blame, our upbringing and life experiences for the good and bad traits we wind up with. But, as the song says, it ain't necessarily so.

The traits singled out by personality tests appear to be at least moderately inheritable. Identical twins share about 50 percent of the same personality traits, the same percentage that they share when it comes to measuring intelligence. And identical twins reared apart are more similar in personality to one another than are siblings or fraternal twins who are raised together. In fact, people raised in the same family are just about as different as any two people picked at random off the street. If you have brothers and sisters, you know what I mean.

But why would upbringing have so little an effect on personality? One reason is that siblings have very different experiences growing up within the same family. For example, my sister, who is 10 years younger than me, felt like an only child growing up. On the other hand, my two-years-younger brother and I felt like the dynamic duo. And my sister and I have very different experiences relating to my parents' divorce. I was 20 when it happened; my sister was only 10.

Don't Be So Temperamental

Did your mother compare you to the Tasmanian devil as a child? Did you have the attention span of a gnat? Hey, you aren't to blame—and neither are your parents. Since the 1950s, researchers have found that newborns and infants vary widely in the following nine temperaments:

- **Activity level.** The amount of physical motion exhibited during the day.

- **Persistence.** The extent of continuation of behavior with or without interruption.

- **Distractibility.** The ease of being interrupted by sound, light, or other unrelated behavior.

- **Initial Reaction.** Response to novel situations, whether approaching or withdrawing.

- **Adaptability.** The ease of changing behavior in a socially desirable direction.

- **Mood.** The quality of emotional expression, positive or negative.

- **Intensity.** The amount of energy exhibited in emotional expression.

- **Sensitivity.** The degree to which a person reacts to light, sound, and so on.

- **Regularity.** The extent to which patterns of eating, sleeping, elimination, and so on, are consistent or inconsistent from day to day.

Even newborns differ widely in these categories of behavior, and these temperament characteristics are an important aspect of a person's individuality. They also have an effect on how we experience our upbringing. Each sibling in a family comes into the world with a unique temperament, which may lead us to choose very different friends, activities, and life experiences. With all these variables, maybe no two people ever grow up in the "same" family!

Personality by Birth Order

If you aren't like the other members of your family, then who are you most like? Well, for starters, numerous studies suggest that you're likely to share some of the same personality traits with other people who share the same birth order. If you were the firstborn in your family, for example, you're probably like other kids who entered their families first—you're a member of the family of firstborns!

Because firstborns are older, they're likely to be bigger, stronger, more knowledge-able, and more competent than later-born children. They're first to receive privileges, first to grow up, and, alas, the first to be asked to take care of younger siblings.

The firstborns' privileged position makes them special, and at times, burdens them—and their personalities are likely to reflect this mixed bag. For example, they tend to be leaders, but they also may be hard to get along with and are most likely to feel insecure and jealous. Perhaps that's because they never get over their younger siblings invading their territory! More U.S. presidents have been firstborns than any other birth order, and, as we all know, some of them (who shall remain nameless) have had some unresolved personality issues.

> **Insight**
>
> Think all the "birth order" stuff is nonsense? Mention it to the next Ph.D. you meet. About 90 percent of people with doctorates in the United States are first-borns or only children!

Middle children tend to be diplomats, while last-borns are the rebels—with or without a cause. Having been picked on and dominated by firstborns, later children are more likely to support liberal causes, be open to new ideas and experiences, and support innovative ideas in science and politics. Later-born children are also more agreeable and more sociable—firstborns may be most likely to achieve, but later-borns are clearly most popular.

Personality by Gender

No, men do not have personalities from Mars and women personalities from Venus. The uniqueness of our own personalities, and the diversity of personality traits within each gender, far outweigh any personality differences based on gender. However, numerous cross-cultural studies suggest that members of each gender are more likely to share a few common personality traits.

The most consistent difference by far is that women are easier to get along with. In every study in every country, women score higher on agreeableness, and lower on antagonism, than men. To be specific, about 84 percent of women score higher on measures of the ability to get along with others than the average man (and guys, it's just your bad luck if you married into the other 16 percent).

But it's not all bad news for men. After years of trying to get "equal pay for equal work," we are at the point where this is finally happening in the United States. Yet men still tend to earn more. Why? Social equality issues aside, men seem to develop personality traits that encourage risk-taking, and, in general, risk-taking jobs often pay more. (Think firefighter versus preschool teacher, or salesperson on commission versus salesperson receiving an hourly wage.)

Look Out, I'm Culture Bound!

Would you have the same personality if you were brought up in a different culture? Maybe not. Our culture shapes the development of our personality in many ways—by encouraging differing parenting strategies, communicating certain values, reinforcing certain behaviors, and teaching social rituals. In fact, some researchers think that various cultures have a "national character" that permeates social interactions and results in the tendency for certain personality characteristics to develop in members of that culture.

For example, although there are no definitive culture traits that define Americans, the following are some general attitudes/traits that are often cited by expatriates who've survived the culture shock of living in the United States—and are helping their compadres who are about to do the same:

- **Friendly.** Accepting of strangers.

- **Open.** Share personal information easily, little need for personal privacy.

- **Insular.** Unaware of other cultures (but often curious and interested).

- **Fast-paced and impatient.** In a hurry, place a premium on time.

- **Assertive.** Make little effort to hide thoughts and feelings.

- **Noisy.** Uncomfortable with silence, play music when studying, and so on.

Understanding different cultures can be a great help in avoiding the "labels" that can easily be attributed to a person who behaves in a way that is unexpected. The Japanese cultural value of respectfully allowing a person to "save face" by communicating bad news indirectly was often misinterpreted as dishonesty or manipulation before cultural-awareness training for executives came into vogue.

Disturbing Personalities

So far, we've spent our time talking about normal personalities and how we get them. But how does an *abnormal* personality develop? And when does an eccentric personality become a personality disorder?

We're All a Little Bit "Off"

Personality disorders are chronic mental disorders that affect a person's ability to function in everyday activities. While most people can live pretty normally with mildly self-defeating personality traits (to some extent, we all do), during times of increased stress the symptoms of a personality disorder will gain strength and begin to seriously interfere with their functioning. Personality disorders are at the extreme end of the continuum.

def•i•ni•tion

A **personality disorder** is a long-standing, inflexible, and maladaptive pattern of thinking, perceiving, or behaving that usually causes serious problems in the person's social or work environment.

For example, just about everyone enjoys attention. And we all know someone who hogs the limelight or seems to be constantly seeking approval or recognition. But although we might not like such people or find them pleasant to be around, their personality traits don't necessarily indicate a clinical disorder. Sure, they might be self-centered or have a narcissistic view of the world, but that's not the same as having narcissistic personality disorder.

But It's All About Me and My Needs!

People with narcissistic personality disorder have a grandiose sense of self-importance, a preoccupation with fantasies of success or power, and a constant need for attention and admiration. They might "overreact" to the mildest criticism, defeat, or rejection. In addition, they're likely to have an unrealistic sense of entitlement and a limited ability to empathize with others. This lack of empathy, tendency to exploit others, and lack of insight almost always results in serious relationship problems. As you can see, these are not people who are merely "selfish"; they're people who genuinely can't relate to others.

Before you start diagnosing friends and family, however, keep in mind that true personality disorders are usually severe enough to interfere with a person's life in some way. A hunger for the limelight can be healthy if it's channeled in the right direction; without it, many of our greatest actors might not have chosen acting as a profession. And some of our greatest inventors, artists, business leaders, and reformers could be considered quite eccentric if you take a closer look at them—people who take a stand often don't conform to the norm. Think of Margaret Sanger, whom you met at the start of this chapter. Her personality was considered to be disturbed because of her views on "free love." Today, she's a hero.

How Personality Disorders Develop

Mental-health professionals disagree about the prevalence and makeup of personality disorders, and they can be pretty darned hard to treat. But there are a few things that are generally accepted as true on the subject.

For one thing, it's largely accepted that personality disorders are recognizable by the time a person reaches late adolescence or early adulthood—and that there are no "personality disorders" among children because their personalities are still being shaped. It's also true that no one knows exactly what causes personality disorders. It may be a combination of parental upbringing, one's innate personality, and social development, as well as genetic and biological factors.

For example, while we know there was no obvious physical abuse in serial murderer Ted Bundy's childhood, some form of emotional abuse that contributed to his antisocial personality disorder could perhaps be traced to the lies perpetrated by his family: his "parents" were actually his grandparents and his "sister" was, in fact, his mother.

> **Psychobabble**
>
> Do plastic-surgery candidates have more personality disorders? According to a recent study, up to 70 percent of plastic-surgery candidates meet the criteria for at least one personality disorder—most commonly, narcissistic personality disorder and obsessive-compulsive personality disorder.

What's Your Tonic?

Psychological disorders are often classified as either *ego-dystonic* or *ego-syntonic*. What's that mean in English? Well, behaviors, thoughts, or feelings that upset you and make you uncomfortable are ego-dystonic. You don't like them, you don't want them, and that makes you more likely to seek treatment for them.

But often personality disorders are ego-syntonic: as far as you're concerned, the thoughts, behaviors, and feelings you're having fit in with your sense of who you are. That means you can have what everyone *else* considers a disorder—they don't like it, and you make them uncomfortable—but as far as you're concerned, it's everyone else's problem, not yours. And if you think you're okay, you won't be very likely to seek treatment, and will probably resist it if it's forced on you.

Playing the Best Treatment Odds with Personality Disorders

For years, it was believed that personality disorders could be almost impossible to treat. Now we know that they can be difficult and time-consuming to treat, but not impossible.

The treatment of choice is psychotherapy. Specifically, the most effective treatment tends to focus on reducing self-defeating behaviors, improving interpersonal relationships, and teaching the client to handle difficult emotions (for example, by learning to mentally observe one's feelings rather than getting overwhelmed by them). Therapy that is structured around these goals tends to be more useful than unstructured techniques like free association (where the therapist works with whatever comes to the client's mind) or supportive psychotherapy (where the therapist provides consistency, support, and a hopeful attitude rather than directing active behavioral change).

Insight

New research suggests that the main benefit of treatment of personality disorders may be to speed up a recovery process that occurs naturally as we age. About 90 percent of clients diagnosed with borderline personality disorder in their 20s no longer meet the criteria by midlife—even without treatment.

Medications for personality disorders are usually aimed at symptoms associated with the disorder, such as the impulsivity and unstable moods associated with borderline personality disorder. Popular antidepressants include the SSRI category (serotonin-specific reuptake inhibitors) like Prozac, Paxil, Effexor, and so on. However, they appear to have little impact on the personality disorder itself.

In this chapter, you've learned how difficult it can be to predict someone's behavior no matter how well you think you know them. However, personality tests are one tool that can help us understand how traits lead to behavioral patterns. In the next chapter, you'll learn about the methods people use to protect their personalities and defend themselves emotionally.

Psychobabble
For a detailed description of the personality disorders, check out http://psychcentral.com/personality.

The Least You Need to Know

◆ Your personality is a complex assortment of unique traits that are stable over time and across settings.

◆ Psychologists use both objective and projective personality tests to figure out who we are and sometimes (but not always) predict what we will do.

◆ We all have traits (characteristics of personality that are relatively stable and consistent over time) and we all have states (temporary emotional responses to specific situations).

◆ Personality development is influenced by a number of things, including genetics, environment, culture, birth order, and gender.

◆ Personality disorders are chronic mental disorders that affect a person's ability to function in everyday activities. They are complex, somewhat fuzzy, and can be difficult—but not impossible—to treat.

Chapter 15

Psychic Self-Defense

In This Chapter

- The personalities behind the personality theories
- Understanding your hidden motives and urges
- Strategies for psychic self-defenses
- Exploring the person you were born to be
- Do you believe in destiny?

Joyce is a shy, exhausted-looking young woman who has come to you, a psychologist, for help with her frequent headaches. For the past hour, she's been telling you about her complete devotion to her husband and child, but at a stressful moment in the conversation, she closes her eyes.

When she reopens them, the expression on Joyce's face is completely transformed. She sits up, squarely facing you, and speaks in a confident voice. Suddenly she has become a vivacious and talkative woman who jauntily calls you "Doc." When you ask about her headaches, she looks bewildered and says she's never had a headache in her life. This woman calls herself "Joanna" and says she's single and "a little bit wild." Yes, she knows Joyce; in fact, she feels sorry for her, being saddled with that boring husband and bratty child.

This anecdote illustrates a rare, and somewhat controversial, form of psychological self-defense—dissociative identity disorder, formerly known as multiple personality disorder. It's an extreme example of how a person defends him- or herself against emotional pain, but we all have less dramatic ways of defending and protecting our psyches. In this chapter, we'll look at various theories of personality development, how our conflicts and needs shape who we are, how we protect our psyches, and how our backgrounds and beliefs influence our everyday lives.

Ulterior Motives

While some of Freud's ideas are under attack today, there's no question that Sigmund Freud was the personality pioneer. As a young physician in the late nineteenth century, Freud came to believe that many of his patients' complaints were not due to physical illnesses but to mental conflicts of which they were unaware. On the basis of this insight, he ultimately developed an elaborate model of the mind that he believed explained why, and how, people cope with the psychological stresses of their daily lives.

def•i•ni•tion

A **psychodynamic personality theory** is a model of personality that assumes that inner forces (needs, drives, motives) shape personality and influence behavior.

Freud's theory was the first of the *psychodynamic personality theories*—theories that emphasize the interplay of mental forces (the word *dynamic* refers to energy or force). While each of these theories emphasizes different influences on personality development, they share two beliefs:

♦ That we are often clueless about our real motives

♦ That our minds develop self-protective strategies called defenses, which keep unacceptable or distressing motives, thoughts, and feelings out of our awareness

When Freud talked about hidden motives, he wasn't kidding around. Freud believed that the main causes of behavior lie buried in the unconscious mind. That is, the part of your mind that affects your conscious thought and action but is not itself open to conscious inspection. The differences between my personality and yours, Freud thought, were variations in our unconscious motives, in how these motives pop up in our daily lives, and in the ways that you and I protect ourselves from emotional pain or anxiety.

At center stage in his human drama, Freud put the concept of the unconscious, a kind of psychic storehouse of primitive and repressed impulses. This is not an actual place in our psyches, but rather an important process we learn as a child. The unconscious helps us deal with all these inborn drives and raw psychic energy so that we can grow up to be respectable, law-abiding citizens.

But if people themselves don't know why they do the things they do, how can a psychologist ever hope to help them? Freud was a big believer in the "believe what they do, not what they say" approach to therapy—he thought that by sifting through his patients' behaviors he could make inroads into their unconscious. Because the conscious mind always attempts to act in ways that are logical and rational, Freud did a lot of digging for clues through his patients' most irrational thoughts and behavior—which he felt were generated by the unconscious, or subconscious, mind. Thus, slips of the tongue or the pen, dreams, and random thoughts were the grist for Freud's mill.

> **Insight**
>
> Freud thought that physical and behavioral symptoms were meaningfully related to significant life events. If you are constantly late for a date, or always miss your appointment with your therapist because you "forgot," Freud would say these represent unconscious conflicts that are playing with your conscious life.

According to psychoanalytic theory, at the root of your personality are powerful inner forces that drive your behavior. Personality problems, according to Freud, aren't caused by a lack of motivation. In fact, they're much more likely to be caused by too much motivation—for sex, pleasure, and aggression.

Sex in Overdrive

Some people think Freud was hung up on sex. There's no doubt that Freud thought about sex a lot, wrote about sex a lot, and believed that the sex drive had a powerful influence on the personality. But before you start wondering if Freud had a few skeletons in his sexual closet, it's important to realize that he believed the sex drive to be much more than the simple desire to have sex. He saw it as the human drive toward pleasure-seeking and life-creating activities. He also believed that there were differences in how people channeled their sex drives. Since the most direct ways to express this drive were often unacceptable to the straight-laced Viennese society of his day, people had to channel their energy into something less dangerous.

Freud believed that most of us channel our sex drives into a wide range of thoughts and actions that on the surface are not sexual at all. This idea of channeling sexual energy is reflected in the belief, held by some athletes, that they must abstain from sex while training or before a competition—that they need that energy to win. Some creative people also believe that their creativity is channeled directly from their sex drive.

> **Psychobabble**
>
> Freud may have been on to something with his preoccupation with sex. Modern studies show that, in many cases, an animal even on the verge of starvation will choose a sexually receptive partner over food. As for humans, one psychology professor I know emphasizes that the "Four Fs" are the most basic of human drives. In his words, they are *feeding, fighting, fleeing,* and … reproduction!

As if constantly reining in our sexual impulses wasn't work enough, Freud also believed that human beings were naturally aggressive, and that this aggression, like the sex drive, had to be channeled into more acceptable forms of behavior, or else we'd commit more murders than we already do. In Freud's view, then, people were pretty asocial, forced into society more by necessity than desire, and interacting principally in terms of sex, aggression, and various squashed versions of these drives. And, to Freud's way of thinking, it all begins in childhood.

Urges "R" Us

Freud believed that a person's personality is shaped most strongly during infancy and early childhood. Each of us, he thought, progresses through a series of predictable stages in which we associate pleasure with the stimulation of certain body areas at certain times in our early lives. If we get through them unscathed, we have a chance of turning out okay. However, according to Freud, we can get stuck in any one of these stages because of too much or too little stimulation during that critical time period. This would lead to problems in adult life.

The three stages in Freud's personality play are …

♦ **The oral stage.** In the first year of life, the mouth is the center of pleasure. A baby sucks, drools, and mouths objects like crazy. If the baby gets just enough mouth stimulation, he or she will move on to other pleasure centers. However, babies who are under- or overfed might grow up to be needy, dependent adults. In addition, they might develop some bad habits—overeating, for example, might be a result of getting stuck at the oral stage.

◆ **The anal stage.** From ages one to three—prime toilet training time—babies feel good about the process of elimination, but they also learn that there are pretty strict social rules about bodily functions, self-control, and personal hygiene. Freud would say that people who are stingy and obsessively neat got stuck here. (Whenever I look around my office, I wish I'd gotten stuck here at least for just a little while!)

◆ **The phallic stage.** From the ages of three to six, a child's genitals become the major focus of his or her pleasure. Freud believed that this was the age when boys wanted to marry their moms and kill their dads (the Oedipus complex) and girls wanted to kill their moms and marry their dads (the Electra complex). The way we resolve this conflict, according to Freud, is by identifying more with the same-sex parent.

On the Mat with Freud

Freud thought childhood was no picnic. We have all these inborn drives and urges we have to tame. We have psychosexual minefields we have to navigate. And we have mental forces that are constantly warring with each other. These warring parts of our personality are the *id*, the *ego*, and the *superego*.

What's Id to Ya?

The id is the primitive "Want it, gotta have it" part of your personality. It acts on impulse and pushes for immediate gratification—especially sexual, physical, and emotional pleasures. It never worries about the consequences.

It's a Bird, It's a Plane, It's Superego!

Your superego is the storehouse of values and moral attitudes that you've learned from society as you were growing up. This is your conscience. It develops as you internalize the "no's" of your parents and other grown-up do-gooders who preach against socially undesirable behaviors.

Think of your superego as your inner voice of "oughts" and "should nots." Your superego also includes your *ego ideal*—your view of the person you should try to be. It's that nagging inner voice that constantly critiques your actions and compares them to perfection.

And in This Corner ...

Your ego is your psyche's referee. It tries to find that happy medium between getting what the id wants and doing what the superego thinks is right. When your id and your superego are fighting, your ego looks for a compromise. For example, if you're unprepared for an exam, your id might want to cheat, your superego would worry about the consequences of cheating, and your ego might ask the teacher if you could take the test at a later date.

Given the "personalities" of your id and superego, it's no wonder they don't like each other. The id wants to do what feels good, while the superego wants to put a lid on your id and do what's right. Your ego is the part of your personality that tries to make peace between the other two. It represents your personal view of the way things are: your physical and social reality. Its job is to try to pick actions that will satisfy the id without getting you into big trouble. Sometimes it succeeds and sometimes it doesn't.

Post-Freudian Dynamic Personalities

Not all psychoanalysts share Freud's grim view of human nature. While most agree that the personality battle is won or lost during childhood, not every psychodynamic theorist believes that the battle itself was quite as primordial as Freud would have it. In fact, a lot of neo-Freudians see people simply as social beings just trying to get along with themselves and others.

Forever Jung

Swiss psychologist Carl Jung and Sigmund Freud had a complicated relationship. For many years, Jung was thought to be the heir apparent to the Freudian throne. However, Jung eventually got fed up with Freud's pessimism about human nature and developed a few ideas of his own.

Jung contributed many new and enlightening ideas about personality development. For example, he thought the unconscious was not limited to one person's unique life experiences but was filled with universal psychological truths shared by the whole human race. This *collective unconscious*, in Jung's view, is an inherited storehouse of unconscious ideas and forces common to all human beings.

Jung was also interested in the creative parts of the personality. Sure, he thought sex and aggression were powerful motives, but he also thought that people have an instinctive need to create and self-actualize. And while we might not all be Van Gogh or Cessna, Jung thought we were all predisposed to at least appreciate and intuitively understand myths, art forms, and symbols.

In particular, Jung zoomed in on certain universally recognizable symbols that he labeled *archetypes*. Each archetype is associated with an instinctive tendency to feel and think in a special way. Borrowing from history and mythology, Jung named many images and characters that can be found in ancient and diverse cultures—the hero, the earth mother, the sun god, and the trickster. These, he believed, are archetypes that reside in the collective unconscious of us all.

def•i•ni•tion

According to Carl Jung, an **archetype** is a universal symbol of human experience that is stored in our **collective unconscious,** the storehouse of ideas and forces shared by every human being has who ever lived.

Don't Treat Me Like an Object

One of the most dominant forces in personality theory over the past 50 years is object-relations theory. Object relations is a contemporary psychoanalytic theory that emphasizes the importance of our earliest relations with significant others as the building blocks of our personalities. The basic idea is that our personalities are the byproducts of our mental representation of significant others, ourselves, and the interactions between the two.

It's not that simple, because it's not the actual people that matter so much as our thoughts and ideas about these people. The "objects" in the theory are our internal representations of significant others, and the "relate" part refers to our relationships with them. An *object* in the object-relations theory is an individual who is emotionally important to us. An individual's first objects are his or her parents; later, other members of the family, friends, lovers, and so on become objects in this sense.

To the infant, objects are his or her *perceptions* of other people, and there is one object for each important set of emotions related to each person. So a mother, say, is split in the infant's mind into a good mother who provides food and shelter, and a bad mother who provides punishment or just a feeling of absence when she's not there. Part of an individual's development consists of merging these fragmented objects into more complex objects, which provide a truer intuitive model of the individual. Maturity means, among other things, being able to perceive an individual in terms of all of his or her traits. A mature person views the punishing and the rewarding mother as two aspects of the same individual.

An immature person, however, views the punishing and the rewarding mother as two separate objects. And a person who's in love will only perceive the *good* object of his or her affection, and normally (for a while at least) be unable or highly unwilling to perceive the rest. This phenomenon is known as *splitting*, and is considered a very immature defense mechanism.

Horney's Need for Security

Let's be a little more social, thought Karen Horney. Yeah, we can do all this mumbo-jumbo about internal this and mental-representation that, but the bottom line is how we are actually treated by our parents (particularly our mothers) that starts the personality ball rolling. In particular, she focused on the need for security as a driving force in blossoming personalities. This inborn human need for security can only be filled by other people, and if it isn't filled when we're little, Horney believed that we'll spend the rest of our lives looking for it.

Insight

Penis envy? Puh-leeze! Karen Horney thought women might be much more envious of the superior status and greater power men held in our society. She suggested that Freud should get over his idea that women long for a penis and take a look at the desperate social circumstances in which many women live.

Horney thought the most fundamental human emotion was anxiety—a child's feelings of being isolated and helpless in a potentially hostile world. In Horney's view, parents shape a child's personality by their success or failure in relieving this basic anxiety and helping the child feel secure.

Children who find security with their parents will continue to find security with others later on in life. And children who fail to find security with their parents will grow up feeling insecure and distrustful of others. This distrust will show up in any of three unhappy personality styles of relating or not relating: avoiding others, always giving in to others, or dominating others.

Adler's Quest for Competence

Perhaps Alfred Adler had an inferiority complex. We don't know for sure, but we do know that he thought a lot of other people had one! Adler, a contemporary of Freud and Horney, thought that one of the biggest struggles people face throughout their lives is the need to feel competent. And he believed that we start out with at least one strike against us because of the helpless and dependent state of early childhood. In his view, that helplessness means that we all begin life feeling pretty inferior. The manner in which we learn to cope with or overcome this feeling provides the basis for our lifelong personality.

Adler believed that personal achievements are important because they boost our sense of competence. Psychologically healthy people have a mature sense of their own abilities and worth (self-esteem) and they direct those abilities toward useful achievements.

On the other hand, people who are overwhelmed by a sense of inferiority will constantly think that other people are better than they are and wind up as frustrated underachievers. Or, they may go through life masking their feelings of inferiority behind a snobby attitude and an endless need to prove that they are better than others.

In Adler's view, the first reaction is a classic case of an inferiority complex, and the second is a classic example of a superiority complex, but both are the opposite sides of the same coin!

The Well-Defended Mind

Whew! If you add up Freud's sex and aggression, Jung's creativity, Horney's security, and Adler's competence, one thing becomes quickly apparent—we've all got a lot of needs to meet! And, it's not like the rest of the world is cooperating with us as we go about the business of meeting them. Society says that we can't have sex whenever we want to; we're likely to find out that the relationship we were counting on wasn't as secure as we thought; and the boss doesn't give us the promotion we think we deserve! How do we keep our personalities from getting beaten down while we're building them?

Defenses, my dear Watson. You have them and so do I. I can't tell you how often people, upon learning that I'm a psychologist, start monitoring their every move. There is usually an abrupt and noticeable change of expression when they are told my profession, as if I'm some superpsych who has x-ray vision into their secrets! "Are you going to psychoanalyze me?" they frequently ask in half-jest and half-concern. Believe me, psychologists have all the normal defense mechanisms working, and I, for one, am more than happy to suppress my clinical skills in social settings.

The theory of *defense mechanisms* was most thoroughly developed by Freud's daughter, Anna, who became a psychoanalyst herself. You might think of defense mechanisms as doing for anxiety what endorphins do for physical pain—they reduce its impact.

Anxiety frequently promotes survival, by spurring us to action to overcome a threatening situation. But in some situations it does us more harm than good. Our defense mechanisms are a way to reduce the amount of anxiety we feel, and—to the degree

def•i•ni•tion

A **defense mechanism** is a mental process of self-deception that reduces our awareness of threatening or anxiety-producing thoughts, wishes, or memories.

that they help us worry less about things that aren't worth worrying about, or that we can't do much about anyway—defense mechanisms are helpful. But sometimes they distort reality or keep us from taking action to improve a situation, and that's when they hurt us.

Among the most common defense mechanisms are repression, projection, rationalization, reaction formation, displacement, and sublimation.

Insight

The "serenity prayer" used in alcohol recovery programs is an example of getting the balance right between using defenses to worry less, but not letting them hold us back from progress. It asks for "the serenity to accept the things I cannot change, the courage to change the things I can, and the wisdom to know the difference."

Out of Sight, Out of Mind!

Freud believed that repression was the mind's first line of defense—it lays the foundation for the other defense mechanisms. When painful memories or anxiety-producing thoughts occur, repression is the process of pushing or keeping them out of the mind. Repression is often called a "primitive" defense mechanism because we aren't aware that it's happening. (If we were, that would be *sup*pression.)

Freud visualized repression as the damming-up of a pool of mental energy. And, just as water will leak through any crack in a dam, repressed wishes and memories will leak through the barriers that separate the unconscious from the conscious. But sometimes repression isn't enough, and that's when the other defense mechanisms kick in.

It's Your Problem, Not Mine!

Projection occurs when someone consciously experiences an unconscious drive, wish, or feeling as though it belongs to someone else. For example, a person with intense, unconscious anger may project that anger onto her friend and think it is her friend who is angry.

My husband and I have used this one so often that we eventually developed a code word, "Hello, Mr. Projection," when one of us realizes that our emotional boundaries have gotten confused. If he's in a bad mood or overly stressed, he sometimes thinks

I'm mad at him—and vice versa. The teasing statement "Hello, Mr. Projection" has become our signal to encourage the other to look deep within and see if maybe the source of irritation is really coming from inside ourselves. (Naturally, this kind of humor would only survive in the home of a psychologist!)

The Devil Made Me Do It!

The late comedian Flip Wilson made this line famous. But the devil is not involved in the use of conscious reasoning, or rationalization, to explain away anxiety-provoking thoughts or feelings. A man who cannot face his own violent tendencies may rationalize the beatings he gives his children by convincing himself that his children "asked for it" and that he is only carrying out his fatherly duty. The sexual abuser may rationalize that his four-year-old is "coming on" to him.

Always Keep 'Em Guessing

Reaction formation is an interesting defense mechanism, and it illustrates the paradox of human nature. With reaction formation, the person does or says exactly the opposite of how he or she really feels. The true feelings or wishes are so unacceptable that they are turned into their safer opposite. An example of this mechanism would be a woman who does not want her child but who feels so guilty about her feelings that she becomes an overprotective and smothering mother.

Kicking the Dog Instead of the Boss

When an unconscious wish or drive is unacceptable to the conscious mind, it is frequently redirected toward a more acceptable alternative. A person who wants to have an affair might spend time looking at pornography instead, so as not to "cross the line" into infidelity. A man who discovers that his beloved wife has a terminal illness might yell at the garage mechanic for not taking better care of his car because he'd be considered a heel if he yelled at his dying wife.

On a conscious level, punching your pillow is an often-used "displacement" remedy to get rid of anger and hostility. It's also a pretty good idea, since by venting your anger that way you're less likely to hit anybody else.

If You Can't Beat 'Em, Join 'Em

Sublimation is a little like displacement, but instead of turning unacceptable urges into their opposites, it seeks to find an acceptable use to which those urges can be put.

Martin Luther King Jr. channeled his anger into political activism against discrimination and racial injustice and had a worldwide impact. Orson Welles channeled his narcissism into a phenomenally creative acting and directing career. Each of these men directed their aggressive or otherwise unacceptable energies into activities that are valued by society.

The Best Defense

You might be interested to know which of these defense mechanisms works best. Lots of studies have been done with this goal in mind. While the effectiveness of the defense mechanism somewhat depends upon the situation you're in, there do seem to be some that generally promote more effective coping than others.

Projection, not surprisingly, is one of the least effective defense mechanisms. Not only does it block self-awareness, it also often interferes with interpersonal relationships. For instance, you'd tire pretty quickly if your partner always thought relationship conflict was *your* problem. Repression and reaction formation distort reality less than projection does, and they can lead to somewhat more effective coping, but they still use up unnecessary amounts of psychic energy.

Two of the best defenses are suppression and humor. Suppression—the conscious avoidance of negative thinking—is different from repression. Unlike repression, you're still aware of negative information and can think about it whenever you choose to do so. And humor relieves anxiety and simultaneously enables you to face feared ideas because you're poking fun at them.

Ultimately, however, the best defense is no defense at all. Many people learn that once they face a painful memory or a fearful situation, the reality is not as bad as it first seemed.

> **Brain Buster**
>
> There's a dangerous difference between looking on the bright side and outright denial. Driving recklessly because you believe that you would never get into a car crash, or having unprotected sex out of a sense of invulnerability, are examples of unrealistic, self-deluding optimism. And no, teenagers aren't the only ones who have it.

> **Psychobabble**
>
> Robbie Robertson, rock-and-roll songwriter and guitarist with The Band, suffered from stage fright before each performance. He even wrote a song about it, called "Stage Fright." This is one good way to practice sublimation! Robertson's fear never prevented him from being one of the most acclaimed guitarists in rock history.

Freeing the Psychic Balloons!

While psychodynamic theorists see personality development as a battle, the humanists think of it as a natural, free-flowing process that is sometimes weighed down by outside forces. The humanists are much more optimistic about human nature than the Freudians. To them, we're not so much driven by unconscious conflicts and defenses against anxiety as we are inspired to adapt, learn, and grow. Free the psychic balloons, they proclaim, and our personalities will fly!

Humanists focus on the innate qualities within us that influence our behavior, while they view environmental influences as barriers or blocks, like strings tying down balloons. Once people are freed from their negative situations, humanists would argue, their natural tendency to learn and grow (the actualizing tendency) should actively guide them to choose life-fulfilling situations.

Humanistic personality theorists believe that the motivation for behavior comes from a unique blend of biological and learned tendencies to develop and change and grow positively. *Self-actualization* is a constant striving to realize your full potential, to fully develop your abilities and talents. This innate quest for self-fulfillment and the realization of your unique potential is a useful guiding force that moves you toward generally positive behaviors.

Problems arise, however, when your drive for self-actualization conflicts with your need for approval—from yourself and from others—especially when you feel that certain obligations or conditions must be met in order to gain that approval. For example, if you're a natural-born artist, your drive for self-actualization might be sabotaged if you fear disapproval from one of your parents. Or you might take up sports, not because you want to play but because you need approval from your father.

The Personality Habit

All this stuff about free-loving balloons is a bit much for social-cognitive psychologists. According to the social-cognitivists, personalities are shaped by beliefs and habits of thought acquired through each individual's unique experiences in the social environment.

These learned beliefs and habits may be conscious, but they're tricky. In fact, over time they may be so ingrained and automatic that they exert their influence without us even realizing it. To social-cognitive theorists, "unconscious" refers only to automatic mental processes, not to thoughts that are barred from consciousness by our defense mechanisms. The self-talk we engage in every day is a good example of automatic ways of thinking that influence how we feel and what we do—until we stop and listen to ourselves, we might not even know what our self-talk is saying.

Learned beliefs and habits of thinking either increase or decrease our ability to take control of our lives and accomplish the tasks we wish to accomplish. If, for instance, I kept telling myself that I could not write this book because I had too much else to do, I might have given up before I got started. Instead, I told myself I *could* write it— if I reorganized my life to make room for it. Voilà! The book *did* happen!

Let's take a look at three of our thinking habits that have a tremendous impact on our lives:

- Locus of control

- Self-efficacy

- Optimism

Psychobabble

Just because you became more practical with age doesn't mean that you can't keep your dreams alive. Childhood dreams can provide valuable clues to long-lost parts of ourselves. Take a minute and think back on the first three things you wanted to be when you grew up. Former vet-wannabes make great pet owners or animal activists. And, if you wanted to be a ballerina, are you still dancing? If not, why not give it a try?

Who's in the Driver's Seat?

Clinical psychologist Julian Rotter was a major player in developing the social-cognitive school of psychology. Influenced by Alfred Adler's interest in competence and achievement, Rotter found that people behaved differently on tests or games depending upon whether they believed that success depended on luck or skill. If you believe that your success depends on your skill, you're likely to work harder and get better. To the degree that you believe success depends on luck, you're less likely to work hard.

Rotter found that people's beliefs about their control over the rewards depend on the situation—and they should. At an early age, you figured out that in some situations you could control what happened, and in others you couldn't. You learned that saying please and thank you usually made people like you better, but that no matter *what* you did, your third-grade teacher had it in for you.

However, in some situations, the degree to which your reward depends on your own efforts is not readily apparent. If you bomb a test, for example, it could be that you didn't study hard enough, or maybe it was because the test was unfair and biased. Rotter found that in these situations, people behave differently according to their general disposition, acquired from their personal experiences, to believe that rewards either are or are not *usually* controlled by their own efforts. He called this disposition the *locus of control*.

People who believe that they can control their own fate are said to have an internal locus of control. People who believe life is essentially a crapshoot have an external locus of control. Not surprisingly, when tested, people who score toward the internal end on locus of control try to control their own fate more often than those who score at the external end.

def•i•ni•tion

A **locus of control** is a person's perception of the usual source of control over rewards. An internal locus of control means we believe that our behavior determines our fate; an external locus of control means we think that our fate is controlled by external forces (destiny, luck, or the gods).

How Good a Driver Are You?

Albert Bandura's self-efficacy is not the same as Rotter's locus of control (although it sounds similar). Self-efficacy refers to your sense of your ability to perform a particular task. If you *think* you can do it, then you have high self-efficacy. If you don't, then you have low self-efficacy for that particular task. Locus of control, on the other hand, refers to your belief about whether your ability will do you any good.

Take singing, for example. You might believe that your voice is so fabulous that Barbra Streisand could learn a few things from you. At the same time, you might believe that your chances of "being discovered" as a singing talent are determined by some cosmic roll of the dice. In this situation, you have high self-efficacy but an external locus of control.

Bandura's self-efficacy concept certainly has educational and child-rearing implications. For example, some studies suggest that improving self-efficacy actually improves performance—students who are told that they are good in math do better even when their original scores were no higher than their peers'. And parents know that highlighting a child's abilities and effort leads to greater long-term achievement than using methods that point out inability or failure. But, then, you don't need a Ph.D. to realize that!

Better Living Through Genetics?

What about the role of genes in determining your personality? Well, sorry, but you can't blame a people-pleasing personality on a "dependency" gene; on the other hand, you can take full credit for developing your conscientiousness and extroversion. While there are biological parts of our personalities, we have some control over how they take shape.

Here's how it works: genes do appear to provide some of the "raw material," e.g., temperament, that makes it easier for certain personality traits to blossom. A baby with an easy temperament may more easily develop an optimistic outlook, while an irritable infant may grow into an emotionally expressive child. These temperamental genes appear to interact in very complicated ways, though; in fact, any one gene is likely to account for only 1 or 2 percent of the variability in any given personality trait.

Being of Two Minds

We started out this chapter with Joyce/Joanna, a make-believe example of *dissociative identity disorder*, or DID. A person with DID has two or more distinct personalities ("alters") that coexist and control his or her behavior. The "alters" occur spontaneously and involuntarily, can be male or female, and operate more or less independently of each other.

def•i•ni•tion

Dissociative identity disorder (formerly known as multiple personality disorder) is a psychological disorder in which two or more distinct personalities coexist in the same person at different times.

There are plenty of mental-health professionals who don't believe DID actually exists, but those who do believe it exists agree on some common themes. First of all, it's agreed that a person develops multiple personalities before age 12. It's also generally accepted that while the child is still in the process of mapping out his or her collection of beliefs, morals, and experiences, severe trauma can cause parts of the psyche to split off from each other, forming alternative personalities, or "alters." Memory and other aspects of consciousness are divided up among the "alters" at the time of such splits.

No one knows why some people form multiple personalities and others don't, but when it does happen, it's usually in response to severe, repetitive physical or sexual abuse—more than 80 percent of all documented multiple personalities appear to have been created in response to such traumatic events. Continuous emotional abuse or neglect may also be a cause.

Dissociative identity disorder is a very confusing problem to have. Any dissociative disorder disrupts the continuity of life—people report "missing time." They are unable to account for certain times of the day, or they are told they've done things they don't remember. If you've ever been awakened while sleepwalking, you've had a glimpse of how frightening it can be to come to your senses and not know where you are or how you got there—something that people suffering from DID have to deal with regularly.

Psychobabble

Sybil, starring Sally Field, was one of the first movies to claim to look at a real-life example of multiple personality disorder—but was it true? Dr. Herbert Spiegel, who also treated "Sybil" (Shirley Ardell Mason), believes that the therapist featured in the film, Cornelia Wilbur, actually suggested the personalities as part of Shirley's therapy and that the patient adopted them with the help of hypnosis and sodium pentothal. Shirley apparently had no DID symptoms before her therapy began.

Multiples in Multiple Cultures?

DID, as defined by the current diagnostic manual of mental disorders, appears to be limited to the United States and, to a much lesser extent, other Western countries exposed to the U.S. media and time (roughly, the period from 1976 through 1996). Across cultures, there is no clear link between multiplicity, dissociation, or recovered memories, or between multiplicity and sexual abuse.

However, cross-cultural evidence suggests that a small fraction of humans everywhere experience themselves as multiple and that this multiplicity is not generally perceived as mental illness. In fact, people who claim multiplicity in other cultures often perceive their other selves as independent souls or spirits, such as shamans who claim to communicate with and be possessed by gods or spirits. Some religions may also attribute some illnesses to spirit possession. Those who recover from possession may go on to become shamans; this could be seen as a transition from dysfunctional to functional multiplicity. While such evidence suggests a common psychological mechanism for multiplicity, it also highlights the influence of the surrounding culture on the perception and subjective experience of multiplicity.

Playing the Odds: Getting the Best Treatment for DID

Because of the controversial nature of DID, the first order of business is establishing a correct diagnosis. As a result, many clinicians use numerous sources, including psychological testing and a carefully structured clinical interview, to ensure that they are not confusing other forms of dissociation (or, for that matter, a client with a personality disorder) with DID.

Once a diagnosis is made, the preferred treatment for DID is psychotherapy, with initial goals being client safety, a reduction in problematic symptoms, and increased communication and coordination among the different "alters." Medication, when used at all, is more of a stop-gap measure to help clients deal with the painful emotions as they work through traumatic memories. The ultimate goal is to reintegrate all personalities back into the initial, or core, personality.

We human beings have amazing ways of expressing our personalities and coping with the curveballs life throws at us. And just as our personalities are always changing and growing, our theories about how personality develops continue to evolve. Freud was certainly right about one thing—we'll probably never uncover all the layers of the human psyche. In the next chapter, we'll take a look at the various ways that human psyches can get out of whack. We'll talk about what's normal, what's not, and who decides which is which.

The Least You Need to Know

- Freud, the father of psychoanalysis, believed that personalities developed through a battle between primitive urges and the need to get along with others.

- According to Freud, children pass through three predictable stages of psycho-sexual development—the oral stage, the anal stage, and the phallic stage.

- Freud identified three parts of the personality: the id, the superego, and the ego.

- Jung, Horney, and Adler believed that humans are driven by needs for creativity, security, and competence.

- Defense mechanisms help us cope with unbearable thoughts, feelings, and wishes. Some of these are repression, projection, rationalization, reaction formation, displacement, and sublimation.

- Humanist psychologists believe that we are born with healthy personalities that sometimes get stifled by the needs of others and the demands of our environment.

- Social-cognitive psychologists believe that our personalities arise out of the beliefs and attitudes we develop through our unique life experiences.

- Studies in genetics show that, while we're born with certain temperaments, any one gene has very little effect on a particular personality trait.

Part 5

Just What Is Normal, Anyway?

Get ready for a wild ride! This section deals with the tricky question of what's normal and what's not. How do clinical psychologists identify mental illness? How do they determine the best way to treat it? And, on the flip side, what is happiness and how do psychologists promote it? In these chapters, you'll learn all about psychological diagnoses—how they're made and what they mean. You'll also learn how to build up those mental muscles so that when life's challenges throw you for a loop, you can bounce back and party hardy. In the end, you'll have a good idea of what you can do to take charge of your own life—you'll learn when and how self-improvement techniques can make a positive difference in your life!

Chapter 16

Are You Out of Your *Mind?*

In This Chapter

- ◆ What's normal, and what's not
- ◆ MUUDI-ing the waters of the mind
- ◆ Why labels should come with warnings
- ◆ A "classy" diagnosis
- ◆ The perils of pleading insanity

In 1973, psychologist Dr. David Rosenhan and seven other sane individuals faked mental illness to gain admission to a total of 12 different psychiatric hospitals. It wasn't hard; they all complained of hearing voices that said "empty, hollow, thud." Other than this one symptom, they answered every question honestly. Once in the hospital, they behaved normally—just as they would have outside the hospital. When asked about "the voices," they said they no longer heard them.

You'd think the hospital's staff would have soon realized that these individuals had never been "crazy" or, if they had been, that they weren't any longer. But you'd be wrong. The only people who suspected anything were the other patients, who'd say, "You're not crazy. I bet you're a reporter doing research on the hospital."

Worse still was the way the staff consistently responded to these men. They talked about the patients in front of them, as if they couldn't hear or understand what was being said. And in the hospital notes, normal behavior was often written up as symptoms of emotional instability. For example, the pseudopatients each kept a journal of his experience. No one on staff asked about it, but they'd make notes on the patients' charts about "excessive writing."

In this chapter, you'll learn how psychiatric labels are made—what psychologists define as abnormal, how diagnoses are classified, and the pros and cons of our current classification system. And you'll learn how difficult it is to get rid of the label "mentally ill" once it's been applied. You'll get a sense of the "politics" of mental illness, and its implications for anyone trying to overcome mental illness. You'll know not only what psychiatric diagnoses are currently in use, but also why you should use them with caution.

A warning! Don't succumb to the "psychology student's disease"—a tendency to discover in yourself the symptoms of every disorder discussed in the book. By the time I had finished my first abnormal psychology course, the only mental illness I could rule out for sure was anorexia (I weighed too much and loved to eat!). Forewarned is forearmed.

Meet Abby Normal

In a hilarious scene in the movie *Young Frankenstein*, Igor mistakenly chooses a physically abnormal brain for Dr. Frankenstein's experiments. The resulting "monster" looks physically abnormal, is intellectually impaired, and certainly doesn't know how to win friends and influence people.

> **Insight**
>
> A major National Institute of Mental Health study found that, in any given month, about 15 percent of the population is suffering from a diagnosable mental health problem, and almost one out of every three people will suffer from one in the course of a lifetime.

If this movie were coming from a psychological framework, the underlying message would be that the monster's abnormal behavior came about as a result of his abnormal brain. This biological perspective of mental illness has dominated research on mental illness for the past 15 years.

But what exactly *is* abnormal? Have you ever worried excessively, felt depressed for no apparent reason, or felt afraid of something that you knew couldn't really hurt you? I certainly have—I have been known to mow people down in my frantic need to get away from a harmless cockroach. A few irrational fears, and occasional periods of worry or sadness, seem to be part of life. The challenge is in knowing how many are too many, and how long is too long.

Mental-health professionals face a difficult task when they try to come up with a definition of mental illness. It is hard to determine at what point eccentric or free-spirited behavior becomes a marker of mental illness. But when a person begins to behave in a way that causes significant personal distress and disrupts his or her ability to function effectively at work or at home, it seems obvious that something must be done. So mental-health professionals need to designate some point at which a person's behavior crosses the (imaginary) line between health and illness. This cutoff point is called a diagnosis.

Psychological diagnoses are interpretations based on a person's behavior. In order for someone to receive a psychological diagnosis, that person must have had the problem for some time—to make certain that it's not just a temporary state (see Chapter 15). For some diagnoses, like clinical depression, the minimum time period could be as short as two weeks; for personality disorders, the time frame must be at least two years.

def•i•ni•tion

A **psychological diagnosis** is a label used to identify and describe a mental disorder, based on information collected by observation, testing, and analysis. It is also a judgment about a person's current level of functioning.

In addition, the person's behavioral problems must be bad enough to disrupt normal daily activities. Maybe you've started waking up in the middle of the night and you can't go back to sleep. Maybe you're calling in sick at work a lot, or maybe you're drinking too much. Whatever the problem is, to warrant a psychological diagnosis, it must be severe enough that you would function a lot better without it.

How Psychologists MUUDI the Waters

Clinical psychologists generally evaluate a person's behavior according to five basic criteria: is it maladaptive, unpredictable, unconventional, distressing, or irrational? If at least two of these criteria are present, it sets off a warning bell for the psychologist to look more closely at the person's symptoms. In the world of diagnosis, this is how mental-health professionals often MUUDI the waters of the mind.

- ◆ **Maladaptive.** The person fails to adapt to the demands of everyday life, either by acting counter to his or her own well-being or against the goals and needs of society.

♦ **Unpredictable.** The person loses control or acts erratically from one situation to another. For example, the child who suddenly smashes a toy for no apparent reason is behaving unpredictably.

♦ **Unconventional.** Behavior that psychologists define as unconventional is both rare and undesirable. Geniuses may be eccentric, but a psychologist wouldn't apply the term *unconventional* unless their behavior violates social standards of what is morally acceptable or desirable.

♦ **Distressing.** The person is suffering from severe personal distress or intensely negative emotions. If a person is nervous before an exam, it's normal; if he or she throws up, can't concentrate, and eventually gets up and walks out, that's abnormal.

♦ **Irrational.** The person acts in ways that are incomprehensible to others. Hearing voices or believing that you're overweight at 95 pounds are examples of "irrational" behavior.

Of course, there's another factor involved in any psychological diagnosis—the level of discomfort in the person making the judgment! Certainly, what is defined as "abnormal" partly depends on the comfort level of the society in which we live. A person who hears voices in the United States is much more likely to be labeled "mentally ill" than someone who lives in a culture that views hallucinations as a form of spiritual guidance.

Sick Societies

For hundreds of years, most societies have had a "sick" view of mental illness—they saw abnormal behavior as a sign of evil. Throughout the Middle Ages, for example, concepts of mental illness were intertwined with superstition and religion, and the outcome wasn't pretty. How'd you like having holes drilled in your head to let the evil spirits out?

Until the end of the eighteenth century, the mentally ill in Western cultures were viewed as mindless beasts who could only be controlled with chains and physical discipline. "Psychiatric hospitals" were nothing more than jail cells, when they weren't amusement parks—curious visitors could sometimes pay to view the mentally ill like animals in a zoo. (Except that in modern zoos, we treat the animals more kindly.)

Psychobabble

In Salem, Massachusetts, in 1692, several young girls began experiencing convulsions, nausea, and weakness. They reported sensations of being bitten or pinched, and some became temporarily blind or deaf. Believing that the girls' symptoms were the work of the devil, villagers became caught up in a witchcraft panic that led to the execution of more than 20 men and women believed to be witches. Theories have ranged from ergot poisoning, a fungus that grows on rye and is a source of LSD, to diagnoses of the principle "witnesses" as having histrionic personality disorder or other disorders.

In the 1700s, however, Phillipe Pinel began preaching that the mentally ill were neither immoral nor demonically possessed—they were simply suffering from a sickness. Believing that disorders of thought, mood, and behavior were similar to physical illnesses, he developed the first system to classify psychological disorders. His classifications were a huge step forward because they made it easier for clinicians to identify and design treatments for common disorders.

It wasn't until 1896, however, that the first truly comprehensive system of classifying psychological disorders was created by German psychiatrist Emil Kraeplin. When psychiatrists today speak of "mental illness" and talk of treating "patients," they are borrowing from Kraeplin's medical view of the origins of mental illness. While Kraeplin's medical approach helped reduce the stigma of mental illness, it also slowed down the discovery of the psychological, social, and environmental influences on mental-health problems. It took Sigmund Freud to swing attention back in that direction.

Insight

Good news. A 2004 study found that 76 percent of U.S. managers believe that an employee's acknowledgment of depression would not prevent him or her from getting ahead. The bad news? Only 41 percent of employees believe this.

Psychology Today

Well, today's psychologists have ruled out evil spirits as the source of mental illness—but that's just about as far as we've come. The search for the causes of mental illness is still alive and well, and it's currently led by teams divided into two camps: the biological team and the psychological team.

Walking the Biological Beat

The biological team follows the medical model in assuming that psychological problems are directly attributable to underlying brain or nervous system disorders. The brain is a complex and delicate organ; subtle alterations in its tissue or its chemical messengers can have a dramatic influence on a person's mental health. For example, tumors in certain areas of the brain can cause extremely violent behavior; an autopsy of Charles Joseph Whitman, the "Texas tower" sniper who gunned down 45 people before being killed by two police officers, revealed one. And having too little or too much of even one neurotransmitter can mean the difference between happiness and despair.

The biological approach to mental illness is responsible for developing the powerful psychiatric medications that are available today, some of which enable people to live normal, satisfying lives. Years ago, those same people would have spent their lives chained to the wall of an insane asylum.

Pulling for the Psychological Team

The psychological team, of course, focuses on the causal role of social or psychological factors in the development of *psychopathology*. They search for the personal experiences, traumas, conflicts, parenting styles, and so forth that lead to psychological disorders. A therapist relying on the psychodynamic perspective, for example, might focus on a person's past actions and relationships and the conflicts in these. Behaviorists would examine problem behaviors and the conditions in the environment that keep them in place, while therapists using the cognitive approach would investigate unhealthy reasoning or poor problem solving and its impact on our lives.

def•i•ni•tion

Psychopathology is the clinical term for an abnormality or disorder in thought, emotion, or behavior.

Putting It All Together

Luckily for all of us, the biological and psychological camps are beginning to work together. Both are becoming increasingly aware that psychopathology is the product of a complex interaction between biology and psychology. This is often called the *diathesis-stress* model.

A person might have a genetic susceptibility for depression (biology), but doesn't get depressed until his or her divorce (psychology). In fact, many mental illnesses seem to work this way; a person is vulnerable to a mental illness because of faulty hormones or neurotransmitters, but certain stresses or maladaptive coping strategies are necessary for the illness to fully develop.

def•i•ni•tion

The **diathesis-stress** model of mental illness says that individuals who have a biological predisposition to a certain mental disorder will tend to develop it when under stress.

Of course, it's pretty useless to argue about what *causes* mental illness unless you are in agreement about what it *is*. To create greater consistency among clinicians with various theoretical backgrounds, psychologists and psychiatrists have developed a system of diagnosis and classification that provides precise descriptions of symptoms. At its best, our classification system provides an objective framework for evaluating a person's behavior and picking the most effective treatment. At its worst, it promotes labeling and focuses on the illness rather than on the person who has it.

DSM-IV-TR: The Mental Health Catalog

Without an agreed-upon system to identify people whose disorders are similar to each other, the accumulation of knowledge about causes and effective treatments would be impossible. The system that is currently in vogue is the *DSM-IV-TR*. The "DSM" stands for *Diagnostic and Statistical Manual of Mental Disorders*, and the "IV" means that this is the fourth attempt to get it right. The "TR" stands for "text revision," meaning this was a minor revision (which is why it wasn't version "V") and that the changes were made to some of the descriptions of the disorders but not to the classifications of the disorders themselves. Diagnosis is always a work in progress.

The first version of *DSM* appeared in 1952 and listed several dozen mental illnesses. In 1968, *DSM-II* was published. One of the improvements of this new version was to make the diagnoses more compatible with the international classification system, the World Health Organization's International Classification of

Insight

The current *DSM-IV-TR* attempts to be more culturally sensitive, with even an appendix of disorders apparently only found in certain cultures (for instance, "ghost sickness," a condition associated with some Native American tribes and characterized by very specific psychological and physical symptoms).

Diseases. The *DSM-IV* appeared in 1994, and in 2000 the *DSM-IV-TR*, an expanded but diagnostically compatible version of the *DSM-IV*, was introduced.

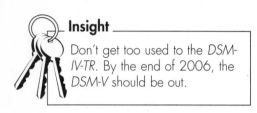

Insight

Don't get too used to the *DSM-IV-TR*. By the end of 2006, the *DSM-V* should be out.

As classification systems go, *DSM-IV-TR* isn't too shabby. First of all, it's pretty reliable: the agreement among diagnosticians as to who has or doesn't have a particular disorder is pretty high. And that's an important point—after all, they must be able to agree on the diagnosis before they compare the individuals who have it.

But is the *DSM-IV-TR* clinically meaningful? That's still a matter of debate. Critics argue that two people with the same diagnosis may suffer in very different ways and respond to different treatments.

Shopping in the *DSM-IV-TR* Catalog

The *DSM-IV-TR* lists more than 200 mental illnesses, grouped under 16 diagnostic categories, summarized as follows. As you review these categories, remember that in order for a diagnostic decision to be made, classification systems must designate some arbitrary cutoff point; below that point you don't have a disorder, and above it you do. In real life, though, mental health and emotional challenges are on a continuum.

- **Anxiety disorders.** A group of disorders in which either fear or anxiety is a major symptom. Examples include panic disorder, phobias, obsessive-compulsive disorder, and post-traumatic stress disorder.

- **Mood disorders.** Disorders characterized by depression or mania. Examples include major depression, bipolar disorder (formerly called manic-depression), dysthymia, and cyclothymia.

- **Somataform disorders.** Disorders in which physical symptoms arise from psychological problems. Examples include somatization disorder and conversion disorder.

- **Substance-related disorders.** Disorders caused by drugs, including alcohol, cocaine, amphetamines, or opiates. Examples include amphetamine withdrawal and alcohol dependence.

- **Dissociative disorders.** Disorders in which a part of one's experience is separated from one's conscious memory or identity. Examples include dissociative identity disorder and psychogenic amnesia.

- **Psychotic disorders.** Disorders characterized by a loss of contact with reality, either through hallucinations, delusions, or inappropriate emotions. Examples include schizophrenia and delusional disorder.

- **Sexual and gender identity disorders.** Sexual disorders are disorders of sexual functioning. Examples include fetishism, exhibitionism, and psychosexual dysfunction. Gender identity disorders involve a persistent desire to be, or appear to be, a member of the opposite sex.

- **Eating disorders.** Disorders marked by excessive concern about weight gain accompanied by extreme undereating, overeating, or purging. Examples include anorexia nervosa and bulimia nervosa.

- **Sleep disorders.** Disorders involving disrupted sleep, sleepwalking, fear of nightmares, or fear of sleep. Examples include insomnia and sleep-wake disorder.

- **Impulse control disorders.** Disorders in which impulsive behaviors harm the self or others. Example include intermittent explosive disorder, kleptomania, and pathological gambling.

- **Disorders usually first diagnosed in infancy, childhood, or adolescence.** A wide range of disorders that appear before adulthood. Examples include mental retardation, learning disorders, and language development disorders.

- **Adjustment disorder.** An extreme emotional reaction to a stressor that occurred within the previous month (much greater than most people would experience).

- **Personality disorders.** Long-term disorders characterized by rigid, maladaptive personality traits. Examples include antisocial personality disorder, histrionic personality disorder, and narcissistic personality disorder.

- **Delirium, dementia, amnestic, and other cognitive disorders.** A diverse group of disorders of memory and cognition that is caused by identifiable brain damage. Examples include Alzheimer's disease, intellectual impairment due to stroke or head injury, and delirium (change in consciousness) as a result of a drug overdose.

- **Mental disorders due to a general medical condition.** A group of mental disorders that can be directly traced to a medical cause. Examples include personality changes due to frontal lobe injury, psychotic disorder due to epilepsy, and depression secondary to diabetes.

- **Factitious disorders.** Physical or psychological symptoms that are faked in order to assume the "sick" role. Examples include making up physical complaints, exaggerating genuine medical symptoms, or self-inflicting wounds and then seeking medical treatment.

Warning: Labels Can Be Hazardous to Your Health

Pretend that you and I are getting ready to go out with another friend of mine, Jan. You've never met Jan, so you're asking me for a little bit of information about her in preparation for our dinner together. I'm singing her praises: "She's really smart, she's headed up the corporate ladder, she's funny, generous, and attractive. Oh, and by the way, she suffers from depression and is on Prozac." Did your level of enthusiasm drop a little with that last remark?

If so, you're like most of us. Diagnosing and labeling may be essential for the scientific study of mental illness. Insurance companies may require them. However, they should be used with caution—studies have shown that labels can be harmful to your mental health.

The Trouble with Tunnel Vision

When we meet a person who is labeled as having a mental disorder, we're often blinded to the qualities of the person that aren't captured by the label. For example, now that Jan has the label "depressed," you're less likely to notice her sense of humor.

Unfortunately, this tunnel vision isn't limited to the layperson—psychotherapists are as susceptible to it as anyone else. In one study, a group of psychotherapists watched a videotape of a man talking about his personal problems. The ones who were told that he was a patient rated his mental health far more negatively than those who were given no such information. Even children treat each other based on labels; a child labeled as having attention deficit disorder, for example, is often ostracized even if he or she doesn't really have the disorder.

Insight

The movie *Frances* is a disturbing and controversial look at the life of actress Frances Farmer and her involuntary commitment to a mental hospital. Not only will you see a stunning performance by Jessica Lange, but you'll also become a mental health activist for life.

That's a Person Under That Label!

Worse still, these labels can hurt the people who carry them. In another experiment, former patients in a psychiatric hospital were found to be much more socially inept if they believed that their psychiatric treatment was known to the person with whom they were interacting.

Obviously, mental-health professionals should continually evaluate the pros and cons of psychiatric labels. And both professionals *and* laypersons should work hard to use language that distinguishes the person from his or her diagnosis. It is dangerous and damaging to call someone "an anorexic" or "a schizophrenic." Such language implies that the diagnosis sums up the entire person. If I truly had my way, we'd say, "Joni has received the diagnosis of anorexia nervosa from a mental-health professional." That way, the person is distinct from the illness, *and* we'd be acknowledging that the diagnosis itself is a judgment made by a fallible human being. It's subjective and never completely reliable.

Psychobabble

In the nineteenth century, Samuel Cartwright argued that slaves were suffering from two forms of mental illness: 1) drapetomania, an uncontrollable urge to escape from slavery, and 2) dyasthesia aethiopica, which included symptoms such as being disobedient, talking back, refusing to work, and fighting back when being beaten. I can think of a few labels that might fit Mr. Cartwright; how about you?

The Gender Politics of Mental Illness

Before I get completely off my soapbox, I should tell you a story. In the 1970s, a study asked a number of mental-health professionals to describe a mentally healthy man. Adjectives like *assertive* and *confident* were used. These same people were asked to describe a mentally healthy woman. This time words like *warm, sensitive, nurturing* appeared. Then came the biggest challenge: describe a mentally healthy *person*. Want to know what happened? The mentally healthy person had the same traits as the mentally healthy man. So where does that leave those of us of the female persuasion?

Gender differences in mental health diagnoses exist, and their causes have been debated ever since they were noticed. Although there is little difference between men and women in the overall prevalence of mental illness, large gender differences are found for specific disorders. Women are much more likely to be diagnosed with anxiety and mood disorders, and men are more likely than women to be diagnosed with substance-abuse problems and antisocial personality disorder. (Although this is changing as roles change; analysis of mental-health data collected between 1950 and 1980 found that, as employment for men and women became more similar, the gender gap in anxiety and mood disorders declined.)

Without getting dragged into the nature-nurture debate again, let's consider a few explanations for why this might be so. It is possible that such differences might directly come from biological differences between the sexes. Most attention, though, has been paid to the sociocultural explanations for these differences, such as self-reporting differences, biased observers, and gender-based differences in life experiences.

Generally speaking, men are much less likely to seek treatment for emotional problems and more reluctant to admit to psychological distress. For instance, experiments have shown that when men and women are subjected to the same stressful situation, such as a final exam, men show physical signs of distress equal to or greater than female peers but are much less likely to admit to it during interviews or on questionnaires. In addition, women receive more social permission to express sadness and fear, while men have more freedom to express anger.

Psychologists are people, too, with their own biases, opinions, and values. These biases may at times influence their clinical decisions. For example, studies suggest that diagnoses may sometimes be circular; because some diagnoses occur more frequently in men and women, clinicians may expect to find them. And, not surprisingly, they find what they are looking for!

Are You Insane?

On March 30, 1981, John W. Hinckley Jr. shot President Ronald Reagan. His defense attorneys did not dispute that he had planned and committed the act. Instead, they argued that he was not guilty by reason of insanity. Specifically, they argued that Hinckley's life was controlled by his pathological obsession with the movie *Taxi Driver*, starring Jodie Foster. In that movie, Foster's character is terrorized by a stalker, who eventually gets into a shootout. The defense attorney argued that Hinckley was schizophrenic, and that the movie was the force behind his assassination attempt against the president. The jury believed it.

Mental Illness vs. Insanity

Mental illness is a medical decision. Insanity, on the other hand, is a legal one. To be insane, a person must be unable to control her behavior and be unaware that her behavior is wrong. If Mr. X, on trial for shooting his boss, truly believed he needed to defend himself against a corporate conspiracy that was ruining his life, he might honestly think that his actions were justified; in fact, he might believe that his actions would protect others from receiving similar treatment. Serial killers like Ted Bundy, on the other hand, do bizarre things but have a clear awareness that their behavior is morally and socially wrong.

The insanity defense is based on the principle that punishment is justified only if the defendant is capable of understanding and controlling his or her behavior. Because some people suffering from a mental disorder are not capable of knowing or choosing right from wrong, the insanity defense prevents them from going to prison.

The Perils of Pleading Insanity

Despite popular belief, the insanity defense is not the easy way out. Defendants rarely enter pleas of "not guilty by reason of insanity," probably because it works less than 1 percent of the time. Also, defendants who are successful may, over time, wish they hadn't been. Their "successful" defense gets them confined to a mental institution until their sanity is established. Some of these defendants spend more time in a mental institution than they would have served in prison. There's an excellent movie on the subject, appropriately entitled *Nuts*.

Stigma Is a Dirty Word

If you missed Tom Cruise railing against psychiatrists and antidepressants in 2005, you were probably either suffering from a power outage or engaging in a media strike. After Brooke Shields publicized her agonizing battle with postpartum depression, Mr. Cruise criticized her "misguided" use of antidepressants and stated that she was irresponsible for promoting the use of psychotropic medication; instead, he stated that vitamins, a proper diet, and exercise should have been her drugs of choice. In reality, while Cruise was correct in that exercise and proper diet can certainly be effective with *mild* depression, trying to treat a suicidal individual with a bowl of Wheaties and a run around the block is not likely to cut the mustard.

In spite of numerous public education campaigns, you can still find major American newspapers running articles that advise the depressed to "Buck up," "Throw away your antidepressants," or "Go away and sulk until you're ready to be sociable." Such stigmatizing

> **Insight**
>
> Television is our number-one source of information about mental illness—and, unfortunately, it's an extremely poor one. While mentally ill individuals are much more likely to hurt themselves than others, mentally ill characters on prime-time television are portrayed as violent 70 percent of the time.

attitudes lead many who would benefit from treatment to avoid getting it and to hide their pain from friends and family members. Tipper Gore, who went public about her own experience with depression after her son's near-fatal car crash, probably thought long and hard about the possible impact of her disclosure on the Gore campaign. No one, it seems, is immune from the stigma of mental illness.

These attitudes ignore the fact that many mental illnesses have a biological basis. Nearly 25 percent of us see mental illness as a personal shortcoming, and 60 percent of employers say that they would "never" hire a candidate who had been diagnosed with depression for an executive job. It seems that, so far, psychology has done a better job at diagnosing individual problems than "treating" the society that condemns them.

Five Things You Can Do to Fight Stigma

You might not be a psychologist, but there's a lot you can do to improve our *society's* mental health. Here are five:

♦ Wise up. Mental illness is not a character flaw, a lack of willpower, or a luxury. People with mental illness are much more likely to be victims, not perpetrators of crime. And people who suffer from a mental illness can be just as effective as people with a physical illness. (Do the names Winston Churchill and Abraham Lincoln ring a bell?)

♦ Avoid using slang like "crazy," "loony," or "nuts" to describe people or situations, even if you're just kidding around.

♦ Be a media watchdog. Fire off letters to editors, writers, and producers who include demeaning expressions or inaccurate descriptions of mental illness in their work.

♦ Don't be afraid to tell someone if you're concerned about his emotional well-being or if you know he's received psychiatric treatment. Asking about someone's mental health problems does not make him worse.

♦ Take charge of your own mental health. If you've struggled with depression or anxiety for a while, get some help.

The Least You Need to Know

◆ Many mental illnesses are a complex interaction between a biological predisposition and stressful life events.

◆ Diagnoses are labels that mental-health professionals use to group together people who have the same symptoms and behaviors.

◆ The most popular classification system in the United States is the *DSM-IV-TR.* It lists more than 200 mental diagnoses, which can be grouped into 16 categories.

◆ While mental illness is a medical decision, insanity—the inability to control one's behavior and distinguish between right and wrong—is strictly a legal determination.

◆ The stigma of mental illness is one of the greatest barriers people face in finding the courage to get help for mental problems.

Chapter **17**

Look on the Bright Side

In This Chapter

- Moving from surviving to thriving
- Joining the "hardy" party and making all Cs"
- Raising children who bounce back from tough times
- Learning how to go with the flow
- Discovering why you should watch comedies

In 1998, APA president Martin Seligman was working in his garden when he had an epiphany that "the entire psychology profession was 'half-baked.'" The catalyst for this unsettling revelation was his five-year-old daughter, Nikki, who had joined her weed-pulling father in their garden. However, while his goal was to leave the garden with fewer weeds in it than when he arrived, hers was to incorporate each pile of pulled weeds into her spontaneous song-and-dance routine by throwing them up in the air.

A self-confessed grouch, Dr. Seligman yelled at his daughter for her unproductive shenanigans. "Daddy," she said in response. "do you remember before my fifth birthday? From the time I was three to the time I was five, I was a whiner. I whined every day. When I turned five, I decided not to whine anymore. That was the hardest thing I've ever done. And if I can stop whining, you can stop being such a grouch."

Nikki's proclamation triggered a little self-analysis in her father and ultimately led to some questions about the field of psychology. Dr. Seligman wondered why it was that his psychological training had little to offer Nikki by way of encouraging a positive attitude or strengthening the will she'd already evinced. "What about the positive aspects of human nature that so often make life such a thrilling, rewarding experience?" he wondered. Once psychology got hurting people back in the game of life, how could psychology help them win? And so began the field of positive psychology.

This chapter is about building the human strengths that make a good life better, help us thrive in the face of adversity, and act as buffers against mental illness—strengths like resilience, optimism, and the capacity for flow and insight. We'll discover how exercising our mental muscles can do as much for our psyche as physical exercise can do for our bodies, and how we can help our children develop the psyches to deal with life's curveballs.

Going Back to Square One

By redirecting the focus from illness to strength, Dr. Seligman was bringing psychology back to its roots. Before World War II, psychology understood itself as having three specific missions: 1) diagnosing and treating mental illness, 2) maximizing the happiness and productivity of all people, and 3) identifying and nurturing extraordinary talents and qualities. Psychological research routinely looked at positive human aspects such as the nature of genius, effective parenting, and marital happiness; for example, the great Carl Jung did a lot of work on our innate human need to discover a true and rewarding meaning to life.

After the war, however, psychology began to increasingly concern itself with the diagnosis and treatment of mental illness. World War II left thousands of soldiers psychologically damaged. In 1946, the Veteran's Administration was founded, and scores of psychologists began treating mental illness through the VA system.

A year later, the National Institute of Mental Health was founded. Given the state and orientation of the health professions at the time, the NIMH was naturally conceived of and created upon the medical model of healing disease. In turn, then, the institute began rewarding significant grant money to those academics and/or psychologists whose research was about pathology.

Suddenly it paid to think a lot less about happiness, productivity, and giftedness, and a lot more about disease, dysfunction, and deviation from the norm. And to a large extent, this investment in mental illness paid off. Tremendous strides have been made in understanding and treating mental illness. There has been an explosion in research on psychological disorders and the negative effects of environmental stressors such as parental divorce, death, and physical and sexual abuse. A great number of disorders that 50 years ago seemed unfathomable have since yielded their mysteries to science and can now be either cured or substantially relieved.

> **Insight**
>
> Recent research has found that optimism may reduce the risk of health problems and may actually help a person recover after experiencing a serious life-changing event like the death of a family member. Pessimists are more likely to emotionally distance themselves from upsetting events rather than actively take control of what parts of a tragedy (or its aftermath) they can.

Keeping It Real

Given psychology's recent focus on trauma and disease, it should come as no surprise that in the psychological literature over the last 30 years, there have been over 50,000 abstracts containing the keyword "depression," but fewer than 1,000 that mention "joy." And yet, in real life, positive events and interactions occur much more frequently than negative ones. For example, when asked how often different social events happened in the past week from a list of eight positive (e.g., a friend, romantic partner, or family member complimented me) and eight negative ones (e.g., a friend, family member, or romantic partner insulted me), participants reported that the negative interactions occurred an average of 5.9 times and the positive interactions occurred 19.0 times—3.2 positive events for every 1 negative event.

Indeed, because positive events occur more often, their impact in the long run may be greater than negative ones, even though the impact of any single positive experience may be more subtle than that of a solo unpleasant one. In a 2001 study, two researchers found that Catholic nuns who wrote happier essays in their early 20s lived longer than nuns whose essays lacked positive emotional content.

Don't get confused, though. "Positive" doesn't mean unrealistic. In fact, while it has been well documented that happy adults tend to live longer, make more friends, and achieve more at work, new research suggests that a relentlessly positive outlook may make us less motivated and less conscientious. Mildly negative moods can help us be more critical and analytical, giving us vital feedback about the need to shift directions or change our strategy. And those of us who are constantly happy may not have the internal gauge that tells us when we need to apply more effort or energy to get what we want; in the long run, this may not serve us well.

Neither does "positive" mean denial. There is a very real negative side of life that, for virtually all of us, results in a certain degree of emotional pain. People in denial hide under their covers: they avoid facing facts and resist their feelings. On the other hand, a positive spin on life's crises means the opposite; it means not distracting oneself by dwelling on what might have happened, and confronting problems by focusing on solutions.

> **Brain Buster**
>
> For chronic worriers, thinking through the "worst-case scenario" and having a plan in advance can actually work better than trying to see the glass as "half full." On the other hand, those of us who aren't anxious do well to set high expectations and then avoid thinking about what might happen.

What positive psychology research does tell us is that we can learn to create more pleasurable life experiences (satisfaction with the past, happiness in the present, and hope for the future) and that there are certain traits that can help us individually thrive in the face of life's toughest challenges. We can use these traits to create the kind of families and institutions that will foster the best in all of us. These are the kinds of things that keep positive psychologists up at night!

Don't Just Follow Your Bliss—Create It!

As we've seen, positive psychology is not about denial, boundless optimism, or eternally cheerful emotions. It is intended as a research-based approach to understanding and building emotional well-being, and finding meaningful, measurable, and attainable ways to be happy.

Seligman, in fact, talks about three different forms of happiness: the pleasant life, the good life, and the meaningful life. The pleasant life is what most of us think of when we consider whether we are happy or not in any given moment; it's the "feel good" part of happiness. When we don't feel happy, we are more likely to take shortcuts to alter our moods—through drugs, mindless entertainment, food, and so on.

However, there are other paths to happiness: the good life and the meaningful life. Both of these can be reached by recognizing, and harnessing, our strengths. The good life comes through deep engagement in work, family life, or other activities. The meaningful life comes through finding a purpose in our existence, whether it's through spirituality or a cause greater than oneself. Of course, positive psychologists would also encourage us to avoid the negative while we're pursuing the positive; it's hard to be upbeat when we're watching endless hours of tragedy on the news, living at the hub of a gossip circle, or talking excessively about a political smear campaign.

> **Insight**
>
> A study of lottery winners showed that within months of their initial elation, they were exactly as happy (or unhappy) as they'd been before they'd won. Research shows that our mood is largely dependent on genes. However, while we may inherit a potential range of good cheer, we can develop ways to make sure we are at the upper end of that range.

From Surviving to Thriving

Trisha Meili, the "Central Park jogger," was given last rites after her rape and savage beating in New York. Only the soles of her feet were unbruised. Multiple gashes split Meili's scalp; an eye socket was fractured in 21 places. She could not breathe on her own, lost most of her blood, and had severe brain damage.

But she didn't die. In fact, she thrived. She pushed herself through an accelerated rehabilitation and returned to work despite not feeling 100 percent mentally or physically. She was promoted to vice-president. She gathered the strength to testify at two criminal trials of the five teenagers accused of assaulting her, and later coped with the knowledge that she had unwittingly testified against innocent men. Today she's a motivational speaker and volunteer who talks about her healing to medical and mental-health groups, patients, and others recovering from traumatic changes.

Meili will never be 100 percent her old self. But her life is rewarding, she feels a sense of purpose, and she's happy.

The "Hardy" Partiers

Amazing as Meili's mega-recovery might seem, it came as no surprise to *resilience* researchers, the psychologists who spend their time studying what separates those of us who thrive under adversity from those of us who barely keep our heads above water. Even before that fateful day in Central Park, Meili's personal

def•i•ni•tion

> **Resilience** is the ability to thrive, mature, and increase competence in the face of risk and adversity.

history suggested that she had developed coping strategies similar to those identified by Dr. Salvatore R. Maddi as characteristic of the "hardy personality."

Here's how he did it. In 1981 Illinois Bell Telephone downsized from 26,000 employees to just over half that many in one year. The remaining employees faced changing job descriptions, company goals, and supervisors. Dr. Maddi and his research team, who were already studying more than 400 supervisors, managers, and executives at IBT before the downsizing, were able to continue following them until 1987. Results revealed that about two thirds of the employees in the study suffered significant performance, leadership, and health declines as the result of extreme stress. However, the other one third actually thrived during the upheaval despite experiencing the same amount of disruption and stressful events as their co-workers. These employees maintained their health, happiness, and performance and felt renewed enthusiasm.

Insight

Research indicates that our genes influence how rosy our disposition naturally is. However, we can all learn ways to be resilient, to stay in the present, keep things in perspective, and work on the problems at hand.

But why? What made the two groups so different? Dr. Maddi found that those who thrived maintained three key beliefs that helped them turn adversity into an advantage: commitment, control, and challenge attitudes. The commitment attitude led them to strive to be involved in ongoing events, rather than feeling isolated. The control attitude led them to struggle and try to influence outcomes, rather than lapse into passivity and powerlessness. And the challenge attitude led them to view changes, whether positive or negative, as opportunities for learning.

Raising Tiggers Who Bounce Back from Stress

Resilience, the ability to bounce back during tough times, is a skill that we can develop no matter what age we are. Of course, it helps if we get a leg up from the beginning. Here are some ways that parents can plant the seeds of resilience that will bloom into an ongoing sense of challenge, commitment, and control.

Commitment starts with the right connections. Help your child develop empathy by having empathy for your child. For example, before you utter parenting words like "try harder" or "speak up," think about how you would feel if someone gave that advice to you. Which is more likely to foster resilience in a shy child: "If you don't start speaking up, your teacher is going to think you don't care" or "Many kids who have trouble speaking in front of a group at the beginning of the year feel more comfortable as they get to know their classmates"? The latter statement is more likely to give the child a sense of hope and understanding—two things she needs to develop a sense of optimism.

A sense of control starts with a balanced perspective between what we can change and what we can't. When your child has a new problem or challenge, ask her to write down all the possible actions she could take to solve—or at least change—the problem. And don't forget to address the self-talk that goes along with the problem; one of the greatest strengths any parent can give a child is helping him or her learn to recognize—and gain control over—the internal dialogue that takes place as we go through every day.

Challenge starts with self-confidence. Identify and nurture your child's strengths; every kid needs to feel capable and good about himself. And one of the best ways you can grow your kid's confidence is to ask him for help. In fact, when 1,500 adults were asked, "What is your favorite positive memory of school?" the number-one positive memory was when they were asked to help out. Feeling like they can make a positive difference makes kids more confident, more hopeful, and more resilient.

Brain Buster

Increase your family optimism by having each member keep track of the positive events in his or her life. For example, for the next month, have each family member keep a daily log of three things that went well and why. Share them with each other once a week.

Going with the Flow at Work

There were times when I was writing this book when I was so intensely engrossed in what I was doing that I lost track of time and felt slightly disoriented when briefly (but, alas, frequently) interrupted by one of my children. When I found an interesting tidbit to include, I felt pure, unadulterated joy. In fact, I was enjoying this process so much that I felt like I was going through withdrawal when I had to turn off my computer and put my attention elsewhere.

According to Dr. Mihaly Csikszentmihalyi, a psychology professor at the University of Chicago who pioneered research on optimal experiences, I was in a state of effortless concentration and enjoyment called *flow*. And, given the right circumstances, we can all learn to reach it.

def•i•ni•tion

According to Mihaly Csikszentmihalyi, **flow** is the sense of effortless action we feel when we are totally absorbed in a task.

This complete immersion in an experience can happen in any number of circumstances—singing in a choir, dancing, performing a complicated surgical operation, or playing with a baby. Athletes often call it "being in the zone." These exceptional moments provide flashes of intense living against the dull background of everyday life.

But where do we find it and how do we get more of it? Apparently, we tend to enter flow during a certain set of circumstances—when the activity provides us with a clear set of goals, clearly outlined responses or actions, and unambiguous and immediate feedback. As a result, it is easier to enter flow in games like tennis or poker, or activities like mountain climbing or piano playing, than it is in the muddier circumstances of day-to-day life that are filled with multitasking, ongoing projects, and unclear feedback. Flow also happens when the challenge we are tackling is pretty compatible with our skill level; if it's too easy, we get bored, and if it's too hard, we get frustrated.

Believe it or not, people find flow most often when they are at work. In some ways, this isn't surprising: work is more like a game than most other things we do, in that it usually has clear goals and rules and we get feedback in terms of supervisor feedback, sales figures, or task completion. A job also tends to encourage concentration and prevent distractions, and ideally, its difficulties match the worker's skills.

Nevertheless, research suggests that we aren't obtaining flow at work as often as we could. Short of making a dramatic career switch, there are many ways to make our job produce more flow. And the secret may lie in the way we approach the job. Here are some examples:

Try turning a job with repetitive tasks into an efficiency or productivity game. Let's say you're waiting tables while waiting for that big Hollywood agent to discover you. What would make your job more efficient, easier, faster, or more tip-inducing? What additional steps could make your customers happier? Is it possible that you might enjoy working more if you spent the same amount of attention trying to find ways to accomplish more on the job than you do daydreaming about your future life on the big screen?

Use the secrets of flow to tackle work stress. Successful people often make lists or flowcharts of all the things they have to do, and quickly decide which tasks they can delegate or forget, and which ones they have to tackle personally, and in what order. The next step is to match your skills with whatever challenges have been identified. There will be tasks you feel incompetent to deal with. Can you learn the skills required in time? Can you get help? Can the task be transformed, or broken into simpler parts? Usually the answer to one of these questions will provide a solution that transforms a potentially stressful situation into a flow experience.

Watch Two Simpsons and Call Me in the Morning

After the birth of my oldest son, I went into a serious postpartum funk. Recovering from a C-section with a colicky infant, the joys of motherhood were not readily apparent to me, a fact about which I felt frightened and ashamed. Luckily for me, one of my mentors, a fellow psychologist, came to visit me shortly after I came home from the hospital. In talking about how she coped with the stress of sleep deprivation and bawling babies, she casually mentioned that she had rented a lot of funny movies. To this day, I can't watch John Candy in *Planes, Trains, and Automobiles* without flashing back to myself 11 years ago—bloodshot eyes, saggy and sore tummy and all—sitting on the couch and howling with laughter. Perhaps laughter really is the best medicine.

Escaping into John Candy's world didn't change my challenges of adjusting to motherhood; it just helped me see reality in a different light. From a mental-health standpoint, humor helps us get a perspective rather than wallow in the cognitive distortion ("My life is over!") that often accompanies emotional distress. In other words, humor helps us adjust the meaning of an event so that it is not so overwhelming.

Here are some additional things we can do to improve our mood, enjoyment of life, and mental health:

- Attempt to laugh at situations rather than bemoan them—this helps improve our disposition and the dispositions of those around us.

- Use cathartic laughter to release pent-up feelings of anger and frustration in socially acceptable ways.

- Lower anxiety by visualizing a humorous situation to replace the view of an anxiety-producing situation.

Laughter also improves our physical well-being. Countless studies show that people who laugh more live longer and feel better throughout the course of their lives. In fact, for Norman Cousins, diagnosed in the mid-1960s with a degenerative disease that causes the breakdown of the tissues that bind together the body's cells, it was a matter of life and death. Cousins, barely able to move and given but a few months to live, checked himself out of the hospital, stopped taking drugs, and self-prescribed a new regime of pain killers: lots of vitamin C and a minimum of one Laurel and Hardy movie per day. He found that 15 minutes of laughing and guffawing could provide him with up to two hours of pain relief. He gradually regained his health and eventually resumed his job as editor of the *Saturday Review*.

The increase of our pain threshold during and after bouts of laughter has since been confirmed in many studies. Besides triggering the release of endorphins (the body's natural pain killer), laughter also removes stress hormones and boosts our immune function by raising T-cell levels, disease-fighting proteins called Gamma-interferon, and B-cells, which produce antibodies that destroy disease. Laughter is also a solid cardiovascular workout: it increases our heart's activity, stimulates our circulation, and, afterward, helps our bodies relax. He who laughs best doesn't only laugh last—he lives longer!

In this chapter, we've explored positive psychology—the science of investigating what can make an okay life better and what qualities increase the odds that we'll bounce back from adversity. We've examined ways we can increase the amount of pleasure in our lives, be more resilient, find more flow in our work, and use laughter to boost our mental and physical health.

> **Psychobabble**
>
> In 1995, Bombay physician Dr. Madan Kataria, a.k.a. the "The Guru of Giggling," formed The Laughter Club International. Together, thousands of members of LCI clubs all over the world get together for a communal crack-up. For more information, check out Dr. Kataria's website at www.laughteryoga.org.

But what if our life isn't okay? What if we find ourselves staring down into such a black hole of depression that we can't get out of bed in the morning? What if we're so anxious that we haven't slept for weeks and are starting to wonder if life is worth living? In Chapter 18, we'll take a look at what state-of-the-art weapons psychology has to help us conquer, or at least control, mental illness.

The Least You Need to Know

- Whereas traditional psychology has been very much about understanding and fixing what goes wrong with the human psyche, positive psychology focuses on discovering, and nurturing, what's right with it.

- Just as we can systematically learn to undo negative ways of responding to stress, we can also learn ways to become stronger, braver, wiser, more resilient, and ultimately happier, too.

- Dr. Salvatore Maddi discovered the "hardy personality," a cluster of coping attitudes that help individuals bounce back from the toughest adversity. These include an ongoing commitment to others, a sense of control over one's life, and a pattern of viewing adversity as a challenge rather than a crisis.

- "Flow" is a term coined by Dr. Mihaly Csikszentmihalyi to describe the pleasant state we all experience when we're so involved in what we're doing that we, in essence, lose ourselves.

- Countless studies show the power of laughter to enhance our physical and mental well-being.

Weapons Against Mental Dysfunction

In This Chapter

- Discovering how psychiatric meds can smooth out moods and lift your spirits
- Finding out the shocking truth about shock therapy
- Learning what all good therapists (and therapies) have in common
- Investigating the latest trends in the psychotherapy business

Irene was an isolated 29-year-old woman with two children, an unemployed and substance-abusing husband, and a severe case of depression. For help she turned to Dr. Aaron Beck, a pioneer in treating depression with psychotherapy.

After six months with Dr. Beck, Irene was practically a new woman. She joined a tennis club, got a job as a waitress, and enrolled in a college course. She also left her husband when he refused to participate in couples' therapy and continued to treat her badly. Dr. Beck pronounced his client "depression free" and Irene proclaimed her therapy was money well spent.

On the other hand, Julie's depression had been unresponsive to antidepressants, lithium, and years of psychotherapy. Desperate at age 32, she tried electroshock therapy. "It's a miracle," she says. "Years ago I would have been locked up in a mental hospital. Today, my depression has lifted and I'm doing better than a lot of people who never suffered from depression."

In this chapter, we'll explore the two paths people travel when they're seeking help for emotional problems: biological and psychotherapeutic. The former involves medical treatments, including psychotropic drugs, electroconvulsive (shock) therapy, and psychosurgery. The other consists of the various "talking cures," which may involve one-on-one counseling, couples or family therapy, or group sessions. We'll explore the myths and realities of psychiatric medications and take a look at some of the more controversial treatments from yesterday and today. We'll also take a look at the who, what, when, where, and whys of psychotherapy and how new trends can help you get the most bang for your treatment buck.

def•i•ni•tion

In psychotherapy, the **patient** or **client** is the person seeking professional help. Medically or biologically oriented therapists generally use the term *patient*, while those who tend to think of psychological disorders as problems with living generally use the term *client*.

Better Living Through Chemistry

Psychiatrists use their understanding of the physical structure of the brain to alter the mind. If you think of the mind as a computer, then you can think of biological treatments as trying to fix the hardware (the brain) to heal the mind (the software). And one of the most effective ways to bring a misfiring brain back to normal is through psychiatric medication. The right dose of the right medication can dissolve hallucinations, douse depression, level out moods, and soothe anxiety.

It all started in France. In the 1950s, French psychiatrists Jean Delay and Pierre Deniker used chlorpromazine to treat the symptoms of schizophrenia and started a whole new era in the treatment of mental disorders. Today, psychiatric medications are available for just about any disorder ranging from attention deficit disorder to depression. In fact, antidepressants are so widely prescribed that we've been dubbed the "Prozac generation."

Considering the short time they've been around, psychiatric medications have made dramatic changes in the treatment of mental disorders. People who, years ago, might have spent many years in mental hospitals because of crippling mental illness may now only go in for brief treatment, or might receive all their treatment at an outpatient clinic.

Psychotherapeutic medications also may make other kinds of treatment more effective. Someone who is too depressed to talk, for instance, can't get much benefit from psychotherapy or counseling; but often, the right medication will improve symptoms so that the person can respond better.

Another benefit from these medications is an increased understanding of the causes of mental illness. Scientists have learned a great deal more about the workings of the brain as a result of their investigations into how psychotherapeutic medications relieve disorders such as psychosis, depression, anxiety, obsessive-compulsive disorder, and panic disorder.

> **Insight**
>
> Challenging recent claims linking antidepressant use to suicidal behavior, a February 2005 UCLA study showed that American suicide rates have dropped steadily since the introduction of Prozac and other serotonin reuptake inhibitor (SSRI) drugs, and caution that regulatory actions to limit SSRI prescriptions may actually increase death rates from untreated depression, the number-one cause of suicide.

Can't You Get the Dose Right?

On the other hand, medication evaluation is not an exact science, and that can be frustrating. How long someone must take a psychotherapeutic medication depends on the disorder. Many depressed and anxious people may need medication for a single period, perhaps for several months, and then never have to take it again. For some conditions, such as schizophrenia or manic-depressive illness, a person may have to take medication indefinitely or, perhaps, intermittently.

But the biggest barrier to psychiatric medication is fear and confusion about what the drug might do. Having a frank conversation with your health-care physician (not to mention doing some personal research on the internet) about side effects, length of time you need to be on it, and so on, is a good way to channel this fear.

> **Psychobabble**
>
> Complaining about your medical treatment? Count your blessings. In the twelfth century, physicians often tried to cure their patients' problems by drilling holes in their skulls to let out "bad spirits."

Choosing Your Drugs Carefully

Before we move along to other biological treatments of psychological disorders, let's nail down some basic information to help keep all these drugs straight. Medications that are used to treat psychological disorders are classified according to their clinical class, chemical class, and action:

- ◆ Clinical class is the drug's purpose, such as antipsychotic, antidepressant, sedative, or antianxiety. Valium is clinically classed as a sedative/hypnotic, Zyprexa and Clozaril are antipsychotics, Xanax is clinically classed as an antianxiety drug, and Prozac is clinically classed as an antidepressant.

- ◆ Chemical class is what the drug is made of. Xanax and Valium are chemically classed as benzodiazepines, for example. (*Benzo* means amphetamine and *diazepine* means relaxant.)

- ◆ Action refers to what the drug does. For example, Prozac works as a selective serotonin reuptake inhibitor, rather than as a direct stimulant to the nervous system, like Ritalin.

There's plenty of information available about these medications, and one place to look them up quickly is on the Internet. Try www.intelihealth.com and click on its drug-information section. The *Physicians' Desk Reference* at your local library is also a good source. And before you take any meds, ask your doctor these questions:

1. What is the goal of this medication and how does it work?

2. For how long will I need to take it?

3. When can I expect to feel better?

4. What are the side effects?

5. What are my treatment alternatives?

6. What happens when I stop taking it?

7. Is this FDA drug approved for the disorder and patient demographics for which I might use it?

> **Insight**
>
> If you're taking psychiatric medication, never go off it "cold turkey" no matter how good you feel. Any medication changes should take place under medical supervision.

> **Insight**
>
> Psychotropic medications can successfully combat symptoms of depression, anxiety, and psychosis. However, anyone who talks about suicide should be closely monitored by a mental-health professional. A review of more than 71,000 patients in clinical trials of 52 psychotropic medications found an equal risk of suicide among those assigned medication and those taking placebos.

Kiddy Candy?

About 15 percent of U.S. children below age 18—about 9 million—have a mental-health problem severe enough to interfere with their ability to function. Mental-health treatment—including psychotropic medication—can be for these kids a lifesaver as long as the risks are taken as seriously as the rewards.

For instance, in 2004, the U.S. Food and Drug Administration (FDA) warned that people with heart problems—especially children—should not take the hyperactivity drug Adderall; and in 2005, Cyalert, an attention deficit/hyperactivity disorder (ADHD) medication that has been around for 30 years, was taken off the market completely. In 2004, the FDA required all antidepressants to carry "black box" warnings that they "may increase the risk of suicidal thinking and behavior" in children who take them.

A survey of primary care doctors giving children stimulants, commonly prescribed for ADHD, found multiple psychiatric medicines prescribed in about 5 percent of office visits during 1993–1994. That surged to 25 percent of visits in 1997–1998.

The trend is raising worries about potential unknown side effects according to a study in the August 2005 issue of *Psychiatry*. The study found that the most frequent combination included stimulants such as Ritalin, Dexedrine, and Adderall used along with other psychotropic medication.

The ABCs of ECT

Does the thought of electric shock therapy give you the heebie-jeebies? I hate to admit it, but even with the clinical knowledge I have, it's hard for me to stomach the thought of shocking someone. But for some people who suffer major depression so profound that suicidal thoughts have begun, *electroconvulsive therapy* (*ECT*, commonly called shock therapy) can be a viable option.

Insight

About 70 percent of those suffering from major depression who have not responded to other treatments get better with ECT. Sometimes the depression goes away for good; other times it reoccurs after several months.

ECT has split the psychiatric community since it was pioneered more than 50 years ago and, back then, its bad reputation was well deserved. Before modern procedures were invented, the seizure induced by the electric shock was so violent that the muscular contractions would break bones. Today ECT is painless and quite safe. Patients are given drugs to block muscle and nerve activity so that no pain or muscular contractions occur. Doctors may disagree about when, or whether, ECT should be used, but all agree that the technology has steadily improved.

Still, some patients complain of lifelong memory lapses after ECT. Studies on the brain show no evidence of permanent memory loss, nor do brain scans show any chemical or structural changes after repeated ECT shocks. However, until this discrepancy between science and personal anecdote is resolved, ECT will continue to be seen as a treatment alternative that should come only after medications and therapy have been tried and have failed.

Frances Farmer Doesn't Live Here Anymore

Is there any word scarier than "lobotomy"? When physician Gottlieb Burhardt first performed the operation in 1892 on six schizophrenic patients, a few became calmer afterward—but two died. Small wonder that for the next 40 years doctors weren't eager to duplicate Dr. Burhardt's efforts. That view shifted, however, when several research labs in the United States began making amazing discoveries about the role of the temporal and frontal lobes in controlling emotional behavior and aggressiveness.

From the late 1930s to the early 1950s, thousands of men and women were subjected to a prefrontal lobotomy, in which the front portions of their frontal lobes were surgically separated from the rest of their brain. The operation was used to treat people with severe cases of schizophrenia, bipolar disorder, depression, obsessive-compulsive disorder, and pathological violence. (At the time lobotomies were so highly regarded that in 1949 the Portuguese neurosurgeon who pioneered the new technique, Antonio Egas Moniz, was awarded the Nobel Prize.)

Sadly, while lobotomies did relieve patients of their incapacitating emotions, it also left them with lifelong deficits in their ability to make plans and follow through with them; they became ghosts of their former selves. Sometimes, it seems, the very parts of ourselves that are the most troublesome are inseparably linked to the parts that make us uniquely human.

Psychosurgery Revised

Although lobotomies are no longer performed, there are a rare few individuals who are helped by a new kind of psychosurgery known as *cingulotomy*. The cingulum, a small structure in the limbic system known to be involved in emotionality, is partially destroyed with radio-frequency current applied through fine wire electrodes temporarily implanted in the brain. Follow-up studies suggest that these operations most often reduce or abolish major depression and obsessive-compulsive disorder and have rarely left the patient worse off than before.

Cingulotomy, like the earlier lobotomy, is still controversial, but to someone who has been seriously depressed for many years, and who has gotten no relief from ECT and every antidepressant medication on the market, it's something to consider. Blessedly, this degree of treatment failure rarely happens. And, no matter how you feel about it, cingulotomy does help.

Winning the Battle with the Talking Cures

Whenever I used to travel on business, the person sitting next to me on the plane or train would inevitably ask, "What do you do for a living?" and like an idiot, I always said "psychologist." Before you could blink an eye, my seatmate would be deep into a discussion of his or her latest problems. Out of desperation, I finally learned my lesson. Now I tell my travel mates that I'm a funeral director—and my travels are much more peaceful.

While travelers are often willing to unload their inner feelings to a captive audience (and a stranger) on a train, bus, or plane, people often feel shame and embarrassment about going into psychotherapy. Even if they think it's okay for someone else, they often resist the idea for themselves—as if this would be an admission of some personal flaw. And the media doesn't help. When we see therapist and client hopping into the sack on television, it's no wonder no one wants to see a "shrink."

Media misrepresentations and invalid stereotypes about therapy are everywhere. But the fact is that a person's experience of therapy will depend on what brought him or her there. Just as a physician would treat cancer differently from a cold, a psychotherapist will treat schizophrenia differently from a fear of riding down escalators.

Between these extremes lies a variety of psychological problems that might drive a person to seek help. Some are short-lived but intense, such as a loss or a divorce. Some are mild but persistent and energy draining over time, such as dysthymia or chronic worrying. And some problems are frustratingly repetitive, like realizing you're dating the same loser but with a different name. What all these problems have in common is that the person dealing with them feels they exceed his or her coping skills. For whatever reason, they just can't see the light at the end of the tunnel. And, believe me, they've looked and looked for it before they come in for help.

The SCAT Team to the Rescue

Your mom is driving you batty, so you call your best friend and ask her what to do. You wouldn't dream of making a career move without talking it over with your college mentor. And when you're feeling down, you hang around after church because talking with your minister makes you feel better. These are your informal "counselors," the ones who help you deal with most of your routine frustrations and conflicts.

No matter how good a listener your best friend is, however, there is something to be said for the skills and knowledge that formal psychological training provides. A SWAT team may rescue hostages kidnapped during a bank robbery, but when people are held captive by their problems, they turn to the SCAT team: school workers, counselors, and therapists. Here are the five kinds of mental-health professionals who most often help us deal with problems when our friends and families can't:

- *Counseling psychologists* specialize in the problems of daily living. They often work in community settings such as schools, clinics, and businesses, and they deal with challenges like relationship conflicts, choosing a vocation, school problems, and stress.

- *Clinical psychologists* are trained to treat individuals who suffer from more severe conditions, such as clinical depression, eating disorders, and anxiety.

- *Psychiatrists* are medical doctors who specialize in the treatment of emotional and mental disorders. These physicians generally treat more severe conditions and, in these days of managed care, are most likely to prescribe medication for psychiatric disorders.

- *Clinical social workers* are mental-health professionals with specialized training in the social context of people's problems. Clinical social workers often work with family problems, like child abuse, and their work often involves entire families in the therapy.

- *Counselors or therapists* are mental-health professionals covering a wide range of specializations and expertise. *Pastoral counselors* are members of a religious group or ministry trained to specialize in the treatment of psychological disorders. Marital and family therapists are often Master's-degreed professionals who have chosen to focus on family/couple problems, while drug and alcohol counselors often have specialized training in the addictions.

Finding a Partner for the Dance of Therapy

What do good therapists have in common? To some extent, it depends upon the client. In a good therapeutic relationship, there's a unique and somewhat illusive chemistry that develops between therapist and client. A good therapist for you, in other words, might not be a good therapist for me. But all good therapists share certain common traits, including the following:

- They listen and you talk.

- They keep their problems to themselves and deal with their own issues outside of your therapy session.

- They don't answer the phone or nod off while you are spilling your guts.

- They can be completely objective about what you are saying.

- They apologize if they make a mistake.

- They protect your confidences: they wouldn't spill the beans about what the two of you talk about if you dragged them over hot coals.

A good therapist would also make a good friend, but don't make that common mistake. Your therapist is *not* your friend. Friends have needs and agendas of their own that may not always coincide with yours.

The Therapeutic Relationship

Nevertheless, you and the therapist have a relationship, and the quality of that relationship is perhaps the biggest determinant in whether you benefit from therapy. In fact, study after study shows that the "fit" between therapist and client is far more valuable than any bag of therapeutic tricks. The ability to trust your therapist, to work as allies on the same team, and to share similar values and goals are the key ingredients to therapy that works.

Unfortunately, it isn't always easy to find a good therapist. Your first therapy session is like a blind date; you never know for sure what you're going to get. However, there are some guidelines you can use that will improve the odds that your "first date" with a therapist will turn into a trusting relationship. Let's examine what you should look for when picking a therapist and what you can expect when you get to his or her office.

Guidelines for Finding a Therapist

The best approach to finding a good therapist is the same one you'd use when seeking any professional services. Here are the basic steps to take:

◆ *Get personal referrals*, particularly from a friend or colleague who has had a problem similar to yours. If you can't find a therapist this way, then check with your doctor or hospital social work department.

◆ *Interview the therapist over the phone*. Remember, you are hiring this person to be your therapist and you need to make sure she is qualified.

◆ *Ask questions*. Be sure to ask what her specialties are, how many people she's seen with the same problem as yours, and her treatment philosophy. One person may be a fabulous therapist for substance-abuse problems, but she may have no experience with depression.

◆ *Trust your instincts*. If you don't like the person or don't feel comfortable after a few sessions, switch therapists.

What to Expect When You're Going to Therapy

Lots of what you do in therapy will depend upon the problem you're seeking help for, the therapist's style and theoretical orientation, and the nature of the relationship the two of you develop. And no matter what problem brought you to the therapist's office, you can expect to work on the four following goals:

> **Insight**
>
> How does your therapist rate? If you're not sure, go to www. cybercouch.com/library/ rati.tag.html and check out Dr. Thomas Grugle's "Rate Your Therapist" quiz.

1. *Figuring out what's wrong*. You might think you know what's wrong; after all, that's what brought you to therapy in the first place. And most of the time, you do. However, this can be trickier than you might think. A client who comes in to deal with problems on the job may come to realize that he is drinking six vodka and tonics a day. So is the job his problem or is it his drinking? Good therapists will do a thorough clinical interview and ask you all kinds of questions that might seem completely irrelevant. This enables the therapist to make a diagnosis that's helpful as a starting point.

2. *Figuring out what caused the problem and why you still have it*. Is your problem genetic? Does it run in your family? When did it start? What keeps it going on or coming back again?

3. *Figuring out what's likely to happen in the future.* There is no crystal ball involved in treatment. Therapists are not psychic, but they try to gauge what or who might take longer to treat and how to keep the problem from happening again. Anorexia, for example, tends to be a long-term problem, and the therapist and client need to be realistic about treatment.

4. *Figuring out how to get rid of it or make it better.* What kind of therapy would work best on the client's particular problem? What does the client's social and professional environment look like? And how can the family or support system help?

> **Psychobabble**
>
> When you visualize yourself in a therapist's office, you might not picture yourself flapping your arms like a bird while your therapist accompanies your movements with drumbeats. However, shamanism, an ancient spiritual tradition that combines healing with contacting the spirit world, is becoming increasingly popular among Western therapists.

Talking It Out

While medications have helped people solve mental problems by acting on the brain, psychotherapy works on the mind. Talk therapy reprograms the thoughts, feelings, and behaviors that interfere with your ability to maximize your potential and get along in the world. No matter how much your genes may be stacked against you, the die is not cast at birth. Your environment can serve as either a powerful buffer or a risk factor.

There are four major types of "talk," or psychotherapy: psychodynamic, behavioral, cognitive, and "group" therapies. Though different in approach and process, each has the same goals: to provide people with a rational explanation of their problem; to offer a very real basis for very real hope; and to achieve their success through a positive, one-on-one relationship between the client and his or her therapist.

The psychotherapist is, in effect, like the patient's driving instructor. He or she can give advice—they can talk about how traffic lights work, and they can explain the importance of a properly executed U-turn and how to merge correctly—but ultimately it's the patient who must drive her own car.

One instructor might concentrate on helping a student unlearn reckless driving habits, while a second might tackle fears of getting behind the wheel. Yet a third might bring new drivers together so that they can support each other. But no matter what, all of the "instructors" have the same purpose: to bring forth their patient's inner Dale Earnhardt, and point them down the road.

To help you narrow down and understand your options, here is a table comparing and contrasting the four primary types of therapies:

Types of Therapy	Cause of Disorder	Goal	Common Techniques
Psychodynamic (Psychoanalysis, Client-centered therapy, Gestalt therapy)	A childhood during which the person was either forced to disown parts of him- or herself (or his or her feelings); as an adult the person is either in conflict with these hidden parts or has repressed them	Give people a better awareness and understanding of their feelings, motivations, and actions so they will be better adjusted	Interpreting and analyzing one's dreams, role-playing different parts of oneself, working with a therapist who fully accepts all aspects of the client, and mirrors the client's thoughts and feelings
Behavior	Learning the wrong behavior	Teach people how to behave in a more satisfying way	Rewarding adaptive behavior through behavior contracts, modeling, getting rid of fears through gradual exposure to them

Types of Therapy	Cause of Disorder	Goal	Common Techniques
Cognitive	Self-defeating ways of thinking; inaccurate views of the world	Identify and correct erroneous ways of thinking	Consciously replacing negative thoughts with positive, coping thoughts, rationally examining and changing negative or inaccurate thinking
Group	Relationship problems that cause personal distress	To identify ways of relating to others that cause problems and learn to relate more effectively; also to use other people as a motivator/support for behavior change	Family therapy, group therapy, couples therapy, self-help groups

No matter which kind of therapy you choose, always remember that there are numerous things you can do to enhance the odds that your therapy will work, including working with your therapist to set clear treatment goals, deciding on how progress will be evaluated, monitoring progress carefully, and revising treatment plans.

Looking Ahead ... to Now

Psychotherapy continues to evolve its applications and methodologies. Currently, for instance, there is an emergence of three trends—the use of scientific evidence to drive treatment decisions, shorter stays in therapy, and the use of technology.

Short, Sweet, and to the Point

Many therapists are now utilizing recently developed therapeutic techniques that focus less on the therapeutic process and more on results. They concentrate less on their patient's childhood and more on their current life experiences and relationships. They provide more directive guidance and feedback—and will often even prescribe homework to speed up the process!

> **Insight**
>
> Research shows that many people, with many common mental-health concerns, will begin experiencing positive gains in therapy in as little as six to twelve sessions. At one session per week, that translates into feeling better in between two to three months.

For people who don't need more intensive treatment, these sort of "McTherapies" can prove very satisfactory indeed; for example, a review of more than 30 years of short-term (between 7 and 40 sessions) psychodynamic therapies found that 92 percent of the treated adults were better off than similar individuals who received no treatment.

Getting Wired

It's only natural that the work of therapists would be influenced and modified by modern technology. These days a lot of us spend at least as much time communicating via our cell phones and computers as we do face to face. While the use of the Internet and other communication technologies for the purposes of therapeutic counseling is new, it's surely here to stay: already, 70–80 percent of psychologists say they rely on "telephone therapy" for at least some of their patients. Increasingly, therapists are delivering clinical services on the Internet, or via satellite. And while the jury is still out on how effective online therapy is, preliminary evidence suggests that "telehealth" may provide new opportunities for effective low-cost treatment.

> **Insight**
>
> For many illnesses, the combination of medication and psychotherapy seems to be more effective than either one used by itself.

Considering the Evidence

In the past, mental-health specialists tended to choose a certain theoretical orientation and then treat all patients under this umbrella. So whether you were having marital problems or a panic attack, a psychoanalyst would treat you the same way—by interpreting your dreams, listening to your free associations, and so forth.

Enter the new kid on the block, Evidence Based Therapy (EBT), which says that the kind of treatment you get should be based on the problem you have—not based on the expertise or theoretical bent of your therapist. If research shows that cognitive behavioral therapy works best for anxiety disorders, for example, then that's the kind of therapy your therapist should start with.

But Does It Work?

Of course therapy works! Why else would I be writing this book? Aside from Woody Allen, most of the people I know who have been to therapy know it works. Don't take my word for it, though; thousands of studies have been done, and here's what they have to say:

- *Psychotherapy works.* About 75 percent to 80 percent of people in therapy show greater improvement than the average person in a control group.

- *The outcomes of therapy tend to be maintained.* Numerous follow-up studies have tracked patients after leaving treatment for periods ranging from six months to over five years. These studies are fairly consistent in demonstrating that treatment effects are enduring.

- *Some therapies work better for some problems.* Fear and anxiety seem to respond best to behavioral and cognitive therapies, while humanistic therapies do wonders for self-esteem, and psychodynamic therapy can help underachievers.

- *The therapist matters.* Some therapists do much better than others, and the difference seems to be in their personalities rather than in their credentials. Therapists who are warm, understanding, and strongly motivated to help are much more effective with their clients than therapists who don't have those qualities.

- *Therapy is for better and worse.* Despite overall favorable results, about 5 to 10 percent of patients get worse during treatment, and an additional 15 to 25 percent show no benefit.

So there you have it: the mechanistic (drugs, ECT, psychosurgery) and the idealistic (using therapy to change thoughts, behavior, and feelings). Both can be useful and both have their pros and cons. Both use different means to get to the same goal—leading a better, happier, and more productive life. In the next chapter we'll go from our general overview of mental-health help to tackling—and treating—two of the most common and most painful disorders that can dampen the light of even the brightest psyche—depression and anxiety.

The Least You Need to Know

◆ Psychiatric medications are often a critical part of the treatment for depression, schizophrenia, and bipolar disorder, and can also be helpful with anxiety disorders but, especially in children, the rewards should outweigh the risks.

◆ The techniques used in electroconvulsive treatment and psychosurgery are much safer than they used to be, but are still used only when less invasive treatments fail.

◆ For therapy to be effective, you must have a good relationship with your therapist.

◆ There are several types of talk therapy, including psychodynamic psychotherapy, behavioral therapy, cognitive therapy, and existential-humanistic therapy.

◆ A new model for treatment is emerging called Evidence Based Therapy (EBT), which seeks to combine different empirically proven techniques from various psychological disciplines.

Part **6**

Between a Rock and a Hard Place

This section is about the major mental illnesses—mood disorders, psychoses, and addictions. You'll learn the difference between a funk and a major depression, find out how normal behavior spirals out of control, and separate the myths and realities of schizophrenia. You'll also learn what treatments give sufferers the best bang for their treatment buck—and how even the most severe diagnoses don't have the gloomy prognoses they used to.

Chapter 19

Mood Swingers and Scaredy Cats

In This Chapter

- Exploring the difference between a major funk and a major depression
- Swinging along with your mood swings
- Dealing with depression in others
- Feeling phobic
- Obsessing compulsively

"I'm afraid the black dog has really got me …. It crouches in the corner of the room, waits for me to make a move. Or lies at the foot of the bed, like a shadow, until I try to get up. Growls and will not let me up …."

So begins the prologue of Cathy Kronkite's candid book, *On the Edge of Darkness: Conversations About Conquering Depression*, in which she talks about her own experience with depression and shares countless interviews with other celebrities who've had similar experiences. They're not hard to find: Queen Elizabeth, Elton John, Patti Duke, Tipper Gore. Not to mention one out of every 20 of us regular U.S. citizens.

In this chapter, we'll explore affective disorders, a family of illnesses in which the main symptom is a disturbance of mood; anxiety and depression are two examples. You'll discover the difference between a bad mood and major depression and you'll see where you fall on the mood continuum. You'll learn about the mood swings in manic depression, the low-level sadness of dysthymia, and the gentler ups and downs of cyclothymia. You'll also meet the four anxiety disorders, discover what "panicking" really means, and learn what to do when obsessive thoughts won't go away.

Being Psychologically Correct

You may or may not be politically correct, but please, try to be psychologically correct. When you have a bad day and are sharing it with a friend or loved one, try to say you are "in a funk," "have got the blues," or are in a "bad mood." Please, oh please, don't call it *depression*.

When the word *depression* is used to describe everything from a passing mood to a chronic illness, it creates confusion for all of us. Bad moods or grief over a loss are normal parts of life; they aren't pleasant, but we get through them with time. Clinical depression, also called unipolar disorder, is a different animal altogether. Depression can kill you.

As long as we use the terms interchangeably, when someone tells you she is suffering from depression, you're likely to misunderstand what she's saying. "So what?" you think. "I was depressed yesterday, too, and I snapped out of it." Not if you were experiencing a major depression, you didn't. Episodes of untreated depression typically last several months, and invade every part of your life. Let's take a look at what clinical depression really is.

In a Major Funk

You don't feel hopeful or happy about anything in your life. You feel like you're moving in slow motion. Nothing tastes good. Getting up in the morning requires a lot of effort. You find yourself crying over nothing, or at something that wouldn't normally bother you; maybe you can't cry at all any more, even if you want to. These are the faces of clinical depression.

Major depression, the common term for clinical depression, is an equal opportunity illness. It affects 1 in 20 Americans every year, about twice as many women as men. It hits people at all socioeconomic levels and ethnic backgrounds. It can creep up on you or grab you by the throat. Major depression is debilitating and dangerous—an overwhelming sadness that lasts at least two weeks and is severe enough to interfere with a person's life.

When mental-health professionals assess someone for depression, they look for specific signs that differ from the blues everyone feels at one time or another, or the grief we experience over the loss of a loved one. If you went to your physician and complained of depression, he or she would look for five or more of the following symptoms.

Insight

Reason number one to get help for depression is this: children of depressed parents are more likely to have medical problems and to be depressed themselves.

◆ Loss of interest in things you used to enjoy, including sex.

◆ Feeling sad, blue, or down in the dumps.

◆ Feeling either slowed down or so restless you can't sit still.

◆ Changes in appetite.

◆ Thoughts of death or suicide.

◆ Problems concentrating, remembering, or making decisions.

◆ Loss of energy or feeling tired all the time.

◆ Feeling worthless or guilty.

◆ Trouble sleeping, or sleeping all the time.

One of the first two symptoms is mandatory—the depression must cause significant emotional distress or disrupt your daily life. But the first symptom that many people notice, in either themselves or in depressed friends or family members, is a change in sleep patterns.

The problem with lists of clinical symptoms is that they sound so clinical. A list of symptoms can't capture the personal experience of living with depression. Here are some real-world examples of what a depressed person might say:

> "I just don't want to be around anyone. I keep making excuses to my friends. I know I'm hurting their feelings, but I don't want to be a downer to them and I just can't pretend anymore that I'm up."

> "I can't remember the last time I laughed. I have so much to be thankful for, so why can't I just snap out of it?"

Brain Buster

Untreated depression is one of the top three workplace problems. Fifty percent of people with depression report work-related problems, and it costs the United States 200 million sick days each year.

"It takes me a week to do what I used to do in a day. Some days I don't get out of bed until noon."

"I feel so bad that sometimes I wish I were dead. Yeah, I guess I've had thoughts of killing myself; anything would be better than this."

As you can see, these thoughts and feelings are not typical of being down in the dumps. You might want to pull the covers up over your head when you're in a bad mood, but you don't think about suicide. Why do some people bounce back from a minor funk, while others slide into a downward spiral that takes months to crawl out of? Let's take a look at what causes depression and who's likely to get it.

Why Me?

Depression can run in families. However, depression can also occur in people whose family history is clean of depressive genes, and we may all be vulnerable to depression if our life circumstances are tough enough.

Many people with depression can point to an incident or situation that they believe has triggered their unhappiness. While the specific life events vary, they almost always involve loss—loss of physical health, loss of a loved one, loss of a job, or loss of self-confidence or self-control. Obviously, not everyone who goes through a divorce or loses a job becomes depressed; most often, it's the double whammy of depressive genes and a stressful life event that triggers the first clinical depression.

Insight

Many physical illnesses can mimic psychological problems. If you suddenly find yourself feeling depressed or experiencing unusual emotional symptoms, it is critical that you get a medical check-up. It can save your life.

As you can see, the question "Is depression mostly physical or psychological?" is a moot one. Clinical depression can be triggered by either physical or psychological events. Most commonly, both seem to be involved; remember our diathesis-stress model from Chapter 16? However it begins, depression can quickly develop into a set of physical and psychological problems that feed on each other and grow.

How Bad Is Your Mood?

You might think a person would know if he or she is depressed, but that often isn't true. Depression can develop gradually, so that a person may slip into a clinical depression without fully realizing how far down he's fallen. If you've ever had a cold that gradually turned into bronchitis or pneumonia, you've experienced the medical version of this phenomenon—because the progression from cold to pneumonia was gradual, you may not have appreciated exactly how bad you really felt until you finally felt better. Depression can be like that, too.

Here's a handy quiz to assess your own mood. Place the number that most accurately reflects your responses to the following statements in the blank.

Mood Assessment Quiz

1 = never   4 = often

2 = rarely   5 = always

3 = sometimes

_____ I have been more unhappy than usual over the past month.

_____ I don't seem to have much energy.

_____ I don't get very much pleasure from anything.

_____ It is hard to get things done that I used to accomplish easily.

_____ I have been more angry or irritated over the past few weeks.

_____ I feel worse in the morning than in the afternoon.

_____ Lately, I feel like crying at the drop of a hat.

_____ I have been sleeping poorly for the past month.

_____ I feel pretty hopeless about my life getting any better.

_____ I can't seem to concentrate like I usually do.

Now let's total up your score and see what kind of mood you're in. Here's how to interpret your score:

continues

---

continued

20 or less. You seem to be on the "happy" end of the mood spectrum. Rarely does a bad mood get you down for long, and when it does, it usually doesn't keep you from doing the things you need to do. What's your secret?

21–30. Although life is manageable, you may find that your moods are a little more volatile than usual. Maybe you're going through a stressful time or a bumpy relationship. Whatever the reason, take good care of yourself, get regular exercise, and try some of the depression buffers (see the next section of this chapter).

31–40. Bad moods seem to grip you more often than most people. If some of the depression buffers aren't working, or if you're having trouble getting your normal activities done, consider talking to a professional. It can't hurt!

41–50. Although this is not a professional tool, your score worries me. Life is much harder than it has to be, and it seems like depression has you pretty firmly in its grasp. There is no need to suffer needlessly; depression is much more treatable than many physical illnesses. It's time to find that out for yourself.

Depression Buffers

Whether you're in a really bad mood or a major depression, there are things you can do that will help you ride the situation out. These 10 depression buffers can be useful either as a bad mood buster or as some additional self-help strategies while you're getting the professional help you need.

- ◆ Don't hide out in your house or apartment for more than a few hours. Depressive thoughts can worsen when no one else is around.

- ◆ Don't make major life decisions until you feel better. If you have to make one, talk it over with at least two people you trust.

- ◆ Structure your mornings as much as possible. Get up and take a shower every day, even if you don't feel like it.

- ◆ Avoid drugs and alcohol. They can make depression worse.

◆ If you've lost your appetite, eat small snacks during the day rather than trying to force yourself to eat a big meal.

◆ Take notes and make lists. Having trouble concentrating is common with depression, so don't trust your memory even if it's normally better than an elephant's.

◆ If you wake up during the middle of the night, get out of bed and do something (read inspirational material, for example).

◆ At the minimum, go for a 20-minute walk every day. Exercise and exposure to natural sunlight can be helpful in reducing mild depression.

◆ Give yourself a break. Don't expect to do all the things you normally do.

◆ Make a date to get some help. If you've been depressed for two weeks or more, talk to someone—your physician, your minister, or a therapist.

Brain Buster

Severe depression heightens the risk of dying after a heart attack or stroke, and reduces the quality of life (and possibly the survival time) for cancer and AIDS patients. And a majority of depressed people who go untreated seriously consider suicide, with up to 17 percent eventually succeeding in killing themselves.

When Someone You Love Is Depressed

When someone you love is depressed, you worry. You probably also feel frustrated, overwhelmed, and confused. You may find yourself asking, "Why can't he or she just snap out of it?" Or you may think there's something you should be able to do to cure your loved one's problems.

Sadly, no one can "cure" someone else's depression, but there are things you can say that will help, and things you can say that will hurt. Even if you've got the best of intentions, telling someone, "Don't worry; be happy," or "Just get over it" is not going to earn you brownie points—plus it trivializes a serious illness. Would you tell someone with cancer to "just get over it"? I don't think so.

There are much more useful things you can say to help people suffering from depression. Let them know you care, and that you're sorry about their pain. Make sure they know that they're not alone; you're there to help! And let them know they aren't "crazy"; depression can hit the smartest and most well-adjusted people.

On the other hand, if you're not careful, you can end up saying things that just make the situation worse. Some good "don'ts": don't point out everything they have to be thankful for; it will just make them feel worse. Avoid dismissing comments like, "It's all in your head," or advice like, "Pull yourself together." And don't say, "I know just how you feel!" unless you have really suffered from clinical depression in the past and want to talk about treatments that helped you.

Low-Level Sadness

When I was 25, I started feeling worse and worse physically and mentally for about six weeks. I was sure that I must be experiencing some psychological problem. When I finally saw the doctor, he took one look in my ears, diagnosed my ear infection, and after five days of antibiotics, I was back to my rambunctious self. But my instinct to look for a psychological cause for my distress wasn't entirely misplaced. *Dysthymia* is like having a low-grade emotional "infection" that saps your mood, drains your energy, and takes a lot of life's pleasure away.

Dysthymic disorder, or dysthymia, is a mild to moderate level of depression that lasts at least two years. It often causes a poor appetite or overeating, difficulty sleeping or sleeping too much, low energy, fatigue, and feelings of hopelessness. But people with dysthymic disorder may have periods of normal mood that can last up to two months. Even though this type of depression is mild, it's kind of like carrying around a ball and chain; you're still able to do what you have to, but it sure makes it harder.

No one knows what causes dysthymic disorder, but it's fairly common. Up to 3 percent of the U.S. population suffers from dysthymia. It can begin at any time, from childhood to adulthood, and it seems to affect more women than men. Although the cause is unknown, there may be changes in the brain that involve the neurotransmitter serotonin. In addition, personality problems, medical problems, and chronic life stresses may also play a role.

Riding the Mood Roller Coaster

Bipolar disorder, commonly called manic depression, is a psychological disorder that affects about 1 percent of the population of every country in the world, including the United States; this distribution is very different from major depression, which varies remarkably from country to country. And unlike major depression, men and women are equally likely to get it.

Bipolar disorder is characterized by extreme mood swings. While all of us have "up" days and "down" days, individuals with bipolar disorder will be severely up sometimes, severely down sometimes, and in the middle some or most of the time. The hallmark of the disorder is the alternation between periods of mania and periods of depression.

The depressive end of bipolar disorder looks much like it does with major depression. For this reason, it's the manic part of bipolar disorder that determines the diagnosis. Although there are a few cases of mania without depression, there is no current formal diagnosis of mania alone. Apparently, the mental-health community embraces the "what goes up must come down" philosophy. Anyone who has a manic episode will be diagnosed with bipolar disorder.

> **Psychobabble**
>
> Check out Kay Redfield Jamison's book *Touched with Fire* to get a fascinating look at the link between creativity and mood disorders. And for an up-close-and-personal encounter with bipolar disorder, read her autobiography, *An Unquiet Mind.*

When mania first starts, it can be productive and fun. Imagine being in a great mood, full of energy and inspiration. Dr. John Kelso, one of the leading researchers in bipolar disorder, suspects that the reason evolution has passed along the bipolar gene is the increased creativity and energy that a mild level of mania (hypomania) bestows on us. The problem is, of course, that the person can't stay at the level forever. In a full-blown manic episode, the person may …

- ◆ Become so restless that he or she can't sit still.
- ◆ Be unable to concentrate on anything, going back and forth from one thing to another without finishing anything.
- ◆ Have racing thoughts and rapid, disconnected speech.
- ◆ Develop paranoid ideas or extremely religious ideas and thoughts.
- ◆ Be extremely impulsive and put him- or herself at risk through increased sexuality, financial extravagance, or an obsessive interest in some venture or hobby.
- ◆ Become highly irritable or easily excitable.
- ◆ Have grandiose delusions.
- ◆ Suffer profound weight loss.
- ◆ Stay awake for days and be unable to sleep.

Cyclothymia is similar to bipolar disorder because it is characterized by mood swings from mania to depression. However, there are important distinctions between the two. A person with cyclothymia experiences symptoms of hypomania but never a full-blown manic episode. Hypomanic symptoms are exactly the same as the symptoms of a manic episode, but milder. A hypomanic episode does not disrupt the person's ability to function, doesn't require hospitalization, and doesn't include hallucinations or delusions.

Likewise, although depression is a part of cyclothymia, the symptoms are never severe enough to meet the criteria for a major depressive episode. For cyclothymia to be diagnosed, hypomanic and depressive symptoms must alternate for at least two years. Treatment depends upon the severity of the disorder—mild symptoms may respond to psychotherapy and more severe mood problems may need lithium or antidepressants.

Moody Children

"All children are happy." "Children have nothing to worry about." "Childhood is the best time of your life." These statements may seem absurd to you, but for years they reflected the attitudes of the mental-health community. It was only in the 1980s that mood disorders in children were included in the category of diagnosed psychiatric illnesses.

There're a Lot of Troubled Kids out There

There is increasing evidence that major depression can develop in children—and that it occurs in teenagers much more often than we once thought. Seven to 14 percent of children will experience an episode of major depression before age 15; 20 percent to 30 percent of adults with bipolar disorder have their first episode before age 20; and an estimated 2,000 teenagers commit suicide each year.

The major ingredients of mood disorders are the same in children and adults, although children may express their symptoms differently. Unlike adults, children may not have the words to accurately describe how they feel, and therefore may exhibit more behavioral problems. In other words, children are more likely to "show" you their problems than to talk about them.

Is It Moodiness or Depression?

Although most preschoolers are unhappy when their wishes aren't granted, there are definite signs when the problem is more than simple disappointment or moodiness. Depressed preschoolers may be frequently tearful or irritable for no apparent reason. They may seem unusually serious and lack the bounce of their peers. And of most concern, they may make frequent nega-tive self-statements ("I hate myself"; "I wish I were dead") and do things that are self-destructive (such as hitting them-selves).

Depressed older children and teenagers often display behavioral problems. They may be irri-table and aggressive, be disruptive at school, and have declining grades. Parents may com-plain that nothing pleases the child, and that he seems to hate himself and everything around him. A teenager who isolates himself in his room and has deteriorating grades and few friends is not just going through a stage; he or she may be clinically depressed.

Brain Buster

People used to believe that "people who talk about sui-cide never really do it." This is a dangerous error! Most people who commit suicide talk about it first. Talking or joking about sui-cide, acting in a reckless or dangerous manner, giving away possessions, or expressing feel-ings of hopelessness are common signs of suicidal plans.

Playing the Odds: Getting the Best Bang for the Depression Treatment Buck

The treatment of choice for depression depends on the type of depression and how severe it is.

For major depression, there are two options that, independently, work about equally well: a type of psychotherapy called *cognitive-behavioral therapy (CBT)*, and antidepres-sant medication. Together, CBT and antidepressants are the most effective weapon in the battle against the "black dog" of major depression; they work for 80 to 90 percent of the clients who use them.

CBT is a type of therapy that focuses on the *thinking* that affects our mood. For exam-ple, you see a friend on the street and you wave, but she doesn't wave back. What will you think? Well, if you think, "Dang, Diane is blind as a bat!" you'll feel one way. If you think, "Diane must not like me anymore," you'll feel much worse. CBT helps individuals with depression challenge the self-defeating thoughts (I'm worthless; I'll never feel better; there's nothing I can do about my situation) that either contribute to, or cause, their depressed mood.

In general, the more severe the depression, the more likely it is that the client will benefit from medication. Medications most often involve the commonly used serotonin-specific re-uptake inhibitors, or SSRIs; think Prozac, Paxil, and Zoloft, among others. (Good news? Almost impossible to overdose. Bad news? They often involve negative sexual side effects.) There are the tricyclic antidepressants: Elavil, Pamelor, and similar meds, which are cheaper but tend to have yuckier side effects, take longer to kick in, and can be used to overdose. Whatever the medication, the goal is to get the brain chemistry back in balance.

Medications are the treatment of choice for bipolar disorder, a.k.a. manic depression. Despite Tom Cruise claiming that "there's no such thing as a chemical imbalance," in these types of mood disorders, the brain's chemistry is actually affected. (I guess there aren't too many psychopharmacology classes in acting school.) The best treatment odds for bipolar disorder are mood stabilizers, with lithium continuing to the line of first defense. Newer medications, especially anticonvulsants like Depakote or Tegretol, are showing promising results but are still used primarily when lithium isn't effective.

What about alternative treatments? Well, the bottle of St. John's wort you buy isn't FDA-regulated; that means it could contain a high amount of the active ingredient— or none at all! If it does work, you have to take it three times a day and stay out of the sun. A better choice for an over-the-counter supplement might be DHEA (dehydroepiandrosterone), but please talk to your physician first!

Brain Buster

A neurological pacemaker is a new, last-ditch treatment for severe depression that is unresponsive to psychotropic medication. Functioning much like a pacemaker does to regulate the heartbeat, it stimulates the neurotransmitters (serotonin, dopamine, norepinephrine) involved in the regulation of mood.

Does ECT (see Chapter 18) sound too scary to you? Clinical trials are taking place with other nondrug therapies, like *transcranial magnetic stimulation (TMS)*, *magnetic stimulation therapy (MST)*, and *vagus nerve stimulation (VNS)*. The first two involve magnetic fields; the last one involves stimulation of an important nerve. Again, the final goal is to somehow "knock" an out-of-whack brain back into balance.

I'm Always Anxious About *Everything*

If you've ever found yourself unable to relax or get to sleep at night because of worries, you know some of the toll anxiety can take. Everyone experiences anxiety or fear in certain life situations, but 15 percent of the population has, at some point in their lives, experienced anxiety that was severe enough to disrupt their lives.

When a person feels anxious or worried most of the time for a period of at least six months, it's quite possible that he or she is suffering from generalized anxiety disorder. The anxiety might focus on a specific circumstance, such as unrealistic money worries or an inexplicable fear that a loved one will die or be injured. Or it might be a general apprehension that something bad is about to happen. For example, a person suffering from generalized anxiety disorder might start calling the emergency rooms if her spouse was late coming home from work.

In addition to the emotional discomfort, a person with generalized anxiety disorder often experiences a number of physical symptoms. She feels tense all the time, is easily startled, is unusually attentive to the cause or source of the anxiety, and may lie awake at night worrying. You can imagine what an energy drain this would be over time, and people who suffer from generalized anxiety disorder often report fatigue and tiredness. They literally wear themselves out with worry.

> **Insight**
>
> Although suicide is most commonly associated with depression, studies show that severe anxiety often leads to suicidal thoughts. They also show that when panic attacks occur along with depression, a person may be at high risk for suicide.

Hit-and-Run Fear

With generalized anxiety disorder, a person worries about everything. With *panic disorder*, on the other hand, the person never knows when an attack will occur. Panic disorder is one of the most confusing and terrifying psychological disorders.

In the Path of an Onrushing Train

People who've had panic attacks often say that it feels like a train is bearing down on them at top speed and they can't move out of the way. In their heads they know there's no train, but their body responds as if there is; their hearts race, their mouths

def•i•ni•tion

Panic disorder is an anxiety disorder during which the person experiences recurrent episodes of intense anxiety and physical arousal that lasts up to 10 minutes.

get dry, their blood pressure rises, and they feel as if they're going to die—or at the very least, lose their minds.

Sufferers of panic disorder experience unexpected but severe bouts of anxiety, from out of the blue, at least several times a month. They can happen anywhere; during a romantic dinner with your spouse, at the grocery store, or in the middle of an aerobics class. And, wham! There you go again.

Panic-Attack Pile-Up

As you might imagine, it wouldn't take too many of these emotional whacks upside the head before you started worrying about when the next one will happen. For many people with panic attacks, this anticipatory anxiety is as bad as the panic attack itself. They can never relax because there's always a chance that the next terrifying fear will be triggered out of the blue. They may avoid any place where they've had an attack, in hopes that this will cut down the odds of having another one. But this can lead to even worse problems, as you'll see when we talk about agoraphobia later in this chapter.

Panic disorder has a strong biological component. For some reason, the normal "fight-or-flight" response begins misfiring. And the disorder tends to run in families. Once it starts, the frightening physical symptoms snowball into a psychological nightmare, characterized by constant worry ("When will it happen again?"), catastrophic thinking ("What if I go crazy?"), and self-doubt ("I can't handle another one").

Psychobabble

Charles Darwin's theory of evolution may have been partly inspired by a psychological disorder. According to an article in the *Journal of the American Medical Association*, at least two psychiatrists think the "strange illness" that led to Darwin's famous reclusiveness, which focused his time and energy on his studies, was, in fact, panic disorder and agoraphobia.

Stuck in the House All Day

To look at Kim Basinger, it's hard to imagine she has a care in the world. She's beautiful. She's smart. She's an Academy Award winner. And she's a recovering agoraphobic.

Individuals with agoraphobia experience anxiety in public places where escape might be difficult or embarrassing. They are controlled by the fear that if they panic or become frightened outside the home, they'll either embarrass themselves or become paralyzed with their fear. As a result, they may gradually narrow their world until they literally become prisoners in their own homes. They cannot hold a job or carry out normal daily activities because their fear limits their ability to maintain contact with the outside world.

People don't just wake up one day with agoraphobia. It often starts out with panic attacks that are terrifying and random. Maybe someone is shopping at the mall and has a panic attack. She leaves immediately and feels better. But the next time she needs to go to the mall for something, she starts to feel a little anxious. "What if it happens again?" a little voice whispers. The mere thought of going through another panic attack—or the fear of public humiliation—sends chills up her spine. Maybe she decides go to a different mall, just in case. Everything is fine, but a few weeks later she has a panic attack there, too.

Over time, you can see how a person might become more and more afraid to venture out. After all, if a panic attack could happen anywhere, no place is 100 percent safe. At least at home no one will see it happen.

Meet the Phobia Family

If your house is on fire or you're being mugged, fear is a rational reaction. It gives you an edge to get out of the house or away from your attacker. In contrast, a person with a phobia suffers from an ongoing, irrational fear of something that is so strong it creates a compelling desire to avoid it. Common phobias include the fear of heights (acrophobia), the fear of cramped spaces (claustrophobia), and the fear of snakes (ophidiophobia).

The Five Most Common Phobias

Name	Percentage of Phobias
Agoraphobia (fear of crowds or public places)	10–50%
Social phobia (fear of embarrassing oneself in public)	10%

continues

The Five Most Common Phobias (continued)

Name	Percentage of Phobias
Fear of inanimate objects (heights, storms, closed spaces)	20%
Illness-injury (death, cancer)	15–25%
Animals (snakes, dogs, insects)	5–15%

In addition to phobias that center on places or things, there's also social phobia. Social phobia is a pervasive and ongoing fear of social or performance situations in which the person might either be under scrutiny from others (public speaking, speaking to authority figures) or around strangers (going to parties, striking up conversations, dating). The sufferer will generally experience a lot of anxiety in these situations, and the fear of embarrassment and humiliation can lead him to avoid having to face such situations. Unlike a simple phobia, which is limited to specific objects such as dogs or flying, social phobias are more complex, because the fear of embarrassment or humiliation can lead to an avoidance of numerous situations and settings.

Insight

Okay, you movie fans, check out Jack Nicholson in *As Good As It Gets*. For once, the person with a psychiatric disorder is not portrayed as "crazy or violent." He isn't cured by the love of a good woman, although she does inspire him to get help. And, at the end of the movie, he's taken charge of his obsessive-compulsive disorder—and gets the girl, to boot! Hooray for Hollywood!

Do you have a phobia? One out of every eight Americans will develop a phobia at some point in his or her life. Some of those phobias gradually go away by themselves and some of us just live with them.

Most people just live with their phobias, unless the fears begin to interfere with their lives in some way. For example, if you were considering a run for public office, a fear of public speaking (one form of social phobia) would be a real drag. It would also be a bummer if your fear kept you from going for a promotion because you knew you'd have to speak before a group.

On the other hand, if you're a computer programmer, the fear of public speaking might be a nuisance, but it wouldn't necessarily interfere with your life in any way. My fear of insects is a lot less cumbersome now that I live in California—with those Texas-size cockroaches in Dallas, I would either have had to face up to my fear sooner or later, or risk my husband tiring of being stuck with endless pest control duty and squirting *me* with the bug spray!

This Can't Be as Good as It Gets

You know the feeling. You've just locked the door and gotten in your car to head to the movie. You're running late and you don't want to miss the beginning. But, just as you're backing out of the driveway, an unwanted thought creeps in. "Did I turn off the stove?" You mentally retrace your movements and you're 95 percent sure you did. But horrible images of your house in flames still dance through your head. What if you forgot? What if your house burns down while you're watching *Star Wars?* Odds are you'll give up and run back in the house to check—or spend much of the movie wishing you had.

We all have moments like this—it's pretty normal. But what if you ran back in the house, saw that you turned off the stove, got back in your car—and had the exact same level of doubt and fear about burning the house down? And, what if that fear surfaced every single time you left the house, even though you knew it was irrational and illogical? What if these fears made you so miserable if you didn't check that you often gave in? Welcome to obsessive-compulsive disorder (OCD).

My Obsessions Compelled Me to Do It!

Obsessive-compulsive disorder is an illness that traps people in endless cycles of repetitive thoughts (obsessions) and behaviors (compulsions). We all have habits and routines that help us organize our daily lives; people with OCD develop patterns of behavior that take up too much time and interfere with their daily lives. This could mean checking to make sure that the stove is off 100 times before leaving for work, or washing your hands for hours after using a public toilet because of a profound fear of germs.

These behaviors are prompted by obsessive thoughts—unwanted and intrusive ideas, images, and impulses that run through your mind over and over again. When you're in the grip of such obsessive thoughts, you're likely to respond with compulsive behaviors that are intended to control or alleviate the obsession. You might perform these compulsive behaviors—often called rituals—according to "rules" you make up to try to control the nervous feelings that come along with the obsessive thoughts. Rituals like this do make the nervous feelings go away, but usually only for a short while. Then fear and discomfort return, and you find yourself repeating the routine all over again.

Playing the Odds: Overcoming Anxiety and OCD

Simple phobias are the easiest phobias to treat. The systematic desensitization technique you learned about in Chapter 7 usually works in a few hair-raising sessions.

But with generalized anxiety disorder, agoraphobia, panic attacks, and obsessive-compulsive disorder, we're back to the treatments of choice mentioned for the depressive disorders: cognitive-behavioral therapy and medications. There's even some overlap in the medications, although some are different.

In addition to CBT, self-calming talk can be particularly effective with panic attacks, while behavior therapy aimed at reducing compulsive acts can be really helpful in OCD. Training in relaxation is very helpful with many anxiety disorders.

The SSRI drugs are often used with OCD, but so are medications like Anafranil. Benzodiazapines like Valium and Xanax will help treat anxiety in the short run, but in the long run they can be dangerously addictive. Generally, they are used in conjunction with psychotherapy.

What's the prognosis for recovery? For simple phobias, the odds are almost 100 percent, if you stick with the treatment. Anxiety disorders? Closer to the numbers for depression: about 80–90 percent with full treatment. OCD? About 60 percent respond to medications; the response rate is higher with psychotherapy added in.

An important rule to remember is that many people give up on treatment too soon. Whether you're suffering from anxiety, depression, or anything else, please, for your sake and your family's sake, stick with it!

In this chapter, we've examined the range of mood disorders. While most of us haven't been clinically depressed or anxious, we all know what it feels like to have the blues or to feel nervous. In the next chapter, we'll take a look at a mental illness whose symptoms—hallucinations, disorganization, delusions—most of us will never experience. We'll explore the fascinating, complex, and misunderstood condition known as schizophrenia.

The Least You Need to Know

- Clinical depression is a psychological disorder that lasts for at least two weeks, causes significant emotional distress, and interferes with a person's ability to conduct normal activities.

- The best treatments for depression are a combination of antidepressant medication and psychotherapy.

- Dysthymia is a low-grade sadness that lasts for at least two years and responds well to antidepressants.

- Bipolar disorder—commonly called manic depression—is characterized by extreme mood swings of "highs" and "lows." Cyclothymia is a milder version of the disorder.

- Children can get depressed, too, and are more likely to "show" their illness through behavioral problems and a declining school performance.

- Anxiety disorders generally respond to cognitive behavioral psychotherapy or medication.

Chapter 20

Postcards from the Edge of Reality

In This Chapter

- ◆ Scoping out schizophrenia
- ◆ Curious conditions: hallucinations, delusions, and other strange things
- ◆ Learning about the family tie
- ◆ When you think they're out to get you

More than 30 years ago, Frederick Frese was locked up inside an Ohio mental hospital. A college graduate and Marine, Frese had been guarding atomic weapons in Jacksonville, Florida, when he developed the belief that enemy nations had hypnotized American leaders in a plot to take over the U.S. atomic weapons supply. He was diagnosed with paranoid schizophrenia.

Twelve years later, Frese was the chief psychologist for the same mental-health system that had once confined him. He was also happily married and had four children. Despite 10 further hospitalizations, Frese had earned a Master's degree and a doctorate. The moral of the story is this: a mental illness is not a death sentence.

This chapter is about one of the most challenging, elusive, and maligned mental illnesses: schizophrenia. Here you'll learn about the different types, their symptoms and causes, and new groundbreaking treatments for this difficult condition. And you'll learn about paranoia in all its forms and why you can't just talk someone out of his or her suspicious beliefs. Finally, you'll see why anatomy is never destiny: someone with a biological vulnerability to schizophrenia can take steps to minimize the risk of getting it.

The General Scoop on Schizophrenia

Schizophrenia is the disorder people usually mean when they talk about "crazy," "psychotic," or "insane." It is probably the most famous mental illness, or at least it runs a close second to dissociative identity disorder, which we discussed in Chapter 13. It's also not very well understood by the general public—when it's portrayed in the media, it's often linked to a violent crime. Although violence by a mentally ill person is rare, it is most likely to happen with someone with a diagnosis of paranoid schizophrenia.

def•i•ni•tion

Schizophrenia is a severe mental disorder characterized by a breakdown in perceptual and thought processes, often including hallucinations and delusions.

Schizophrenia is also the most costly of all mental illnesses. People with this illness make up the majority of all patients hospitalized with mental disorders. It strikes approximately 1 percent of the U.S. population, generally in adolescence and young adulthood, and this percentage rate holds true for many other countries as well.

Schizophrenia is not a rare mental disorder. In the United States alone, there are as many people with schizophrenia as the combined populations of Wyoming, Vermont, Delaware, and Hawaii. It is equally common in men and women, although, for some reason, it tends to hit men earlier (between the ages of 18 and 25) and women later (26 to 45). It can strike as early as childhood, but is extremely unlikely to suddenly occur after age 50.

It is also a scary diagnosis to receive. While the treatment for schizophrenia has improved dramatically over the past few decades, it is often a tough battle to win. Mental-health professionals often talk about the "one third" prognosis for schizophrenia: one third make a full recovery and lead a normal life; one third make a partial recovery; and one third face a slow, downhill spiral of the disease throughout the rest of his or her life.

The Split Personality

Much of what is known about schizophrenia comes from the Swiss psychiatrist who "discovered" it: Eugen Bleuler. He was the first person to use the label *schizophrenia* to describe the devastating symptoms he saw in the people who suffered from this illness. The term comes from the Greek words *schizo*, which means "split" and *phrenum*, which means "mind." Bleuler observed that patients with schizophrenia often acted as if different parts of their minds were split off from each other, and each part was just doing its own thing.

For example, patients with schizophrenia might be listening to auditory hallucinations and thus be unable to attend to anything going on around them. Or they might talk about the recent death of a loved one—but smile or laugh as they're doing so. This "splitting" of the various functions of the brain can lead to bizarre and disorganized thoughts and actions. Our sense of who we are depends on our attention, emotions, thoughts, behaviors, perceptions, and motivations all working in harmony with each other—or at least being on the same page.

Brain Buster

Don't believe what you see in the movies and on television! You are not going to get ambushed by a homicidal stranger suffering from schizophrenia. When violence does occur, which is rare, it's almost always directed at a family member—not at strangers.

Unfortunately, while many of Bleuler's insights still apply today, his choice of names leaves a lot to be desired. Many of us commonly confuse schizophrenia with dissociative identity disorder (DID), although the two have little in common. Someone in the acute stages of schizophrenia has one mind that may not be in touch with reality. A person with DID, on the other hand, sees reality pretty clearly, but has at least two distinct personalities that compete for dominance.

Schizophrenia from the Inside Out

Schizophrenia can literally put a person in another world. In the acute stage of the illness, the differences in thinking, altered sensory experiences, and disruptions in the ability to relate to others gives the person a drastically different experience of the world than you or I have. The essence of schizophrenia is *impaired reality testing:* the person is unable to tell the difference between fact and imagination or fantasy.

What's Real?

So how do you tell the difference between fantasy and reality? How do you normally tell the difference between your wish that a co-worker had the "hots" for you and the harsh reality that, in fact, she's happily married? Or how about dreams? When you wake up from a dream in which you vacationed in Tahiti, how do you know you weren't really there? If these sound like silly questions, it's because you take for granted the mental processes on which you rely to make sense of the world every day. You can trust yours; someone with schizophrenia sometimes can't.

Most of us evaluate the reality of our inner worlds against the outer one. You notice that, despite your fond daydreams of office romance, your co-worker is merely cordial and polite to you, and frequently talks about her fabulous husband. Or you wake up in your bed with no sunburn, and can easily calculate the odds against the likelihood that you traveled to and from Tahiti overnight.

When the Dream Defeats Reality

Someone with schizophrenia reverses this procedure. Inner experiences are the criteria against which they test the validity of their outer world. So, for example, if a person with schizophrenia hears a voice within his head, he believes it is real even though he can't see the speaker anywhere nearby and there is no other evidence that this voice is real. The voice is more real than the external evidence that suggests it is imagined. And if that voice orders him to go out into the street to alert people that enemy missiles are about to strike the city, he will do so. To him, this voice is as real as your boss's voice on Monday morning.

Delusions and Hallucinations: The Devastating Duo

No two sufferers of schizophrenia have exactly the same symptoms. In fact, many mental-health professionals believe schizophrenia is a cluster of several distinct illnesses. However, there are some similarities that these illnesses all share, and it's these similarities that professionals look for when they're trying to figure out what the problem is and how to help.

To receive a diagnosis of schizophrenia, a person has to have a serious, long-lasting decline in his ability to work, care for himself, and connect with other people. In addition, he must have at least two of the five following symptoms: delusions, hallucinations, disorganized speech, extremely disorganized behavior, and what clinicians call "negative" signs. Let's take a look at them.

Delusions

Delusions are basically false ideas that a person believes to be true. These ideas cannot be verified objectively, but the person suffering from schizophrenia believes them in the face of all reason. Delusional beliefs can be outlandish (such as believing that you can control the space shuttle) or they might just be unrealistic or untrue (such as believing that your partner is being unfaithful to you even though she is home every night and has given you absolutely no reason to think this). If you've ever been extremely jealous, you can see how easy it might be to slide down the slippery slope into delusion.

Some common types of delusions in schizophrenia are …

- ◆ **Delusions of persecution.** These are beliefs that others are plotting against you, or that you are being watched, followed, persecuted, or attacked.

- ◆ **Delusions of grandeur.** These are beliefs in one's own extraordinary importance. If you think you're Jesus Christ or the Queen of England, then you're suffering from a delusion of grandeur. Sometimes delusions are based on something going on in the person's real life: it is not unusual for a schizophrenic who is also HIV-positive to believe that he or she knows the "cure" for AIDS.

- ◆ **Delusions of being controlled.** These are beliefs that your thoughts or movements are being controlled by radio waves or by invisible wires, like a puppet.

> **Insight**
>
> The person most at risk for schizophrenic violence is the person who suffers from it. Forty percent of people with schizophrenia attempt suicide, and 10 percent succeed in the attempt.

Hallucinations

As you learned in Chapter 6, hallucinations are imagined sensory perceptions that are thought to be real. The most common hallucinations with schizophrenia are auditory—the hearing of voices. For example, a person might hear a running commentary on her behavior, or several voices having a conversation.

Hallucinations and delusions can occur together, as can several different *types* of delusions. For example, a person who believes she's the Queen of England might also believe that others are plotting to overthrow the throne. Or a man who has delusions of persecution may also hear the voice of his imagined persecutor threatening or insulting him. Clearly, these symptoms severely impair a person's ability to function in the day-to-day world. They are what psychologists call symptoms of *psychosis*.

def•i•ni•tion

Psychosis (also called "psychotic disorder") is a general term for a severe mental disorder that prevents an accurate understanding of and interaction with reality due to impaired thoughts, inappropriate emotions, and distorted perceptions.

Sufferers of schizophrenia can be pretty creative in their battle against hallucinations and often develop elaborate rituals to control them. Some can stop the voices by humming to themselves, counting, or holding their mouth in a certain way.

Mental-health professionals may use rituals to help. For instance, in one mental-health hospital, the psychiatrist convinced a man with hallucinations to wear a towel on his head to "block" the radio signals he was convinced were being beamed at him. It worked, and the man learned to arrange the towel creatively so it appeared to be a turban!

Interestingly enough, auditory hallucinations in schizophrenia occur through the same mechanism that produces vividly imagined speech sounds in everyone. For example, if you "rehearse" an argument before you face the person you're angry with, or if you imagine how your boss's voice will sound after you ask her to double your salary, you're generating the imagined sound by the same means that is used to create auditory hallucinations.

Insight

Auditory hallucinations (hearing something that isn't there) are common in schizophrenia and other psychotic disorders. However, contrary to what Hollywood would have you believe, *visual* hallucinations (seeing something that isn't there) are not usually part of schizophrenia. Visual hallucinations are usually related to medication problems, diseases of the brain, or street-drug use.

Disorganized Speech

The speech of people with schizophrenia often reflects the level of disorganization in their thinking. They may jump wildly and illogically from one idea to another, a phenomenon known as a *flight of ideas*. Or they may suddenly start rhyming. For example, a person may begin talking about the school bell ringing and suddenly jump to "sing, fling, wing, ding, the school bells always ring." Such speech patterns represent a disturbance in the logical thought processes.

Grossly Disorganized Behavior

We're not talking about something as minor as wearing messy clothes or forgetting to write things down so that you'll remember them. Grossly disorganized behavior is behavior that is completely inappropriate for the situation, such as wearing layers of wool clothes on a hot day or behaving in a silly manner at a funeral. Other examples of grossly disorganized behavior are the failure, or inability, to prepare a simple meal or to dress oneself.

Changes in Emotions

The earliest emotional changes seen in schizophrenia are rapid changes in mood and an exaggeration of normal feelings, particularly of guilt and fear. As the schizophrenia gets worse, the person may exhibit strange or bizarrely inappropriate emotions. For example, he or she might burst into laughter at news of a death, or burst into tears at a joke. Or the person may seem to lack emotions at all, and gradually become more detached and apathetic toward other people.

Negatively Speaking

Psychologists often talk about "positive" and "negative" signs of schizophrenia, but don't confuse these terms with "good" and "bad." In this case, *positive* means a sign that is present that shouldn't be— something that is *not* there in people without the condition. *Negative* is a sign that should be there, but isn't— something that *is* there in people without the condition.

Delusions, hallucinations, and disorganized speech and behavior are all positive signs of schizophrenia. When they are present, the illness is said to be in the acute (or psychotic) phase. When such symptoms subside, the illness is said to be in the residual phase.

> **Insight**
>
> Sometimes a person in the midst of psychosis needs to be hospitalized until his or her symptoms are under control. While people can be hospitalized against their will, they must present a clear danger to themselves or to others and refuse voluntary admission before involuntary commitment is considered.

People suffering from schizophrenia exhibit negative signs—they lack certain behaviors, thoughts, feelings, and drives that most people have. They may move more slowly than their peers do. Their speech may lack spontaneity and their range of emotional expression may be restricted. They may lose touch with basic drives such as hunger or thirst, and lose the normal pleasure that comes from satisfying them. For the person with schizophrenia, these symptoms cause real problems in coping with day-to-day life. To date, psychiatric medications have been much more effective at eliminating the positive signs of schizophrenia than at alleviating the negative signs.

Psychobabble

Never bet against the power of the human spirit. When John Nash received the 1994 Nobel Prize for economics, few people would have known that he had been diagnosed with paranoid schizophrenia more than three decades earlier, or that he had spent some 20 years of his life in and out of psychiatric hospitals.

The Faces of Schizophrenia

One of schizophrenia's challenges for psychologists is that it appears in many different guises. Two people with the same diagnosis may share very few of the same symptoms. One might hear taunting voices and attribute them to a specific (delusional) source. Another may just seem to indulge in silly and inappropriate behavior and not make a lot of sense. Researchers have tried to determine which symptoms are most likely to go together, and have come up with three different clusters of symptoms:

- Clusters of positive symptoms—usually a combination of delusions and hallucinations

- Clusters of disorganized symptoms—for example, a combination of illogical speech and disorganized behaviors

- Clusters of negative symptoms

According to the *Diagnostic and Statistical Manual of Mental Disorders* (*DSM-IV-TR*), here's how mental-health professionals classify the diverse symptoms of schizophrenia:

The Many Faces of Schizophrenia

The Type of Symptoms	What It Looks Like
Disorganized	Inappropriate behavior and emotions, incoherent speech, random delusions or hallucinations.

The Type of Symptoms	What It Looks Like
Catatonic	Bizarre movements, either a frozen or rigid posture or very excitable movements.
Paranoid	Behavior is more organized, delusions and hallucinations centered around a theme of persecution or grandiosity.
Undifferentiated	A grab-bag category, mixed set of symptoms, unusual thinking with features from other categories.
Residual	No positive symptoms appear, but the person still shows some signs like flattened affect and social withdrawal.

What Causes Schizophrenia?

Ever since it was discovered, scientists have been trying to figure out why people get schizophrenia. In fact, because of its seriousness, schizophrenia has been more fully studied than any other mental disorder. But while we've ruled out some possible causes—for instance, we know that poor family communication does *not* cause the disorder, which means we've quit blaming mothers, fortunately—we still haven't gotten to the root of the problem. Probably because there's more than one root.

The Biological Connection

One thing we know for certain is that schizophrenia is as much a medical illness as diabetes, multiple sclerosis, and cancer. On PET scans and other brain scans, the brain of a person with severe schizophrenia looks significantly different. But what causes this?

In the early 1970s, neuroscientists thought they were on to something—they thought schizophrenia might be caused by having too much of the neurotransmitter dopamine in the brain. Alas, while dopamine is involved in schizophrenia, neuroscientists now know it's not simply a matter of how much or how little you have—in fact, the way dopamine is distributed and what it does are far more important factors. Unusual patterns of dopamine activity, perhaps including overactivity in some areas and under-activity in others, may be partly responsible for schizophrenia. (For a refresher on the role of neurotransmitters, return to Chapter 2.)

In addition, glutamate, a chemical that's part of another brain-signaling system, may contribute to psychosis, thought disorder, and schizophrenia.

So, like cancer, schizophrenia probably has more than one cause. Let's take a look at the extent to which four other factors play a role in the onset of schizophrenia:

◆ Genes

◆ Prenatal development

◆ Home life

◆ Cultural influences

Family Links

If someone in your family has schizophrenia, you're about four times more likely to get it than someone whose family doesn't have it lurking in the gene pool. If one identical twin has schizophrenia, the other twin has a 50-50 chance of getting it, too. The siblings of a nontwin or a fraternal twin with the disease have a 9 percent chance of developing the illness, while the child of one parent with schizophrenia has a 13 percent chance. And a child whose parents both suffer from the disease has a 46 percent chance of developing it.

Brain Buster

Approximately one third of the 600,000 homeless people in the United States have been diagnosed with a serious mental illness, including schizophrenia and other psychotic disorders.

However, the fact that even people with the exact same genes (identical twins) share it only half the time also points out the obvious fact that our genes don't necessarily "make" us get schizophrenia. If the disease were completely genetic in origin, both twins would always get the disease. Obviously, therefore, other factors must be involved.

Prenatal Effects

Prenatal or birth trauma may stack the deck against someone with a genetic vulnerability to schizophrenia. When one identical twin develops schizophrenia, it is more likely to be the one who had the more difficult birth. Prenatal viral infections or lack of nutrition also put a baby at risk. But even here, the sequence of cause and effect isn't completely straightforward—trauma alone is not enough to cause the problem. According to one long-term study, prenatal and birth traumas were related to the later development of schizophrenia in babies whose mothers had schizophrenia but *not* in the babies who weren't genetically at risk.

Oddly enough, two risk factors for schizophrenia are place and season of birth. Babies born in February and March have a 10 percent above-average risk for schizophrenia, while babies born in August and September have a 10 percent lower risk than average. And here's a reason to move out of the city—an urban birth puts a child at twice the risk for schizophrenia, compared with babies born in rural areas.

Effects of the Home Environment

A chaotic family environment can contribute to schizophrenia but it doesn't cause the disease. A study of adopted children in Finland found that when high-risk children (whose biological mothers had schizophrenia) were adopted by parents with poor communication skills, they had more bizarre or unusual thoughts than did high-risk children whose parents communicated in a calmer, more organized fashion. There was no such difference found for low-risk children, however, so communication styles alone can't account for the onset of schizophrenia.

Other research has focused on the effects of criticism and negative attitudes or feelings expressed about and toward a person with schizophrenia by his or her family members. Other things being equal, the greater the expressed anger and hostility toward someone with schizophrenia, the more likely that his or her symptoms will worsen and the person will require hospitalization. So these factors can intensify the symptoms of the disease, but once again, they don't appear to be the cause of it.

Cultural Influences

You can't blame American culture for causing schizophrenia—the disease looks remarkably the same across cultures. The prevalence of symptoms, the average age of onset, and the sex difference in age of onset (men getting it earlier than women) are similar despite wide variations in the ways people live.

However, Western culture may make it harder to get well. Patients in developing countries get better much faster than they do in developed countries like the United States, and this holds true for every category of schizophrenia, using every measure of recovery. In fact, in one study of 1,379 patients across 10 countries, 63 percent of the patients in developing countries, compared with only 37 percent in the developed countries, showed a full recovery within a two-year period.

One possible explanation for this difference in recovery patterns is the different cultural attitudes toward mental illness. Family members in developing countries are more accepting of a family member with schizophrenia—and so is the culture in which the family lives. They are much less likely to label the person as "sick" or to think of schizophrenia as a permanent condition. They may call it "a case of nerves," which sounds more benign, and they may be more likely to tie it to experiences that everyone has had.

Insight

There is no reliable way to predict whether a young person will develop schizophrenia. However, an unusually large number of children who are at risk for schizophrenia show attention deficits similar to their adult counterparts. Once again, however, the connection isn't a simple one of cause and effect: most people with attention deficit disorder do not develop schizophrenia.

Perhaps more importantly, the social organization common to non-Western cultures provides more support for a person suffering from schizophrenia and for his or her family. Extended families provide more resources and care, which helps caregivers be more nurturing and tolerant. And nonindustrialized, more agriculturally based cultures can be more flexible in allowing a person with schizophrenia to play a useful role in the family economy by performing chores on the family farm. These social factors are generally unavailable in highly individualistic, nonagricultural societies like the United States.

When Schizophrenia Happens in Childhood

The appearance of schizophrenia before age 12 is rare—less than $\frac{1}{60}$ as common as adult-onset schizophrenia. Some children who develop the illness seem to be different from their peers at an early age; about 30 percent have on-and-off symptoms in the first years of life. As a group, they are more anxious and disruptive than their peers, and are more likely to exhibit behaviors frequently seen in pervasive developmental disorders such as autism—rocking, arm flapping, or other unusual, repetitive behaviors. Most of them also show delays in learning language and other skills.

Childhood schizophrenia tends to develop gradually, without the sudden onset of psychotic symptoms—called a psychotic break—that we see in adults and adolescents. Hallucinations, delusions, and disorganized thinking almost always occur after age seven. Once the schizophrenia starts, its symptoms often parallel those seen in adults and older adolescents.

A significant drop in I.Q. during early childhood (between ages four and seven) may signal an increased risk of psychotic symptoms in adulthood. The *American Journal of*

Psychiatry reported a study of 547 Americans born between 1959 and 1966. A decline in I.Q. between ages four and seven was associated with psychotic symptoms 16 years later. This was seven times higher than for individuals whose childhood I.Q. did not decline.

Who Gets Better?

One thing should be clear by now: the human spirit is stronger than any psychiatric illness. But as a clinician I know that some people with a serious mental illness get better, some coast along, and some get worse. My job is to push my clients into the first category as hard as I can.

Studies of the outcome of treatment suggest some things that make a good recovery more likely, and a few others that work against a happy ending. A person with little or no family history of schizophrenia—as was true for Mr. Frese at the start of this chapter—is more likely to have a better treatment outcome than someone whose family genes are stacked against her. Another good sign is having lived a normal and productive life before the onset of schizophrenia. And early intervention is critical: the sooner someone gets help for his first psychotic episode, the more likely he is to avoid future crashes.

> **Brain Buster**
>
> While the term *nervous breakdown* was once commonly used by physicians as a generic term for any acute mental problem, in reality it is so vague as to be meaningless as a description of a psychological disorder. The term has been used to describe emotional problems ranging from a severe stress reaction (like post-traumatic stress disorder) to debilitating depression or psychosis.

On the downside, if schizophrenia strikes at an early age and there's a strong family history of the disease, the person may have a tough road to recovery. The gender of the patient makes a difference, too: for some reason, men tend to do worse than women. In addition, patients who have a lot of *negative* signs—such as apathy and withdrawal from others—often have a harder time than those who do not. Last but not least, the greater the number of relapses a patient suffers, the lower his chances for complete recovery. And, of course, while getting effective treatment for schizophrenia is the first step, sticking to it is the rest of the game.

Schizophrenia tends to scare everyone—the person who has it, the family that hears the diagnosis, and the mental-health professional who's treating it. Fortunately, we have a whole new arsenal in our war on schizophrenia and, finally, it's a war we're starting to win.

Playing the Odds: Schizophrenia

What's the treatment of choice? Three words: medication, medication, medication. When schizophrenia is treated right from the start, remission rates are as high as 80 to 85 percent. As with diabetes, medication is used to control the symptoms, not to cure the disease itself. But when the symptoms are under control, a person with schizophrenia can lead a normal life. The sooner treatment is begun after the first psychotic episode, the greater the chance that medication will get the symptoms under control.

The medications used to treat schizophrenia are called antipsychotic or neuroleptic drugs. These drugs help restore the function of the brain to normal levels. And they have an encouragingly high success rate: on average, a person with schizophrenia who takes medication has a 60 percent chance of not being rehospitalized. Without medication, those odds drop to 20 percent.

Treatment of schizophrenia improved drastically in the 1990s, with the advent of new antipsychotic medications called *atypical antipsychotics*. Some of the commonly used ones include Clozaril, Zyprexa, Seroquel, and Risperdal. For patients who don't respond to these medications, new research suggests that topiramate, a drug that blocks glutamate, can be an effective add-on.

The biggest problem with schizophrenia is not that the drugs don't work; they usually do. The biggest problem occurs when people don't take the medications. A common cycle is a full-blown psychotic episode, resulting in a trip to the emergency room or the psych hospital. The person is medicated, improves, and is released. And eventually she either (1) feels so good that she decides she doesn't need the medications anymore, or (2) has unpleasant side effects and therefore stops taking the meds. In both cases, the person stops the medications. Gradually, the symptoms come back, and the cycle starts again.

Because psychotherapy alone doesn't work at all when someone is having a psychotic episode, it traditionally hasn't been considered an important part of the treatment for schizophrenia. But cognitive-behavioral therapy that focuses on medication adherence (consistently and correctly taking the drugs) can be a crucial part of treatment. Family and group support can also be very effective. Psychodynamic therapy, however, can actually make the condition worse!

Clearing Up Any Remaining Confusion

We've already cleared up the confusion between schizophrenia and multiple-personality disorder. However, because of the common use of generic words like *nervous breakdown* and *psychotic break*, schizophrenia is often confused with a number of other, very different mental illnesses. Let's clear up the confusion once and for all.

Schizophrenia is *not* …

- **Bipolar disorder (manic depression).** This is a periodic, recurrent mood disorder of extreme highs and lows interspersed with periods of complete normalcy. It does not involve negative signs or fixed delusions.

- **Schizoaffective disorder.** This disorder has symptoms of schizophrenia and bipolar disorder. It involves a disturbance of mood (depression, anxiety) on top of the usual signs of schizophrenia.

- **Brief reactive psychosis.** While this disorder has symptoms similar to schizophrenia, it lasts for less than two weeks and is generally brought on by extreme stress. An example is postpartum psychosis.

- **Personality disorders.** Schizoid and schizotypal personality disorders share some of the odd behaviors and impaired relationships as are found in schizophrenia, but there are no breaks with reality and the person who has such a disorder can still function more or less competently in society.

- **Creativity.** Extremely creative people may have unusual thoughts and views and may behave in ways that other people consider to be eccentric, but the creative person remains in control of his or her thought processes.

- **Diseases afflicting the brain.** Hallucinations or delusions can be caused by brain infection or tumors. But once the infection is treated or the tumor is removed, these symptoms will end without the need for continued medication.

The Perils of Paranoia

One of my all-time favorite bumper stickers says, "Just because I'm paranoid doesn't mean they're not out to get me." This humorous bumper sticker illustrates how often (although certainly not always) there can be a grain of truth in the most irrational beliefs.

Dealing with Distress

Suppose Mr. Smith worked for a national pharmacy chain for 30 years, was an exemplary employee, and never missed a day's work. One day he comes to work to discover that the pharmacy chain has been bought out and he's abruptly laid off from work. Understandably, he feels hurt and betrayed. He spends hours thinking about what's happened to him and how, after all his years of service to the company, something like this could have happened to him.

From Distress to Delusion

So far, Mr. Smith's reactions are perfectly normal. But what if, after a while, his thoughts take a stranger turn? Unemployed and isolated in his apartment, he begins to believe that his layoff has nothing to do with the company buyout and begins to wonder if his former employer was engaged in a systematic plot to destroy his life and take away his sanity. He begins to believe that company agents are tampering with his mail, following him, and even tapping his phone.

> **Insight**
>
> There's more than one condition that has paranoid symptoms. There's paranoid schizophrenia, paranoid delusional disorder, and paranoid personality disorder. Each is a different condition, with different preferred treatments.

Mr. Smith has developed a paranoid delusion. This is a serious psychological diagnosis—it's not what most people mean when they use the term *paranoid* casually, to refer to simple suspiciousness. When a person is suspicious based on past personal experience or observation, it is inappropriate to call him or her paranoid. In fact, mental-health clinicians only use the term when a person's suspiciousness or mistrust is either highly exaggerated or completely unwarranted.

Because paranoia is common in many psychiatric disorders, it can be difficult to fit the symptoms to the right diagnosis. We've already explored one diagnosis in which paranoia plays a part—paranoid schizophrenia. Now let's talk about another disorder in which paranoia reaches delusional proportions.

> **Insight**
>
> Here's a good reason to lay off "uppers" such as cocaine and amphetamines. They can greatly increase the symptoms of schizophrenia in people who already have them and, at high doses, can induce those symptoms in people who do not. And the abuse of drugs like amphetamines, LSD, and PCP can also cause paranoid thinking and behavior.

Paranoid Delusional Disorder

Someone with a paranoid *personality* might frequently suspect colleagues of making jokes at his or her expense. People with paranoid *delusions*, on the other hand, might believe that their colleagues are poisoning them, drugging them, spying on them, or plotting a grand conspiracy to smear their name. There's a big difference between the two.

The Green-Eyed Monster

Not all people who suffer paranoid delusions are convinced that they're going to be harmed or killed. Jealousy can become delusional, for example. I once knew a man who truly believed that his wife had gotten into an automobile accident deliberately—in an attempt to cover up her rendezvous with her lover. This is more than a simple fear that a loved one might find somebody new—this man took *everything* as a sign that his partner was unfaithful. Although his beliefs might sound almost comical, the genuine emotional distress his delusion caused both him and his partner was no laughing matter.

The Strange Psyche of the Stalker

On rare occasions, you read about a celebrity whose life is plagued by a stalker. Late-night talk-show host David Letterman was stalked for years by such a woman. She phoned him, she wrote him love letters, and she became a constant and unwelcome presence in his life. Despite Letterman's consistent failure to respond to her proclamations of love, she continued to believe that he really loved her. She was arrested, hospitalized, and eventually killed herself.

This woman was in the grip of a powerful form of paranoia—an erotic delusion. No amount of external evidence could shake her in her belief that Letterman returned her love. A paranoid delusion like hers is an extreme example of the power that our beliefs can hold over our entire lives.

> **Brain Buster**
>
> Don't confuse paranoid schizophrenia with paranoid delusional disorder. The latter is not accompanied by hallucinations or generally disorganized behavior. In fact, except for actions and thoughts that center around the specific delusion, the person with paranoid delusional disorder can often function normally.

The Origins of Paranoid Delusions

Families of people with paranoid delusional disorder do not have higher than normal rates of schizophrenia or depression. A person suffering from the disorder, however, is more likely to come from a family in which other members have the same problem: twins are more likely to share paranoia than regular siblings, and paranoid disorders are more common among relatives. Although we don't know exactly what causes paranoia, we do know that certain drugs make it worse. And there's bad news for *all* of us these days—some studies show that paranoia has increasingly become more common over the past 100 years. Just being alive at the start of the new millennium puts some of us at risk!

There are other factors at work as well. Stress, for example, can trigger paranoia or make it worse. Prisoners of war, immigrants, and other people living under extreme stress all show a higher likelihood of developing paranoid delusions. Even "normal" people can suffer from a short-lived form of paranoia, called acute paranoia, when they are thrust into highly stressful new situations. The relationship between stress and paranoia is complex, but it appears that a person can be genetically predisposed to paranoia and that stress is likely to trigger it.

Playing the Odds: Delusional Disorders

Delusional disorders can actually be one of several types: erotomanic (like Letterman's stalker), grandiose, jealous, persecutory (the fictitious Mr. Smith), or somatic (odd beliefs about bodily function). Unlike schizophrenia, these disorders commonly occur later in life—middle age and beyond. Delusional disorders are commonly far less disruptive to day-to-day living than is schizophrenia. They are also less common: most estimates say perhaps less than one third of 1 percent of the population has a delusional disorder.

Treatment prognosis, however, may be worse. Paranoia, by its very nature, involves the belief that the problem is *out there* rather than inside oneself. As a result, many people with these disorders refuse treatment, and, unless they are a clear and present danger to themselves or others, treatment cannot be forced upon them. Both medications (from antidepressants to antipsychotics) and psychotherapy (usually psychodynamic) have been used with some success, but many people with the disorders simply drop out of treatment early.

The Least You Need to Know

◆ Schizophrenia is a serious medical illness that affects about 1 percent of the global population.

◆ Common symptoms of schizophrenia are delusions, hallucinations, disorganized speech, disorganized behavior, and inappropriate emotions.

◆ Schizophrenia is a disease of the brain—much as diabetes or cancer are diseases of the body—and its symptoms can be controlled with medication.

◆ The odds of getting schizophrenia are greater if one or more members of your family have it. Prenatal birth trauma and living in a chaotic home may also contribute.

◆ Paranoia is a symptom found in many psychiatric disorders, including paranoid schizophrenia, paranoid delusional disorder, and paranoid personality disorder.

◆ Paranoid delusional disorder is characterized by a highly exaggerated and unwarranted mistrust and suspicion of others, but it does not involve hallucinations or other psychotic symptoms.

Chapter 21

Outta Control!

In This Chapter

- Why does normal behavior go haywire?
- Food fights: dealing with eating disorders
- The trouble with booze
- Dangerous impulses: pyromania, kleptomania, and compulsive gambling

In June 2004, Mary-Kate Olsen entered treatment for anorexia, after denying for months that she was too thin or had an eating disorder. In 1983, 32-year-old singer Karen Carpenter died from heart failure, the result of complications she had sustained during her eight-year battle with anorexia nervosa. Why do young, talented, beautiful women starve themselves? Why can't they "see" that they're dangerously thin?

Back in 1983 we didn't understand the seriousness of anorexia nervosa. Today, the news of another death from anorexia still saddens us, but isn't such a shock. Eating disorders in general (especially anorexia) are the most deadly of the psychiatric disorders. Without treatment, a serious eating disorder will kill about 20 percent of the people who have it.

In this chapter, we'll look at a group of disorders that share a common theme: they all start out with normal or common behaviors. Most of us have dieted, drunk alcohol, or gambled—but most us don't develop an eating disorder or an addiction to alcohol or gambling. Similarly, although young children are often fascinated by fire and, at least once, might take something that doesn't belong to them, they rarely grow up to become fire setters or kleptomaniacs. In this chapter, we'll explore when, why, and how these behaviors get out of control, what can be done to prevent it, and how people with addictions or impulse control disorders can kick the habit.

What's Eating You?

Many people think of eating disorders as stemming from an unhealthy desire for a perfect body. If that were true, the disorders would be a lot easier to get rid of. You might be surprised to know that eating disorders are not about vanity and not really about weight at all. They are complex psychological illnesses in which people try to control the conflict and stress in their lives by controlling their food intake. The food, weight, and body-image issues are obvious symptoms of deeper problems.

Insight

A person with an *eating disorder* develops a pathological relationship with food—she may eat extreme amounts of food in a single sitting, she may starve herself, or she may prevent her body from digesting her food by purging or using laxatives.

Typically, people who develop an eating disorder are at a difficult time in their lives. Let's use a fictitious person, whom we'll call Suzanne, as an example of how the eating disorder ball gets rolling. Suzanne came from a family in which a slim physique was a prized attribute. Luckily, she never had to worry about her weight—until she graduated from college.

Her first job required a move to a new city, and she was cut off from family and her old friends. She had to work long hours, so she had little chance to make new friends, and no time to exercise.

At 23, Suzanne was lonely, homesick, and terrified of failing at her first job. After six months, she was horrified to learn that she had gained 10 pounds. Her life already felt out of control, now her weight was out of control, too!

Over time, all of her anxiety, self-doubt, and feelings of failure and inadequacy became tied to her weight. She began making herself vomit after her business dinners and started bingeing as a way to comfort herself in her lonely apartment on weekends. What would have been a difficult time in anyone's life gradually turned into an anorexic nightmare. If it had lasted long enough, Suzanne could have died.

Wasting Away to Nothing

Anorexia nervosa is hard to understand because we relate it to dieting. Think back to a time when you were on a diet. Maybe you crash dieted to get ready for the senior prom. Maybe you shed a few pounds for your tenth high school reunion. Most of us think *diet* is truly a four-letter word. Sure, you'd have sympathy for anyone who had trouble sticking to a diet, but most of us find it less easy to see how it could be hard to *quit* one!

Anorexia is a lot more complicated than an out-of-control diet. It's a pattern of self-starvation that occurs primarily in young girls in Western cultures from middle and upper socioeconomic classes; in fact, anorexia and bulimia are extremely rare in non-Western countries.

With anorexia, the strong desire to be thin, which plagues most American women, turns into an obsession. Someone with this disorder is terrified of becoming obese. The problem is compounded by the fact that people with anorexia have lost their ability to see themselves objectively. You or I can look at a person and tell whether he or she is plump or skinny, but people with anorexia feel fat no matter what their actual weight is. Even when they're close to death, they'll point out areas of their bodies where they "need" to lose weight.

A person with anorexia may also be trying to cope with feelings of powerlessness: she may feel that if she can't control what is happening around her, at least she can control her weight. Each morning, the number on the bathroom scale determines whether she has succeeded or failed in her goal for thinness. She feels powerful and in control when she can make herself lose weight.

And sometimes, focusing on calories and losing weight is a way of blocking out feelings and emotions. It's easier to diet than it is to deal with problems directly. In addition, people with anorexia usually have low self-esteem and sometimes feel that they don't deserve to eat.

A person with anorexia will often deny that anything is wrong. He might say that he doesn't get hungry. If you try to get him help, he'll fight you, because he is likely to see therapy as a way to force him to eat.

Psychobabble

Writer O. Henry wrote a short story featuring a New York model whose measurements were even better than "the required 38-25-42 standard." In current American terms, this is a size 12 or 14 bust, a size 4 waist, and a size 14 to 16 rear! Think she could get a modeling job today?

Before getting help, a person with an eating disorder can do some significant damage to himself—in ways you might never have imagined. For example, parents of young children often keep syrup of ipecac around the house in case of accidental poisoning, because it causes immediate vomiting. About 300,000 people with anorexia and bulimia, however, use it for another reason—to get rid of unwanted food. Some physicians believe that many mysterious heart failures in patients with anorexia and bulimia may actually be due to ipecac abuse.

The Food Roller Coaster

Have you ever overeaten because you were stressed? Then, consumed with guilt, you pulled yourself up by your bootstraps and dieted like crazy the next day? Maybe you even consciously added up the extra calories you ate the day before and made sure you deprived yourself of the same amount. Welcome to food games.

To some extent, we play that kind of give-and-take all the time. We "splurge" at birthdays and we "cut back" after the holidays. These are mini-versions of the big eating-disorder roller coaster, *bulimia nervosa*. Bulimia takes the "splurging" and "cutting back" to extremes.

def•i•ni•tion

Bulimia nervosa is a disorder in which a person binges (overeats) and purges (attempts to get rid of the food).

Bulimia nervosa is a cycle of binge eating followed by some method of trying to rid the body of unwanted calories—through fasting, vomiting, laxatives, diuretics, diet pills, or even excessive exercise. People with bulimia are amazingly different in how they define a binge; although most of us have the image of a young woman locking herself in her apartment and eating her way through her entire refrigerator, another person may define a "binge" as eating foods that are normally prohibited from his or her diet.

The psychological dynamics of bulimia nervosa are different from those associated with anorexia. In bulimia, food often becomes a person's only source of comfort and a way to hide or suppress uncomfortable feelings. Unlike many people suffering from anorexia, people with bulimia are often well aware that they have a problem, but they may be too ashamed or scared to get help.

Perhaps the best-known sufferer of this eating disorder in recent years was Princess Diana. In the 1990s, she brought much-needed attention to the emotional and physical costs of bulimia nervosa when she publicly divulged her own struggle with this illness.

I Just Can't Quit Eating

Compulsive overeating, or as professionals call it, *binge-eating disorder*, is the other side of the eating-disorder coin. It's characterized by uncontrollable eating and conse-quent weight gain. A person who compul-sively overeats uses food as a way to cope with stress, emotional conflicts, and daily problems. The food blocks out feelings and emotions, but at a price—compulsive overeaters usually feel out of control and are aware that their eating patterns are abnormal. Like people with bulimia, people who compulsively overeat recognize that they have a problem, but are often too ashamed of their "lack of discipline" with regard to food to seek help with the problem.

def•i•ni•tion

Binge-eating disorder is the official diagnosis given a person who eats a large amount of food within two hours, at least two days a week for six months, with-out purging in any way to lose or maintain his or her weight. This disorder is commonly called com-pulsive overeating.

"Comfort" Food Gone Wrong

Compulsive overeating usually starts in early childhood, when eating patterns are formed. Perhaps a child watches a parent overeat in response to stress. When he falls and skins his knee, he is treated to an ice cream sundae. When he feels mad, a grand-parent suggests that he "treat himself" to a special food. Over time, the child learns that food is useful for a lot more than helping him grow—it can soothe hurt feelings, melt away loneliness, and push down unpleasant feelings.

Most people who become compulsive eaters have never learned the proper way to deal with stressful situations, and so they use food instead as a way of coping. In addition, whereas a person with bulimia is terrified of getting fat, people who compulsively overeat often find comfort in their excess weight. They use fat as a barrier that pro-tects them from other people getting too close. This is especially common in people who have been victims of sexual abuse.

The Vicious Binge-Diet Cycle

But no matter how much emotional protection a large body size may provide for someone who compulsively overeats, she's likely to be disgusted by her excess weight and undisciplined eating habits. So her binges are usually followed by feelings of pow-erlessness, guilt, shame, and failure. The more weight she gains, the harder she diets, and her drastic dieting usually leads to the next binge. This vicious cycle can go on and on—unless she gets help or begins to address the underlying emotional issues that trigger her out-of-control eating.

Many people with binge-eating disorder complain that their problem isn't taken seriously enough—and rightly so. Most people who have an overeating problem are directed to diet centers and health spas, where they lose weight and then regain it—but that only addresses a part of the problem. It does nothing to help them overcome the emotional issues underlying the overeating in the first place.

And it's important that those issues be addressed. Although most eating-disorder fatalities are due to starvation, bingeing itself can be fatal. A 23-year-old model, who had starved herself down to 84 pounds, died in London after gaining 19 pounds in a single binge. In fact, people with bulimia as well as those with binge eating disorder have been known to binge so severely that the abdominal wall ruptures; they literally split open from the inside out from massive amounts of food. Clearly, compulsive overeating can be a serious problem with life-threatening medical complications, just like anorexia and bulimia.

We Might Look Different, but We Have a Lot in Common

A woman who weighs 210 pounds looks dramatically different than a woman who weighs 75 pounds—on the outside, at least. But put these two women in a dark room and listen to them talk, and you might not be able to tell them apart. They share a pathological relationship with food and eating, no matter which eating disorder they're struggling with. And there are other common elements shared by anorexia, bulimia, and binge-eating disorder, as well.

Common circumstances and risk factors include …

- Family problems or a troubled home life

- Major life changes (divorce, death of a loved one, a move)

- Romantic or social problems

- Abuse or trauma (especially physical or sexual)

These disorders are also similar in the kinds of physical dangers they can cause for their sufferers. These include disruptions in blood sugar levels, kidney infection and failure, liver failure, poor circulation, heart problems, vitamin and mineral deficiencies, weakness, fertility problems, impaired digestion, and osteoporosis or arthritis. Dental problems are also common, particularly in bulimia, as the stomach acids produced by repeated vomiting eat away the tooth enamel.

An Ounce of Prevention Is Worth a Pound of Cure

There is an environmental factor that plays a role in the development of eating disorders: family attitudes toward food and eating. If one or both parents are stressed about how to deal with their own anxieties about their body or weight, they can unintentionally pass them along to their children. Conversely, parents can provide a healthy, balanced role model for their children.

If you're committed to teaching healthy eating habits and a positive *body image* to your children, then you need to know that you're swimming upstream—just look at all the media messages that bombard your child every day. By the time your child is six, she will have formed a definite prejudice against obesity and a clear idea that thin is in. Throw in a few fashion magazines and, by the time she reaches adolescence, she's a lucky girl indeed if she's managed to escape our culture's beauty obsession unscathed.

def•i•ni•tion

Your **body image** is the subjective way you view your physical appearance. It consists of a complex array of thoughts, feelings, and behaviors.

There are things you can do, though, to at least buffer your children against this culture's bondage to beauty and to decrease the risk that they'll develop eating disorders. For example, you can teach your children to eat healthfully and to view food as nothing more than an enjoyable source of energy for their bodies. And you can teach your children to appreciate all the things their bodies can do—and not just to obsess about how they look.

Ten Seeds That Grow Healthy Eaters

Here are 10 do's and don'ts that you can use to help prevent your child from developing an eating disorder. Here's a warning: these tips are not for the fainthearted—and they may require you to do a little body-image work of your own!

- **Don't** make disparaging comments about your child's weight or body size. Parents' comments about their children's weight plays a direct role in the number of times a child tries to diet, their self-esteem, and their concern about weight gain.

- **Don't** soothe your child with food. If he's hurt, let him cry, put a Band-Aid on it, or give him a punching bag to work his feelings out on. Just don't give him a cookie! One of the easiest mistakes we make is to teach our kids to equate food with emotion. Food is not love, pride, sadness, or a friend. It is something our bodies need for fuel to keep us healthy and strong.

Insight

Because power struggles around food are common in eating disorders, family therapy is a critical part of effective treatment for adolescents suffering with an eating disorder.

- **Don't** use food as a regular reward. If your children do something good, give them hugs, kisses, and praise, or spend special time with them. Don't use a trip to McDonald's or a hot fudge sundae as a regular reward.

- **Don't** withhold food as punishment or force your children to eat when they're not hungry. This teaches them not to trust their own bodily cues for hunger and fullness.

- **Do** engage in fun physical activity as a family and limit the amount of television your family watches.

- **Do** provide structure for your child's eating. Eat around the same time each day and provide a well-balanced meal. Let your child determine how much he or she eats.

- **Don't** forbid any foods. "Junk food" in moderation is fine. Restricting sweets from your children's diet will only backfire and make them want them more, especially as they approach school age and see other children eating and enjoying candy, cookies, and chips.

- **Do** set an example. Kids learn their lifestyles from the people around them, and thinking "Do what I say, not what I do" will not get you very far.

- **Don't** *ever* put your child on a diet unless it is for medical reasons. While most teenagers who diet don't develop an eating disorder, dieting during adolescence is the best predictor of whether any one teenager will subsequently develop a problematic relationship with food. If your child is complaining about feeling "fat," then encourage her to become more physically active and to feel better about her body image.

Playing the Odds: Battling Eating Disorders

The road to recovery for someone with an eating disorder is often bumpy. Unlike alcohol or drugs, we can't just quit eating "cold turkey." For better or worse, we have to have a relationship with food for the rest of our lives. In addition, because there is no one cause for eating disorders, there isn't one cure, either. Whether you're suffering from anorexia, bulimia, or binge-eating disorder, the *treatment of choice* is a team of professionals who work together to tackle all the different parts of the illness.

The recommended team consists of a physician, a psychiatrist or psychologist, and a nutritionist, at the minimum. Outpatient treatment can work if the disorder is not life threatening, but hospitalization or inpatient psychiatric treatment may be helpful if the person's weight is dangerously low or if he just can't stop the self-destructive behaviors on his own.

Psychotherapy is a critical component of treatment, and you want a specialist for this disorder. Two types of therapy appear particularly beneficial: *cognitive-behavioral therapy (CBT)*, which has been discussed in previous chapters, and *interpersonal* therapy. Interpersonal psychotherapy focuses on a person's relationships with other people, a core issue for many people with eating disorders. While some professionals advocate hard-core behavior therapy (eat this much, get this reward), others criticize this as keeping the focus on eating as a control issue.

In the past, *medications* had little place in the treatment of eating disorders. Newer studies show that many people benefit from them. The SSRI medications discussed in treatment of depression and anxiety appear to work well in some people, as do some of the tricyclic antidepressants.

What's the prognosis? With extensive treatment, about 60 percent of people with eating disorders recover. While we're working to get this number higher, there is hope; the earlier the treatment begins, the better!

When Someone You Love Has an Eating Disorder

Eating disorders don't just hurt the people who have them. Disorders also make life hard for their families, who spend a lot of time worrying about them, trying to get help, and, oftentimes, getting into energy-draining food battles in an attempt to "fix" their loved one's eating problem. When someone has an eating disorder, it can be hard to know when to step in and where to draw the line.

And if you *do* step in to help a family member with an eating disorder, your help is often unappreciated. That doesn't mean, however, that you shouldn't try. Silence can be deadly, and a compassionate talk with your troubled loved one about worrisome behaviors can at least plant seeds that could later blossom into the recognition of the need for treatment. Here are eight ways to help someone with an eating disorder and still keep your sanity:

- Know your limits. You can be a friend and you can be supportive. You can encourage the person to get help. But you cannot make the person get help or change before he or she is ready. You are not responsible for his or her recovery.

- Provide information and encourage the person to get help. Offer to go along for the first visit to a therapist or doctor.

- Refrain from comments like "you're too thin" or "you don't have to worry about your weight." Do not give advice about weight loss. And whatever you do, *never* say, "I'm glad you've put on a few pounds."

- Do not ignore behavior that concerns you. If you see clear signs that someone has been purging (for example, she always heads to the bathroom right after a meal), tell her in a nonjudgmental way and express your concern.

- Avoid power struggles over food—you will never win them.

- Do not let the person control when, where, or what *you* eat. For example, if you live together, don't quit buying certain foods if he asks you to, or change your eating schedule in the hope that he will eat more.

- No matter how tempting it is, don't nag, beg, bribe, threaten, or manipulate.

- Get support for yourself. Being in a relationship with someone who has an eating disorder can take its toll.

Eat, Drink, and Be ... Addicted?

"First the man takes the drink, then the drink takes a drink, and then the drink takes the man." This Japanese proverb applies to at least one out of every ten people in the United States. Four out of ten Americans have alcoholism in their family. Odds are, you personally know someone who is addicted to alcohol—a friend, a family member, or a co-worker. Although tens of thousands of people attend Alcoholics Anonymous every week, there are a lot more alcoholics secretly drinking their lives away.

Of course, not all drinking is problem drinking. The National Institute on Alcohol Abuse and Alcoholism defines moderate drinking as an average of two drinks a day or less. But 15 million Americans exceed this drinking limit. And the 15 percent of men and 3 percent of women who drink more than four drinks a day are on the slippery slope to alcohol dependence.

The Road to Alcoholism

There are many different ways that a person might wind up with an addiction to alcohol. Some people drink till they're drunk from the time they take their first drink—immediately acting in ways that are destructive to themselves and their relationships. Others start with acceptable social drinking that gradually spirals out of control. But no matter how they start, alcoholics end up at the same place—with their lives revolving around booze.

Alcoholism is not always progressive, although it usually is. And it generally takes some remarkably predictable steps in its development:

- **Step One.** Quickly or gradually, the drinker comes to depend upon the mood-altering qualities of alcohol. Drinks perk him up, relieve anxiety and stress, make special occasions more fun, and temporarily take away the blues. Maybe the drinker gulps a few drinks before the party or has a double before dinner. The drinking might still be under control, but the amount of alcohol consumed gradually increases.

- **Step Two.** The drinker's life starts to revolve around alcohol. The urge to drink starts earlier in the day, and the person begins to prefer alcohol-related activities and to hang around with friends who drink. An increasing tolerance for alcohol is accompanied by *blackouts* and an increasing loss of control.

def•i•ni•tion

Blackouts are a type of amnesia in which the person can still function (drive or make dinner) but later can't remember what happened. A blackout is always a symptom that should be taken *very* seriously.

During the middle stages of alcoholism, some drinkers may try to stop on their own. Before the "denial" sets in, they may begin to be secretly ashamed of their behavior and may be aware that life is getting out of control. They may try to monitor their alcohol consumption, switch brands, or limit drinking to a certain time of day. As their strategies fail, they may begin to deny their powerlessness and instead rationalize that they could quit if they "really wanted to."

Relationship problems, financial difficulties, and work problems all provide excuses for having a drink.

◆ **Step Three.** The later stages of alcoholism are often characterized by an obsession with alcohol—to the exclusion of almost everything else. As relationships and financial responsibilities deteriorate, guilt and remorse are alleviated with more alcohol. The person in the late stages of alcoholism may drink around the clock. Without help, the alcoholic may eventually drink him- or herself to death.

Are You Hitting the Booze Too Hard?

Even today, when people think of alcoholics, they tend to picture a wild-eyed, disheveled bum. But they'd be wrong. Alcohol abuse can sneak up on anyone. You can be a problem drinker and still not drink more than the people you hang out with. You can be the life of the party, and let no one know that you keep drinking when you go home. You can have a problem with alcohol and still get up and go to work the next day.

Assessing Your Intake

Because of the misguided stereotypes we have of what alcoholics are like, it can be difficult to identify the point at which "normal" social drinking becomes problem drinking. The following quiz may help you assess your own alcohol use or abuse.

Respond to the following questions using the number key below:

1 = never   4 = often

2 = rarely   5 = almost always

3 = sometimes

1. Have you ever awakened the next day after partying the night before and not been able to remember part of the evening? ____

2. Is it hard to stop drinking after you've had one or two drinks? ____

3. Does someone you care about worry or complain about your drinking? ____

4. Do you ever feel guilty about your drinking? ____

5. Have you ever gotten in trouble at work because of your drinking? ____

6. Has your drinking caused problems between you and your spouse, parent, or other friend/relative? ____

7. Have you ever blown off your responsibilities for two or more days in a row because you were drinking? ____

8. Do you drink before noon? ____

9. Do people close to you say you have a problem with alcohol? ____

10. Do you drink more than most people you know? ____

Now, total up your answers. Here's how to assess your score:

10–15: We all have problems, but alcohol probably isn't one of yours. When it comes to booze, you can usually take it or leave it—and most of the time, you leave it before it takes hold of you.

16–20: It might surprise you that, despite your relatively low score, I'm urging you to take a close look at the role alcohol plays in your life. Even if it "rarely" causes blackouts or arguments, the numbers show that you're experiencing negative consequences from drinking, and that's enough for me to consider raising a red flag.

21–30: Consider the red flag truly raised. Remember the Japanese proverb at the beginning of this section? If your score is over 25, you are at least at the "drink takes a drink" stage half of the time you use alcohol.

31 or higher: I am worried about your alcohol use. And, judging by your answers, you are worried about it, too. Why not err on the side of caution and talk to a professional—or attend an AA meeting just to see what's it's like?

Why Can't I Handle My Liquor?

Alcoholism isn't fair. Some people can drink like a fish and never develop a drinking problem. For others, alcohol is like a hypnotic poison—it quickly puts them under its spell, dramatically changes their behavior, and causes blackouts and other physical problems. Why can some of us handle liquor so much better than others?

To some extent, the answer may lie in our genes. There's no question that alcoholism runs in families. Identical twins reared apart are more likely to share alcoholism than fraternal twins living in the same family. A child of an alcoholic has four times the risk of becoming an alcoholic than the a child of a nonalcoholic—even when raised by teetotalers. At the very least, some of us inherit a predisposition to alcoholism.

> **Brain Buster**
>
> Have you got an alcohol problem? The best way to find out is to get input from friends, family members, or co-workers. Their input is important because it is hard to objectively assess the pros and cons of a behavior that you've found to be very enjoyable or that you've used to cope with problems in your life.

Alcohol dependence is also more prevalent in some cultures. Ever heard the saying, "God invented whiskey to keep the Irish from taking over the world?" People with this Anglo-Saxon ancestry do, in fact, seem to have higher rates of alcoholism, as do many people of Native American ancestry. Conversely, many Asian groups appear to have relatively low rates of alcoholism.

Alcoholism is not like a cold, however—you can't catch it from your family. Most people who develop an addiction to alcohol start out with a genetic predisposition, but the actual progression of a drinking problem is triggered by stressful life events. Developing effective stress-management strategies is one way to buffer yourself against life's tornadoes. And there's no two ways around it: it pays to stay away from the booze. No matter how many studies you read touting the heart benefits of a glass of wine a day, you're better off exercising regularly than risking addiction.

Playing the Odds: Overcoming Alcohol Dependence

The *treatment of choice* for addiction is the self-help support group. While there are different types of these, the best known is Alcoholics Anonymous (AA).

AA is a worldwide self-help support group of individuals recovering from alcohol addiction. It was started in 1935 by two alcoholics, Bill W. and Dr. Bob, after all of their professional treatment programs had failed. Neither one of them ever drank again.

In an informal survey of AA members, 29 percent said they had remained sober for more than five years, 38 percent for one to five years, and 33 percent for less than a year. Overall recovery rates suggest that between 20 percent and 35 percent of alcohol-dependent adults will completely recover, another third of them will struggle, and the rest are likely to die prematurely or remain alcohol-dependent.

Worried that no one will really understand you? Not only are there general AA groups, but in cities there are often specialty AA groups as well: nonsmoking, gay or lesbian, single parents, physician or lawyer-only, and HIV-positive are just some of the AA groups that are out there.

Like eating disorders treatment, however, a treatment team can significantly boost the odds of recovery. Physical withdrawal from alcohol can be fatal if not closely supervised, so some professionals routinely recommend inpatient treatment for detoxification (detox). *Psychotherapy* can be an important part of treatment, especially when used in conjunction with a support group.

What about medications? The old treatment rule was the three "A's"—abstinence, AA, and Antabuse. While the first two are still recommended, the medication Antabuse, which made you vomit violently if you consumed alcohol, has been largely replaced by new medications aimed at reducing the cravings. Perhaps the most promising of these drugs is naltraxone. It can't stop someone from picking up that bottle, but it can help reduce the urge to.

> **Brain Buster**
>
> Depression and alcohol don't mix. Although most people with alcohol problems are not clinically depressed, the substantial minority who suffer from depression are much more likely to relapse if they don't get treatment for the depression along with treatment for alcoholism. And substance abusers who are depressed are much more likely to commit suicide.

Helping a Loved One with a Drinking Problem

Most people have heard about 12-step programs—there's one for just about every compulsive behavior out there, from narcotics abuse to gambling. And, of course, there's the granddaddy of all 12-step programs: the one that AA introduced. Here's my own recommended 12 steps for coping when someone you love has a drinking problem.

1. Don't try to control your loved one's drinking. Don't hide or get rid of the booze; she will only replace it and feel justified in her anger.

2. Don't bail your loved one out of trouble or lie for him to cover up his drinking. Let him suffer the consequences.

3. Don't blame yourself. You didn't cause your loved one to start drinking, and you can't make her stop.

4. Don't make threats unless you've thought them through and intend to carry them out.

5. Don't try to be your loved one's therapist. Express your concern about his alcohol use in terms of the problems you see it creating, not by labeling him with the term *alcoholic*.

6. Don't nag, preach, or lecture. You'll only wear yourself out and your loved one won't appreciate it, anyway.

7. Take care of yourself. Read as much as you can about alcoholism and the traps that family members can fall into.

8. Don't drink with your loved one in the hope that he will drink less.

9. Support any and every attempt that your loved one makes to get help—even if it's not the method you would choose.

10. Offer as much love and support as you can without sacrificing yourself or neglecting your own needs.

11. Give Al-Anon a try. It's a self-help group for the friends and families of alcoholics. You'll find that it's helpful to be around other people who are dealing with the same issues you are. There are even specialized groups like Ala-Teen, aimed just at teenagers.

12. Don't give up. Contrary to popular belief, not everyone with an alcohol problem has to hit bottom and lose everything before she sees the light.

I Can't Control My Impulses

Okay, let's admit it. At some time in our lives, we've all behaved impulsively. Most of us have said or done something in our lives that, looking back, seems completely out of character, something we regret. Maybe we blamed our behavior on the full moon or our first love. However we tried to explain it to ourselves, the fact is that we all commit impulsive actions once in a while.

People suffering from impulse-control disorders, however, have to live with the consequences of their rash actions *all the time*. They repeatedly fail in their attempts to resist temptation and wind up doing something that could be harmful to themselves or others.

The immediate payoff for impulsive behavior is usually a release of tension: by acting impulsively, you can "blow off steam" or feel an immediate sense of pleasure and gratification. Later, however, you're likely to feel regret or guilt or, if the behavior has gone on over time, you may find yourself constantly having to rationalize or justify your actions. The long-term consequences, whether it's jail or financial ruin, are much harder to escape.

Let's take a look at three impulse-control disorders that can get people into a lot of trouble: kleptomania, pyromania, and compulsive gambling.

I Just Had to Take It!

Kleptomania is a psychological disorder whereby a person literally cannot resist the impulse to steal objects that are not needed for personal use or for their monetary value. We're not talking about a plain old shoplifter or common criminal. In fact, the stolen objects are often discarded or given away or, if the person suffers enough remorse, returned surreptitiously at a later date. It is the act of stealing that is the "goal," not the object that is stolen.

For people with kleptomania, stealing provides a relief of tension. They'll report feeling increasingly tense before the theft and an immediate sense of relief or pleasure after the act is committed. They don't really want to steal—they know that stealing is wrong and senseless, and they often feel depressed and guilty afterward. However, when tension builds, they can't resist.

> **Psychobabble**
>
> Winona Ryder isn't the only star-studded shoplifter. Miss America 1945, Bess Myerson, and actress Hedy Lamarr were both arrested for taking store items that they didn't need and could easily afford to pay for.

Pyromania

My four-year-old son is fascinated with fire; he loves watching the flames dance in the fireplace and wants to be a firefighter when he grows up. While I don't mind his career choice, I'm counting on his fascination with fire to die down as he grows older. For people with pyromania, however, it never does.

Pyromania is characterized by well-planned fire-setting on at least more than one occasion. Like all impulse-control disorders, the fire-setting is a response to emotional tension and serves as a way for the person to find relief. In addition to setting actual fires, people with pyromania often set off false alarms, hang out around fire stations, follow fire trucks, and watch neighborhood fires.

> **Brain Buster**
>
> Take it seriously if your kid is a fire-starter! Persistent fire-setting and cruelty to animals are considered two of the biggest red flags for children and teens; a high number of individuals in prison for violent offenses have a history of one or both.

Pathological Gambling

There's a big difference between taking a trip to Las Vegas and developing a problem with compulsive gambling. Social gambling typically occurs with friends or colleagues, lasts for a fixed amount of time, and results in affordable (although unwelcome) financial losses.

Compulsive gambling, on the other hand, is out of control. Compulsive gamblers are obsessed with gambling. They gamble with money that they can't afford to lose, and use gambling either to escape from problems or to get a "high." People who compulsively gamble truly feel compelled to roll the dice. They'll lie to friends, family members, or therapists to conceal the extent to which their behavior is affecting their job or their relationships.

> **Brain Buster**
>
> Between 1 percent and 3 percent of the U.S. adult population is believed to have a problem with compulsive gambling.

Unlike other addictive disorders, this one is very likely to hit in older age. Many retirees become addicted and lose a lifetime of savings before they seek treatment or before family members realize what's going on.

Playing the Odds: Getting Control over Impulse Disorders

While it may not seem like drinking too much, setting a fire, or spending the week's paycheck at the casino could be treated the same, in fact, they are. The first line of defense is always *abstinence*—staying away from the temptation! Avoid the first drink that leads to the tenth one, avoid the casino, and don't touch the matches.

Next, the self-help support groups, or 12-step groups, exist for gambling as well. People with pyromania or kleptomania are more likely to have to rely on individual or group psychotherapy.

Antidepressants may be helpful if there is an underlying depression, which there often is. What's the prognosis? Truthfully, it's not really known for pyromania and kleptomania. For compulsive gambling, the prognosis appears similar to that of alcohol dependence—possibly with more financial consequences and fewer physical ones.

In this chapter, we've explored a number of behaviors that, when taken to excess, can become serious psychological disorders. Whether the addiction is food, alcohol, or setting fires, these disorders can have serious psychological, physical, and, sometimes, legal consequences. With the right treatment, people with one of these disorders can also get better.

The Never-Ending Story

As you finish this book, you may think that you've learned more about human psychology than you wanted to know—or, perhaps, you've learned just enough to make you a psychology student for life. I hope that you now have a better sense of understanding about yourself and others, and how to learn what you need to know to improve your life—in any situation.

We've looked at the good, the bad, and the ugly of human nature. You've learned about neurons and neurotransmitters, how children grow and how adults survive. You've seen how people can buckle under stress and rise above the toughest problems.

Maybe you'd like to relocate to Mars now that you've gotten a closer look at what makes humans tick. Or, just maybe, you're convinced that the human condition is a good one after all. Because one thing that psychology teaches us is that, if we expect good from people, they usually deliver. If we let people know we care, they usually care back. And if we ask for their help, they will almost always grant it. We are still evolving, but let's hope that we never lose that special and mysterious complexity that makes us all too human.

The Least You Need to Know

- ◆ Eating disorders are not about dieting, vanity, or weight; they're complex psychological disorders in which eating is used to cope with other problems.

- ◆ The three eating disorders are anorexia nervosa, bulimia nervosa, and binge-eating disorder.

- ◆ All eating-disorder sufferers have a lot in common and they're all at risk for a number of life-threatening medical problems.

- ◆ Alcoholism can start out slowly or quickly, but its progression is surprisingly predictable, until the person ultimately centers his or her life around drinking.

- ◆ Kleptomania (compulsive stealing), pyromania (compulsive fire-setting), and compulsive gambling are all impulse-control disorders that can have serious emotional, social, and legal consequences.

Glossary

affective disorders   A family of illnesses in which the primary symptom is a disturbance of mood; also called "mood disorders."

alienist   A specialist who treated mental and nervous disorders before the science of psychology was developed.

amnesia   The partial or complete loss of memory; psychologically based amnesia can be triggered by a traumatic event; memory almost always returns after a few days.

anorexia nervosa   A pattern of self-starvation that occurs primarily in young girls in Western cultures from middle and upper socioeconomic classes.

appetizer effect   Hunger that is stimulated by external stimuli, such as the smell or sight of food or food advertisements.

archetype   In Jungian theory, a universal symbol of human experience that is stored in the collective unconscious, the storehouse of ideas and forces shared by every human being has who ever lived.

aspirational groups   Social groups we don't yet belong to, but in which we would like to be accepted.

attention   A state of focused awareness coupled with a readiness to respond.

attribution theory   A system of explanations for the causes of individual and social behavior.

behavior modification   The application of principles of operant and classical conditioning to change a person's behavior in a more adaptive direction.

binge-eating disorder   The official diagnosis given a person who eats a large amount of food within two hours, at least two days a week for six months, without purging in any way to lose or maintain her weight. This disorder is commonly called compulsive overeating.

bipedalism   The ability to walk upright on two legs.

bipolar disorder   (Commonly called manic depression.) A psychological disorder characterized by extreme mood swings of "highs" and "lows."

blackout   A type of amnesia in which the person can still function (drive or make dinner) but later can't remember what happened.

body dysmorphia disorder   The severe preoccupation with slight or imaginary defects of the body, an obsession with body image.

body image   A complex array of thoughts, feelings, and behaviors that make up the subjective way a person views his or her physical appearance.

bulimia nervosa   A disorder in which a person binges (overeats) and purges (attempts to get rid of the food).

burnout   A unique pattern of emotional symptoms often found in professionals who have high-intensity contact with others on a daily basis; it is characterized by exhaustion, a sense of failure, and a tendency to relate to others in a depersonalized and detached manner.

cingulotomy   A form of psychosurgery that uses radio frequency current to destroy the cingulum, a small structure in the brain known to be involved in emotionality.

circadian rhythm   The clock that regulates your sleep/wake cycle.

classical conditioning   When two stimuli become so closely associated that one of them can elicit the same reactive behavior as the other.

cognitive dissonance   The inner conflict we experience when we do something that is counter to our prior values, beliefs, and feelings.

cognitive model   A hypothetical representation of how cognitive processes work.

cognitive processes   The mental abilities that enable us to know and understand the things around us; they include attending, thinking, remembering, and reasoning.

collective unconscious   The storehouse of ideas and forces shared by every human being who has ever lived.

consciousness   Our awareness of ourselves and all the things that we think, feel, and do.

contingency management   A technique designed to change behavior by modifying the consequences.

counterconditioning   A behavioral modification technique in which a new response is substituted for an unwanted or ineffective one.

cyclothymia   A disorder in which a person experiences the symptoms of bipolar disorder, but in a milder form. The symptoms are not severe enough to disrupt normal functioning and don't include hallucinations or delusions.

declarative memory   The portion of memory that stores information and facts.

defense mechanism   A mental process of self-deception that reduces an individual's awareness of threatening or anxiety-producing thoughts, wishes, or memories.

demand characteristics   Situational cues that influence our perceptions and our behaviors. For example, most of us would automatically obey the directions of a police officer or the advice or our physician because we have been taught to do so.

diathesis-stress model   The psychological theory that says predisposing biological factors interact with life stressors in the environment to cause illness.

diffusion of responsibility   A weakening of each person's sense of personal responsibility and obligation to help. It happens when one person perceives that the responsibility is shared with other group members.

dissociative disorder   A psychological disorder characterized by a disturbance in the integration of identity, memory, or consciousness.

dissociative identity disorder   (Better known as multiple personality disorder.) A psychological disorder in which two or more distinct personalities coexist in the same person at different times.

dual diagnosis   A term used to describe a person with two or more simultaneous mental-health problems, such as a person suffering from alcohol dependence and major depression. It is also referred to as coexisting disorders.

dysthymia   A psychological disorder in which the feelings of depression are less severe than those in major depression, but last for at least a two-year period.

ego   Freud's term for the part of our personality that focuses on self-preservation and the appropriate channeling of our basic instincts.

emotional intelligence   The ability to successfully understand and use emotions. It involves a group of skills, including the ability to motivate ourselves, regulate our moods, control our impulses, and empathize with others.

encephalization   The development of a larger brain during the course of evolution.

event-related potential (ERP)   The measurable change in brain waves in response to a particular stimulus.

explicit memory   The ability to retain information that we've put real effort into learning.

false memory syndrome   A pattern of thoughts, feelings, and actions based on a mistaken or inaccurate memory for traumatic experiences that a person claims to have previously repressed.

flow   The sense of effortless action we feel when we are totally absorbed in a task.

Freudian slip   A mistake or substitution of either spoken or written words. Freud believed that such "slips" come from subconscious wishes that pop up unexpectedly through unintentional words. By analyzing these "slips," a person might get some clues into her inner thoughts or "real" intent or wishes.

fundamental attribution error   A tendency to overestimate the influence of personality or other internal traits and to underestimate situational factors in explaining other people's behavior.

gender dysphoria   A clinical illness characterized by a desire to be, or insistence that one is, of the opposite sex; men have this disorder two to three times more often than women.

General Adaptation Response (GAS)   A pattern of general physical responses that are triggered by any stressors, no matter what kind.

genome   The full complement of an organism's genetic material, in other words, a blueprint for building all the structures and directing all the processes for the lifetime of that organism.

habituation   The process whereby a person becomes so accustomed to a stimulus that he or she ignores it and attends instead to less familiar stimuli.

hypnotizability   A measure of how susceptible a person is to entering a hypnotic state.

hypothesis   An answer to a question, based on theoretical assumptions, that can be tested to see if the answer can be proven wrong.

id   Freud's term for the uninhibited pleasure-seeker in one's personality.

implicit memory   The ability to remember information that we haven't deliberately tried to learn.

impression management   All the ways in which people try to control the perceptions other people have of us.

judgment   The process of using available information to form opinions, draw conclusions, and evaluate people and situations.

language acquisition devices (LADs)   The preprogrammed instructions for learning a language that some linguists believe all infants are born with.

language acquisition support system (LASS)   The circumstances that facilitate the efficient acquisition of language.

latent content (of a dream)   The meaning that lies hidden underneath the dream—its symbols, images, and actions.

learning   Any process through which experience at one time can change our behavior at another.

locus of control   A person's perception of the usual source of control over rewards; an internal locus of control means that we believe our behavior determines our fate; an external locus of control means that we think our fate is controlled by external forces (destiny, luck, or the gods).

manifest content (of a dream)   The literal story told by a dream.

maturation   The process of growth typical of all members of a species who are reared in the usual environment of the species.

mental retardation   A condition in which a person has significantly impaired intelligence in combination with problems in living (taking care of oneself, getting along with others, and doing other age-appropriate tasks).

mnemonics   Short verbal strategies that improve and expand our ability to remember new information by storing it with familiar and previously encoded information.

morality A system of beliefs, values, and underlying judgments about the rightness of human acts.

motivation The physical and psychological process that drives us toward a certain goal.

natural selection The Darwinian principle that says the best-adapted traits are the ones that will be passed along from one generation to another in a species. Creatures with less well-adapted traits will die out before they can reproduce, so their poorly adapted traits will eventually disappear from the population.

nerve A bundle of sensory or motor neurons that exist anywhere outside the central nervous system. You have 43 pairs of them—12 pairs from the brain and 31 pairs from the spinal cord.

neuron A nerve that specializes in information processing.

neuropsychologist A psychologist specially trained in identification, assessment, and possible rehabilitation of brain damage.

neurotransmitter Biochemical substances that stimulate other neurons. More than 60 substances have been identified as neurotransmitters. Among these are dopamine, norepinephrine, and serotonin.

off-labeling The process of prescribing a medication that has not been approved or extensively studied for safety and/or efficacy.

operant conditioning Encouraging voluntary behavior that attempts to influence control over the environment. When a rat learns that pressing a lever gets more food, it has been operant conditioned to push the lever.

panic disorder An anxiety disorder during which a person experiences recurrent episodes of intense anxiety and physical arousal that last up to 10 minutes.

paresis A disease of the brain contracted by a syphilis-caused infection of the central nervous system that is characterized by dementia and paralysis.

personality The unique bundle of all the psychological qualities that consistently influence an individual's usual behavior across situations and time.

personality disorder A long-standing, inflexible, and maladaptive pattern of thinking, perceiving, or behaving that usually causes serious problems in a person's social or work environment.

prejudice A learned negative attitude toward a person based on his or her membership in a particular group.

procedural memory   The long-term memory of how things are done.

psychoanalysis   The field of psychology that specializes in applying Freudian principles to the treatment of psychological disorders.

psychoanalyst   Specialist in Freud's school of psychological treatment; one must complete an intensive post-graduate training program, specializing in psychoanalytic theory and practice (including undergoing one's own analysis).

psychodynamic personality theory   A model of personality that assumes that inner forces (needs, drives, motives) shape personality and influence behavior.

psychological diagnosis   A label used to identify and describe a mental disorder, based on information collected by observation, testing, and analysis. It is also a judgment about a person's current level of functioning.

psychoneuroimmunology   The study of the interactions between the brain, the body, the emotions, and the immune system.

psychopathology   The clinical term for an abnormality or disorder in thought, emotion, or behavior.

psychophysics   The study of psychological reactions to physical stimuli.

psychosis   (Also called "psychotic disorder.") A general term for a severe mental disorder that prevents an accurate understanding and interaction with reality due to impaired thoughts, inappropriate emotions, and distorted perceptions.

reasoning   A process of realistic, goal-directed thinking in which conclusions are drawn from a set of facts.

reference group   Any group that a person uses to compare and evaluate himself against, from age-related peers to supermodels on the covers of fashion magazines.

reinforcement   A consequence that increases the occurrence of a particular behavior over time. Reinforcement can be either positive (a hug, a raise in pay) or negative (a punishment).

REM sleep   Sleep that is characterized by rapid eye movement, brain activity close to that of wakefulness, and a complete absence of muscle tone. Most dreaming takes place during REM sleep.

reference group   A group to whom a person looks to get information about what attitudes and behaviors are acceptable or appropriate. It can be a formal group (church or club) or an informal group (peers or family).

repressed memory   The memory of a traumatic event retained in the unconscious mind, where it is said to affect conscious thoughts, feelings, and behaviors even though there is no conscious memory of the alleged trauma.

resilience   The ability to thrive, mature, and increase competence in the face of risk and adversity.

retrieval cues   Mental or environmental aids that help us retrieve information from long-term memory.

savant ability   An exceptional skill in a narrow area, such as doing calculations or composing music, that is significantly higher than the person's overall level of functioning.

schizophrenia   A severe mental disorder characterized by a breakdown in perceptual and thought processes, often including hallucinations and delusions.

scientific method   A way of answering questions that helps remove bias from the study. First you form your question into a statement that can be proven false, and then you test it against observable facts. Other researchers who doubt your findings can duplicate your test and see if they get the same results.

self-actualization   The constant striving to realize your full potential.

self-concept   A person's awareness of his or her identity as a distinct and unique individual.

self-fulfilling prophecies   Predictions about a behavior or event that actually shape its outcome in the expected direction.

self-monitoring   The degree to which we vary our self-presentation to match the people we're with.

self-serving bias   A tendency to accept credit when things turn out well, and to blame the situation or other people when things go badly.

shaping   A process of rewarding small steps that are in the direction of the desired behavior.

signal detection theory   The assumption that the ability to perceive environmental stimuli is influenced by both physical and psychological factors.

situationism   The assumption that situational factors can have subtle and powerful effects on our thoughts, feelings, and actions.

social comparison   The process of comparing ourselves with others to identify our own unique abilities.

social psychology   The study of how people are influenced by their interactions and relationships with other people.

somatization   The tendency to channel emotions into physical complaints; instead of feeling angry, you might get a headache. A hypochondriac is an extreme example of somatization.

somatoform disorder   A mental disorder in which a person experiences symptoms of physical illness but has no medical disease that could cause them.

state   A temporary emotional condition.

stimulus generalization   When an individual who has become conditioned to respond to one stimulus in a certain way will also respond in that same way to any similar stimuli.

stress   A general term that includes all the physical, behavioral, emotional, and cognitive responses we make to a disruptive internal or external event.

stressors   The events that trigger a stress response.

superego   Freud's term for an individual's social conscience.

tardive dyskinesia   An unusual disturbance in motor control (especially of the facial muscles) that can be caused by long-term use of antipsychotic medication.

theory   A set of assumptions about a question.

think-aloud protocols   A research method during which subjects are asked to describe their problem-solving strategy at the time that they are actually trying to solve a real-life problem.

trait   A stable characteristic that influences an individual's thoughts, feelings, and behavior.

Appendix B

Psychology Resources

Mental Health Advocacy Groups

National Mental Health Association
1021 Prince Street
Alexandria, VA 22314-2971
www.nmha.org.index/cfm

National Alliance for the Mentally Ill
www.nami.org

National Mental Health Consumer's Self-Help Clearinghouse
www.libertynet.org/mha/cl_house.html

General Online Psychology Resources

American Psychological Association
www.apa.org

American Psychological Society
www.psychologicalscience.org

Self-Help and Psychology Magazine
www.shpm.com

Internet Mental Health
www.mentalhealth.com

At Health
www.athealth.com

Health Touch
www.healthtouch.com

KEN Consumer Information
www.mentalhealth.org/consumer/index.html

Psych Central
http://psychcentral.com

Psych Web
www.psywww.com

PsychRef
http://maple.lemoyne.edu/~hevern/psychref.html

Psychology Today
www.PsychologyToday.com

Mental Health Net
www.cmhc.com

Mental Health Infosource
www.mhsource.com

Sites That Have Lists of Psychology Links and Online Resources

Cyber Psych
www.cyber.psych.com

Encyclopedia of Psychology
www.psychology.org/links/resources/MetaSites/index/html

Psych Central
www.psychcentral.com

Resources for Specific Problems

Alcohol Resources

Alcoholics Anonymous
www.alcoholics-anonymous.org

Depression Resources

Depression and Related Affective Disorders Association (DRADA)
Meyer 3-181
600 N. Wolfe Street
Baltimore, MD 21287-7381
Online contact: drada@welchink.welch.jhu.edu

Depressive and Bipolar Support Alliance (formerly National Depressive and Manic Depressive Association)
730 North Franklin Street, Suite 501
Chicago, IL 60610-3526
1-800-826-3632
312-642-7243
www.dbsalliance.org

National Organization for Seasonal Affective Disorder (NOSAD)
P.O. Box 40190
Washington, DC 20016

Depression After Delivery
P.O. Box 1282
Morrisville, PA 19067
1-800-944-4773
www.beharenet.com/dadinc

Postpartum Support International
927 North Kellog Avenue
Santa Barbara, CA 93111
805-967-7376
Online contact: THONIKMAN@compuserve.com

Wing of Madness: A Depression Guide
www.wingofmadness.com

Dr. Ivan's Depression Central
www.psycom.net/depression.central.html

Bipolar Resources

Moodswing.org
www.moodswing.org

Anxiety Resources

Anxiety Disorders Association of America
11900 Parklawn Drive, Suite 1200
Rockville, MD 20852
www.adaa.org

Anxiety Disorders Education Program
www.nimh.nih.gov/anxiety

Obsessive-Compulsive Foundation, Inc.
P.O. Box 70
Milford, CT 06460-0070
203-878-5669
Online contact: JPHS28A@prodigy.com
http://pages.prodigy.com/alwillen.ocf.html

Eating Disorders Resources

American Anorexia Bulimia Association
www.abainc.org

Anorexia Nervosa and Related Disorders, Inc.
www.anred.com

National Eating Disorders Association (NEDO)
6655 South Yale Avenue
Tulsa, OK 74136
918-481-4044
www.laureate.com/nedo/nedointro.asp

Overeater's Anonymous World Service Office
6075 Zenith Court NE
Rio Rancho, NM 87124
505-891-2664
http://recovery.hiway.net

The Something Fishy Website on Eating Disorders
www.something-fishy.org/top/html

Schizophrenia

Schizophrenia Home Page
www.scizophrenia.com

Mental Wellness
www.mentalwellness.com

NAMI Consumer and Family Guide to Schizophrenia Treatment
www.nami.org/disorders/treatment/html

Therapy Resources

California Board of Psychology: A Consumer Guide to the Mental Health
Professions
www.psychboard.ca.gov/pubs/consumer.html

Counselling Resource
http://counsellingresource.com

Finding a Therapist
1-800-THERAPIST

Psychology Today magazine's FREE Find-a-Therapist database
www.PsychologyToday.com

Rating a Therapist
www.cybercouch.com/library/rati.tag.html

I.Q. Sites

World's Greatest Geniuses
http://home8.swipnet.se/~we80790/Index.html

Mensa
www.mensa.org/workout

Personality and I.Q. Self-Assessment

Personality Psychology Links
www.wesleyan.edu/spn/person.html#online

Personality and I.Q. Tests
members.aol.com/HOON4R/personality.html

ABC's Personal Growth
www.helpself.com

Online I.Q., Personality, Political Tests, and Novelty Games
http://universityoflife.com/serious.html

Positive Psychology Websites

Authentic Happiness Website
www.authentichappiness.org

Positive Psychology Center
www.positivepsychology.org

Quality of Life Research Center
http://qlrc.cgu.edu

Values in Action Institute
www.viastrengths.org

Questions About Psychiatric Medicine

Medications—Health Center's Pharmacy Page
www.health-center.com/english/pharmacy/meds/default/html

Index

E

N

T